For Michael S. Green—Raconteur Extraordinaire and Dear Friend

NEW PERSPECTIVES ON CIVIL WAR-ERA KENTUCKY

NEW
PERSPECTIVES
ON
CIVIL WAR-ERA
KENTUCKY

EDITED BY JOHN DAVID SMITH

UNIVERSITY PRESS OF KENTUCKY

Scholarly publisher for the Commonwealth, serving Bellarmine University, Berea College, Centre College of Kentucky, Eastern Kentucky University, The Filson Historical Society, Georgetown College, Kentucky Historical Society, Kentucky State University, Morehead State University, Murray State University, Northern Kentucky University, Spalding University, Transylvania University, University of Kentucky, University of Louisville, University of Pikeville, and Western Kentucky University. All rights reserved.

Editorial and Sales Offices: The University Press of Kentucky
663 South Limestone Street, Lexington, Kentucky 40508-4008
www.kentuckypress.com

Portions of this book previously appeared in *The Register of the Kentucky Historical Society* and are reprinted here by permission.

Library of Congress Cataloging-in-Publication Data

Names: Smith, John David, 1949- editor.
Title: New perspectives on Civil War-era Kentucky / edited by John David Smith.
Description: Lexington, Kentucky : University Press of Kentucky, [2023] | Includes
    bibliographical references. | Summary: [available online]
Identifiers: LCCN 2023006248 | ISBN 9780813197463 (hardcover ; alk. paper) |
    ISBN 9780813197807 (paperback ; alk. paper) | ISBN 9780813197814 (epub)
Subjects: LCSH: Unionists (United States Civil War)—Kentucky. | African
    Americans—Kentucky—History—19th century. | Slavery—Kentucky—History. |
    Kentucky—History—Civil War, 1861–1865. | Kentucky—History—1865–
Classification: LCC F455 .N49 2023 | DDC 976.9/03—dc23/eng/20230216
LC record available at https://lccn.loc.gov/2023006248

This book is printed on acid-free paper meeting
the requirements of the American National Standard
for Permanence in Paper for Printed Library Materials.

∞

Manufactured in the United States of America.

ASSOCIATION
of UNIVERSITY
PRESSES

Member of the Association
of University Presses

CONTENTS

INTRODUCTION: "TRULY A HOUSE DIVIDED DURING THE CIVIL WAR"

By John David Smith

In 1960, as Americans prepared for the Civil War Centennial, the esteemed southern historian C. Vann Woodward, then teaching at The Johns Hopkins University, informed Robert Penn Warren that Kentucky stood "between revelation-happy Yank and deduction-bitten Reb, Alsace-Lorraine of pragmatism between the crusaders."[1] In a few words Woodward touched upon a theme common to students of Civil War-era Kentucky.

During the crisis of the Union, Kentuckians unabashedly proclaimed their exceptionalism and their pragmatism. First its leaders declared neutrality. Then, after Confederate troops either "invaded" or "liberated" (depending on one's perspective) the commonwealth, state leaders reluctantly established a tense rapprochement with Abraham Lincoln's government. From 1863 onward the president's Emancipation Proclamation, and later the Federal recruitment of U.S. Colored Troops (USCT) in the state, sparked intense opposition to the national government generally and to the president in particular. Unquestionably Lincoln considered Kentucky, his native state, the most important and troublesome of the so-called loyal slave states. For their part, Kentucky politicians repeatedly tested Lincoln, pledging allegiance to slavery and white supremacy and to the Union. By 1863, however, Lincoln had determined that slavery and the Union were

I thank the following persons for providing valuable assistance in preparing this introduction: Thomas H. Appleton Jr., Amanda Binder, David W. Blight, Nelson L. Dawson, James S. Humphreys, James C. Klotter, Patrick A. Lewis, William H. Mulligan Jr., Ashley Runyon, and Paul Telljohann.

[1] C. Vann Woodward to Robert Penn Warren, September 4, 1960, Robert Penn Warren Papers, Beinecke Library, Yale University.

incompatible. The loyal slave states quickly were proving themselves an anachronism and an oxymoron.

Meanwhile, prosouthern Kentuckians coquettishly kept Confederate president Jefferson Davis, another Kentucky native, hopeful that their state would join the ranks of the Rebels. Many white Kentuckians identified and sympathized openly with Davis's government. Significantly, Kentucky had by far the largest slave population among the border states. In 1860 its 225,483 slaves constituted 19.5 percent of the state's population. In contrast, Missouri's 114,931 bondsmen constituted but 9.7 percent of its population. "Sure enough," writes Stephen Aron, "when the test of southern nationalism came, Kentucky failed by staying in the Union, though, of course, this decision was bitterly contested, and the state was truly a house divided during the Civil War."[2] Between 25,000 and 40,000 Kentucky volunteers donned Confederate gray. Between 90,000 and 100,000 men, volunteers and draftees alike, wore Union blue.[3]

Scholars have long recognized Kentucky's strategic value, as well as that of Maryland and Missouri, to combatants blue and gray. Writing in 1927, the political scientist Edward Conrad Smith, reflecting on the importance of the border land during the Civil War, remarked, "This great homogenous section, extending almost the whole width of the country, had in it the power to determine the outcome of the Civil War. . . . For both the Federal and the Confederate governments the attitude of this section afforded easily the most important domestic problem of the war."[4] Although Maryland and Missouri, positioned respectively near the nation's capital and at the "Gateway to the West," were vital to Lincoln, he considered the commonwealth the crown jewel of the Union slave states. As James C. Klotter has explained, "Given the state's sizable population, rich agricultural stores, and

[2] Stephen Aron, "Putting Kentucky in Its Place," in *Bluegrass Renaissance: The History and Culture of Central Kentucky, 1792–1852,* ed. James C. Klotter and Daniel Rowland (Lexington, Ky., 2012), 45.

[3] Lowell H. Harrison and James C. Klotter, *A New History of Kentucky* (Lexington, Ky., 1997), 195.

[4] Edward Conrad Smith, *The Borderland in the Civil War* (New York, 1927), 2–3.

natural Ohio River defense line, its decision would prove vital for the eventual success of the United States."[5] And so it did.

For all its complexity, drama, and importance, historians have paid surprisingly short shrift to the story of the borderland in the Civil War. According to Klotter, "It is almost as if those places [Kentucky and Missouri] existed in some kind of scholarly Star Trek Neutral Zone, not to be visited, at any cost. Over the years only an occasional monograph or a section in a state textbook survey has told their stories."[6] For Kentucky, E. Merton Coulter's *The Civil War and Readjustment in Kentucky,* published almost a century ago, continues to control Kentucky Civil War-era historiography, if not the disputed buffer between the United Federation of Planets and the Romulan Star Empire.[7]

Given the rich archival resources available both in Kentucky and nationally, and a strong secondary historical literature, the absence of a thorough, up-to-date monograph on Kentucky and the Civil War era remains inexplicable. To be sure, over the last fifty years scholars have taken steps to update Coulter's venerable although terribly outdated work.

In the 1970s Lowell H. Harrison and Ross A. Webb authored short, general interest books on the Civil War and Reconstruction in the commonwealth, respectively. Two books on Kentucky's emancipation experience appeared in the 1980s: Victor B. Howard's *Black Liberation in Kentucky* and Richard D. Sears's *"A Practical Recognition of the Brotherhood of Man."* Ira Berlin and his colleagues at the University of Maryland's Freedmen and Southern Society Project followed with the multivolume *Freedom: A Documentary History of Emancipation, 1861–1867,* containing invaluable primary source material on

---

[5] James C. Klotter, "Central Kentucky's 'Athens of the West' Image in the Nation and in History," in Klotter and Rowland, eds., *Bluegrass Renaissance,* 28.

[6] James C. Klotter, "Rebels on the Border: Civil War, Emancipation, and the Reconstruction of Kentucky and Missouri," *Civil War Book Review* 14, no. 3 (summer 2012), digitalcommons.lsu.edu/cwbr/vol14/iss3 (accessed September 23, 2022).

[7] On the endurance of Coulter's 1926 work, see John David Smith, "E. Merton Coulter, the 'Dunning School,' and *The Civil War and Readjustment in Kentucky,*" *Register of the Kentucky Historical Society* 86 (1988): 52–69 (hereafter *Register*).

emancipation and black recruitment in the commonwealth. In the following years a number of important works on Civil War Kentucky appeared, including articles by J. Michael Rhyne and books by Lowell H. Harrison, *Lincoln of Kentucky,* Earl J. Hess, *Banners to the Breeze: The Kentucky Campaign, Corinth, and Stones River,* Kent Masterson Brown, ed., *The Civil War in Kentucky: Battle for the Bluegrass State,* Richard D. Sears, *Camp Nelson, Kentucky: A Civil War History,* Darrel E. Bigham, *On Jordan's Banks: Emancipation and Its Aftermath in the Ohio River Valley,* Brian D. McKnight, *Contested Borderland: The Civil War in Appalachian Kentucky and Virginia,* Bruce S. Allardice and Lawrence Lee Hewitt, eds., *Kentuckians in Gray: Confederate Generals and Field Officers of the Bluegrass State,* and Kent T. Dollar, Larry H. Whiteaker, and W. Calvin Dickinson, eds., *Sister States, Enemy States: The Civil War in Kentucky and Tennessee.*[8] Especially important books by Andrew Slap, Anne E. Marshall, Rusty Williams, and Aaron Astor appeared in the new century. They treated various aspects of Civil

---

[8] J. Michael Rhyne, "'We Are Mobbed & Beat': Regulator Violence Against Free Black Households in Kentucky's Bluegrass Region, 1865–1867," *Ohio Valley History: The Journal of the Cincinnati Historical Society* 2 (2002): 30–42; J. Michael Rhyne, "'Conduct . . . Inexcusable and Unjustifiable': Bound Children, Battered Freedwomen, and the Limits of Emancipation in Kentucky's Bluegrass Region," *Journal of Social History* 42 (2008): 319–40; Lowell H. Harrison, *The Civil War in Kentucky* (Lexington, Ky., 1975); Ross A. Webb, *Kentucky in the Reconstruction Era* (Lexington, Ky., 1979); Victor B. Howard, *Black Liberation in Kentucky: Emancipation and Freedom, 1862–1884* (Lexington, Ky., 1983); Richard D. Sears, *"A Practical Recognition of the Brotherhood of Man": John G. Fee and the Camp Nelson Experience* (Berea, Ky., 1986); Ira Berlin, ed., *Freedom: A Documentary History of Emancipation, 1861–1867,* series II, *The Black Military Experience* (Cambridge, Eng., 1982), series I, vol. I, *The Destruction of Slavery* (Cambridge, Eng., 1985), series I, vol. II, *The Wartime Genesis of Free Labor: The Upper South* (Cambridge, Eng., 1993); Lowell H. Harrison, *Lincoln of Kentucky* (Lexington, Ky., 2000); Earl J. Hess, *Banners to the Breeze: The Kentucky Campaign, Corinth, and Stones River* (Lincoln, Neb., 2000); Kent Masterson Brown, ed., *The Civil War in Kentucky: Battle for the Bluegrass State* (Mason City, Iowa, 2000); Richard D. Sears, *Camp Nelson, Kentucky: A Civil War History* (Lexington, Ky., 2002); Darrel E. Bigham, *On Jordan's Banks: Emancipation and Its Aftermath in the Ohio River Valley* (Lexington, Ky., 2006); Brian D. McKnight, *Contested Borderland: The Civil War in Appalachian Kentucky and Virginia* (Lexington, Ky., 2006); Bruce S. Allardice and Lawrence Lee Hewitt, eds., *Kentuckians in Gray: Confederate Generals and Field Officers of the Bluegrass State* (Lexington, Ky., 2008); and Kent T. Dollar, Larry H. Whiteaker, and W. Calvin Dickinson, eds., *Sister States, Enemy States: The Civil War in Kentucky and Tennessee* (Lexington, Ky., 2009). On the influence of Lexington on the state's military and political leaders, see Joshua H. Leet and Karen M. Leet, *Civil War Lexington, Kentucky: Bluegrass Breeding Ground of Power* (Charleston, S.C., 2011).

War-era Kentucky life and collective memory.[9] Significantly, two major books on Kentucky and the Civil War published in 2011—William C. Harris's *Lincoln and the Border States: Preserving the Union* and Elizabeth D. Leonard's *Lincoln's Forgotten Ally: Judge Advocate General Joseph Holt of Kentucky*—shared the prestigious 2012 Gilder Lehrman Lincoln Prize.[10]

In 2012 the *Register of the Kentucky Historical Society* published a special Civil War Sesquicentennial number that built atop these works and added considerably to interpretations of Kentucky's Civil War history as Americans reflected on the war along America's antebellum "dividing line."[11] *New Perspectives on Civil War–Era Kentucky* reprints the ten articles that appeared in the *Register* with an expanded and revised introductory essay by the editor and an afterword by Benjamin Lewis Fitzpatrick. The authors ask penetrating questions, and their pieces bristle with first-rate research and interpretation. They underscore the high quality and vibrancy of today's scholarship on Kentucky and the Civil War and Reconstruction era.

In his essay James C. Klotter traces what he terms the "spirit" of Henry Clay, who died in 1852, before, during, and following the secession crisis. "Like Banquo's Ghost in *Macbeth*," Klotter writes, "Clay haunted the secession crisis, warning of evil in several ways." Clay, the great compromising nationalist, "had done his job too well, for his actions remained vivid in the psyche of the populace," but effective compromise was not to be. For decades Clay had opposed disunion, emphasizing the deleterious impact "secession, or separation" would have on Kentucky, positioned at the crossroads between North and South. Clay urged majority rule, moderation, and negotiation

[9] Andrew L. Slap, ed., *Reconstructing Appalachia: The Civil War's Aftermath* (Lexington, Ky., 2010); Anne E. Marshall, *Creating a Confederate Kentucky: The Lost Cause and Civil War Memory in a Border State* (Chapel Hill, 2010); Rusty Williams, *My Old Kentucky Confederate Home: A Respectable Place for Civil War Veterans* (Lexington, Ky., 2010); and Aaron Astor, *Rebels on the Border: Civil War, Emancipation, and the Reconstruction of Kentucky and Missouri* (Baton Rouge, 2012).

[10] William C. Harris, *Lincoln and the Border States: Preserving the Union* (Lawrence, Kans., 2011); Elizabeth D. Leonard, *Lincoln's Forgotten Ally: Judge Advocate General Joseph Holt of Kentucky* (Chapel Hill, 2011).

[11] Mark Yost, "Behind the Dividing Line of Slavery," *Wall Street Journal*, December 1, 2011.

on slavery and other divisive sectional matters—reason not treason. According to Klotter, "the lingering influence of Henry Clay on the South and on Kentucky decision-making, and the resulting influence of Kentucky on the other border states . . . may have been one of the crucial factors in the Civil War."

In their articles Luke E. Harlow and Aaron Astor probe different aspects of Kentucky Unionism during the Civil War era. Harlow relies on religious sources to connect proslavery arguments and political neutrality during the sectional conflict. Challenged by both southern proslavery secessionists and northern abolitionists, conservative white Kentucky Christians, Harlow writes, blamed abolitionists for the war and the possibility of whites' worst fear: emancipation. They advocated neutrality as a means of preserving "the Union on Christian slaveholding grounds—even as they sided socially and culturally with the South." This set the scene, he concludes, for a postwar Confederate memory of the conflict.

Astor examines closely the role of slavery both as a labor system and as an ideological force in shaping conservative Unionist political culture in the commonwealth. Like Harlow, he interprets political Unionism as resulting from the "dual threats" of radical abolitionism and secessionism. Conservative Unionists viewed the sectional crisis pragmatically, weighing the costs of secession as greater than the benefits. Drawing on what they considered "the great strength of the American Republic and the compromises that allowed the nation to grow to its prosperous status," they expected to withstand radicalism North and South. According to Astor, Kentucky Unionists were totally unprepared, however, for real and imagined threats to their social order from the commonwealth's slaves (57 percent of Kentucky's male slaves of military-age enlisted in the Union army). Ultimately, Unionists calculated that "slavery would be best preserved within the Union, coupled with a viable two-party system that tended to soften debate away from the maximalist positions of Radical Republicans in the North and fire-eaters of the Deep South."

In his article Christopher Phillips examines what he terms the "dominion system" of establishing and maintaining Federal authority in Kentucky. He defines this as a "system of sorts, a knot of counter-insurgency measures initiated, although never routinized, by both state and Federal governments and implemented by low-level, often volunteer, post commanders." In practice Federal commanders used the "dominion system" to identify loyal and disloyal Kentuckians and to punish Rebel sympathizers. They employed various methods of doing so, including mobilizing Unionist civilian informants, declaring martial law, making arrests, requiring oaths of allegiance, assessing levies on private property, suppressing newspapers, and regulating trade. Such harsh measures, Phillips concludes, were the price Abraham Lincoln's government forced Kentuckians to pay to keep the peace and to retain their commonwealth in the Union fold.

Christopher Waldrep probes the "static" constitutional views of Garrett Davis, who in December 1861 occupied John C. Breckinridge's U.S. Senate seat. Davis fiercely defended the Union against traitors and worked closely with Lincoln until March 1862, when they split over specific protections for states' rights over slavery. After joining other border state politicians in rejecting Lincoln's July 1862 gradual emancipation initiative, Davis objected forcefully to Lincoln's Emancipation Proclamation, which he considered "mischievous and revolutionary"—a threat to constitutional liberty. In 1864 Davis bitterly charged Lincoln with various constitutional usurpations of power—suppressing free press, free speech, and free suffrage in the 1863 Kentucky state elections, and plotting what Waldrep terms "the unconstitutional and total subversion of slavery." For Davis the Thirteenth Amendment proved most disastrous because it abolished slavery in loyal slave states like Kentucky. "To Davis," Waldrep argues, "the fact that his enemies had the power to graft their emancipationist vision onto the Constitution in defiance of the Founders' original intent did not legitimize the Constitution or make them less insane."

Unlike Davis, Kentuckian Joseph Holt, the subject of Elizabeth Leonard's essay, supported emancipation, "hard war," and the suppression of civil liberties if needed to defeat the Rebels. As Lincoln's judge advocate general, Holt adjudicated military law in much the same way that the attorney general determined civil law. In the thousands of judgments Holt considered during the war, he vigorously supported the president's understanding of adapting the Constitution in ways that would preserve the Union. Accordingly, he justified limitations on civil liberties and extending the legal powers of the military justice system. "Tolerance and magnanimity," Leonard concludes, "would simply have to wait until the war was over, the South was punished, treason was crushed, and the future of the freedpeople was secure."

In his sweeping article, Benjamin Franklin Cooling looks anew at the fraternal or fratricidal (depending on one's perspective) Kentucky-Tennessee relationship during the Civil War era. He does so through the interpretive, speculative, and theoretical lens of contemporary U.S. foreign policy, using paradigms of failing and failed states, paroxysms of violence, social dislocation and revolution, privation and destruction, and reconstitution and readjustment. Cooling concludes that during the Civil War era the Bluegrass and Volunteer states were fraternal *and* fratricidal—antebellum brothers who became enemies during the war. Ironically, both states experienced the hard hand of Federal administration during and after the contest. During the war, Cooling explains, "Their administrations saw a swirl of violence, human degradation and prejudice, and disruption of governance, economics, and institutions that demand better accounting of cost and result."

Anne E. Marshall's close reading of Kentucky women's Civil War diaries identifies important themes that connect gender and home front conditions in the war-torn commonwealth. The diarists whose work she assesses, whether Unionist or secessionist, commented on real or perceived enemies almost daily, thereby providing poignant bird's-eye views of all manner of wartime drama. Frances Peter, a Unionist, for example, spied on the goings-on of Confederates, especially those of Henrietta Hunt Morgan, at the home of John Hunt Morgan across the Little College Lot from her Lexington home. Like Miss Peter, Martha Buford Jones, who lived near Versailles, participated in a gendered communication network, but with like-minded spouses of Kentucky Confederates, not women with pro-Union sympathies. Female diarists on both sides of the sectional divide recorded all manner of strained personal and family relationships. They also commented on military affairs and politics, especially concerning emancipation, slavery, and the recruitment of African American soldiers. Marshall observes that, taken collectively, Kentucky female diarists highlighted "the high stakes of women's disloyalty in the war, and the readiness of Union army officials to quell it." Beyond this, the women themselves "became embattled participants in the eyes of both military officials and their fellow citizens."

In her article, Patricia A. Hoskins studies the activities of the Freedmen's Bureau in the Jackson Purchase during the early years of Reconstruction. This pro-Confederate section of the commonwealth "was stuck in a violent cycle" exacerbated by fiercely divided loyalties, and what local white citizens considered the inflammatory presence of Federal soldiers, especially African American troops, and ex-slave refugees. To protect these vulnerable groups, and to provide humanitarian relief for the destitute and people of color, in late 1865 the Bureau of Refugees, Freedmen, and Abandoned Lands (Freedmen's Bureau) established subdistricts in Kentucky, with headquarters in Lexington, Louisville, and Paducah. Although the Federal agency successfully established schools and courts for the freedpeople and regulated child labor, its activities sparked all manner of racial violence by whites against blacks in western Kentucky. Hoskins concludes that the Freedmen's Bureau in Kentucky, underfunded, understaffed, and under supported by the U.S. Army, "failed to achieve its intended reforms." It never proved capable of surmounting the virulent racism of whites directed at the freedpeople.

Although white Kentuckians resisted black freedom (universal emancipation came only after ratification of the Thirteenth Amendment in December 1865), over the next century, as Peter Wallenstein narrates in his essay, native black Kentuckians asserted themselves politically. Wallenstein uncovers Kentucky-born black persons serving in state legislatures across the South, in the Midwest, and finally in the commonwealth itself. Astonishingly, unlike in other southern states, no African American won election to the Kentucky legislature during Radical Reconstruction. Not until 1935 did voters elect an

African American, Charles W. Anderson Jr. of Louisville, to its General Assembly. Anderson and African Americans who followed him, including Georgia M. Powers, the first black Kentuckian elected to the state senate, challenged Jim Crow, first in education, and then in public accommodations. Although the commonwealth, according to Wallenstein, "came late to the party among the slave states of 1860 in electing a black candidate as a state legislator," the state "had black representation during most legislative sessions from the 1930s," unlike all of the former Confederate states.

******

In 2014, following the publication of the special Civil War Sesquicentennial number of the *Register*, I published an analysis of the state of Kentucky Civil War historiography and enumerated more than a dozen suggestions for future topics needing additional research and reflection.[12] Over the last decade the volume of historical scholarship on Civil War-era Kentucky has not only kept pace with previous years, but has mushroomed and veered in new directions, mirroring historiographical and methodological trends in other research fields as well as in Civil War studies.

In 2019, for example, the *Register* published a special number, "The Civil War Governors of Kentucky," with a dozen articles showcasing the rich sources of the *Civil War Governors of Kentucky Digital Documentary Edition*. Drawing upon a fully searchable online database of roughly 40,000 letters, petitions, pardon applications, and other documents from Kentuckians to the four Civil War governors, the authors unearthed a rich archive of the daily lives of men and women, black and white, rich and poor, urban and rural. The articles cover such diverse topics as emotional trauma, guerrilla warfare, alcohol consumption, prostitution, hunger, immigration, and the meaning of the Union to Kentucky residents.[13] As Edward R. Crowther has

[12] John David Smith, "Whither Kentucky Civil War and Reconstruction Scholarship?" *Register* 112 (2014): 223–47.

[13] "The Civil War Governors of Kentucky," *Register* 117 (2019): 151–370. The authors include Stephen Berry, Lesley J. Gordon, David Gleeson, Anne Sarah Rubin, Amy Murrell

observed, "In recent years, Civil War era scholars have turned to studying the border between the United States and the Confederate States to further elucidate the nature of union and secession in ways that complicate a simple binary of north versus south."[14]

A prime example of the new borderland research is *The Rivers Ran Backward: The Civil War and the Remaking of the American Middle Border* (New York, 2016) by Christopher Phillips. He frames the conflict in the commonwealth within the context of the burgeoning field of comparative and borderland studies—in this case, the western middle border region: Kentucky, Missouri, Illinois, Indiana, and Ohio.[15] Phillips argues that along the middle border "the Civil War was the catalytic event in a long struggle between collectivism, imperfectly recognized as northern progressivism, and individualism, equally imperfectly recognized as southern traditionalism. Because the war's meaning was the most contingent in this place, these conflicts entwined into bitter, persistent legacies that were only deepened over a century of politics, formal and informal, surrounding the conflict" (8). Kentucky and Missouri contained persons with varying attitudes toward race and slavery, including colonizationists, emancipationists, secessionists, conditional Unionists, and unconditional Unionists, all of whom disagreed widely on vexing questions of region, nation, sovereignty, and patriotism. While during the secession crisis conservatives in both states hoped for neutral status in the sectional divide, troop movements by the Confederates quickly proved neutrality to

Taylor, Mark Wahlgren Summers, Kenneth Noe, Diane Miller Sommerville, Crystal Feimster, Luther Adams, Carole Emberton, and Patrick A. Lewis.

[14] Edward R. Crowther, review of April E. Holm, *A Kingdom Divided: Evangelicals, Loyalty, and Sectionalism in the Civil War Era*, in *Civil War Book Review* 20 (2018): article 23, https://digitalcommons.lsu.edu/cwbr/vol20/iss2/23 (accessed September 23, 2022). In her study of Kentucky's secession crisis, Shae Smith Cox identifies economic interests and the influence of old Whig ideology in Kentucky's on again, off again neutrality stance. See "Kentucky's Conflict as a Border State during the Secession Crisis" (master's thesis, Oklahoma State University, 2013).

[15] Phillips also published a general synthesis on this topic. See *The Civil War in the Border South* (Santa Barbara, Calif., 2013). Other recent studies that treat the border South during the war include Matthew Salafia, *Slavery's Borderland: Freedom and Bondage Along the Ohio River* (Philadelphia, 2013); Andrew J. Torget, *Seeds of Empire: Cotton, Slavery, and the Transformation of the Texas Borderlands, 1800–1850* (Chapel Hill, 2015); and Bridget Ford, *Bonds of Union: Religion, Race, and Politics in a Civil War Borderland* (Chapel Hill, 2016).

be unrealistic and Kentuckians cast their lot with the Union. As Matthew Salafia has explained regarding Kentucky, "In a state plagued by division, neutrality had little chance for success." By war's end, around 70,000 white Kentuckians brandished arms for the Yankees and between 30,000 and 40,000 fought for the Rebels.[16]

Books by Stephen I. Rockenbach and April E. Holm broaden recent analyses of sectional questions across the Kentuckiana borderland. Rockenbach's *War upon Our Border: Two Ohio Valley Communities Navigate the Civil War* (Charlottesville, 2016) is a micro-intraregional study that compares all aspects of the war, including historical memory and military, political, and social history, in Corydon, Indiana, and Frankfort, Kentucky. While residents in both towns generally supported the Union, as the war dragged on white residents in Frankfort opposed emancipation and its challenges to white racial supremacy. Guerrilla raids and material losses ultimately convinced citizens in Corydon to welcome emancipation as a force in shortening the war.

Focusing largely on Baptist, Methodist, and Presbyterian churches in Missouri and Kentucky, in *A Kingdom Divided: Evangelicals, Loyalty, and Sectionalism in the Civil War Era* (Baton Rouge, 2017) Holm charts attempts by border state evangelicals to remain politically neutral on slavery, even following divisions of these denominations into northern and southern wings. During the war, Federal officials used oaths and other tests of patriotism to pressure border evangelicals to declare their loyalty to the Union. This encouraged their turn in the postwar decades to join southern evangelicals in defending slavery, states' rights, and the ideals of "Lost Cause" ideologues.

Such sentiments were not new. During the war Unionist leaders in Kentucky and in the other loyal slave states had consistently complained against what they deemed usurpations of unconstitutional

---

[16] Salafia, *Slavery's Borderland*, 247, 249. For an interpretive study of the meandering path toward Kentucky neutrality, 1860–1861, see James W. Finck, *Divided Loyalties: Kentucky's Struggle for Armed Neutrality in the Civil War* (Eldorado Hills, Calif., 2012). Also see Robert Goebel, "'The Men of the West Want No Disunion': The 1860 Union Meetings in Louisville, Columbus, and Cincinnati," *Ohio Valley History* 21 (2021): 3–24.

power by Lincoln's government. Many had sided with the Union precisely because they assumed that the Federal government would uphold chattel slavery as a constitutional right.[17] For example, Democratic politicians bitterly opposed the July 1862 Confiscation Act, the 1863 Emancipation Proclamation, the arming of blacks as Federal soldiers after 1863, conscription, the suspension of the writ of habeas corpus, military occupation, martial law, and, later, Reconstruction.[18] As Michael D. Robinson avers in his *A Union Indivisible: Secession and the Politics of Slavery in the Border South* (Chapel Hill, 2017), "Unionists had kept their states in the Union, but the exigencies of civil war had irrevocably destroyed proslavery Unionism and [Henry] Clay's America" (208). According to Stephen Rockenbach, "as the war progressed and transitioned from a war to preserve the Union to a crusade to end slavery, the complex mixture of allegiances in Kentucky shifted. Emancipation, and more importantly black military service, upset the unique balancing act of Unionism in Kentucky. Although Unionists believed that they could protect white citizens' right to property and black labor by remaining loyal, they were mistaken as resistance to Federal authority, a hallmark of Bluegrass Confederates, proved to be the best method for retaining white supremacy in Kentucky."[19]

Perhaps not surprisingly, during the war 87,000 Kentucky males avoided military service completely. "In a war," Phillips writes, "that appeared to offer no winners, most [white Kentuckians and Missourians] found no side to serve them, so they served none but their own" (205). A disproportionately large number of black Kentuckians, however, wore the Union blue. In May 1864 the War Department removed previous restrictions on slave enlistments from the loyal slave states. "Kentucky's contribution," writes Phillips, "was nothing short of remarkable. More than 24,000 of the state's African Americans,

---

[17] Salafia, *Slavery's Borderland,* 310n21.

[18] For a recent account of Kentucky's armed neutrality in 1861 and Democrats wartime debates over slavery, states' rights, federalism, and union, consult J. Matthew Gallman, *The Cacophony of Politics: Northern Democrats and the American Civil War* (Charlottesville, 2021).

[19] Stephen Rockenbach, "'The Weeds and the Flowers Are Closely Mixed': Allegiance, Law, and White Supremacy in Kentucky's Bluegrass Region, 1861–1865," *Register* 111 (2013): 589.

. . . constituting 57 percent of the state's black men of military age, enlisted in the Federal armies" (259). William H. Mulligan Jr.'s 2018 article on the 4th U.S. Colored Heavy Artillery documents how the army employed black soldiers not only as armed troops, but as fatigue laborers and recruiters in pro-Confederate western Kentucky and Tennessee. His work adds to the growing scholarship on African Americans soldiers in the state during the war.[20]

Surprisingly, few recent works study military actions and campaigns in the commonwealth. In *Conquered: Why the Army of Tennessee Failed* (Chapel Hill, 2019), Larry J. Daniel revises previous historians' negative assessments of Confederate generals Edmund Kirby Smith and Braxton Bragg in their fall 1862 Kentucky campaign. Focusing on "the myth that Kentucky was a sleeping giant of secessionism primed to be awakened" (37), Daniel hypothesizes that if the Confederate icon Gen. Robert E. Lee had commanded the Army of Tennessee, his presence might have persuaded more Kentuckians to enlist in Rebel gray. "But," he adds, "it might conversely have also driven a far greater number into the Northern ranks. . . . To offset the manpower disparity in the West, the Confederacy needed Kentucky to supply as many men as Tennessee. In terms of the percentage of whites who fought for the South, Kentucky ranked dead last" (326–27).

Several essays in Kent T. Dollar, Larry H. Whiteaker, and W. Calvin Dickinson's edited *Border Wars: The Civil War in Tennessee and Kentucky* (Kent, Ohio, 2015) treat Kentuckians and their military affairs. Aaron Astor compares prewar local militias in Lexington, Kentucky, and Clarksville, Tennessee, and their later conversion into regiments in the Confederate Army of Tennessee. Scott Tarnowieckyi blames the Union army for failing to protect residents around Henderson, Owensboro, Hopkinsville, Madisonville, and Morganfield from bands of Confederate irregular troops in 1864 and 1865. William A. Penn's *Kentucky Rebel Town: The Civil War Battles of Cynthiana and Harrison County* (Lexington, Ky., 2016) treats Rebel brigadier general John

---

[20] William H. Mulligan Jr., "African American Troops in Far West Kentucky during the Civil War: Recruitment and Service of the Fourth U.S. Heavy Artillery Colored," *Journal of the Jackson Purchase Historical Society* 45 (2018): 32–43.

Hunt Morgan's 1862 and 1864 raids on Union troops in Cynthiana, Kentucky.[21] J. Michael Crane explains how the combined efforts of the U.S. Army, Confederate guerrillas, and the agency of enslaved persons contributed to the eradication of slavery in the Henderson, Kentucky, area.[22] Stuart W. Sanders has written several short works on the Civil War in Kentucky, including the Battle of Mill Springs in January 1862 and Perryville in October of that year.[23]

Contemporary scholars have paid more attention to Kentuckians' diverse ethnic and religious cultures, defined broadly, than to their military history. For example, Joseph R. Reinhart, David T. Gleeson, and Lee Shai Weissbach have published articles on German, Irish, and Jewish persons, respectively, during the war.[24]

Luke E. Harlow's *Religion, Race, and the Making of Confederate Kentucky, 1830–1880* (Cambridge, Eng., 2016) joins Anne E. Marshall's and Jacob F. Lee's earlier work on the processes whereby white Kentuckians metaphorically "became" Confederates following Appomattox.[25] Harlow argues that before the Civil War white Kentuckians operated in a "neutral" middle ground between anti- and proslavery ideologies, allowing them eventually to support the Union cause because Americans had long tolerated both evangelical Protestant proslavery and antislavery doctrines. After 1863, however, as

---

[21] Also see William A. Penn's *Rattling Spurs and Broad-Brimmed Hats: The Civil War in Cynthiana and Harrison County, Kentucky* (Midway, Ky., 1995).

[22] J. Michael Crane, "The Demise of Slavery on the Border: Federal Policy and the Union Army in Henderson, Kentucky," *Register* 113 (2015): 601–40.

[23] Stuart W. Sanders, *The Battle of Mill Springs, Kentucky* (Charleston, S.C., 2013); Stuart W. Sanders, *Maney's Confederate Brigade at the Battle of Perryville, Kentucky* (Charleston, S.C., 2014); Stuart W. Sanders, *Perryville Under Fire: The Aftermath of Kentucky's Largest Civil War Battle* (Charleston, S.C., 2012). Also see Stuart W. Sanders, "A Name Worth a Division: Simon Bolivar Buckner and the 1862 Kentucky Campaign," in *Confederate Generals in the Western Theater*, ed. Lawrence Lee Hewitt and Arthur W. Bergeron Jr., 4 vols. (Knoxville, 2010–2018), 3:121–50.

[24] Joseph R. Reinhart, "Louisville's Germans in the Civil War Era," *Register* 117 (2019): 437–84; David T. Gleeson, "'An Unfortunate Son of Erin': The Irish in Civil War Kentucky," ibid., 197–214; Lee Shai Weissbach, "Kentucky Jewry during the Civil War," ibid., 110 (2012): 165–84. Also see a brief chapter on Civil War-era Germans in *Germans in Louisville: A History*, ed. C. Robert Ullrich and Victoria A. Ullrich (Charleston, S.C., 2015).

[25] Jacob F. Lee, "Unionism, Emancipation, and the Origins of Kentucky's Confederate Identity," *Register* 111 (2013): 199–233.

the conflict in Kentucky and elsewhere became a war of black liberation, white Kentuckians assumed a proslavery and pro-Confederate stance. "Racist religion accomplished after the Civil War what was impossible before: it created cultural and political solidarity with the white South" (15).[26]

Patrick A. Lewis's *For Slavery and Union: Benjamin Buckner and Kentucky Loyalties in the Civil War* (Lexington, Ky., 2019) interprets the life of Benjamin Forsyth Buckner, a battle-tested Union officer and later a U.S. senator, as a window to why many white Kentuckians supported the northern cause after Fort Sumter. Like Buckner, they donned the Union blue to protect African American slavery in Kentucky and to maintain "The Union as it was, the Constitution as it is," not to free their bondspeople. After 1863, however, Buckner and others concluded that preserving the Union proved indefensible after Abraham Lincoln issued his final Emancipation Proclamation. Following his resignation from the 20th Kentucky Infantry Regiment in April 1863, Buckner continued to oppose political and racial change in the commonwealth.[27] Like other proslavery Unionists, he opposed racial equality, including granting suffrage to the freedpeople.

Dan Lee and Brad Asher chronicle the lives of controversial Kentuckians who served as Union officers but who differed dramatically on the question of emancipation and the recruitment of African American troops in the state. Lee's *Wolford's Cavalry: The Colonel, the War in the West, and the Emancipation Question in Kentucky* (Lincoln, Neb., 2016) chronicles how Frank L. Wolford (1817–1895), the brave, gallant, resourceful, and once revered commander of the esteemed 1st Kentucky Volunteer Cavalry, ruined his military career and long-term reputation by conducting a "personal war" of words against Lincoln for his emancipation project, especially the recruitment of black troops in the commonwealth (189). Dishonorably

---

[26] On the origins of Kentucky's antislavery evangelicals, see Andrew Landreth, "Friends of Humanity, Enemies of Bondage: Kentucky's Antislavery Evangelicals and Their Legacy," *Journal of the Jackson Purchase Historical Society* 44 (2017): 11–25.

[27] See Patrick A. Lewis's "'All Men of Decency Ought to Quit the Army': Benjamin F. Buckner, Manhood, and Proslavery Unionism in Kentucky," *Register* 107 (2009): 513–49.

discharged from the army for his disloyal and patriotic speeches, and later arrested three times, Wolford proved relentless in criticizing Federal military policy and the president (even after meeting Lincoln in Washington in June 1864). Following the war, Wolford joined other white conservative Unionists in denouncing emancipation. He worked as a lawyer and served as Kentucky's adjutant general and in the U.S. House of Representatives. But Wolford could never shed his notoriety for having slandered the martyred Lincoln, who in fact had treated him with considerable magnanimity.

In *The Most Hated Man in Kentucky: The Lost Cause and the Legacy of Union General Stephen Burbridge* (Lexington, Ky., 2021), Asher examines the life and labor of Stephen Gano Burbridge (1831–1894), the native Kentuckian who commanded Union army activities in the state from March 1864 until February 1865. His many critics charged Burbridge with ruling military affairs in the commonwealth with an unusually heavy hand. He employed retaliatory executions of Confederate partisans, banished, harassed, and imprisoned pro-southern political partisans, suppressed newspapers that supported the Rebels, and interfered with the marketing of Kentucky crops. But his enemies considered Burbridge's recruitment and use of men of the USCT as his most egregious acts. After the war, Asher maintains, "attacking Burbridge was a surefire way to keep picking the scab of Kentucky's wartime grievances, reminding the white population of the injustices wrought in the name of military necessity and of the misbegotten objective of emancipation" (2).[28]

Historians in the second decade of the new century have paid increasing attention to the Civil War in western Kentucky, especially to the state's so-called "South Carolina"—the pro-secessionist, pro-Confederate Jackson Purchase region. In 2020, George Humphreys argued that historians of Kentucky should take into greater account regional differences within the commonwealth when assessing secession and the war's meaning. "Kentucky historiography requires a lighter touch in order to more easily recognize the distinctive paths

---

[28] On Burbridge, also see Bryan S. Bush, *Butcher Burbridge: Union General Stephen Burbridge and His Reign of Terror Over Kentucky* (Morley, Mo., 2008).

of its many regions" during and after the war, he wrote. Responding to the hypothetical question, "Is there any Kentucky history outside of the Bluegrass?" Matthew E. Stanley responded affirmatively. Aware that "far western Kentucky was a wartime social and political outlier," he insisted that nonetheless "its story is far from marginal."[29]

Several historians, in addition to Patricia Hoskins, whose essay on the Freedmen's Bureau appears in this book, have worked to unravel the history of the Civil War in the Purchase, the portion of the commonwealth bounded by the Mississippi River to the west, the Ohio River to the north, and the Tennessee River to the east.[30] Among current scholars, Dan Lee and Berry Craig have led the way in addressing the significance of this microregion, the storm center of secessionist and guerrilla activities in Kentucky's Civil War history.

In 2014 Lee published a preliminary study, *The Civil War in the Jackson Purchase, 1861–1862: The Pro-Confederate Struggle and Defeat in Southwest Kentucky* (Jefferson, N.C., 2014), and Craig published *Kentucky Confederates: Secession, Civil War, and the Jackson Purchase* (Lexington, Ky., 2014). Craig made the case that this far western region of the state was far and away the most pro-Confederate section in a largely Unionist state. He establishes its vibrant, late antebellum slave trade, its residents' overwhelming support for neutrality in 1861 and soon after joining the southern Confederacy. The fall of Paducah, the region's primary city, in early September 1861 to Brig. Gen. Ulysses S. Grant's forces essentially left the Jackson Purchase under Federal military control for the rest of the conflict. That said, pro-Confederate irregular troops in the area constantly harassed Union occupation forces, and, ironically, from 1863 onward white

[29] George Humphreys, review of Luke E. Harlow, *Religion, Race, and the Making of Confederate Kentucky, 1830–1880,* in *Journal of the Jackson Purchase Historical Society* 47 (2020): 84; Matthew E. Stanley, review of Berry Craig, *Kentucky Confederates: Secession, Civil War, and the Jackson Purchase,* in *Journal of Southern History* 81 (2015): 990.

[30] Hoskins also contextualizes the increased presence of Federal military garrisons, trade restrictions, and penalties in "Guerrilla Warfare and the Federal Occupation in the Jackson Purchase Region of Kentucky, 1862–64," in Dollar, Whiteaker, and Dickinson, *Border Wars,* 89–110.

Kentuckians increasingly gravitated toward the pro-Confederate sympathies of residents of the Purchase. "While the Purchase was Kentucky's only Rebel region," Craig explains, "most of the rest of the state moved towards the Purchase perspective following the Emancipation Proclamation and the enlistment of African American soldiers, both of which almost every white Kentuckian bitterly opposed. The shift became even more pronounced after Confederate surrender" (293).[31]

Perhaps not surprisingly, contemporary historians have devoted considerable attention to race relations in Civil War-era Kentucky. This subject has long attracted researchers because many white Kentuckians considered emancipation, especially its economic, political, and social consequences, the most salient question hovering over the state like a miasma. They assumed naively, according to modern scholars, that because their state never seceded from the Union, and because the Emancipation Proclamation did not apply to the commonwealth, that the status of the state's slaves and race relations in the state generally would remain unchanged after the war. This pipedream burst early in the war as Confederate and Union troops entered the state and slaves either fled northward to freedom or to Federal army lines seeking protection and work. According to Col. Marcellus Mundy, both a Kentucky slaveholder and a Union officer stationed in Louisville, Federal troops had become "a mere negro freeing machine."[32]

Yet slavery continued throughout the war, and slaveholders watched with dismay as they gradually lost control over their human

---

[31] Additional books on the war and the Jackson Purchase include John Philip Cashon, *Paducah and the Civil War* (Charleston, S.C., 2016); Dieter C. Ullrich and Berry Craig, *Unconditional Unionist: The Hazardous Life of Lucian Anderson, Kentucky Congressman* (Jefferson, N.C., 2016); Berry Craig, *Kentucky's Rebel Press: Pro-Confederate Media and the Secession Crisis* (Lexington, Ky., 2018); Dieter C. Ullrich and Berry Craig, *General E. A. Paine in Western Kentucky: Assessing the "Reign of Terror" of the Summer of 1864* (Jefferson, N.C., 2018).

[32] Col. M[arcellus] Mundy to Capt. A. C. Semple, April 4, 1863, in *Freedom: A Documentary History of Emancipation, 1861–1867*, series I, vol. I, *The Destruction of Slavery*, ed. Ira Berlin, Barbara J. Fields, Thavolia Glymph, Joesph P. Reidy, and Leslie S. Rowland (Cambridge, Eng., 1985), 570. Mundy commanded the 23rd Kentucky Infantry.

chattel.[33] After 1863 no question proved more volatile in Kentucky than the recruitment—sometimes by force—of enslaved men to serve in the USCT or as laborers. By war's end only Confederate Louisiana contributed more black men to the USCT than the commonwealth. And as several of the authors mentioned in this introduction argue, after the war Kentuckians quickly transitioned from identifying as residents of a "loyal" slave state to aligning ideologically with the former Confederates.

Much scholarly work focuses on how blacks and whites responded to the challenges and opportunities of emancipation as the commonwealth emerged as a bastion of white supremacy. James Oakes's *Freedom National: The Destruction of Slavery in the United States, 1861–1865* (New York, 2013) details the emancipation experience in Kentucky, which he dubbed "the graveyard of antislavery hopes for the Border States." "In Kentucky every escalation of federal pressure to abolish slavery produced an equal and opposite proslavery backlash." The state's "civil and military leaders did everything they could do to thwart the Union antislavery policy. In no other state was the civil war over slavery *within* the Union army so visceral" (486).

Elizabeth D. Leonard, in *Slaves, Slaveholders, and a Kentucky Community's Struggle toward Freedom* (Lexington, Ky., 2019), provides a microstudy of the meandering path a small group of enslaved men from Breckinridge County, Kentucky, took to serving in the 118th USCT and their postwar lives as freemen amid whites who resented their newfound status. In their books, Chandra Manning and Amy Murrell Taylor trace how refugees, formerly enslaved persons in Kentucky and elsewhere, traversed the fragile and perilous moments of self-emancipation to find temporary freedom but hardship and misfortune in improvised Union army contraband camps. While free at last, figuratively if not legally, black families struggled in crowded, makeshift camps and towns, physical spaces lacking the basic necessities of life, including housing, fresh water, adequate sanitation, food,

---

[33] On slavery's continuing presence in wartime Kentucky, see Timothy Ross Talbott, "Telling Testimony: Slave Advertisements in Kentucky's Civil War Newspapers," *Ohio Valley History* 16 (2016): 28–47.

clothing, and medical care. Ex-slave refugees lived under degrees of constant deprivation, struggle, and uncertainty as they coped with the paternalism and racism of the U.S. Army, northern missionaries, and aid workers, and worse, the fear of re-enslavement from Confederate raiders and partisans.

Despite these challenges, ex-slave refugees constructed ad hoc orphan asylums, churches, gardens, homes, and freedmen's schools. Regardless of their agency, theirs was a fragile and chaotic birth of freedom, one circumscribed by innumerable humanitarian crises. Their small steps toward economic and social freedom required great courage and dignity from those who survived the ordeal. Taylor pays special attention to the history of Camp Nelson, Kentucky's large recruitment and training center for the USCT in Jessamine County, and a hospital, supply depot, and refugee camp for their wives and children.[34] In 2013, Camp Nelson became a National Historic Landmark, and on October 25, 2018, the National Park Service renamed the site Camp Nelson National Monument and placed the facility under its administrative control.[35]

Despite the dramatic increase of interest by historians in the importance of gender in historical analyses, the roles of women and men, of feminism and masculinity, have attracted surprisingly little scholarship by historians of the war in the Bluegrass State. For starters, students should consult unpublished dissertations by Kristen Lenore Streater and Adrian Schultze Buser Willett.[36]

---

[34] W. Stephen McBride examines the challenging circumstances of females at Camp Nelson in "African American Women, Power, and Freedom in the Contested Landscape of Camp Nelson, Kentucky," in *Archaeology and Preservation of Gendered Landscapes,* ed. Sherene Baugher and Suzanne M. Spence-Wood (New York, 2010), 95–112.

[35] Chandra Manning, *Troubled Refuge: Struggling for Freedom in the Civil War* (New York, 2016); Amy Murrell Taylor, *Embattled Freedom: Journeys through the Civil War's Slave Refugee Camps* (Chapel Hill, 2018); Mark Smith, "A Chaotic Birth of Freedom," *Wall Street Journal,* August 27–28, 2016; https://www.nps.gov/cane/learn/news/campnelsondesignated.htm (accessed January 3, 2022).

[36] Kristen Lenore Streater, "She-Rebels on the Border: Gender and Politics in Civil War Kentucky" (Ph.D. diss., University of Kentucky, 2001); Adrian Schultze Buser Willett, "'Our House was Divided': Kentucky Women and the Civil War'" (Ph.D. diss., Indiana University, 2008). On available source materials for research, see Eric Willey, "Documenting Women's Civil War Experiences in the Ohio Valley at the Filson," *Ohio Valley History* 13 (2013): 70–76.

In 2000, John David Smith and William Cooper Jr. published *A Union Woman in Civil War Kentucky: The Diary of Frances Dallam Peter* (Lexington, Ky., 2000), and nine years later Nancy Disher Baird published *Josie Underwood's Civil War Diary* (Lexington, Ky., 2009). These texts document the *Weltanschauung* of two young, elite, Unionist proslavery women caught in the complicated throes of internecine war in the Bluegrass region and south-central, Kentucky, respectively.[37] More recently Amber C. Nicholson studied the conflicting loyalties of another female diarist, Hopkinsville, Kentucky's Ellen Wallace. Long committed both to slavery and the Union cause, war weariness and the specter of emancipation (she referred to the freedpeople as "black monsters") converted Wallace to the Confederate cause.[38]

In *Family, Law, and Inheritance in America: A Social and Legal History of Nineteenth-Century Kentucky* (Cambridge, Eng., 2013) Yvonne Pitts devotes considerable attention to gender in the commonwealth. Throughout the nineteenth century white women struggled to control property because Kentucky's Court of Appeals employed formalist readings of the law, "imposing particularly onerous burdens on women" (144). Wills, Pitts explains, served to assure the orderly transmission of real and chattel property. Pitts considers Kentucky a "rich ground for studying women's access to property and authority" (23). Because of Kentucky's laws restricting women's access to

---

[37] Baird also edited Underwood's second diary treating her later life. See Nancy D. Baird, "Josie Underwood's Civil War: An Introduction," *Register* 112 (2014): 335–49, and "Josie Underwood's Civil War Diary, Part Two," ibid., 351–493. For comparative analyses of the Peter and Underwood diaries, see Anne E. Marshall, "A 'Sisters' War': Kentucky Women and Their Civil War Diaries," *Register* 110 (2012): 481–502; Andrea S. Watkins, "Josie Underwood and Frances Dallam Peter (1840–1923; 1843–1864): Two Union Women in Civil War Kentucky," in *Kentucky Women: Their Lives and Times,* ed. Melissa A. McEuen and Thomas H. Appleton Jr. (Athens, Ga., 2015), 99–118; and Tanfer Emin Tunc, "Food on the Borderlands: Josie Underwood's Civil War Diary and the Kentucky Home Front, 1860–1862," *War and Society* 36 (2017): 81–97.

[38] Amber C. Nicholson, "Border State, Divided Loyalties: The Politics of Ellen Wallace, Kentucky Slave Owner, During the Civil War" (master's thesis, University of New Orleans, 2011), 35. Additional studies of Kentucky women in this period include William Kuby, "Mary Jane Warfield Clay (1815–1900): Wifely Devotion, Divorce, and Rebirth in Nineteenth-Century Kentucky," in *Kentucky Women,* ed. McEuen and Appleton, 59–80, and Angela Esco Elder, "Emilie Todd Helm (1836–1930) and Mary Todd Lincoln (1818–1882): 'We Weep Over Our Dead Together,'" in ibid., 81–98.

property, women proved to be especially vulnerable to constraints as testamentary beneficiaries.

Other probate challenge cases occurred when testators manumitted slaves, made interracial gifts, and recognized concubines. Pitts notes correctly that by emancipating slaves through wills, testators challenged conventional racial hierarchies, ostensibly recognizing slaves as persons, not property. Interestingly, in cases where they were the party defending a will, slaves possessed legal standing and, accordingly, played an active role in the legal system—a system generally reserved for whites. According to Pitts, manumission will challenge cases "concocted a potent evidentiary stew of racial and gendered transgressions" in the state (62).

More recently, in *Marriage on the Border: Love, Mutuality, and Divorce in the Upper South during the Civil War* (Lexington, Ky., 2020), Allison Dorothy Fredette examines the nexus between intraregional identity and the structure of marital roles in Kentucky, Virginia, and western Virginia (later West Virginia). Choosing six communities for in-depth archival research—Kentucky's Franklin and Warren Counties, Tazewell, Fauquier, and Amelia Counties in eastern Virginia, and western Virginia's Ohio County—she discovered "a language of domesticity and mutuality" among women and men that shaped their marital bonds and, when necessary, facilitated their divorce (20). Men and women generally formed relationships based on separate, unequal spheres but in marriages that were mutually dependent.

Fredette maintains that "contractualism, . . . the growing view of marriage as not a permanent, sacramental institution but a contractual one with rules, procedures, and escape clauses, allowed more men and women to file for divorce and to use a variety of causes to explain their decision" in the borderlands of Kentucky and western Virginia than in more traditional, patriarchal eastern Virginia (21). "In postbellum Kentucky and West Virginia, residents used the same rhetoric and cited the same motivations for separation as in their antebellum cases, reflecting a continued desire for mutuality and individualism in their relationships, while [eastern] Virginians decried the breakdown of racial mastery, connected this breakdown with potential disruptions to their hierarchical households, and demanded mastery and loyalty from both former slaves and spouses" (22–23). Fredette also discovered that the Civil War, often considered a cultural dividing line for families, generally had minimal impact on the culture of divorces either along the border or in eastern Virginia.[39]

Four decades ago James C. Klotter identified the opportunity for researchers to address more fully Civil War-era guerrilla warfare in the state—a lacuna that historians have worked hard to fill.[40] Students should consult Brian McKnight's *Confederate Outlaw: Champ Ferguson and the Civil War in Appalachi*a (Baton Rouge, 2011); T. R. C. Hutton's account of "guerrillaism" in Breathitt, County, Kentucky, *Bloody Breathitt: Politics and Violence in the Appalachian South* (Lexington, Ky, 2013); articles by Berry Craig and Dieter Ullrich on Confederate partisan warfare in western Kentucky; Stuart W. Sanders's account of a Union soldier-turned-Rebel bushwhacker; Stephen Rockenbach's "Home Rebels, Amnesty, and Antiguerrilla Operations in Kentucky in 1864"; J. Michael Rhyne's "'A Blood Stained Sin': Slavery, Freedom, and Guerrilla Warfare in the Bluegrass Region of Kentucky, 1863–65"; and Scott A. Tarnowieckyi's "'Branded by the Lincolnites as Guerrillas': Adam Rankin Johnson, Guerrilla Identity, and Irregular Warfare in the Lower Green River Valley in 1862."[41] In 2018, the

---

[39] Also see Allison Dorothy Fredette, "'One Pillar of the Social Fabric May Still Stand Firm': Border South Marriages in the Emancipation Era," in *Rethinking American Emancipation: Legacies of Slavery and the Quest for Black Freedom,* ed. William A. Link and James J. Broomall (Cambridge, Eng., 2016), 93–118.

[40] James C. Klotter, "Clio in the Commonwealth: The Status of Kentucky History," *Register* 80 (1982): 75.

[41] Berry Craig and Dieter Ullrich, "Captain Thomas Jones Gregory, Guerrilla Hunter," *Journal of the Jackson Purchase Historical Society* 45 (2018): 44–61; Stuart W. Sanders, "The Radicalization of 'Bloody-Handed' Bill Davison: How a Union Soldier became a Pro-Confederate Bushwhacker," *Register* 116 (2018): 183–208; Stephen Rockenbach, "Home Rebels, Amnesty, and Antiguerrilla Operations in Kentucky in 1864," in *The Guerrilla Hunters: Irregular Conflicts during the Civil War,* ed. Brian D. McKnight and Barton A. Myers (Baton Rouge, 2017), 77–100; J. Michael Rhyne, "'A Blood Stained Sin': Slavery, Freedom, and Guerrilla Warfare in the Bluegrass Region of Kentucky, 1863–65," *Register* 112 (2014): 553–87; and Scott A. Tarnowieckyi, "'Branded by the Lincolnites as Guerrillas': Adam Rankin Johnon, Guerrilla Identity, and Irregular Warfare in the Lower Green River Valley in 1862," *Register* 113 (2015): 641–73. For context, readers also will benefit from the essays in Matthew C. Hulbert and Joseph

editors of *Ohio Valley History* devoted an entire number to irregular military actions, including hit and run attacks on enemy soldiers and civilians, that occurred throughout the state.[42] That same year the *Register of the Kentucky Historical Society* also published a special issue on "Irregular Violence and Trauma in Civil War Kentucky."[43]

Klotter also urged historians to devote more effort to questions pertaining to the economy, "business in uncertain times," freedom of the press, martial law, and what he termed "changing patterns of social life."[44] In 1999 he noted that scholars needed to investigate wartime policy—state political actions, such as formation of the State Guard, economic actions, and loyalty oaths—and to pay more attention to conflicts on the commonwealth's home front.[45] While some of these omissions in the scholarship have been addressed over time, others remain untapped, including the history of working-class whites, especially Appalachian folk, women, nonelite women, and agriculturists, black and white, throughout the state. Careful research also needs to be conducted to determine which Kentuckians supported each side in the conflict, possibly evaluating their demographic, economic, and social profiles by counties, communities, and families. Challenges facing Freedmen's Bureau agents in guaranteeing racial justice and the racial violence directed at blacks that enveloped the state during the period remain virtually unexplored.[46] So too are many of the topics

M. Beilein Jr., eds., *The Civil War Guerrilla: Unfolding the Black Flag in History, Memory, and Myth* (Lexington, Ky., 2015).

[42] "Guerrilla Warfare Was the Norm: Toward a New Vision of Civil War Kentucky," *Ohio Valley History* 18 (2018): 3–74. See articles by Andrew Fialka, Barton A. Myers, Matthew Christopher Hulbert, James M. Prichard, Lorien Foote, and Brian Matthew Jordan.

[43] "Irregular Violence and Trauma in Civil War Kentucky," *Register* 116 (2018): 151–236. See articles by Matthew Christopher Hulbert, Joseph M. Beilein Jr., Stuart W. Sanders, and Andrew Fialka. An additional work is Gerald W. Fischer, *Guerrilla Warfare in Civil War Kentucky* (Sikeston, Mo., 2014).

[44] Klotter, "Clio in the Commonwealth: The Status of Kentucky History," 76.

[45] James C. Klotter, "Moving Kentucky History into the Twentieth Century: Where Should We Go From Here?" *Register* 97 (1999): 89–90, 109–10.

[46] For recent work on both topics, see Rand Dotson, "The Murder of Peter Banford and the Campaign against the Freedmen's Bureau in Kentucky's Bluegrass Region," *Register* 118 (2020): 447–87, and William A. Blair, *The Record of Murders and Outrages: Racial Violence and the Fight over Truth at the Dawn of Reconstruction* (Chapel Hill, 2021).

I mentioned in 2014 that still cry out for exploration and analysis.[47] Remarkably, historians still seem intimidated, overawed by the prospect of writing a complete study of the Civil War and Reconstruction in the commonwealth. Accordingly, Coulter's very outmoded work, reflecting the racial biases, research methodologies, and sources of the 1920s—not the 2020s—continues to reign.

But as Brad Asher observed recently, scholarship on Civil War-era Kentucky finally has begun keeping pace with the scholarship of the last two generations of historians who write in the field. "This work has overturned the Lost Cause view of the war, reevaluating claims of southern military prowess, Confederate unity, and northern brutality . . . it has reversed the tendency to downplay slavery as a cause of the war and emancipation as an ultimate and important objective of the Union war effort. It has elevated the crucial role, and the self-liberating actions of slaves in making the case for abolition, and it has revisited the reputation of the Radical Republicans, even as it noted the persistence and virulence of northern racism and antiblack attitudes."[48] Also, significantly, the pioneer work of Marshall and Harlow has influenced recent scholars increasingly to agree that "the supreme irony" of Rebel defeat "was that Confederates, so ostracized during the war, ultimately won a considerable portion of the peace."[49]

Although Kentucky may not have been the "Alsace-Lorraine of pragmatism between the crusaders," before, during, and after the Civil War the strategically positioned commonwealth charted its own unique course as part of and apart from its fellow southern states. One only needs to reflect on Kentucky's "favored nation" status by Lincoln, its Unionism built atop states' rights, its unwillingness to emancipate its slaves, its obstructionism in recruiting USCT, its reign of racial terror during and after Reconstruction, its persistent "uncivil

---

[47] These include a full-scale social history of the war, a study of Louisville and the war, work on the conflict in eastern Kentucky, and research on the Republican Party in the state during the "long" Reconstruction. See Smith, "Whither Kentucky Civil War and Reconstruction Scholarship?" 240–44.

[48] Asher, *The Most Hated Man in Kentucky*, 7.

[49] Stanley, review of Craig, *Kentucky Confederates*, 991.

war" conducted by guerrillas and partisans, and its unwillingness to ratify the Thirteenth, Fourteenth, and Fifteenth Amendments until 1976. Then one can begin to understand Kentucky's so-called brand of Bluegrass exceptionalism.[50]

[50] For an interpretation of Kentucky's pre–Civil War history, its stance on secession, and the state's alleged exceptionalism, see Gary R. Matthews, *More American than Southern: Kentucky, Slavery, and the War for an American Ideology, 1828–1861* (Knoxville, 2014). On race, reunion, and Reconstruction in Kentucky, see Aaron Astor, "'I Wanted a Gun': Black Soldiers and White Violence in Civil War and Postwar Kentucky and Missouri," in *The Great Task Remaining Before Us: Reconstruction as America's Continuing Civil War*, ed. Paul A. Cimbala and Randall M. Miller (New York, 2010), 30n53; Anne E. Marshall, "'The Rebel Spirit in Kentucky': The Politics of Readjustment in a Border State, 1865–1868," ibid., 54n68.

KENTUCKY, THE CIVIL WAR, AND THE SPIRIT OF HENRY CLAY

By James C. Klotter

Henry Clay was dying. The Great Compromiser could not compromise that situation. In November 1851, after a twelve-day trip, he had arrived in Washington, D.C., the site of his last great effort at keeping the Union intact, just the year before. Many accolades had come his way following the resulting Compromise of 1850. Now he had returned to Congress to do his duty as senator and also to argue a potentially lucrative case before the U.S. Supreme Court. But almost immediately on his return, Clay began to experience increasingly bad health. He made a brief appearance in the Senate but returned no more; he turned over his oral arguments before the court to an ally, and they split the resulting sizable fee that followed a favorable decision. All the while, Clay's health worsened. He began to spit up blood and could not sleep because of the constant coughing. The man who once exuded energy and vitality now complained of a lack of strength, no appetite, and a constant cold. Clay took opiates to help him get some rest and, displaying his famous wit amid the ad-

JAMES C. KLOTTER is the state historian of Kentucky and professor emeritus of history of Georgetown College, where he taught for twenty years. Before that, he was at the Kentucky Historical Society for a quarter of a century, retiring as the executive director. Dr. Klotter has authored or edited some twenty books, including *The Breckinridges of Kentucky* (1986); *Kentucky: Portrait in Paradox, 1900-1950* (1996); *Kentucky Justice, Southern Honor, and American Manhood* (2003); and two 2018 works, *Henry Clay: The Man Who Would Be President* and a revision (with Craig Friend) of his *New History of Kentucky*. He wishes to thank Lindsey Apple and Harold Tallant for their critiques and aid.

versity, noted that he had "nearly emptied an apothecary shop" with the various medicines he took. Seldom venturing from his room in the National Hotel, he resigned his Senate seat in December, effective the next September. Ever the politician, Clay had chosen that date to ensure that a Whig administration would choose his successor early, rather than the Democrats who would soon take the reins of state office.[1]

By January 1852, Clay told a fellow member of Congress that his situation remained "very critical." Two months after that, Clay reported to his wife Lucretia, back in Kentucky, that "I may linger for months, but I cannot get well." He told her that while he had expected he would return to the folds of family and home, he had not the strength to make the taxing trip. As the last days approached, Clay stressed he was ready to go, though, he said with a smile perhaps, "I welcome death but do not desire an exciting one." Finally, in the late morning of June 29, 1852, at the age of seventy-five, Henry Clay died, in the arms of his country, in the nation's capital, hoping that his last compromise would bind the bleeding sections together and keep his beloved Union intact but fearful that it would not.[2]

For almost a half-century, Henry Clay had served the United States well, as representative, Speaker of the House, senator, diplomat, secretary of state, spokesman for the American System, twice-rejected Whig presidential hopeful, three-time presidential nominee, respected party chief, Great Pacificator, and honored leader—but never as president. But even his many enemies respected the record he had forged, and Clay became the first person to lie in state in the

---

[1] J. Winston Coleman Jr., *Last Days, Death, and Funeral of Henry Clay* (Lexington, Ky., 1951), 27nn3-4; Henry Clay to James B. Clay, January 3, [1852], box 39, Papers of Henry Clay and Family, Library of Congress, Washington, D.C. (hereafter Clay Family Papers); Henry Clay to Lucretia Clay, February 27, November 19, 1851, January 4, 12, 1852; Clay to John M. Clay, February 28, 1852, all in James F. Hopkins et al., eds., *The Papers of Henry Clay*, 11 vols. (Lexington, 1959-92), vol. 10, *Candidate, Compromiser, Elder Statesman, January 1, 1844–June 29, 1852* (Lexington, 1991), 876, 933, 943, 947, 956 (hereafter *Clay Papers*).

[2] Henry Clay to Garrett Davis, January 12, 1852; to Lucretia Clay, March 22, April 25, 1852, all in *Clay Papers*, 10:943, 961, 966; Clay to James B. Clay, February 18, 1851, box 39, Clay Family Papers; George R. Poage, *Henry Clay and the Whig Party* (Chapel Hill, 1936), 275.

capitol. Then his casket made its roundabout way back to Kentucky, covering twelve hundred miles and passing through five state capitals, so that the crowds of Americans could honor their hero one more time and offer one last farewell. The body was interred in the Lexington Cemetery on July 10, 1852, before a crowd of as many as thirty thousand people. Henry Clay had finally returned home, one last time. But his service to his country had not ended with his death. The United States would need his spirit again and again.[3]

For as the nation mourned Clay, it also worried. He had dominated his political world as perhaps no one else of his generation, usually building up rather than tearing down, creating rather than destroying, producing optimism rather than pessimism. Clay had helped frame the Missouri Compromises of 1820-21, had forged the 1833 Compromise after South Carolina and Andrew Jackson had taken the nation to the edge of conflict, and had crafted the peace plan that eventually became the Compromise of 1850. With his presence in Washington, D.C., no more, with his ability to craft workable plans now absent, with his eloquent voice calling for reason now stilled, could the nation remain one and united?[4]

Symbolically, the answer to that question seemed to be suggested in regard to Clay's own estate, Ashland. Purchased by a son, James B. Clay, after the father's death, the home had been structurally unsound and the son had razed the property. A *Cincinnati Gazette* reporter visited the site in the late summer of 1854 and found only a brick wall in the parlor still standing, and workmen had begun to level even that: "All . . . that remains of the old homestead of the statesman is a pile of bricks and rubbish." Only a carriage remained

---

[3] Coleman, *Last Days*, 9-14; David S. Reynolds, *Waking Giant: America in the Age of Jackson* (New York, 2008), 9. For in-depth biographies, see Robert V. Remini, *Henry Clay: Statesman for the Union* (New York, 1991) and David S. Heidler and Jeanne T. Heidler, *Henry Clay: The Essential American* (New York, 2010). For excellent, briefer analyses, see the chapter "Henry Clay," in Daniel Walker Howe, *The Political Culture of the American Whigs* (Chicago, 1979), and Merrill D. Peterson, *The Great Triumvirate: Webster, Clay, and Calhoun* (New York, 1987). Numerous earlier biographies and more specialized studies of aspects of Clay's career all add to the story, but no modern source examines in any depth Clay's continuing influence after his death.

[4] James B. Swain, *The Life and Speeches of Henry Clay*, 2 vols. (New York, 1844), 1:197.

of the man who had lived there. Angry, the reporter wrote that the edifice should have been repaired instead as one of America's "shrines of liberty." After the visitor left, the house would, in fact, be rebuilt by 1857, supposedly using many of the same materials and a similar floor plan. But by that time, day after day, year after year, the passion present at the time of Clay's death had grown stronger, the rhetoric shriller, the possibilities of a peaceful resolution dimmer. At Ashland, the bricks that had seen the warm sun of many summers and the soft rain of many autumns had been dismantled. Would the edifice that was the nation suffer the same fate? And if it did, could it emerge, like Ashland, as a reborn, stronger place, built on a new, firmer foundation, looking forward to a better future? Or would the country lie in ruins, a grim reminder of the failures of a generation that did not include Clay?[5]

******

On April 12, 1861, guns echoed across the waters of Charleston Harbor. Union soldiers in Fort Sumter felt the first shock waves from the impact. Soon the shock waves would be felt across America. The Civil War had begun—on the anniversary of the birth of Henry Clay.

Numerous ironies abounded. Not only did the cannon thunder on a day when some citizens across the nation still celebrated the memory of the great peacemaker on his birthday, as they had since his death, but the commander of the fort, Robert Anderson, was from the same state as the Kentuckian. Moreover, the leaders of the two warring sides had both been born in the commonwealth.

Kentucky appeared to be in the middle of the crisis, whether it wanted to be or not. On the Washington Monument in the early 1850s, the state had inscribed the Clay-inspired words: "Under the auspices of heaven & the precepts of Washington, Kentucky will be the last to give up the Union." But in April 1861 would that be the

---

[5] *Cincinnati Gazette*, in *New York Times*, October 3, 1854; *Macon (Ga.) Weekly Telegraph*, July 22, 1865; Coleman, *Last Days*, 23; Charles W. Coleman Jr., "Ashland, the Home of Henry Clay," *Century Magazine*, December, 1886, 168-69; *Remembering Barry Bingham* (n.p., 1990), 109.

case? Forces pulled the state both ways. The sons and daughters who had moved away lived in both North and South. Economic forces tugged it both directions. Transportation routes connected it to both regions. But Kentucky held slaves, like the South, and had the third-highest number of slaveholders of any slave state. Yet people in the commonwealth had also invested their capital in the North. Over the decades, Kentucky had sacrificed for a country "bought by the blood of our fathers." A majority of the dead in the War of 1812 had been Kentuckians; one-time resident Zachary Taylor had led an American army in the Mexican-American War; Henry Clay's son had been killed on a battlefield of that conflict. The nationalism that grew up from those efforts, and from the teachings of Clay, had fought for years with a strong states'-rights outlook within Kentucky as well. Various forces thus pulled Kentucky to support one side or the other as the state sought to find its way. This place that had once been a middle ground between competing cultures during its formative frontier period now became that kind of place once more, as it tried to avoid being a new "dark and bloody ground."[6]

Abraham Lincoln and Jefferson Davis both recognized the di-

[6] *Tenth Annual Celebration of the Birth-Day of Henry Clay . . .* (n.p., 1855); image of Washington Monument inscription at www.nps.gov/wamo/photosmultimedia/upload/WAMC/; E. Merton Coulter, *The Civil War and Readjustment in Kentucky* (Chapel Hill, 1926), 3, 8-13; Lowell H. Harrison, *The Civil War in Kentucky* (Lexington, Ky., 1975), 1-3; J. Stoddard Johnston, *Kentucky*, vol. 9 of *Confederate Military History*, 12 vols. (Atlanta, 1899), 6-17; Bureau of the Census, *Population of the United States in 1860* (Washington, D. C., 1864), 176-79, 594-95; *New York Times*, January 26, 1861; James W. Hammack Jr., *Kentucky and the Second American Revolution: The War of 1812* (Lexington, Ky., 1976), 111-12; James Russell Harris, "Kentuckians in the War of 1812: A Note on Numbers, Losses, and Sources," *Register of the Kentucky Historical Society*, 82 (1984): 277-86 (hereafter *Register*). For general information on Kentucky in the early days of the war, see also Henry Volz III, "Party, State, and Nation: Kentucky and the Coming of the American Civil War" (PhD dissertation, University of Virginia, 1982); Timothy M. Russell, "Neutrality and Ideological Conflict in Kentucky during the First Year of the American Civil War" (PhD dissertation, University of New Mexico, 1989); John Boyd, "Neutrality and Peace: Kentucky and the Secession Crisis of 1861" (PhD dissertation, University of Kentucky, 1999); Aaron Astor, "Belated Confederates: Black Politics, Guerrilla Violence, and the Collapse of Conservative Unionism in Kentucky and Missouri, 1860-1872" (PhD dissertation, Northwestern University, 2006); Thomas C. Mackey, "Not a Pariah, but a Keystone: Kentucky and Secession" in *Sister States, Enemy States: The Civil War in Kentucky and Tennessee*, ed. Kent T. Dollar, Larry H. Whiteaker, and W. Calvin Dickinson (Lexington, Ky., 2009), 25-45.

lemma of their home state and tried to act in such a way as to influence the commonwealth to support their respective causes. Both had similarities in their lives. Both had been born in the state, some eight months and a hundred miles apart. Both had departed the commonwealth when young. Both had continued their Kentucky ties—Davis through education at two state schools, Lincoln through his law partners and friendships. Both married women from Kentucky. Both served in the Black Hawk War. Both served in the U.S. House for one term. Both served as presidential electors. And both experienced numerous setbacks and defeats in their careers. But the differences between the two mattered most. One voted Democrat, the other Whig, then Republican. One supported the expansion of slavery, the other did not. One wanted a new nation, the other a united one.[7]

Davis had served with Clay in Congress and had mostly opposed him vehemently during the crisis of 1850. He recognized that Clay had greater "graces of oratory than any man that ever lived in this country" but respected neither Clay's nationalistic programs nor his efforts at compromise. Lincoln and Clay were another matter, however. Whether the two men ever met is unknown. Lincoln's wife, Mary Todd, knew Clay and could have introduced the two on the several occasions when Lincoln came to Lexington. The man from Illinois certainly heard Clay speak, and apparently Clay inscribed a book to him. But no contemporary evidence links the two. And Lincoln never indicated that they met, something he likely would have noted. But perhaps they did. What is known, however, is that Clay heavily influenced Lincoln's policies, programs, and pronouncements.[8]

On Clay's death, Lincoln had delivered a forty-minute eulogy,

---

[7] Holman Hamilton, *The Three Kentucky Presidents* (Lexington, Ky., 1978), passim; Lowell H. Harrison, *Lincoln of Kentucky* (Lexington, Ky., 2000), vii, 47-49.

[8] "Jefferson Davis: The Ex-Confederate President at Home," *Tyler's Quarterly Magazine*, January 1951, 171-72; Edgar DeWitt Jones, *The Influence of Henry Clay Upon Abraham Lincoln* (Lexington, Ky., 1952), 33-34; William H. Townsend, *Lincoln and the Bluegrass* (Lexington, Ky., 1955), 132-33, 142; Shearer Davis Bowman, "Comparing Henry Clay and Abraham Lincoln," *Register* 106 (2008): 498; "Recent Acquisition Enhances Clay-Lincoln Legacy," *Ashland: The Henry Clay Estate*, Fall 2009, 1.

extolling Clay's devotion to human liberty and his vision for the nation: "Whatever he did, he did for the whole country." And, in fact, Lincoln tried mightily to follow the lead of his fellow Kentuckian. He called party leader Clay his "beau ideal of a statesman" and that did not represent hyperbole. Lincoln told a correspondent that he "loved and revered" Clay and that he repeated his stances on colonization of freed slaves, internal improvements, and the tariff: "I was an old Henry Clay tariff Whig," he later stressed. In the Lincoln-Douglas debates, Lincoln invoked his hero's name numerous times and declared again and again that the Great Compromiser's visions reflected his own. When Lincoln ran for the presidency, the Republican platform mirrored many of Clay's programs. And, after his election, the president-elect took four references into a room with him as he composed his inaugural address. One of the four was Clay's 1850 speech on the compromise. A part of Clay lived on in Lincoln.[9]

Yet, importantly, a major difference existed between Clay and Lincoln. Even though both had publicly expressed opposition to slavery—Clay first did so at age twenty-one, Lincoln at age forty-five—the two diverged on that great question. "Prince Hal" held slaves. Lincoln did not. Clay criticized slavery and advocated gradual emancipation over time. So too did Lincoln. Yet to Clay, the Union was most important and he therefore would compromise on the moral issue of slavery and the lives of millions of humans held in bondage, in order to still the southern dissent, to try to avoid war, and to keep the nation one. Lincoln differed on that score. If Clay wanted to preserve the Union he knew, Lincoln wanted to defend a different kind of Union. As one historian stated, Lincoln "insisted that a Union worth saving was a Union that stood for something more than itself." Although he was no abolitionist, Lincoln recognized that sometimes

[9] Eulogy on Henry Clay, July 6, 1852; First Debate with Stephen A. Douglas at Ottawa, Illinois, August 21, 1858; Lincoln to David Ullman, February 1, 1861; Lincoln to Edward Wallace, October 11, 1859; Speech at Rushville, Illinois, October 20, 1858; speech at Petersburg, Illinois, October 29, 1858, all in Roy P. Basler, ed., *The Collected Works of Abraham Lincoln*, 9 vols. (New Brunswick, N.J., 1953-55), 2:122-32, 3:29-30, 4:184, 3:487, 329, 333; Mark. E. Neely Jr., "American Nationalism in the Image of Henry Clay: Abraham Lincoln's Eulogy on Henry Clay in Context," *Register* 73 (1975): 56; Jones, *Influence of Clay*, 29, 32, 1.

an evil is so great that a people or a nation cannot compromise on the issue. The expansion of slavery was just such an evil. He could not—would not—allow the peculiar institution to spread. That issue would help spark the secession crisis. But even then, Clay may still have influenced Lincoln. Like his model, Lincoln saw that the two sections shared a common language, religion, political heritage, and republican ideology. He also had mostly experienced the South in Kentucky, a place whose Clay-like views may have misled Lincoln on the overall sentiment of the South. As a result, in 1860-61, the new president may have overestimated the extent of southern unionism and underestimated the power of proslavery conviction. Ex-Whigs and ex-Clayites usually did lead the opposition to secession, and they, like Lincoln, expected wiser heads and better counsels to see eventually the fatal errors of secession. But their voices did not win out. And compromise failed. And the war came. And people died.[10]

******

With the coming of war after Fort Sumter, Kentucky had to decide on a course of action. The allies of Lincoln and Davis voiced their appeals, worked to influence the decisions, and labored to move the commonwealth to their side. And in those crucial, desperate days, the voice of Henry Clay once more echoed across Kentucky and the

[10] Richard Hofstadter, *The American Political Tradition and the Men Who Made It* (New York, 1968), 109; Lonnie Maness, "Henry Clay and the Problem of Slavery" (PhD dissertation, Memphis State University, 1980), vi, 253; Andrew Cayton, "To Save the Union," *New York Times Book Review*, July 4, 2010; Brian Dirck, "Lincoln's Kentucky Childhood and Race," *Register* 106 (2008): 318; Robert W. Johannsen, *Lincoln and the South* (Ft. Wayne, Ind., 1989), 15-16; Harrison, *Lincoln of Kentucky*, 122; Ronald C. White Jr., *Lincoln: A Biography* (New York, 2009), 349, 449-51. For the ex-Whig opposition to secession, see, for example, Thomas B. Alexander, "Persistent Whiggery in the Confederate South, 1860-1877," *Journal of Southern History* 27 (1961): 306; Burton Folsom II, "The Politics of Elites: Prominence and Party in Davidson County, Tennessee, 1835-1861," ibid., 39 (1973): 372; William G. Shade, *Democratizing the Old Dominion: Virginia and the Second Party System, 1824-1861* (Charlottesville, Va., 1996), 1, 290-91; James Copeland, "Secession and the Union in Tennessee and Kentucky: A Comparative Analysis," *Border States* 11 (1997) at Border States on-line <http://spider.georgetowncollege.edu/htallant/border/6511/copeland.htm>; Michael F. Holt, *The Rise and Fall of the American Whig Party* (New York, 1999), 983. For an astute discussion of the recent Lincoln scholarship, see John David Smith, "'Gentlemen, I too, am a Kentuckian': Abraham Lincoln, the Lincoln Bicentennial, and Lincoln's Kentucky in Recent Scholarship," *Register* 106 (2008): 433-70.

nation. His words, his beliefs, and his advice became a clarion call to guide the citizenry. At least ten published biographies and collections of his speeches had already been published.[11] Leaders could read Clay's counsels. But, more than that, newspapers reprinted key parts of Clay's talks. People could even purchase an envelope bearing Clay's picture with words regarding secession printed on the image. Other Kentuckians already knew the Great Compromiser's stands as a result of following him politically over the years. Even if dead for almost nine years, Clay lived on through his written words, remembered appeals, and learned behaviors. Many Kentuckians had been well inculcated in Clay's vision of America and had accepted it as their own. As the waves of fear about the future surged across the state and nation, Clay's spirit would prove crucial in keeping Kentucky in the Union—and thus perhaps in winning the war.[12]

Like Banquo's Ghost in *Macbeth*, Henry Clay haunted the secession crisis, warning of evil in several ways. In one sense, Clay had done his job too well, for his actions remained vivid in the psyche of the populace. For when earlier crises had arisen and when the nation had seemed on the verge of conflict, Clay had stepped up and defused the situation. As a friend of Clay later stated, the Great Pacificator would never have accepted the idea of an irrepressible conflict that some spoke of in 1861. A senator who served with Clay wrote in his recollections that had Clay been in Congress in that time, "There

[11] For Clay books in print by the time of the Civil War, see George D. Prentice, *Biography of Henry Clay* (Hartford, Conn., 1831); David Mallory, *The Life and Speeches of the Hon. Henry Clay of Kentucky* (New York, 1843); Swain, *Life of Clay*; Epes Sargent, *The Life and Public Service of Henry Clay . . .* (New York, 1844); Calvin Colton, *The Life and Times of Henry Clay* (New York, 1845); Colton, ed., *The Works of Henry Clay* (New York, 1855); Colton, ed., *The Private Correspondence of Henry Clay* (New York, 1856); Colton, *The Last Seven Years of the Life of Henry Clay* (New York, 1856). Additionally, the Sargent book was updated and expanded by Horace Greeley in a work that appeared in 1852. J. Winston Coleman Jr., *A Bibliography of Kentucky History* (Lexington, Ky., 1949) cites two more works (not examined): Richard Chambers, ed., *Speeches of the Hon. Henry Clay . . .* (Cincinnati, 1842) and A. H. Carrier, *Monument to the Memory of Henry Clay* (Cincinnati, 1856).

[12] Envelope, c. 1861-65, available at http://infoweb.newsbank.com/iw-search/we/HistArchive?p_action=doc&f_content=image . For one example of the range of newspapers reproducing Clay's words, compare *New York Times*, December 26, 1860, with the obscure *Egg Harbor City (N.J.) Atlantic Democrat*, May 15, 1861.

would, I feel sure, have been no civil war." In 1860-61, many expected another Clay to come forward and save the nation. As a eulogist had emphasized at Clay's funeral, if one section sought to rise up against another, the citizens of America should go to Clay's grave and implore God "to raise up from his ashes another *Clay!*" Kentuckian John J. Crittenden had tried to be that man and had invoked both the spirit and the name of Clay: "What do I ask of you more than Mr. Clay himself did?" Crittenden returned to the state and addressed the Kentucky legislature, noting that Clay had stood on the same spot in 1850 and had spoken then "with a prophet's fire." Crittenden quoted the words of union that Clay had uttered, and asked, "What shall we do?" The national answer had been clear. His efforts at compromise, like those of many others, failed. Circumstances had changed, and different solutions were needed. No Clay had arisen from the ashes; no new Clay with the same foresight, will, and force came forward.[13]

Clay's spirit lived on in other ways. His words would be quoted in the crisis, not just in Kentucky but across the nation, and others paraphrased his sentiments without directly citing him. But Clay's own words made it clear how he would have stood on the issue before the people. Almost three decades before the Civil War, Clay had all-too-accurately foreseen what the future could hold, if his generation did not act constructively:

> I wish to see war of no kind; but, above all, do I not desire to see a civil war. When war begins . . . no human foresight is competent to foresee when, or how, or where it is to termi-nate. But when a civil war shall be lighted up . . . , and armies are marching, and commanders are winning their victories, and fleets are in motion . . . , tell me, if you can—tell me, if any human beings can tell its duration? . . . In what state will be left our institutions? In what state our liberties? I want

[13] Robert C. Winthrop, *Memoir of Henry Clay* (Cambridge, Mass., 1880), 2; Henry S. Foote, *Casket of Reminisces* (1874; repr., New York, 1968), 30; "Address of the Rev. Ed. F. Berkley, Funeral of the Hon. H. Clay, July 10, 1852," in Edward F. Berkley Papers, Filson Historical Society, Louisville, Kentucky; Anne Mary Crittenden Coleman, ed., *The Life of John J. Crittenden.* 2 vols. (Philadelphia, 1871), 2:273, 278, 313 (quotes, 278, 313).

no war; above all, no war at home.

Six years later, in a controversial address before Congress, in which he attacked both nullifiers and abolitionists, Clay had once more warned of what could occur without wise actions. He had stressed that "the fraternal bands, which now happily unite us" might be extinguished in the "hazard and uncertainty of war." Then the Great Compromiser had recounted once more the dangers before them. War would produce "desolated fields, conflagrated cities, murdered inhabitants, and the overthrow . . . of human government." No one could win a fratricidal war: "It would be a conquest without laurels, without glory—a self, a suicidal conquest—a conquest of brothers over brothers." A decade after that, Clay had made it clear that his home state would suffer greatly in such a conflict: "Kentucky would become the theater and bear the brunt of the war," one that "would lay waste and devastation her fair fields." In short, Clay had foreseen nothing but sorrow resulting from a civil war. Would that more of his era had heard and believed those words.[14]

But if a division did occur, which side would Clay have taken? How he stood on that question would infl uence the course of Kentucky and the nation almost a decade later. In a series of talks and publicly printed letters in 1850 and 1851, Henry Clay had made his course very clear. In a February 1850 speech before the Senate, he had emphasized that "I am directly opposed to any purpose of secession, or separation. I am for staying in the Union . . . . Here I am within it, and here I mean to stand and die." A few months later, in the heat of summer, Clay once more had reminded his listeners of the uncertainty of war: "All history teaches, that the end of war is never seen in the beginning of war." Who could foresee the consequences or effects of any such conflict? Instead, he had implored Congress to discard passion, jealousy, and pride and sacrifice for the common good of the country by forging a compromise: "What are we—what is any man worth who is not ready and willing to sacrifice

[14] Register of Debates, 22nd Cong., 2nd sess. (1831-33), 472; Congressional Globe, 25th Cong., 3rd sess. (1838-39), 359; Clay to Richard Pindell, February 17, 1849, *Clay Papers*, 10:579.

himself for the benefit of his country when it is necessary?"[15]

After Clay had finished, a South Carolinian arose to take exception to how the speaker had characterized one of the "fire-eaters" in that state. Clay's quick response left little doubt on the contempt he held: "If he pronounced the sentiment attributed to him of raising the standard of disunion and of resistance to the common Government . . . , if he follows that declaration by corresponding overt acts, he will be a traitor, and I hope he meets the fate of a traitor. [Great applause—the galleries]." A few days later, Clay had tried to bring together the factions opposing compromise and had blamed both extremes for their intransigence. But he most faulted those who threatened secession: "I said, and I repeat—and I wish all men who have pens to record it—that if any single State, or the people of any State, choose to raise the standard of disunion and to defy the authority of the Union, I am for maintaining the authority of the Union," by force, if necessary. Even if his own state of Kentucky hoisted the disunion banner, he would oppose it: "I would go against Kentucky herself in that contingency, much as I love her." As William Freehling has noted, that sentiment by a slaveholding Southerner represented a very significant statement. And to those who spoke of their state as their country, Clay had forcefully rejoined that, "This Union is my country; the thirty States are my country," all together as one, as the United States of America. Later in 1850, Clay had returned to the land he loved and had addressed the Kentucky General Assembly. Once more his words would be heard, recorded, and remembered. Noting that he had foreseen "the dark and gathering storm," he hoped that the Compromise of 1850 would protect the country from the threatening clouds of war. To those who asked if he could ever consent to the dissolution of the Union, Clay had exclaimed, "Never—never—never." Those words of 1850 would appear in Clay's published correspondence and would be reprinted during the secession crisis.[16]

[15] Speeches in Senate, February 5-6, and July 22, 1850, both in *Clay Papers*, 10:672, 780-81.

[16] Speech in Senate, July 22, 1850, and Comment in Senate, August 1, 1850, *Clay Papers*, 10:789-90; William W. Freehling, *The Road to Disunion: Secessionists at Bay, 1776-1854* (New

In the last year before his death, Clay had gone even further in his denunciation of the doctrine of secession. He had written several letters on the subject, most of which would appear in his published works and many of which would reappear in newspapers in 1861. In February 1851, for example, Clay had stressed that if rebellion occurred, no one would want to avoid the shedding of blood more than he. But such opposition must be put down in order to preserve "our glorious Union." Otherwise, he had stressed, the nation would break up into "petty, jealous, and belligerent fragments." Did the nation want to return to the days of the failed Articles of Confederation? Did it want to give up a dazzling destiny? Did it want to yield its place as a beacon for others? Three months later, he had remarked, simply, "Secession is treason." "An exclusive reliance upon law and reason" would not work against such actions, and force must be the response.

Finally, in a widely reprinted letter in October and in a speech not long before he made his final trip to Washington, D.C., Clay had advocated putting down illegal resistance to the Union, "at every hazard." Revolution, he agreed, was a fundamental right but not secession. People could revolt against a government only if an "intolerable" tyranny so oppressed them and a blatant injustice so tormented them that they had no other option. But in America, no such situation existed. Citizens voted freely, enjoyed wide rights, and possessed a voice in government. "Metaphysical" secession theorists and "rash men, promoted by ambition" suggested that a state could leave the Union even if it only differed from the view the majority held. To Clay, dedicated to the idea that majority rule provided the best answer in governmental decision-making, such a theory represented extreme error. He had called secession unconstitutional and an "utterly irreconcilable" action within the compact of government. Such an action would be an "atrocious" act of "extreme folly and madness" that would fragment the nation and bring "endless war." Such words made a difference when Kentucky took action a decade

York, 1990), 506; *Mr. Clay's Speech to the General Assembly of Kentucky, 1850* (Frankfort, 1850), 13; *Clay Papers*, 10:830.

later. Union supporters like Robert J. Breckinridge, Joseph Holt, and George D. Prentice echoed the Great Compromiser's calls for opposition to those who advocated secession. Voting Kentuckians knew the words of Clay as well. But would that be enough to keep Kentucky from joining the new Confederate States of America?[17]

******

Kentucky remained torn, distraught, and divided. Speakers for both sides made their appeals. Citing common ties and cultures, pro-Confederate advocates called for Kentuckians to join them in a government dedicated to states' rights and the protection of slave property. Unionists, in turn, argued that no cause existed for secession. A Republican president might sit in Washington, D.C., but he could do little with a Senate and a Supreme Court blocking any actions. Moreover, Unionists stressed, slavery in Kentucky would be more vulnerable if the state joined the Rebels. Under the current federal law, fugitive slaves had to be returned; if a foreign nation operated across the Ohio River, runaways would not be returned. In other words, the Union would better protect slavery. And, said Unionists, if the commonwealth joined the southern cause, it would become—as Clay predicted—a bloody battlefield in the war. A Union meeting in Louisville on April 16, 1861, proclaimed that "the memories of the past, the interests of the present, and the solemn convictions of future duty" should show the folly of following secessionists. But as both sides made their cases to the public, a third alternative found support.[18]

[17] Clay to Francis Lathrop, February 17, 1851; to Thomas Stevenson, May 17, 1851; to Fellow Citizens of New York City, October 3, 1851, *Clay Papers*, 10:861, 891, 923; *Baltimore Sun*, October 18, 1851; James C. Klotter, *The Breckinridges of Kentucky* (Lexington, Ky., 1986), 77-81; Joseph Holt to Joshua Speed, May 31, 1861, Frank Moore, ed., *Rebellion Record*, 11 vols. (New York, 1861-68), 1:289; Thomas D. Clark, "George D. Prentice," in *The Encyclopedia of Louisville*, ed. John E. Kleber (Lexington, 2001), 723. The families of Unionists Breckinridge, Holt, and Prentice all would divide in the war. See Klotter and Clark (above), and Elizabeth D. Leonard, "One Kentuckian's Hard Choice: Joseph Holt and Abraham Lincoln," *Register* 106 (2008): 392-94.

[18] Harrison, *Lincoln of Kentucky*, 126; William W. Freehling, *The South vs. the South* (New York,

As a historian wrote later, "Clay for almost fifty years molded the composite mind of the state." From the "memories of the past" came the words of Clay, calling for compromise, moderation, and reason rather than fury, war, and madness. Kentucky wanted slavery, but it also wanted the Union. Clay had been a slaveholder and a Unionist. Like him, Kentuckians saw no conflict between the two, for even Abraham Lincoln had made it clear at the start of the war that he sought to preserve the Union, not end slavery. No crisis of fear caused people in the commonwealth to worry that their world was slipping away. They saw a still-vibrant two-party system and trusted in the democratic process to protect their interests. After all, in America, a minority that felt ignored on some controversial issue could quickly become the majority after the next election. Clay had helped create an enduring Kentucky mindset that combined a moderate southern outlook with a conservative nationalism. Because of that, many Kentuckians tried harder than most to find some kind of last-minute compromise to the conflict, to serve as mediators between the sections, to return the swords to plowshares. But the two sections did not heed their calls. War raged stronger and stronger.[19]

The war spirit spread across uncommitted areas of the slave South with a white-hot intensity. Other states joined the Confederacy, eventually including the Mother State of Virginia. In that atmosphere, at that time, a vote on that issue in Kentucky might have produced an emotional reaction for secession by citizens caught up in the excitement of the moment. In March 1861, a leading southern sympathizer stated that the state might well side with the Confederacy. if a vote could be taken. But in those crucial months, the Kentucky Unionists outmaneuvered the secessionists. Prosouthern governor

2001), 38; Volz, "Party, State, and Nation," 472; Andrew McClester to [George McClester], May 27, 1861, *Adair County Review* 4 (1990): 50 (letter made available by Eugene Conover of Columbia, Kentucky); Coulter, *Civil War*, 40-41 (quote).

[19] Coulter, *Civil War*, (quote) 4; Steven Channing, *Crisis of Fear: Secession in South Carolina* (New York, 1970); Boyd, "Neutrality and Peace," 114; Volz, "Party, State, and Nation," 7-8, 475, 479; Michael E. Holt, *The Political Crisis of the 1850s* (New York, 1978), 6-8, 230; Gary Matthews, "Beleaguered Loyalties: Kentucky Unionism," in *Sister States, Enemy States,* 12, 15, 22.

Beriah Magoffin first wanted no war, but if that could not be avoided, then he favored secession. Accordingly, he called on the General Assembly to pass legislation that would allow a convention to vote on the issue. But if fortune in war favors the largest army, fortune in politics favors those with the most votes. And the legislature was solidly pro-Union. The spirit of Henry Clay still hovered over the capitol chambers; his voice still echoed down the spiral staircase; his appeals for calm still remained strong. The General Assembly tabled the motion to call a convention by a 54-36 vote in the House. And perhaps some leaders of the Union cause, like ex-Whigs Robert J. Breckinridge and John J. Crittenden, had learned well the art of politics from their friend Clay. The legislature then took a unique step, but one which would prevent a Kentucky vote on secession at those crucial moments. By sizable votes of 69-26 and 13-9—a 70-percent margin—the state resolved, and the governor proclaimed, a policy of "strict neutrality." Kentucky still sought to be an agent to resolve differences and to end the internecine struggle. If the state could do that, editorialized the *Louisville Journal*, it would be entitled to "the gratitude of the present generation and of posterity." But that forlorn hope disguised the fact that neutrality kept armies out of the state and prevented battles on Kentucky soil, and it gave the Union cause a most precious resource—time.[20]

There now existed the United States of America, the Confederate States of America—and Kentucky. Michael Burlingame noted that the state became "a domestic Switzerland," surrounded by war. That declaration of neutrality in May did not stop boys and men from marching off to join one side or the other. Would-be recruits crossed Kentucky north and south to enlist. Meanwhile, the two competing camps continued to make their appeals and operate be-

---

[20] Johnston, *Kentucky*, 25; Boyd, "Neutrality and Peace," 148, 2, 75, 145, 206-7; Coulter, *Civil War*, 29-31, 51, 55-56; Mackey, "Kentucky and Secession," *Sister States, Enemy States*, 34-36; Lowell H. Harrison, "Kentucky," in *The Confederate Governors*, ed. W. Buck Yearns (Athens, Ga., 1985), 83; Susan Lyons Hughes, "Camp Dick Robinson: Holding Kentucky for the Union in 1861," *Perspectives in History* 6 (1991): 49; *Louisville Journal*, April 21, 1861. For an excellent recent analysis, see William C. Harris, *Lincoln and the Border States* (Lawrence, Kans., 2011).

hind the scenes. But time favored the Union. An ally from Kentucky told Lincoln that delay now allowed people "[to] begin to think for themselves," and he saw them daily becoming more supportive of the Union cause. That cause gained strength on the Fourth of July in 1861. On that day, some twenty thousand people filled the city of Lexington to dedicate, at long last, the monument to Henry Clay at the Lexington Cemetery. Work had begun four years earlier, when the cornerstone had been laid on another Fourth of July. Delays had followed. But now the tall shaft with Clay's statue on top was to be formally dedicated. Featured speaker (and Unionist) James Harlan delivered a talk that praised Clay but also emphasized Clay's beliefs and stands on the issue of union or disunion.[21]

All that had an effect. Neutrality provided the delay needed to help passions cool and to let the words of Clay, offered by speakers and the press, take hold. In the end, the nationalistic spirit the Great Pacificator had engendered over the years finally won out. The summer elections produced a huge Union victory. With an even larger pro-Union makeup of 76-24 in the House and 27-11 in the Senate, the legislature could override the governor's veto or even impeach him if needed. That situation, as Garrett Davis, a pro-Union congressman, told the U.S. secretary of war, meant that the state stood poised "for a more active policy." Legislators needed only an incident or excuse to move away from neutrality. That moment came when a Confederate general made an ill-advised military movement into western Kentucky. The General Assembly almost immediately ended the policy of neutrality in September—after four months—and declared Kentucky a loyal member of the United States. They called for the expulsion of Confederates. When the governor vetoed that resolution, they overrode the veto. Angry prosouthern Kentuckians formed their own rump government, with their own governor and, eventually, their own congressmen. Then with admission of the

[21] Michael Burlingame, *Abraham Lincoln: A Life*, 2 vols. (Baltimore, 2008), 2:154-56; Ira Stout to Lincoln, May 1, 1861, Abraham Lincoln Papers at the Library of Congress, available online at the American Memory Project, Library of Congress; Townsend, *Lincoln and the Bluegrass*, 282-83; Coleman, *Last Days*, 20.

group into the Confederacy, Kentucky had a star in both flags. And, as Clay had foreseen, it became a Brothers' War, more so perhaps than anywhere else.[22]

******

The decision of Kentucky to remain a loyal state proved to be one of the most decisive victories the Union achieved. Lincoln's quote that "I think to lose Kentucky is nearly the same as to lose the whole game" has been often noted. But the rest of that comment reveals much as well: "Kentucky gone, we cannot hold Missouri, nor, I think, Maryland. These all against us, and the job on our hands is too large for us." Lincoln knew that the Kentucky decision could mean the difference between Union success or failure. First of all, its geographical position could be crucial to victory. If Kentucky (and Missouri) had gone Confederate, the southern forces would have had a natural defense line at the Ohio and Mississippi Rivers. And since the Ohio had no bridges crossing it at the time, invasion would be more difficult. Moreover, had Missouri joined Kentucky in the Confederacy, southern forces would start much closer to midwestern cities like Chicago and Cincinnati. And had Maryland joined them, then the District of Columbia would have been encircled by hostile states.[23]

In 1861, Kentucky was one of the most important states in the Union. It offered much to the side it supported. The Kentucky population—ninth among the states and third among the fifteen slave states—meant that its men could fill armies. The state also had a very diversified agricultural base that could aid a cause. In 1860, it stood first in the nation in the production of hemp, second in tobacco, third in flax, and fifth in corn and rye. Beyond that, Kentucky held more mules than any state and its thoroughbreds seemed unrivaled.

---

[22] Volz, "Party, State, and Nation," 458-62; Garrett Davis to Simon Cameron, July 15, 1861, Thomas Metcalfe Collection, Kentucky Historical Society Collections, Kentucky Historical Society, Frankfort, Kentucky; Edward C. Smith, *The Borderland in the Civil War* (New York, 1927), 306.

[23] Lincoln to O. H. Browning, September 22, 1861, Basler, ed., *Collected Works*, 4:532-33; Mackey, "Kentucky and Secession," *Sister States, Enemy States*, 26.

Add in the large numbers of hogs and cattle and Kentucky stood preeminent in agriculture among the slave states.[24]

In fact, as William Freehling and others have stressed, the border states that remained loyal—Kentucky, Missouri, Maryland, and Delaware—may have provided the key to Union success. Three of the four largest cities of the South—Baltimore, St. Louis, and Louisville—lay in those states. They held more people than the combined population of the other fourteen largest southern cities. Those border urban areas were also at crucial strategic locations, held sizable manufacturing plants, and served as vital transportation hubs. And those four loyal border states had a population of over three million. Since the eleven slave states that seceded had only about nine million people overall—and some 40 percent of them slaves who would not be fighting for the South but sometimes against it—the addition of the border-state numbers in the southern mix would have greatly enlarged the Confederate fighting pool and made the Confederacy much more competitive on that score. (Of course, not all border-state whites would have fought for the Confederacy, even if their states had declared that way, just as not all Southerners in the seceded states fought for the Confederacy. But official actions would have had an effect and the draft might have operated much better as a result.) In short, the lingering influence of Henry Clay on the South and on Kentucky decision-making, and the resulting influence of Kentucky on the other border states (as enunciated by Lincoln) may have been one of the crucial factors in the Civil War.[25]

******

Henry Clay had warned of the costs of a conflict and his descendants would feel the effects firsthand. The Civil War divided the Clay family as well. One son supported the North; one supported the South, and one vacillated. That pro-Confederate sibling

[24] Coulter, *Civil War*, 16; Burlingame, *Lincoln*, 2:154.
[25] Freehling, *South vs. South*, 23; Mackey, "Kentucky and Secession," *Sister States, Enemy States*, 26-28; 1860 U.S. census, 598-99.

would die in exile during the war. Beyond that, five of Henry Clay's grandchildren took up arms—for both sides. Of those who fought, three—including Henry Clay III—never returned. Nor was Clay's old estate and rebuilt home spared the ravages of war. In October 1862, a skirmish took place on the grounds, literally bringing the war home to the Clays.[26]

That battle between Blue and Gray, in some ways, reinforced the fact that Clay had failed. In the end, he had not framed a political system capable of withstanding the stresses placed on it after his death. His compromises had delayed the conflict enough for the North to gain strength, but, in the end, failed to quiet the sectional controversy and did not succeed in preventing war. His attempts to end the divisive question of slavery as an issue had not borne fruit. And his inability to win the presidency had kept him from strengthening the course of the nation that way. Yet also in the end, Clay succeeded better than that record indicates. Henry Clay's greatest contribution to the United States may have been the continuing influence he had on the mindset of his home state. That proved crucial. In a book published the year after the war ended, a Southerner proclaimed that Kentucky had remained officially a Union state because of Henry Clay, "who, like every great man, left an impress upon his state, which it remained for future even more than contemporary generations to attest." That same year, an article in the *North American Review* recounted how Clay had been quoted frequently in the decision days of 1861 and asked, "Who can estimate the influence of these clear and emphatic utterances?" The writer admitted that no one could truly know "how many wavering minds" those words affected, but he termed the number significant. Defeated in life in his presidential bids, Clay may have achieved his greatest victory after his death.[27]

---

[26] Lindsey Apple, *The Family Legacy of Henry Clay: In the Shadow of a Kentucky Patriarch* (Lexington, Ky., 2011), 109; Henry Clay Simpson Jr., *Josephine Clay* (Louisville, 2001), 60, 37, 51, 60; *Clay Papers*, 10:823n; Basil W. Duke, *History of Morgan's Cavalry* (Cincinnati, 1867), 383-85.

[27] E. A. Pollard, *Southern History of the War,* 2 vols. in 1 (New York, 1866), 194; unsigned review of *The Life of Henry Clay* in *North American Review,* January 1866, 192. The matter of Clay not winning the presidency and having an influence on developments is not a trivial one. One historian argues that had Clay won in 1844, no Mexican-American War would

In his lifetime, writers had recognized Clay's accomplishments but noted that, even then, "posterity will deliver justice if the present generation does not." Earlier, a Lexington paper had pointed out that "history, more durable than brass, or marble, becomes the lasting monument of the statesman." But a one-time enemy of Clay perhaps summed it up best: "They may lay their pedestals of granite . . . [but] he is not dead—he lives . . . . He needs no stone—he desired none. . . . He carved his own statue, he built his own monument." Clay's record, his lasting memory, his influence beyond his own generation, all represent better memorials than the ones in capitol rotundas or in cemeteries or public squares. The best monument to Henry Clay is the fact that the United States remains one country, one nation, one example of a successful democracy, still working, still changing, still trying to reflect the enduring spirit of Henry Clay.[28]

have resulted, no issue of slavery expansion would thus have occurred, and there might have been no Civil War. See Gary J. Kornblith, "Rethinking the Coming of the Civil War: A Counterfactual Exercise," *Journal of American History* 90 (2003): 76-105.

[28] *New York Herald*, November 21, 1850; *Kentucky Reporter* [Lexington, Ky.], October 20, 1823; Thomas Marshall, quoted in Peterson, *Great Triumvirate*, 489.

THE RELIGION OF PROSLAVERY UNIONISM: KENTUCKY WHITES ON THE EVE OF CIVIL WAR

By Luke E. Harlow

On May 6, 1861, just a few weeks after Confederate artillery fired on Fort Sumter and started the Civil War, the Kentucky annual statewide meeting of Baptists, the General Association, petitioned the legislature to "preserve the peace of the state." A report in the *Western Recorder*, the chief organ of the denomination in the Commonwealth, took great pride in noting that the document lacked partisan animus. Demonstrating that Baptists were not "attempt[ing] to make political capital" in that moment of sectional strife, the petition had been affirmed by coreligionists from a variety of perspectives, "Secessionists and Unionists, women and children." The appeal itself called upon Kentucky politicians to "rise above the excitement and confusion of party, and of the times, and deliberately, in the fear of God, seek only, first, the good, the very best possible good, of our Commonwealth, and, then, of other portions of our country." The logic of this argument was straightforward: Kentucky Baptists hoped "to avert from our soil, our homes, our women, and our children, the dreadful scourge of civil war." In the coming conflict, they wanted to remain neutral.[1]

That opinion was common among religious whites and among white Kentuckians as a whole. Located just south of Ohio, Indiana, and Illinois, only 664 miles of the Ohio River were all that separated

LUKE E. HARLOW is an associate professor of history at the University of Tennessee, Knoxville. He is the author of *Religion, Race, and the Making of Confederate Kentucky, 1830-1880*.

[1] "The Lexington Memorial," *Western Recorder*, May 25, 1861.

the slave state of Kentucky from free soil—the longest of any slave state-free state border. Thus "truly a border state" in both geography and politics, Kentucky whites labored to remain detached from the divisive sectional controversy.[2] Their sentiment of neutrality stood out vividly in the notably complicated and controversial presidential election of November 1860. A plurality of the electorate (45.2 percent) sided with the conservative Constitutional Union Party candidate, slaveholder John Bell of Tennessee, over the Southern Democratic Party nominee, native Kentuckian John C. Breckinridge (36.3 percent). The other two candidates, Democrat Stephen A. Douglas and Republican Abraham Lincoln, both from Illinois, received 17.5 and 0.9 percent, respectively. Almost everywhere else in the United States, Constitutional Unionists were unpopular; Kentucky joined only Tennessee and Virginia in giving its largest vote to Bell. The party itself was an amalgam of former Whigs and Know-Nothings and famously ran on a platform that "recognize[d] no political principle other than *the Constitution . . . the Union . . . and the Enforcement of the Laws*." Most significantly, Constitutional Unionists took no stance on the most pressing issue of the day—slavery.[3]

Such reluctance to speak on the slavery question, if unappealing almost everywhere else in the United States, singularly suited a border slave state unwilling to push for secession but also unwilling to tamper with the institution within its boundaries. Slavery, in fact, had much to do with the variety of political conservatism of white Kentuckians. If the Union were to be preserved, it was the Union without modification—that is, the Union as it existed in 1860. In other words, neutral Kentuckians defended a slaveholding nation they refused to leave and opposed changing.[4]

[2] See Lowell H. Harrison, *The Civil War in Kentucky* (Lexington, Ky., 1975), ix.

[3] Lowell H. Harrison and James C. Klotter, *A New History of Kentucky* (Lexington, Ky., 1997), 183-86; James M. McPherson, *Battle Cry of Freedom: The Civil War Era* (New York, 1988), (quote, 221); 1860 Presidential election figures taken from the American Presidency Project, University of California, Santa Barbara, http://www.presidency.ucsb.edu/showelection.php?year=1860. For further analysis of Kentucky voting patterns in the 1860 election, see Harrison, *Civil War in Kentucky*, 4-5.

[4] Lowell Harrison and James Klotter cogently capture the irony of the attempt of Kentuckians to remain disengaged from the sectional crisis: "Neutrality was attractive to

The political neutrality of Kentucky drew considerable justification from religious sources. As elsewhere in the South, white evangelicals represented a preponderant political majority in the Bluegrass State in 1860—perhaps more than 75 percent of the white population and more than 60 percent of the total population.[5] In their view, God had ordained slavery as a properly Christian institution. To be sure, the future course of Kentucky was anything but certain on the eve of the Civil War. As a slave state that bordered free soil, Kentucky fostered a small but vocal evangelical antislavery movement throughout the antebellum era—often connected to colonizationism—which culminated with a failed attempt in 1849 to enter an emancipationist clause in the state constitution.[6] However, while the

many Kentuckians who were uncertain of the path their state should take, although a state had no more right to declare neutrality than it did to secede." See Harrison and Klotter, *New History of Kentucky*, 187, and Gary R. Matthews, "Beleaguered Loyalties: Kentucky Unionism," in *Sister States, Enemy States: The Civil War in Kentucky and Tennessee*, ed. Kent T. Dollar, Larry H. Whiteaker, and W. Calvin Dickinson (Lexington, Ky., 2009), 9-24.

[5] Estimates of evangelical adherence in Kentucky are drawn from church accommodations as a percentage of the state population, given in 1860 U.S. Census, Churches & Religion and General Population, Historical Census Browser, University of Virginia, Geospatial and Statistical Data Center, http://mapserver.lib.virginia.edu/php/start.php?year=1860.

In 1860, Baptists claimed nearly 95,000 members; Methodists numbered nearly 57,000, and Presbyterians counted roughly 10,000. Membership figures on the Christian Churches (followers of the Campbellite/Restorationist movement) are harder to determine for 1860, but they claimed more than 41,000 members in 1846, and it is plausible to estimate that there were more than 50,000 members by 1860. Undeniably, the Christian Churches were the third-largest denomination in Kentucky in the period. See J. H. Spencer, *A History of Kentucky Baptists*, 2 vols. (Cincinnati, 1885), 1:722, and Lewis Collins and Richard H. Collins, *History of Kentucky*, 2 vols. (Covington, Ky., 1874), 1:425-26, 456, 459.

Membership numbers are suggestive, but they vastly undercount the number of religious adherents in nineteenth-century America. Because of relatively restrictive membership standards, most churches saw many more regular church attendees—perhaps double or triple the number—than actual members. As a result, ascertaining the actual number of Christian adherents in the period is highly imprecise. Most careful historians of American religion tend to rely on the U.S. census tally of church accommodations but currently lack effective ways of determining just how many people considered themselves active faith practitioners in the period. See George C. Rable, *God's Almost Chosen Peoples: A Religious History of the American Civil War* (Chapel Hill, 2010), 11-12. For an elucidation of this problem as it applies to antebellum Virginia, see Charles F. Irons, *The Origins of Proslavery Christianity: White and Black Evangelicals in Colonial and Antebellum Virginia* (Chapel Hill, 2008), 3-10.

[6] See Harold D. Tallant, *Evil Necessity: Slavery and Political Culture in Antebellum Kentucky* (Lexington, Ky., 2003), 27-57. See also Lowell H. Harrison, *The Antislavery Movement in Kentucky* (Lexington, Ky., 1978), 29-31; Jeffrey Brooke Allen, "Did Southern Colonizationists Oppose

conservative believers of the state once found themselves arguing over the will of God for American slavery as it existed in reality, they never denied that the Bible sanctioned slavery as a method of social and labor organization for some times and places, if not their own. More significantly, they never fought over white supremacy; no religious conservative in Kentucky dared question the racist foundation upon which antebellum white American society rested. Evangelical Kentuckians—like white evangelicals more broadly in the South— had long rejected abolitionism for committing a two-fold heresy. The first was theological: abolitionists contravened nineteenth-century standards of American evangelical orthodoxy. The second was racial: by demanding an immediate end to slavery, abolitionists threatened the secure social fabric of America, which required the dominance of a pure-race class of white elite leadership.[7]

Since on the eve of the Civil War, the United States remained a nation that protected the rights of slaveholders, when most religious whites in Kentucky spoke of loyalty to the Union, they spoke of a nation they believed served as the civil protector of conservative Christian values, including slavery. It was this belief that drove their commitment to political neutrality in the sectional conflict. From such a perspective, threats to neutrality constituted threats to their faith or, at the very least, threats against the nation that secured their conservative Christian faith. As the Kentucky Baptist press contended throughout 1860, "God has chosen these United States as the theater" of divine beneficence. The American nation stood "elevat[ed] among the kingdoms of the earth," "a monument of the power of Christianity and civilization," "reserved for some grand and holy

Slavery? Kentucky 1816-1850 as a Test Case," *Register of the Kentucky Historical Society* 75 (1977): 92-111 (hereafter *Register*); Carl N. Degler, *The Other South: Southern Dissenters in the Nineteenth Century* (New York, 1974), 22-25; and on the broader appeal of colonization, Ellen Eslinger, "The Brief Career of Rufus W. Bailey, American Colonization Society Agent in Virginia," *Journal of Southern History* 71 (2005): 39-74.

[7] For further explication of these claims, see Luke E. Harlow, "Neither Slavery nor Abolitionism: James M. Pendleton and the Problem of Christian Conservative Antislavery in 1840s Kentucky," *Slavery & Abolition* 27 (2006): 367-89, and "Religion, Race, and Robert J. Breckinridge: The Ideology of an Antislavery Slaveholder, 1830-1860," *Ohio Valley History* 6 (2006): 1-24.

purpose" by "our great Creator." To rend the national fabric would prove disastrous, especially if that rending came through violent and bloody means.[8]

From the view of religiously and politically neutral Kentucky, two major factions poised to fight. On one side were southern proslavery secessionists. On the other side were northern abolitionists. Both were evil because both sought to destroy the Union as it presently existed, but Kentuckians were not evenly poised between the two options. Secession, however undesirable and extreme it might have seemed to many white evangelical Kentuckians in 1860 and 1861, served to preserve Christian slavery and the white supremacy that attended it. If disunion were wrong, the religiously conservative whites of Kentucky at least identified with and understood the position of their coreligionists in the South.

They offered no such empathy, however, for the hostiles from the North. To the Kentucky conservatives, secession remained far less of an evil than that foisted upon the American public by a radical antislavery faction hell-bent on tearing down the most basic foundations of Christian America: its faith, its unity, and its racial stratification, all of which the slavery system secured. As a Virginia Methodist bluntly contended in May 1860, and Kentucky Baptists heartily endorsed, "Abolitionism is the cancer at the very heart of America."[9] It thus constituted the primary threat to Christian America and, by extension, to Kentucky political neutrality.

When contrasted with abolitionists, the longstanding differences proslavery and gradual emancipationist Kentuckians saw between themselves became inconsequential. From the perspective of those white evangelicals who considered themselves true believers in 1860, there was right and wrong on the slavery question. Abolitionism was wrong. Thanks to that "alarming" fiction, as one *Western Recorder* article contended, "Orthodox churches have been affected" by the "corrupt current of mingled errors." The essay—republished from

---

[8] "Prayer for the Preservation of the Union," *Western Recorder*, January 9, 1860; "Thoughts Upon the Present Condition of our Country," ibid., August 18, 1860.

[9] "Northern Apostacy [*sic*]," ibid., May 26, 1860.

the *Christian Advocate* of Richmond, Virginia, chief organ of the Virginia Conference of the Methodist Episcopal Church, South—saw the "evangelical ministry" warped by "widespreading heresies." Classic doctrines of Christianity, including "a particular providence, the special agency of the Spirit in regeneration, the inspiration of the Scriptures," to say nothing of "depravity, regeneration, and the atonement," had all been subverted by the wayward theology of abolitionism.[10]

It was a theological problem freighted with tremendous social and political baggage. "Heresy in religion is a portentous omen," the Methodist author argued. Assuming that the foundation for nineteenth-century American society rested upon classical Christianity, he continued: "A corrupt public conscience is a throne on which Satan sways a terrible dominion. Religion in America has more to fear from the abolition speculations of the North than from any other source in the whole world." True Christians needed to band together to defeat such threats, white religious conservatives maintained. Such unified orthodoxy might not simply preserve the faith. It might also protect the life of the American nation.[11]

It was precisely this sort of religious solidarity against abolitionism that prompted the *Western Recorder* to publish in early January 1861 a sermon by Henry J. Van Dyke (1822-91), noted minister of the First Presbyterian Church of Brooklyn, New York. Just under a month before, Van Dyke had labored to show "the Character and Influence of Abolitionism." His religiously conservative message registered a clear ecumenical appeal, apparent in the strong approbation given by the editors of the *Western Recorder*. Van Dyke, they wrote, delivered a "discourse characterized by the loftiest Christian patriotism, and by its fearless advocacy of God's truth." Indeed, they had "seldom seen a more faithful revelation of the true character of abolitionism." They believed that though Van Dyke was a Presbyterian in the heart of Yankeedom, his commitment to foundational principles of con-

---

[10] Ibid.
[11] Ibid.

servative Protestantism offered a guiding light to Kentucky Baptists.[12]

In the redacted form of Van Dyke's discourse that followed this introduction, he plainly defined the target of his sermon. An abolitionist "believes that slaveholding is sin, and ought therefore to be abolished." That was quite a different position than the one occupied by emancipationists, who, for example, might "believe on political or commercial grounds that slavery is an undesirable system" or find the U.S. Constitution unduly disposed toward "the rights of slaveholders." That antislavery impulse could be tolerated, according to Van Dyke. One was not an abolitionist "unless he believes that slave holding is morally wrong." Advocates for that extreme view, he argued, had no Christian basis for such a claim.[13]

Van Dyke's argument unfolded directly. Abolitionism failed as a proper Christian ideology because it had "no foundation in Scriptures." It was "a historic truth," he contended, that "at the advent of Jesus Christ slavery existed all over the civilized world, and was intimately interwoven with its social and civil institutions." On such a purportedly evil institution, the New Testament remained silent. "Drunkenness and adultery, theft and murder—all the moral wrongs which have ever been known to afflict society, are forbidden by name." Somehow, however, slavery, "according to abolitionism, this greatest of all sins—this sum of all villainies—is never spoken of except in respectful terms." "How," Van Dyke asked his congregation, "can this be accounted for?"[14]

The answer was obvious. Abolitionism led to "utter infidelity." Those under its spell operated from the "assumption, that men are capable of judging beforehand what is to be expected in a Divine revelation." Abolitionists "did not try slavery by the Bible" but rather "tried the Bible by the principles of freedom." Theoretically, those "principles of freedom" drew from the laws of "nature." But really, Van Dyke surmised, natural law was merely code language for

[12] "Character and Influence of Abolitionism," ibid., January 5, 1861.

[13] Ibid. Quotes from longer printed version of the sermon, Henry Jackson Van Dyke, *The Character and Influence of Abolitionism!: A Sermon Preached in the First Presbyterian Church, of Brooklyn, on Sunday Evening, December 9th, 1860*, 2nd ed. (Baltimore, 1860), 5.

[14] "Character and Influence of Abolitionism," *Western Recorder*, January 5, 1861.

"preconceived notions." Abolitionists, in other words, committed the classic first error on the path to heterodoxy—the human claim to understand the mind of God was "the cockatrice's egg, from which in all ages heresies have been hatched." "This is the spider's web," Van Dyke argued, "which men have spun out of their own brains, and clinging to which, they have attempted to swing over the yawning abyss of infidelity." Van Dyke admitted that not all "abolitionism is infidelity," but the "tendencies" within the system were too much to ignore: "Wherever the seed of abolitionism has been sown . . . a plentiful crop of infidelity has sprung up." True believers needed to avoid the bitter "fruit of such principles." Orthodox faith, Van Dyke asserted, demanded no less.[15]

Van Dyke gained little traction for his perspective among his northern coreligionists, but in white evangelical Kentucky it achieved extensive appeal. Moreover, Van Dyke's was not the only opinion about abolitionism from above the Mason-Dixon Line that white religious Kentuckians found laudable.[16] Van Dyke's sermon only briefly alluded to the white supremacist foundation of American slavery, but for the many white Americans—South and North—who agreed with him, it was impossible to extract racism from their critique of abolitionism.[17] Just a few months after publishing Van Dyke's sermon, the *Western Recorder* published a defense of slavery that originally ran in

[15] Ibid.

[16] As a result of his open denunciation of abolitionism, many in the North argued that Van Dyke was a proslavery southern sympathizer. Van Dyke's Unionist credentials, however, had long been established and his opinion on abolitionism does not seem to have affected the opinion of his Brooklyn congregation of his pastoral abilities, where he served until his death in 1891. See Lewis G. Vander Velde, *The Presbyterian Churches and the Federal Union, 1861-1869* (Cambridge, Mass., 1932), 285; Peter J. Parish, "From Necessary Evil to National Blessing: The Northern Protestant Clergy Interpret the Civil War," in *An Uncommon Time: The Civil War and the Northern Home Front,* ed. Paul A. Cimbala and Randall M. Miller (New York, 2002), 78-79; and "Tablet to the Rev. Dr. Van Dyke: Formally Unveiled in the Second Presbyterian Church, Brooklyn," *New York Times,* October 2, 1894.

[17] It is no reach to assume that Van Dyke's own sense of racial superiority pervaded his analysis. In briefly saying that he would bracket questions of race in his sermon, he alluded to a classic racist defense of slavery—its utility as a Christian instrument for the improvement of benighted Africans: "I shall not attempt to show what will be the condition of the African race in this country when the Gospel shall have brought all classes under its complete dominion." Van Dyke, *Character and Influence of Abolitionism,* 11-12.

the *Christian Observer*, a Philadelphia-based, New-School Presbyterian paper that earned a reputation as the only publication in that mostly northern denomination to overtly endorse secession.[18]

Writing anonymously as "A Christian" from the City of Brotherly Love, the author contended, like a slew of other opponents of abolitionists, that "the advocates of the 'higher law' in regard to slavery" rejected the Holy Writ and were only able to "contend against the institution on conscientious grounds." The truth of the Biblical record on slavery, however, became apparent, the author argued, when rational minds looked at the very practical racial need for slavery. Despite possessing "every opportunity . . . the African has no where risen, to any extent in civilization." Freedom was no blessing to American blacks and the writer knew as much, living as he did on the free soil of Philadelphia. "There is a homely adage that 'the proof of the pudding is in the eating,' and when we in Philadelphia see around us a population of at least ten thousand persons of color, the mass of them born in our own State, and enjoying every advantage of civilization," it was impossible for the white mind to countenance that "we find them, with a few avocations, [living] in poverty." If the "degenerate" state of "the free black man, with the great advantage he has in Philadelphia," proved any indication, the writer asked, "how can it be expected that the liberated slave could succeed?" As the northern author contended, and his white Kentucky readers understood, African Americans constituted an unavoidably degraded race. Those abolitionists who argued otherwise rejected "common sense" and "God's law" only to uphold "their pride of opinion." As "A Christian" put it, God "for his wise purposes, permitted the African for centuries to be a barbarian in his own country, and a slave when he left it." "Why," he asked, would anyone "rebel and cavil with the great decree?" American slavery served a fundamentally Christian purpose as "it is now bringing thousands" of African Americans "to the knowledge of the truth as it is in Jesus." It made little sense that immediatist antislavery activists, "'calling themselves

---

[18] On the record of the *Christian Observer* in the sectional crisis, see Vander Velde, *Presbyterian Churches and Federal Union*, 370-71.

Christians' and ministers of Christ interfere to prevent this glorious cause." Abolitionism, asserted the writer, ludicrously pursued the wrongheaded ideal "of giving freedom to the contented and happy slaves." God had chosen one superior race to work for the elevation of one far more inferior. To act against that divine imprimatur represented nothing less than an affront to the will of God.[19]

Much historiographic debate has concerned the extent to which racism pervaded proslavery Christianity, particularly as it concerned readings of Genesis 9:18-27, where the Biblical patriarch Noah pronounces the so-called "Curse of Canaan" or "Curse of Ham" upon his son.[20] While no allusion to race, in any modern sense of the term,

[19] A Christian, "The Bible and Slavery," *Western Recorder*, March 9, 1861.

[20] Mark Noll has argued that the reason the proslavery-antislavery debate was so fierce was because of a "theological crisis" over Biblical interpretation and the role of Providence in the world. In Noll's formulation, because northern and southern Protestants both read the Bible the same way—through the lens of what he calls a "Reformed, literal hermeneutic"—religion was central in the rise of sectional strife: "Two cultures, purporting to read the Bible the same way, were at each other's throats." See Mark A. Noll, *America's God: From Jonathan Edwards to Abraham Lincoln* (New York, 2002), 396. Noll is somewhat sanguine about the possibilities of alternative hermeneutics in the period to solve the Bible-and-slavery dilemma. In *America's God* and also *The Civil War as a Theological Crisis* (Chapel Hill, 2006), he makes this point about African American, Catholic, and some high-church Reformed traditions. In short, the dilemma was profound but perhaps not entirely intractable. There were religious contingencies, though few Americans heeded those voices. Thus, in large part according to Noll, the Civil War came about because of the hermeneutical failures of American Protestantism.

Eugene D. Genovese and Elizabeth Fox-Genovese disagree. The sum of the Genoveses' point is that it has always been impossible to craft an antislavery agenda rooted in the Bible:

Noll offers the arresting argument that a faulty hermeneutic imposed severe rigidity on both proslavery and antislavery theologians and that peculiarly American conditions prevented a turn to the alternative hermeneutics offered by African Americans, Catholics, and certain Reformed Protestants. Noll's illuminating discussion clarifies much, but does not demonstrate how any of the alternatives could ground antislavery Christian doctrine in Scripture.

See Elizabeth Fox-Genovese and Eugene D. Genovese, *The Mind of the Master Class: History and Faith in the Southern Slaveholders' Worldview* (Cambridge, Mass., 2005), 526-27.

Molly Oshatz tries to push the debate further. Implicitly, she agrees with the Genoveses. Her essay, "The Problem of Moral Progress: The Slavery Debates and the Development of Liberal Protestantism in the United States," *Modern Intellectual History* 5 (2008): 225-50, and her book, *Slavery and Sin: The Fight against Slavery and the Rise of Liberal Protestantism* (New York, 2011) show how northern Protestants' inability to ground their antislavery claims in Scripture led to the rise of theological innovation and the concept of "moral progress," which gave rise to theological liberalism. However, Oshatz is careful to distance herself from both the projects of Noll and the Genoveses in "The Problem of Moral Progress," 227n5, where she

exists in the passage—and although there existed little historical prec-
edent for a racialized reading of the text—white nineteenth-century
American interpretations ubiquitously read African American inferiority into the curse, finding therein a foundation for black enslavement.[21] As a pseudonymous "Nannie Grey" contended in a February
1860 *Western Recorder* essay (reprinted from the Richmond, Virginia,
Whig), God's providential racial design for humanity, set forth in
Genesis 9:27, had only recently been fulfilled. The text—"'God' shall
enlarge Japheth, and he shall dwell in the tents of Shem; and Canaan
shall be his servant"—contained a direct, prophetic application to
American racial hierarchy. The first peoples of the North American
continent, the American Indians, "are, undoubtedly, the descendents

contends that: "Noll's focus on hermeneutical and moral failure, and the Genoveses' disparaging
characterization of the incipient liberalism of antislavery Protestants, do not account for the
ways in which the slavery debates necessitated theological innovation."

Charles Irons comes at the issue from a different direction and focuses primarily on the
role of race. He argues that Noll is right about the white Protestants' "faulty hermeneutic,"
which is most blatantly obvious to Irons in proslavery whites' racialized readings of the
Biblical texts. Though they claimed to be reading Scripture at face value, the Bible contains
no references to race. For Irons, "White evangelicals did not constantly adjust their defense
of slavery because they discovered new passages in the Bible or developed new modes of
interpretation, but because the terms of their relationship with black evangelicals changed."
See *Origins of Proslavery Christianity*, 16.

[21] Stacy Davis, *This Strange Story: Jewish and Christian Interpretation of the Curse of Canaan
from Antiquity to 1865* (Lanham, Md., 2008), provides a thoroughgoing analysis of the origins
of the nineteenth-century racist, proslavery reading of the Curse of Canaan. Davis contends
that, while prior Christian exegetes read social stratification into the text, there existed few
precedents for a racialized, proslavery interpretation.

The full text of Genesis 9:18-27 (King James Version) reads:

And the sons of Noah, that went forth of the ark, were Shem, and Ham, and
Japheth: and Ham is the father of Canaan. These are the three sons of Noah: and
of them was the whole earth overspread. And Noah began to be an husbandman,
and he planted a vineyard: And he drank of the wine, and was drunken; and he
was uncovered within his tent. And Ham, the father of Canaan, saw the nakedness
of his father, and told his two brethren without. And Shem and Japheth took a
garment, and laid it upon both their shoulders, and went backward, and covered
the nakedness of their father; and their faces were backward, and they saw not their
father's nakedness. And Noah awoke from his wine, and knew what his younger
son had done unto him. And he said, Cursed be Canaan; a servant of servants
shall he be unto his brethren. And he said, Blessed be the Lord God of Shem;
and Canaan shall be his servant. God shall enlarge Japheth, and he shall dwell in
the tents of Shem; and Canaan shall be his servant.

of Shem." Likewise, Japheth was progenitor of "the Europeans" who had conquered the North American continent and "now dwell in the homes of the Indians." Finally, Canaan's "sons" constituted the population of black slaves. Once, according to Grey, they "lived in the degraded wilds of Africa," but now they had received the "blessing" of becoming the "servant" of Japheth's white offspring—"to be civilized by the enlarged brain of Japheth, for God enlarged him mentally as well as physically." Africa's "miserable inhabitants," Grey argued, had been offered divine provision. Sparing no shortage of abhorrently imaginative racist language, Grey portrayed indigenous Africans to the *Western Recorder*'s white readers as "the thick-lipped, black skinned and wooly headed negro, in a state of barbarism, more degrading that of the brute creation; for he has neither the ingenuity of the beaver, nor the industry of the bee; for he provides neither food nor shelter for himself; but [is] guided by brute instinct alone." The Genesis curse, Grey explicated, had so "literally" and obviously "been fulfilled" that no one could doubt the "truth" the Christian God revealed in the Bible. White religious conservatives in nineteenth-century America thus considered racial distinctions a providential gift, Biblically considered.[22]

Some elite proslavery divines, as historian Eugene Genovese has maintained, found such a strained application of the text for racist ends "feeble." But most contemporary southern whites did not. Drawing from the deep religious well of what Stephen Haynes has called "intuitive racism," proslavery believers read white supremacy directly into the Biblical texts they charged their abolitionist enemies with perverting. Relying on their own common-sense understanding of black inferiority, most whites required no fancy hermeneutical scaffolding to build a racialized theological structure. Simply put,

[22] Nannie Grey, "The Origin of Slavery," *Western Recorder*, February 25, 1860. Versions of this article circulated through a number of southern newspapers in the period. In addition to its interpretation of African American inferiority, the exegesis of the Curse of Canaan was also applied broadly to justify Indian subjugation and, hence, Manifest Destiny. See William G. McLoughlin and Walter H. Conser Jr., "'The First Man was Red'—Cherokee Responses to the Debate Over Indian Origins, 1760-1860," *American Quarterly* 41 (1989): 252.

white Southerners—as well as many Northerners—were unwilling, by and large, to accept a Bible that was not racist.[23]

A March 1861 *Western Recorder* article, also reprinted from the New School Presbyterian, Philadelphia-based *Christian Observer*, demonstrated this point succinctly: "The descendants of Ham are yet in slavery as God willed it, and they will be so until he changes their condition." The divine division of the races led to a "natural dislike or antipathy in the white race to the black, which prevents the amalgamation of the races." While racial hostility would not remain permanent, it would persist until the end of human time. Accordingly, the writer explained that such interracial harmony would not come until the period of millennial global peace arrived with the eschaton—which Christians from many denominations believed in—"when the Lion and the Lamb lie down together." Until then, however, American slavery, "which is now in a very ameliorated form," served as a socially stabilizing force of Christian benevolence. In this writer's telling, African Americans were an uncontrollable people when left to their own baser passions. The enslaved were "happy where they are," because they were "restrained by their owners from the vices so common with the free black man in our cities." Those vices included a host of the most critical problems facing American urban populations; "details of murders, poisonings, arsons" filled the "daily papers." "Our streets at night swarm with prostitutes, swindling in high and low places, dram-drinking, gambling, and every vice that can be enumerated." Comparatively considered, slavery could not be so bad—the Bible approved of it. The Christian God had offered

---

[23] For the first quote, see Eugene D. Genovese, *A Consuming Fire: The Fall of the Confederacy in the Mind of the White Christian South* (Athens, Ga., 1998), 4. On "intuitive racism," see Stephen R. Haynes, *Noah's Curse: The Biblical Justification of American Slavery* (New York, 2002), 126. Part and parcel of the Christian proslavery exegesis of the Curse of Canaan as connoting racial difference was a defense of monogenetic accounts of human origins, as explained in the Biblical record. Reaching for an explanation of a white-dominated racial hierarchy that also upheld the Genesis record on common human ancestry, the racialized interpretation of the curse proved a convincing narrative. See Colin Kidd, *The Forging of Races: Race and Scripture in the Modern World, 1600-2000* (Cambridge, Eng., 2006), 137-51, and David N. Livingstone, *Adam's Ancestors: Race, Religion, and the Politics of Human Origins* (Baltimore, 2008), 180-86.

slavery as a means by which whites could socially control an inferior race unfit, as the example of northern free blacks confirmed, for the responsibility of freedom. Slavery may have been evil, the author opined, but it was certainly "the least of evils."[24]

The proponents of abolitionism, however, did not see the matter that way. "This self-righteous and Pharisaic spirit impedes the cause of the church," a sympathetic northern voice contended. By pushing a racially and theologically heterodox agenda, as a like-minded Presbyterian put it, abolitionists ventured to "plunge our happy nation into a fraternal war." Abolitionism would "let loose the passions and prejudices of men and all the evils which [include] civil war, the slaughter of men and of innocent women and little children." White Kentuckians, long assured of the rationality and importance of neutrality—and equally convinced of the abolitionist syllabus of errors—did not need persuading on this point.[25]

Three days before the secession of South Carolina on December 20, 1860, Duncan Robertson Campbell (1814-65) penned a letter to the *Western Recorder* addressed to a readership broadly defined as the "Christian public, North and South." Campbell, well known to his audience as president of Georgetown College—located in central Kentucky and the flagship institution of Baptist undergraduate education—did not achieve such a prominent position through extremist opinions.[26] His opinion on the sectional crisis was, like that among many of white Kentucky Christians, characteristically moderate. A civil war need not occur, Campbell assured his readership, but it would only be avoided if extreme partisans on both sides of the divide would give up their grievances. Those grievances were manifold, but it was clear from the tone of Campbell's letter that one section had been injured far more than the other. Campbell's prose took up more than three lengthy newspaper columns and offered words of opprobrium for southern secessionists, whom he saw as inaugura-

---

[24] A Christian Father, "Christian Charity," *Western Recorder*, March 23, 1861.

[25] Ibid.; A Christian, "The Bible and Slavery."

[26] For biographical information on Campbell, see Spencer, *History of Kentucky Baptists*, 1:603-4.

tors of nothing less than "revolution." That rebuke of disunionists, however, accounted for only a small fraction of the space devoted to condemning the northern "crusade of abuse" of southern patriots.[27]

Southerners charged that "the present troubles originated with the North." By and large, Campbell wrote, they were right. Because they lived on free soil, Northerners "have ungenerously and offensively assumed to themselves a higher grade of moral Christian character." There had been no shortage in the "torrents of abuse and insult" from Yankee "pulpits," "platforms," and "presses" in the "last fifteen or twenty years." It was not only the "peculiar institution" of the South that came under attack, but "our character also." However, those same northern Christians, Campbell argued, needed to consult the Bible they believed carried so much authoritative value. After a close reading of the text, Yankee believers would have to ask themselves "if the supercilious and proscriptive course" toward abolition, which included much invective "towards Christians at the South, is warranted by the spirit and conduct of Christ and his apostles towards the slaveholders of their day?" On this matter, the slaveholding South could remain assured: the answer was no. Abolitionism drew no "warrant from Scripture." As Hopkinsville educator J. W. Rust claimed, "The pulpit at the North" labored under the "pressure of the 'higher law power.'" It had thus become corrupted: "The great *animus* of the Northern pulpit has been hostile, and in constant activity against the institution of slavery in the South." Abolitionism was a heretical disease that had infected northern churches and twisted traditional Christian messages of love into harangues of hate.[28]

Northerners thus bore the responsibility for "driv[ing] the South to revolution." With the rise of the abolition-minded Republican Party to political dominance in the North, a "section" was now

[27] D. R. Campbell, "To the Christian Public, North and South: Must the Union be broken up?" *Western Recorder*, December 22, 1860.

[28] Ibid.; J. W. Rust, "'My Kingdom is not of this World.' The Irrepressible Conflict," *Western Recorder*, January 5, 1861 (emphasis in original). Rust was one of the most prominent Baptist layman in Kentucky. In 1864, he assumed the presidency of Bethel Female College, a boarding school in Hopkinsville sponsored by the local Bethel Association of Baptist churches, and in 1869 he became co-owner of the *Western Recorder*. See Spencer, *History of Kentucky Baptists*, 1:727.

"wholly controlling" national politics with the "single sentiment of antislavery." Thus, as Duncan Campbell explicated, the South had no recourse, no way to protect its own interests—slavery—but war. The dominant section, the North, held the salve that would heal the deep wounds of the nation. They had to "retrace their steps of aggression" and recognize the rights of masters in the South, which were secured both by the Bible and the U.S. Constitution. Since the abolitionist North had provoked the animosity between the sections, according to Campbell, it was the North that needed to repent. After that—and after "a reasonable time" passed—sectional hostility would cease.[29]

Presbyterian Samuel R. Wilson (1818-86) presented a similar argument in a November 1860 sermon on the sectional crisis: "I believe that in this whole affair Northern men have been really the aggressors, and impartial history will so attest." Wilson, pastor of the First Presbyterian Church in Cincinnati, claimed that his "life-blood" came through "Southern veins," despite being born in the Queen City, having received his education in northern schools, and holding pastorates to date only on free soil. To be sure, Wilson claimed a sizable audience in Kentucky, so much so that he assumed the pulpit of Mulberry Presbyterian Church in Shelby County in 1863 before moving to the First Presbyterian Church in Louisville for a thirteen-year pastorate beginning in 1865. Like religiously conservative Kentuckians, Wilson, just north of the slave line, espoused a conservative Unionist viewpoint. He contended that the election of Lincoln, while the "*immediate occasion*" of the "present threatening movements in the country," was "not the *cause*." Sectional strife came from a deeper source, rooted in the rampant tripartite American sins of "Pride," "Oppression," and "Lawlessness." No region claimed a monopoly on these wrongs, according to Wilson.[30]

Still, Wilson's message of sectional conciliation tended, like those

---

[29] Campbell, "To the Christian Public."

[30] Samuel R. Wilson, *Causes and Remedies of Impending National Calamities* (Cincinnati, 1860), 7-11, 16 (emphasis in original). For biographical information on Wilson, see William E. Connelley and E. M. Coulter, *History of Kentucky*, ed. Charles Kerr, 5 vols. (Chicago, 1922), 3:364-65.

of his Kentucky coreligionists, to highlight the record of northern wrongs. On southern plantations, there persisted "the degradation and oppression" of the enslaved, of which most Americans had been well informed. But, meanwhile, "in New England, with the paeans of liberty sounding in his ears, the emancipated slave freezes and starves and sinks into imbecility; and the philanthropy of his boasted Northern friends, having exhausted itself in denunciation of his master, leaves him to the tender mercies of time and chance." In truth, Wilson allowed, "the black man in our midst is subjected to many unjust disabilities." That acknowledgment, however, did not mean that he advocated, like apostate abolitionists, "either social or civil equality" of the races. Simply, Wilson wanted to point out the hypocrisy of northern immediatist antislavery voices. "The taunting finger," as he put it, "may point to the slave-mart, the whipping-post, and the loose marriage-tie of the slave; and the taunt may be hurled back by an appeal to the pauperism, prostitution, homicides, and divorces of those who, in the philanthropic zeal, have forgotten the admonition of Jesus: 'Judge not, that ye not be judged.'" Southern secessionists, according to Wilson, were guilty of trying to "break up the national Covenant" and could not be lauded for launching a rebellion that, if it failed, "is treason." In Wilson's telling, however, the South had been provoked by "a pulpit teaching the infidel doctrine of a Higher law than God's word residing in the instincts and rational consciousness of man's own soul." If bloodshed were to come from the impending crisis, in the mind of Wilson and the Kentucky white evangelicals whom he would soon pastor, it would be on abolitionist hands.[31]

It was an attempt to avoid the mass spilling of American blood, as well as to preserve slavery and the Union, that led Kentucky senator John J. Crittenden (1786-1863)—like much of his constituency, a Constitutional Unionist—to propose to Congress a famously flawed eleventh-hour compromise on slavery in December 1860. Through a series of constitutional amendments, the slave-free line would be set

---

[31] Wilson, *Causes and Remedies*, 4, 10-11, 15.

at 36°30'. Deep South states could keep slavery; the Fugitive Slave Act would be more strictly enforced; future states entering the nation could determine for themselves whether or not they wanted slavery; and—according to a final provision—these amendments could not be overturned in the future and Congress could not interfere with slavery. Republicans in both houses of Congress rejected the Crittenden Compromise outright, which smacked overtly of other failed attempts to mollify sections of the country on the slavery question, and it looked obviously similar to the Missouri Compromise of 1820. Moreover, it did nothing to stave off the secessionist impulse. Two days after Crittenden submitted his proposal for consideration, South Carolina left the Union.[32]

Still, if the Crittenden Compromise proved offensive beyond the borders of Kentucky, within the state it seemed the only hope for saving the nation. Particularly among the leading religious bodies, neutrality remained the watchword of the day. As right-minded conservatives, the religious whites of Kentucky would not lead the state down the path to bloodshed or national destruction. But it was also clear from their perspective that there were zealots in both North and South who would. Robert J. Breckinridge (1800-71), at that date the most prominent Presbyterian cleric of Kentucky—and also the most cantankerous—argued in a widely published sermon following the South Carolina secession that warfare would be all but unavoidable if "the Cotton States, [follow] the example of South Carolina—or the Northern States adher[e] to extreme purposes in the opposite direction." Such insanity was to be avoided at all costs. As was the case with Crittenden, Breckinridge held the "unalterable conviction" that "the slave line is the only permanent and secure basis of a confederacy for the slave States" and that "the union of free and slave States, in the same confederacy, is the indispensable condition of the peaceful and secure existence of slavery."[33]

---

[32] Harrison and Klotter, *New History of Kentucky*, 185-86.

[33] Robert J. Breckinridge, *Discourse of Dr. Breckinridge Delivered on the Day of National Humiliation, January 4, 1861, at Lexington, Ky.* (Baltimore, 1861), 15.

Similarly, in an article in late 1861 in the *Danville Quarterly Review*, the theological journal associated with the Old-School Presbyterian Danville Theological Seminary and known for its Unionist and emancipationist tone, Breckinridge contended that the only sure security for American slavery came through a collectively unified nation. Breckinridge had chaired the 1849 emancipation convention that called for a revision of the state constitution. His ambition then had been to "whiten" the Commonwealth: his antebellum conservative emancipationism led him to affirm, on the one hand, a commitment both to the maintenance of white supremacy in Kentucky through the colonization of African Americans in Liberia and to a version of a states'-rights doctrine that did not interfere with the interests of slave states further south. The U.S. Constitution, Breckinridge argued in 1861, had guaranteed the rights of southern slaveholders from its inception. The Union, moreover, which enforced those constitutional assurances, had provided Americans with "more than seventy years of unparalleled prosperity." Given these historical and contemporary political realities, the "madness of the whole secession conspiracy" made little sense. Southerners would leave the Union to protect their right to hold slaves, a right they already enjoyed.[34]

As a letter by one of the emerging Baptist orators of Kentucky, Henry McDonald (1832-1904), asked in the *Western Recorder:* "Are Christian men prepared for secession and its bitter fruits? What evil will disunion remedy? As men, as patriots, as Christians, let us weigh well what we do. Are any so blind as to suppose that our rights, civil and religious, can live in the engulfing maelstrom of disunion?" The white religious conservatives of the state maintained that Kentucky would have no part in the endeavor to wreck the Union. In the sectional crisis, moderation was key.[35]

[34] Robert J. Breckinridge, "The Civil War:—Its Nature and End," *Danville Quarterly Review*, December 1861, 645. See also Harlow, "Religion, Race, and Robert J. Breckinridge," 1-24.

[35] Henry McDonald, "The Resolution of the State Convention of Alabama Baptists," *Western Recorder*, December 8, 1860. At the time, McDonald was serving as pastor of Greenburg Baptist Church in south-central Kentucky. His star would rise considerably in coming years, when, beginning in 1870, he served (at times simultaneously) as pastor of Georgetown Baptist

For religious Kentuckians, these matters were never purely political, nor were they only responding to secular developments. Indeed, much of the context for the religious statements of white Kentuckian on disunion came from coreligionists elsewhere in the nation. With regard to secession, Baptists in particular were acutely aware of developments in Alabama, where the state Baptist convention endorsed a secessionist resolution at their November 1860 meeting. The Alabama Baptist statement came out almost immediately in response to the election of Abraham Lincoln, widely believed in the South to be an open assault on the southern way of life enshrined in slavery and, thus, cause to break with the North.[36] Writing to a broad audience of Kentucky Baptists, Henry McDonald found such argumentation tenuous at best. Nothing had happened yet, he contended. "The rights of the people are represented as not merely endangered, but destroyed." Yet Lincoln has "not yet assumed the position to which he has been constitutionally elected," nor has he "done one official act, good or bad." The opinions emanating from Baptists farther south could be characterized unambiguously: "Rhetoric, not reason, war, not peace, angry agitation, not conservatism, rule the day." McDonald asserted that disunion—and certain warfare to follow—needed to be considered far more carefully by Baptists in the United States.[37]

Unlike any other nation in world history, McDonald reminded his readers, the United States had afforded Baptists incredible religious liberties. By contrast, "Pagan, papal, and too often Protestant nations have united to exterminate Baptists." As the historical record

Church, as professor of theology at Western Baptist Theological Institute in Covington, Kentucky, and as professor of moral philosophy at Georgetown College. By 1880, he had accepted the pastorate of the Second Baptist Church of Richmond, Virginia, and held a position at Richmond College. From 1882 to 1900, he led the Second Baptist Church of Atlanta, Georgia, and also served as president of the Southern Baptist Convention Home Mission Board. See Spencer, *History of Kentucky Baptists*, 2:211, and George Braxton Taylor, *Virginia Baptist Ministers*, 5th series, 1902-14 (Lynchburg, Va., 1915), 99-102.

[36] For the broader context on the Alabama Baptist resolution, see Wayne Flynt, *Alabama Baptists: Southern Baptists in the Heart of Dixie* (Tuscaloosa, Ala., 1998), 109-13. On southern attitudes on the election of Lincoln as a rationale for secession, see Charles B. Dew, *Apostles of Disunion: Southern Secession Commissioners and the Causes of the Civil War* (Charlottesville, Va., 2001).

[37] McDonald, "Resolution of the State Convention of Alabama Baptists."

showed, "There is hardly a country in Europe but what has drunk the blood of Baptists, and kindled the fires of persecution against us." In the divinely favored United States, however, "True soul freedom, the yearning of every Baptist heart, and for which we have so nobly suffered, is now realized." "In no other land," McDonald maintained, "is there such fullness of religious freedom." The work of nation-making had been a distinctively Baptist enterprise, as "Baptist blood was shed on every revolutionary battle field." Why, he asked, would American Baptists choose to "desecrate the land where [our fore-bears] sleep by destroying what their lives helped to purchase?" It was unimaginable to McDonald that his coreligionists elsewhere in the South could forget the labors of such a significant generation from less than a century ago. Moreover, considered theologically from a Baptist perspective, the Union stood guardian of an essential doctrinal principle—the liberty of believers to practice their variety of faith as they pleased. By dismissing the Union so cavalierly, as Alabama Baptists did in their resolution against the Union, secessionists risked key aspects of their religious lives.[38]

The *Western Recorder* editors enthusiastically endorsed Henry McDonald's conservative Unionist article. Indeed, the paper argued like McDonald that Abraham Lincoln's election, however unpopular, provided no just provocation for secession. Even as late as March 9, 1861, the Baptist newspaper remained positive in support of the Union. That date came only days after Lincoln took the oath of office on March 4. In addition to publishing the full text of his inaugural address, the paper asserted its viewpoint on the matter—even "though in the estimation of many" civil war was irrepressible, the editors chose "to look on the bright side" and refused to "give up the hope but that all may be well with our whole country." At the time these words appeared in print, however, seven southern states had exited the Union, and it appeared increasingly less plausible that such longing for peace would be realized in the near term.[39]

---

[38] Ibid.
[39] "Apologies," *Western Recorder*, March 9, 1861.

Moreover, even if the *Western Recorder* was the primary dispenser of Baptist opinion in Kentucky, its editors certainly did not speak for all Kentucky Baptists. Just a week after McDonald's December 1860 article appeared in print, the newspaper published an altogether different perspective on "The Crisis" by A. D. Sears (1804-91), a well-known pastor in the western Kentucky town of Hopkinsville. As Sears interpreted the troubles of the day, the nation had been on a collision course since 1845—the year Baptists split along the Mason-Dixon line over the slavery question with the creation of the Southern Baptist Convention. Baptists in the South, who affirmed the Biblically sanctioned Christian right of masters to hold slaves, had been pushed far enough throughout the course of the antebellum era. Given "the aggressions upon the institution of slavery, so constantly and violently made by the people of the North," it was no surprise to Sears that "we would reach the present crisis." Rather, he contended, "The wonder to me is that the people of the South have kept quiet so long." Sears found no fault in the action of the Alabama Baptists. "They are not traitors," he asserted, "[W]e should remember that the men of Alabama and South Carolina are but men, and that as men they have been goaded on by the wrongs of the Northern States to a determination to resist aggression, and to defend their rights at all hazards." Any talk of patriotism, Sears argued, ignored the role of "a mad and infuriated sectional party"—apparent to any reader as abolitionist-influenced Republicans—who had forced the hand of southern secessionists.[40]

The question before the citizens of the Bluegrass State, according to Sears, was whether or not Kentucky would follow the lead of slaveholding states to the South. Kentuckians had a choice. They could "remain silent, and thus lead both the people of the North as well as the South astray." Or, by contrast, Kentucky could take a stand and show that it "would not countenance any attempt to invade the soil of any of the States of the South by Federal troops and that in

[40] A. D. Sears, "The Crisis," *Western Recorder*, December 15, 1860. Sears ranked as one of the more prominent Baptist ministers in Kentucky and Tennessee, carrying on an active ministry in the region for more than forty years. See Spencer, *History of Kentucky Baptists*, 1:267-68.

no event will Kentuckians endorse or sustain measures calculated to involve any of the states in the calamities and horrors of civil war." From Sears's point of view, the choice was plain: "[I]f we are not blind to the spirit of the religion of our Saviour, as well as utterly destitute of all regard to the interests of mankind, we will adopt the latter answer." White Kentucky had not yet made such a decision but, according to Sears, protecting the interests of the white Christian South could not be wrong. Sears did not advocate that Kentucky secede, but he did insist that the state oppose actions to militarily resist the secession of its sister states to the south.[41]

Kentucky never came to officially endorse the Confederate cause, but Sears otherwise reflected clearly the political opinion of Kentucky whites. On April 15, 1861, Kentucky Governor Beriah Magoffin famously rebuffed Lincoln's call for 75,000 troops to support the war effort, four regiments of which would come from the Bluegrass State. Magoffin minced no words in replying to the president: "I say emphatically, Kentucky will furnish no troops for the wicked purpose of subduing her sister Southern states." Then, a month later, the governor followed with a broadcast declaration of Kentucky neutrality, opposing the use of any of the "State Guard" for any purpose other than to "prevent encroachments upon [Kentucky's] soil, her rights, and her sovereignty by either of the belligerent parties." The Kentucky militia, he asserted, existed only to "preserve the peace, safety, prosperity, and happiness and strict neutrality of her people." As a matter of official state policy, Kentucky neither supported southern secession nor northern military efforts to reunite the nation.[42]

For conservative Kentucky whites, Magoffin's declarations represented the political application of the religious values they steadfastly held. Interpreting the war, which had only just begun, Joseph Otis, editor of the *Western Recorder*, wrote that the paper had "but one mission and that mission is peace." Otis fervently declared

41 Ibid.

42 "President Lincoln to Gov. Magoffin," *Western Recorder*, April 20, 1861; "Proclamation of Gov. Magoffin," ibid., May 25, 1861. For the broader political context, see Harrison and Klotter, *New History of Kentucky*, 186-89.

himself "loyal to the Union" but refused to take sides in the fight. Explaining his position, Otis asked his readers, "Shall the cause of Christianity be set back a hundred years to appease fanaticism on one hand or build up a sectional administration on the other? Shall the benign influence of Christian America be forever destroyed throughout the world" simply to achieve "political ends"? "Shame," Otis wrote, "on the Christianity which requires the sword to uphold it; and thrice cursed is that nationality which can live only at the cost of their own citizens, immolated upon the altar of sectional bigotry." As a like-minded Methodist essayist put it, evangelical Northerners and Southerners were bound together by a bond that transcended sectional allegiance: their faith. As "the cry for blood, blood, blood, comes from one section and is sent back with terrible defiance by the other, shall we lift up our voice to augment the wrath and swell the fury? By the grace of God, *never*." Neutrality in the warfare, thus understood, was an important religious value because it meant refusing to take arms against fellow members of a broader Christian fellowship.[43]

At the same time, however, it remained clear whom white religious Kentuckians blamed for stoking the embers of sectional conflagration. Abolitionists, with their heretical views of Christian truth, could never stake claim to a broader fellowship of the orthodox. Right-thinking believers understood that Christian America had been a divine gift. "[W]e were unwilling," Joseph Otis wrote, summing up the late-antebellum political attitude of white religious Kentuckians, "to give our sanction to building up a sectional Christianity, based upon an unrelenting hostility to [the] wise and beneficent institution" of slavery. That is, he could not sanction abolitionism or the political consequences of its principles. After all, slaveholding had been "protected by the Constitution, and blessed and owned of God in the enlightenment and regeneration of many of Africa's sons, who are now heralds of the cross in their benighted fatherland." As reli-

---

[43] Joseph Otis, "Who Will Write The Chapter?" *Western Recorder*, June 1, 1861; "Our Brethren," ibid. (emphasis in original).

gious conservatives in white Kentucky had consistently contended, slavery was a Christianizing force, a quintessential institution for a nation shaped by faith.[44]

The Civil War, brought on by abolitionist agitation, thus threatened the core of Christian America. There was only one solution to the strife, according to Otis. "Christianity, pure and undefiled" was all that could "save our country and once again unite every section in sweet communion." Unfortunately, it seemed to the editor that the moment of Christian influence had passed. In allowing the slavery question—which true believers did not agitate—to fuel sectional antagonism, the properly orthodox had compromised their formidable antebellum base of cultural unity and power. Now, however, "a heterogenous mass, composed of natives and foreigners, and sects of every shade and color, abolitionists, proslavery demagogues, rip-raps, zouaves and infidels" had "assumed a guardianship over the nation." Christian America had been compromised. Otis worried that "the nation's ground of hope, the only palladium of a free people"—white evangelical Christianity—"is forever buried." For the godly in the commonwealth, the open fighting between sections represented the worst of American life. Because of the war, the nation that had served as the guarantor of Christian values could no longer make such assurances.[45]

For this reason, in June 1861 the *Western Recorder* announced in its pages, "Sink or Swim, Live or Die, Survive or Perish, We Are Opposed to this War." That sentiment prevailed more broadly in the state throughout the course of the conflict, but the political neutrality of Kentucky came to an end in September 1861. At that date, following contentious debate between a Union-minded legislature and southern-sympathizing but neutral governor, the legislature passed resolutions against the wishes of Magoffin demanding the removal of Confederate forces that had entered the southwestern part of the state. Formalized support for the Union soon followed, and Kentucky

[44] Otis, "Who Will Write The Chapter?"; Otis, "Our Nation's Ground Of Hope," ibid., June 8, 1861.
[45] Otis, "Our Nation's Ground Of Hope" and "Who Will Write The Chapter?"

remained with the United States throughout the course of the war. In the Russellville conventions of October and November 1861, a sizable group of Confederate sympathizers did, however, organize a provisional government with its capital in Bowling Green, but it operated ineffectually for the next year and only under the protection of the nearby Confederate army. After Confederate forces withdrew from Kentucky the next year, following the battle of Perryville in October 1862, Confederate Kentuckians had to make their claims from beyond state lines and did so with little effect.[46]

By the summer of 1861, no one in Kentucky was certain of the future which the Civil War would bring. Yet war had come and, from the perspective of conservative white Christians in the state, it was an unwelcome presence. They were confident that the fighting, which had only just begun, had irreparably sundered Christian America—the only viable basis for North-South unity. But in point of fact, they argued, it was abolitionism that was responsible for the initial breech.

Conservative Kentuckians had long held antipathy toward those radicalized northern opponents of slavery who, they believed, created the tension between the sections. And they carried that belief with them in the coming years. As the war progressed and turned

---

[46] Harrison and Klotter, *New History of Kentucky*, 190-94; Otis, "Our Nation's Ground Of Hope. The state was dominated politically by conservative Unionists up to 1865. Contrary to older views that suggested that Kentucky Unionism masked a silent majority of Confederate sympathizers, Thomas C. Mackey argues that most Kentuckians were actually Unionist. See Mackey, "Not a Pariah, But a Keystone: Kentucky and Secession," in Dollar, Whiteaker, and Dickinson, eds., *Sister States, Enemy States*, 25-45.

Kentucky did, in spite of its formal Unionism, retain a visible minority of Confederate sympathizers and sent between 25,000 and 40,000 volunteers to fight for the South during the Civil War. However, more than three times that number fought for the Union. That number included, especially after the landmark Union decision in early 1864 to enlist black troops, more than 23,000 once-enslaved African Americans who fought for their own freedom and that of their dependents—though several thousand African Americans began to move toward freedom as early as 1861 and later enlisted in states north of the Ohio River before they were permitted to do so in Kentucky. Estimates of soldiers serving the Confederacy and Union are from Harrison and Klotter, *New History of Kentucky*, 179-80, 195. See also Victor B. Howard, *Black Liberation in Kentucky: Emancipation and Freedom, 1862-1884* (Lexington, Ky., 1983), 45-90; Marion B. Lucas, *From Slavery to Segregation, 1760-1891*, vol. 1 of A *History of Blacks in Kentucky*, 2 vols. (Frankfort, 1992), 146-77, and John David Smith, "Self Emancipation in Kentucky," *Reviews in American History* 12 (1984): 225-29.

from a war to preserve the Union to a war to abolish slavery, white Kentuckians grew increasingly convinced that their antebellum fears of an abolitionist threat were being realized. The religious interpretation of the righteousness of slavery and the inequality of the races, developed and in place before emancipation, thus provided a compelling narrative for white religious Kentuckians to remain neutral in language and support the preservation of the Union on Christian slaveholding grounds—even as they sided socially and culturally with the South. Thus white evangelicalism also drove the developments that were to come in the postbellum years, when white Kentucky ultimately embraced a Confederate memory of the war.[47]

[47] For a similar narrative trajectory, see Patrick A. Lewis, "'All Men of Decency Ought to Quit the Army': Benjamin F. Buckner, Manhood, and Proslavery Unionism in Kentucky," *Register* 107 (2009): 513-49. On the postwar history of Kentucky, see Anne E. Marshall, *Creating a Confederate Kentucky: The Lost Cause and Civil War Memory in a Border State* (Chapel Hill, 2010) and Aaron Astor, *Rebels on the Border: Civil War, Emancipation, and the Reconstruction of Kentucky and Missouri* (Baton Rouge, 2012).

THE CROUCHING LION'S FATE: SLAVE POLITICS AND CONSERVATIVE UNIONISM IN KENTUCKY

By Aaron Astor

In a letter to the *Cincinnati Commercial* five years after the Civil War, a Kentuckian described the vital role his native state played in the Union: "Right here, in the very center of the Mississippi Valley, lying like a crouching lion, stretched east and west, is Kentucky, the thoroughfare of the continent."[1]   The metaphoric crouching lion represented more than just a geographic fulcrum between east and west, and north and south. It also symbolized the political heart of the Union, with its wise and strong tradition of principled compromise. But by 1870, Kentucky had become thoroughly Confederate, both in its partisan habits and its cultural hue. As such, the metaphoric lion stands as a marker of transformation for a state that once prided itself on its spirit of conservative, proslavery Unionism and political moderation but that had become the vanguard of the post-Reconstruction South.

How could a state that fought so hard to preserve the Federal Union embrace a decidedly Confederate identity so soon after the end of the war? In his classic *Civil War and Readjustment in Kentucky*, E. Merton Coulter aptly characterized the conservative Unionism of the state during the first year of war as a product of social, economic, demographic, and political ties between Kentuckians and their neigh-

CHRISTOPHER PHILLIPS is the John and Dorothy Hermanies Professor of American History at the University of Cincinnati. He is the author of seven books, including *The Rivers Ran Backward: The Civil War and the Remaking of the American Middle Border* (New York: Oxford University Press, 2016)

[1] *Cincinnati Commercial*, December 1, 1870, cited in E. Merton Coulter, *The Civil War and Readjustment in Kentucky* (Chapel Hill, 1926), 12.

bors in all directions. But Coulter succumbed to the very myth he described—Kentucky's "secession after the war"—as he located the emerging southern identity of Kentucky with the overbearing Federal military presence in the state in the latter years of the war.[2] The narrative of the destruction of states' rights made for good propaganda in the 1920s "Tragic Era" school of Reconstruction historiography, but it completely missed the real driver of change within the state: the slaves and their insistence upon casting a war of Union as a war of emancipation, regardless of what their conservative Unionist masters may have believed. By running to Union lines during the military campaign of 1862 and then enlisting en masse in the Federal army in 1864, the slaves subverted the conservative Unionist paradigm and fundamentally altered the political culture of the state.

Recent scholarship on post–Civil War Kentucky recognizes the centrality of emancipation—driven primarily by armed slaves—in the creation of a southern identity. Anne Marshall's *Creating a Confederate Kentucky* reveals the ideological weakness among the majority of Kentucky Unionist veterans and the powerful Confederate narrative that privileged the Confederate heritage of the state over its Unionist past.[3] This ideological frailty manifested itself in the virtual abandonment of the memorial field to Confederates, especially as black Kentucky veterans cast the Union cause in emancipationist terms that most white Kentucky Unionists found repugnant. On the ground level, the result was an epidemic of racial violence, mostly targeting black soldiers and their families. J. Michael Rhyne refers to the emergence of Regulator violence in the immediate postwar years as a "rehearsal for redemption," especially as the ex-Confederate states would apply the same methods of terrorism to undermine the power of Radical Republicans.[4] Historians today recognize that the

---

[2] Coulter, *Civil War and Readjustment*, passim.

[3] Anne Marshall, *Creating a Confederate Kentucky: The Lost Cause and Civil War Memory in a Border State* (Chapel Hill, 2010).

[4] J. Michael Rhyne, "Rehearsal for Redemption: The Politics of Racial Violence in Civil War–era Kentucky," C. Ballard Breaux Conference Invited Lecture at the Filson Historical Society, May 19, 2001; see also Rhyne, "Rehearsal for Redemption: The Politics of Post–Emancipation Violence in the Bluegrass Region" (PhD dissertation, University of Cincinnati, 2006).

Kentucky regional orientation and identity shifted after the Civil War and that the emancipation of the 225,000 Kentucky slaves played a central role in that transformation.

But this remarkable shift begs even deeper questions about the nature of conservative Unionism itself. Why did a state with such a strong tradition of compromise and relative moderation on the politics of slavery take such a militant turn over emancipation? What does this reveal about the political culture of conservative, proslavery Unionism prior to the war? And to what extent did forces inside the state undermine the conservative Unionist consensus? The answer to these questions must be located amidst the slave population itself. After all, the challenge to the conservative Unionist order did not emerge out of thin air amidst a large-scale civil war. And despite the contention from outraged slaveholders, slaves did not need Yankee invaders to inform them that freedom was both attractive and attainable. In the form of continual slave resistance, this rebellious spirit had long existed, barely concealed and just under the surface for decades prior to the Civil War. Taking seriously the highly political actions of Kentucky slaves means that historians must reassess the meaning and significance of conservative Unionism itself, both for the state of Kentucky and the nation as a whole.[5] And by connecting the arc of slave resistance to the enlistment of slaves in the Union army, and subsequent efforts by black Kentuckians to create a new social order based on racial equality, historians can come to grips with the fate of the crouching lion.

The Social Basis of Conservative Unionism

The rise of conservative, proslavery Unionism in Kentucky during the late-antebellum era resulted, in many ways, from the transfer of a diversified, small slaveholding class westward from Virginia. What Barbara Fields referred to as the "Middle Ground," a society materially based on small-scale slavery, diversified agricultural holdings,

---

[5] Steven Hahn, *A Nation Under Our Feet: Black Political Struggles in the Rural South from Slavery to the Great Migration* (Cambridge, Mass., 2003). Hahn describes the varied acts of slave resistance as deeply political.

and widespread slave hiring, reemerged in large part across Kentucky and directly informed the development of a conservative Unionist political culture.[6] The local tensions and rhythms of border-state society and the national political context of late antebellum America encouraged white Kentuckians to articulate a specific set of social values that conveyed the fears and aspirations of the small border slaveholding class. These values privileged stability, pragmatism, compromise, and tradition over ideological rigidity and sectional honor, and so helped solidify the regional embrace of conservative Unionism with the outbreak of Civil War.

The social structure of Kentucky slavery facilitated such a political culture. Dispersed smallholdings, diversified farming, and slave hiring characterized the antebellum Kentucky countryside, just as they did in much of colonial Virginia.[7] The smallholdings indicate farms with a mixed-labor force consisting of male household members, hired laborers, and slaves. The relatively dispersed slave population did not mean that white exposure to the slave system was rare. Nor did it indicate that slaveholders were statistically marginal elements among the white, male, voting population. To the contrary, dispersed smallholdings simply indicated a higher *number* of slaveholders and, more importantly, of white family members living in households headed by slaveholders. In 1860, 37.7 percent of the residents of central Kentucky were enslaved with 6.3 slaves per slaveholder in the Bluegrass region. By the time of the Civil War, Kentucky had more slaveholders than any state in the Union except Georgia and Virginia.

There was considerable variation in slaveholding patterns across the state. In the eastern mountains, slaveholdings were few and far between. Slaveholdings were somewhat larger in the southwestern tobacco area around Christian County. The Bluegrass was the slaveholding heartland, with a majority of Woodford Countians held as

---

[6] Barbara Jeanne Fields, *Slavery and Freedom on the Middle Ground: Maryland during the Nineteenth Century* (New Haven, 1985).

[7] Philip Morgan shows slaveholdings in Virginia to be much smaller than in South Carolina. See Philip D. Morgan, *Slave Counterpoint: Black Culture in the Eighteenth-Century Chesapeake and Lowcountry* (Chapel Hill, 1998).

slaves and more than 40 percent of Fayette Countians in bondage. The sizable slave population and small size of slaveholdings meant that roughly half the white population of the Bluegrass region lived in households with slaves.[8] When slave hiring is taken into account, the practices, habits, and values of slaveholding stretched into a majority of white homes.

Slaveholders in Kentucky employed bondmen and bondwomen to plant, cultivate, and harvest tobacco and hemp, as well as corn and wheat. Slaveholders also directed their slaves to tend the livestock, repair fences, build barns, and haul supplies from one end of the farm to another. The work required of slaves depended on the particular crop mix and labor supply of each farmer, and the evidence suggests that slaveholders across Kentucky operated highly diversified farms. The differing labor demands of each crop meant that farmers required a more flexible workforce than existed in the cotton-plantation districts of the Deep South. While tobacco and hemp were highly labor-intensive crops, their time and skill demands differed. With land and slave labor available outside of tobacco and hemp production, Kentucky farmers employed their slaves in the production of wheat and corn as well as the raising of livestock. Horse farmers also employed slaves for skilled work in the stables and saddle shops of the Bluegrass. In the cities and towns of Kentucky, factories processed, packed, and rolled tobacco leaf, constructed hemp rope and bagging, produced woolen and coarse textiles, milled corn and grain, and manufactured many other items for local and regional consumption. Ropewalks in Lexington turned dew-rotted hemp into cotton bagging for sale to the Deep South. In each of these facilities, a combination of white wage workers, free blacks, and slaves—some, but not all of whom, were hired—worked side by side. Factory operators regularly adjusted their workforces in response to changing market demand and labor prices, maintaining both labor flexibility and the social relations of slavery in expanding cities and towns.

[8] 1860 U.S. census, Population and Slave Schedules.

Slaveholders in both rural and urban sections of Kentucky employed slave laborers in the home, as well as in the fields and factories. Slaves formed a domestic workforce intended to relieve white women of the burdens of household drudgery. While some wealthy estates employed armies of mostly female servants in their homesteads, most domestic slaveholders came from relatively humble circumstances and hoped that one or two slaves could help with washing, cooking, and child-rearing. The relatively small slave population of Louisville performed mostly domestic work as well, with most of the work in the bustling Ohio River wharves and factories done by German and Irish immigrants.

A diversified economy centered on cereal production, tobacco processing, hempen bagging, and rope manufacturing created a demand for a more flexible workforce than that normally possessed by slaveholders. To exploit the mixed economy efficiently but maintain the slave system as a viable means of labor and social organization, slaveholders turned to slave hiring. The practice of slave hiring took place wherever slavery existed in the American South, but its incidence was higher in the border and upper South than it was elsewhere.[9] And in urban areas where industrial and domestic demands required seasonable labor to operate the ropewalks and grain mills, slave hiring was even more prevalent.

Detailed information concerning slave hiring is available for Lexington and Fayette County, because the census taker in 1860 accounted for all slaves hired as well as owned. So it is possible to draw some broader conclusions about the prevalence of slave hiring and the effect it had on white business relations, the character of Upper South slavery, and slave community life. In Lexington, as many as 29 percent of slaveholders hired out at least one slave in 1860. However, a greater proportion of slaveholders hired out at least one of their slaves (29 percent) than the proportion of slaves actually hired (12 percent). Many slaveholders in the city owned more than ten slaves,

---

[9] Jonathan D. Martin, *Divided Mastery: Slave Hiring in the American South* (Cambridge, Mass., 2004).

and of those, very few of them hired out more than one or two in a given year. A majority of slaves hired out in the city were female (57 percent), thus confirming Keith C. Barton's analysis of Bourbon County, Kentucky, that most hirees were domestic servants.[10] However, 17 percent of all hired slaves were sent outside the city of Lexington to work the farms of the surrounding Bluegrass. And of those, a slight majority (52 percent) were males, almost certainly hired out to work the hemp and wheat farms of the countryside, but many were also female domestics sent to the estates of outer Fayette County.

While some slaves were hired out to other slaveholders looking to expand their labor force for seasonal demand, most hirers were nonslaveholders who needed one or two extra hands to help with domestic work or in small shops run by carpenters, blacksmiths, and other skilled craftsmen. Slave hiring was a vital component of the slave system in Lexington, as well as other parts of Kentucky. The incidence of slave hiring may have been less in more rural areas—it is doubtful that as many as 29 percent of all rural slaveholders hired out their slaves in a given year—but the practice played a critical role in balancing the social order defined by slavery and the diversified economic demands of the mixed economy of the Border South.

Perhaps most importantly, slave hiring introduced the habits, values, and social relationships of slavery into a far larger portion of the population than would have otherwise been exposed to slavery. Thousands of white families in Kentucky without the wealth to own slaves themselves hired slaves to help around the house or in the fields. Slave hiring gave nonslaveholders a stake in the protection of slavery and encouraged this larger mass of the white population to come to the defense of slavery in the late antebellum era. The widespread practice of slave hiring thus helped extend the political culture of conservative, proslavery Unionism to nonslaveholding elements of the white population.

[10] Keith C. Barton, "'Good Cooks and Washers': Slave Hiring and the Market in Bourbon County, Kentucky," *Journal of American History* 84 (1997): 436-60.

Slavery, Order, and Border State Values

Slavery imposed a distinct racial order that few in the border states dared threaten. Though some offered relatively tepid defenses of slavery, nearly all white Kentuckians feared social chaos and the demise of white civilization if the slave population were to be liberated at once.[11] If any ideal characterized late-antebellum border-state life more than any other, it was the desire for order—social, economic, racial, and, ultimately, political order. The thirst for order in a region challenged by both abolitionism and secessionism stood as the central pillar to antebellum Upper South social thought. It would trump all concerns about sectional honor in the ensuing crisis, revealing a population that embraced slavery and Union.[12]

At the heart of Kentucky values was white supremacy, or more specifically, a belief that Western civilization was a product of characteristics unique to the white race and that all interracial relationships must protect the white race from subjugation or degradation by the black race.[13] Failing to hold the line against attempts at racial equality would yield nothing less than complete reversion to barbarism, which whites believed inevitable wherever blacks lived without white authority. Most white Northerners and Southerners agreed with this racial order, but each section preserved white supremacy differently. Northerners simply excluded African Americans outright—states like Indiana and Illinois legally banned black people from entering in 1860, and many other states placed onerous taxes on blacks who could not prove employment or property ownership—or, failing that, segregated blacks and whites in all facets of social and economic life.[14] White Northerners protected white supremacy by monopolizing the property, power, and labor force of the northern states. White

[11] Harold D. Tallant, *Evil Necessity: Slavery and Political Culture in Antebellum Kentucky* (Lexington, Ky., 2003), 3-6.

[12] On the southern obsession with honor, see Bertram Wyatt-Brown, *Southern Honor: Ethics and Behavior in the Old South* (New York, 1982).

[13] George Fredrickson, *Black Image in the White Mind: The Debate on Afro-American Character and Destiny, 1817–1914* (New York, 1971).

[14] Leon Litwack, *North of Slavery: The Negro in the Free States, 1790–1860* (Chicago, 1961); and Baker, *Affairs of Party*, 212-58.

Southerners, living amidst populations that often included large majorities of African Americans, embraced slavery as the natural system of racial and social control. Without slavery, white Southerners feared, blacks would literally overrun and destroy white civilization, re-creating either Haiti or Africa itself.

Whites in Kentucky embraced a form of white-supremacist ideology that fit the culture of border-slave life. The slave system naturally produced excess slaves not needed to work the fields and factories of the Bluegrass and other Kentucky slaveholding centers, and slaveholders sought a means to control these residual slaves. Kentucky slaveholders either manumitted or, more commonly, sold to the Deep South their excess slaves. Where manumission occurred, it took place very slowly and under the tight control of former masters. A small free-black population emerged in larger towns like Danville, Louisville, and Lexington, but it never grew to the size it had attained in the eastern border states of Maryland and Delaware, where more than half the black population was free by 1860. Moreover, the free-black population in Kentucky remained closely tied to white patrons who posted bond for ex-slaves' rights to remain in the state.[15] The apologists and critics of slavery in Kentucky might have differed as to the efficiency, fairness, or productivity of the slave system, but they all agreed that emancipation without complete colonization would result in total and complete social chaos and very possibly the demise of civilization as they knew it.[16]

More than just a racial system, however, slavery in Kentucky was, as in the lower South, a relationship of production. Hemp producers regularly complained that the crop would die out completely without the aid of male slave labor, especially in the breaking season. Cereal production and livestock-raising also depended materially on slave labor. While examples of profitable free-labor-based corn and wheat

[15] Richard C. Brown, "The Free Blacks of Boyle County, Kentucky, 1850-1860: A Research Note," *Register of the Kentucky Historical Society* 87 (1989): 431.

[16] Harold Tallant cites a slew of central Kentuckians, including proslavery Charles Wickliffe and antislavery Robert J. Breckinridge, as fearing disorder with general emancipation. See Tallant, *Evil Necessity*, 59-90.

production abounded across the Ohio River in 1860, a transition to such a system would have drastically altered landholdings and labor relations on the many large farms in Kentucky. Free labor would have been possible, as emancipationists like Cassius M. Clay argued, but it would have sown great economic disorder for the foreseeable future; after the Civil War the aspirations and actions of slaves to own their own land, rather than toil for others as wage laborers, would confirm the fears of conservative opponents of general emancipation.

Labor exploitation in the farms and factories of Kentucky was certainly a critical way in which the slave system permeated the lives of border-state whites. But slavery was a social system every bit as much as it was an economic system. As such, the slave system mediated relationships within and between households.[17] Kentucky slaveholders regularly spoke of their chattel as "my girl" or "our dear servants," and took very seriously the paternalistic prerogatives of the slaveholding class.[18] Perhaps the exception—slave hiring—accentuates the rule here. Even in the many cases where hiring arrangements intruded market imperatives on an otherwise paternalistic household relationship, some masters insisted that slaves be treated with "humanity and kindness."[19] Incorporating such language into hiring contracts meant more than protecting an investment in property. Owners hoped that their hiring clients would maintain the owner's paternal obligations vis-a-vis their slaves, thus reinforcing the household ties of slave and owner, even when the slave lived outside the master's direct control.

[17] For the definition of "household," see Elizabeth Fox-Genovese, *Within the Plantation Household: Black and White Women of the Old South* (Chapel Hill, 1988), 31-32. As Fox-Genovese notes, the term household extends beyond personal family relationships. As such, it is possible for masters and mistresses to imagine the extension of paternalistic relationships to those who hire their slaves.

[18] For a general description of slavery as a "way of life" based on the paternalistic prerogative, see the classic U. B. Phillips, *American Negro Slavery* (Baton Rouge, 1966), 291-308. For the most comprehensive analysis of slavery as a system characterized by paternalistic relations between slave and slaveholder, see Eugene D. Genovese, *Roll, Jordan, Roll: The World the Slaves Made* (Chapel Hill, 1976), 3-7.

[19] Alexander Jeffrey, Promissory Notes, December 25, 1860 (microfilm Clift, no. 481, Kentucky Historical Society Collections, Kentucky Historical Society, Frankfort, Kentucky (hereafter KHS Collections).

Slave hiring, and slave sale for that matter, complicated and at times threatened the paternalistic relationship between slaves and slaveholder, but it rarely undermined it on a *systemic* level.

Even more important, slave-hiring negotiations underscored the role Upper South slavery played in solidifying the social and political order, including the many nonslaveholders in the Kentucky white population. After all, the persistent practice of slave hiring directly incorporated nonslaveholders into the slave system, with hirers exercising nearly all the racial perquisites that owners possessed. Slave hiring thus dramatically expanded the universe of white Kentucky families directly exposed to the slave system. When the time came to defend slavery from its enemies, slaveholders found plenty of allies among the nonslaveholding white population.

Conservative Unionist Political Culture

As political scientists Sidney Verba and Lucian Pye define it, political culture is "the system of empirical beliefs, expressive symbols, and values which defines the situation in which political action takes place."[20] The conservative Unionist political culture of Kentucky reflected its dominant social system defined by small-scale slaveholding, diverse labor relationships, and market relations to both the free North and the plantation South. This political culture, which venerated the yeoman republic and a slaveholder's democracy, refracted into political parties with differing personalities, habits, and visions of the role of the Federal government. The second party system, pitting Jacksonian Democrats against the Whigs of Henry Clay, survived longer in Kentucky than anywhere else in the Union. The persistence of that party system reflected a stable state political culture—while also reinforcing that stability—even as the political order collapsed in much of the rest of the country by 1861.

The main ideological appeal of the Whigs lay in their championing of Federal investment in national improvements and a protec-

---

[20] Lucian Pye and Sidney Verba, eds., *Political Culture and Political Development* (Princeton, 1965), 8-9.

tive tariff. Henry Clay's American System advocated the Federal construction of the Maysville Road connecting the Bluegrass to the Ohio River, a high tariff to protect Kentucky hemp, and a Federal banking apparatus that would extend credit to Bluegrass businessmen. The Democratic Party of Andrew Jackson also appealed to Kentuckians, especially those in the mountains and in the western Jackson Purchase. A distrust of currency manipulation by eastern bankers and Federal interference in local governance, plus an embrace of a small slaveholders' democracy, linked whites all across the border West to the Democratic Party. A sizable percentage of Kentuckians supported the party of Andrew Jackson because of the Democrats' cultural hue, not any particular policy position.[21] The values of both Democratic and Whiggish whites in the Border South stressed the preservation of the existing order: an economic order based on small-scale production among middling farmers and manufacturers, a social order centered on nurturance of familial relationships, and a racial order based on a white numerical advantage and the circumscription of black life.

Political leaders across Kentucky embraced a moderation that reflected ideological and regional compromise. From the early constitutional debates in 1792, where the founders of Kentucky seriously considered abolishing slavery, to the 1833 Kentucky law banning the importation of slaves, to the presence and relative toleration of outright opponents of slavery like Cassius M. Clay and John G. Fee well into the 1850s, the Kentucky position on slavery had always listed toward the middle of the political spectrum. Kentucky politicians almost universally defended slavery—though as a "necessary evil" and rarely as a "positive good"—but few among them joined in the national southern-rights agitation.[22] Right up through the secession crisis, Kentuckians united in favor of moderation and compromise. Even future top Confederates like John C. Breckinridge and John Hunt Morgan refused to join forces with the new Confederate nation

---

[21] Baker, *Affairs of Party*, 27-70.

[22] This is the essence of Harold Tallant's thesis. See Tallant, *Evil Necessity*.

until September 1861.[23] Morgan, reflecting the moderate politics of Kentucky, went so far as to declare Lincoln's election virtually meaningless. Shortly after the November 1860 election, Morgan wrote to his brother Thomas, "The election is now over and Lincoln is certainly elected. Both Congress and the Senate are Democratic, so he can do nothing even if he wished, but I expect he will make us a good president."[24] Thomas Morgan echoed his brother's moderation when he wrote their mother, "Have any of the Southern States an idea of seceding upon the Election? If there are any I earnestly hope that Kentucky will not figure among them."[25]

A major reason for the general ideological moderation was the social and economic relationship that linked Kentucky to the North. Even more than dependence on the Federal government, ties with the free states of the Old Northwest, as well as Pennsylvania, lent caution to political agitation of the slave issue. From the earliest days of statehood, Louisville emerged as a major Ohio River port, manufacturing center, and railroad town connected by trade to Indiana and Ohio as much as to the South. Legions of German and Irish immigrants lent Louisville a cultural and ethnic identity more like that of Cincinnati than a southern city. Though the Bluegrass trade was more southerly than that out of Louisville, a sizable portion of Lexington horses as well as hemp and woolen manufactures made their way into the Cincinnati and greater Ohio market.[26] Economic ties between Kentucky and the free cities and states of the North tended to moderate the political discourse of the state, even in the more heavily slaveholding Bluegrass heartland.

[23] On Breckinridge as a truly reluctant Confederate, see William C. Davis, *Breckinridge: Statesman, Soldier, Symbol* (Baton Rouge, 1974). For Morgan's decision to enter the war on the side of the South, see James Ramage, *Rebel Raider: The Life of General John Hunt Morgan* (Lexington, Ky., 1986), 40-45.

[24] John Hunt Morgan to Thomas Morgan, November 9, 1860, folder 5, Hunt-Morgan Papers, special collections, University of Kentucky Libraries, Lexington, Kentucky (hereafter special collections, UK).

[25] Thomas Morgan to Henrietta Morgan, undated, ibid.

[26] Coulter, *Civil War and Readjustment in Kentucky*, 16-17. The bulk of the Lexington hemp trade went to the South, especially to cotton planters. But its horses were known throughout the country as the finest stock and were in high demand in the South and the Northwest.

Social and kin ties also linked Kentucky with the free North. Perhaps the most famous example was Abraham Lincoln and his Lexington-born wife Mary Todd. Indeed, the Todd family was one of the oldest and most powerful in Bluegrass society, and the Lincolns regularly visited the Todd family in the decades before the Civil War.[27] Though Lincoln's association with the "black" Republican Party rendered him a political pariah in Kentucky politics in 1860, his Kentucky provenance undoubtedly helped soothe the anxieties of ardent defenders of slavery there.[28] There was a substantial number of emigrants from Kentucky to the Northwest; according to the 1860 census, sixty thousand Kentucky-born citizens followed Lincoln's path into Illinois, sixty-eight thousand to Indiana, fifteen thousand to Ohio, thirteen thousand to Iowa, and six thousand to Kansas.[29] United States senator Garrett Davis of Bourbon County remarked in 1861, "Kentucky has almost peopled the northwestern states, especially Indiana and Illinois. I have no doubt that one fourth of the people of Indiana are either native-born Kentuckians or the sons and daughters of native-born Kentuckians. They are bone of our bone and flesh of our flesh."[30] The political ramifications of these kinship ties across the Ohio River were clear; as one Kentuckian remarked, "What can she do by secession but make war upon the people of Indiana and Illinois many of whom Kentucky gave birth to."[31]

More immediate concerns about an inevitable civil war also strengthened Kentuckians' attachment to the Union. Many Kentuckians distrusted the secessionist movement in the Lower South, because the border would bare the brunt of any ensuing military invasion. Others feared that a "Cotton State Confederacy" would subjugate the economic needs of hemp, tobacco, and cereal producers

[27] On Mary Todd Lincoln and her Kentucky childhood, see Jean H. Baker, *Mary Todd Lincoln: A Biography* (New York, 1987).

[28] On Lincoln's relationship to his state of birth, see Lowell H. Harrison, *Lincoln of Kentucky* (Lexington, Ky., 2000).

[29] 1860 U.S. Census, Population, 616-17. Data compiled and presented in Coulter, *Civil War and Readjustment in Kentucky*, 13.

[30] Quoted in Coulter, ibid., 15.

[31] Ibid.

in the border states to the free-market, slave-importing demands of the cotton-based Lower South. Nostalgic sentiment for the "Union of our fathers"—too strong to sever for ideological purposes—added cultural glue to the Union cause already strengthened by ties to the Old Northwest and fears of cotton-based Confederacy. So long as conservatives in the border believed that Northerners would leave slavery alone, they believed that the ties of Union were too important to abandon.

The Rhetoric of Conservative Unionism

Conservative Unionism developed in response to dual threats. From the North came radical abolitionists declaring slavery the gravest sin of mankind. After John Brown's raid on Harpers Ferry in October 1859, Southerners of all political stripes reacted with horror to three things: the raid itself, the alleged conspiracy of Northerners behind it, and, most importantly, the martyr-like treatment granted Brown after his execution in December. White Kentuckians reacted with especial alarm, considering the location of Brown's raid in northern Virginia and the risk that this event could dramatically escalate sectional tensions. But, as the *Frankfort Commonwealth* reassured its readers, most Northerners reacted to Brown's fanaticism with disgust:

> We are pleased to observe that the Northern press, without the distinction of party, express the most unqualified condemnation of the wicked and insane projects of Brown and his hairbrained associates. The great mass of the Northern people, including the most inveterate Republicans, regard such schemes with as much abhorrence as they do any other conspiracy to murder by wholesale, and it is not going too far to assert that in case there had been any necessity for their aid, thousands of true men in the North would have promptly taken up arms in behalf of the Southern slaveholder against the brutality of the slave.[32]

Even after the martyr-like treatment accorded Brown in many

---

[32] *Frankfort Commonwealth*, October 24, 1859.

sections of the North—and the corresponding shock across most of the southern press—the *Commonwealth* again reassured its conservative Unionist readers that the mass of Northerners remained vigilant in support of sectional peace and a Union where slavery could continue to thrive where it had already existed. "It is pleasing to observe the reaction which is rapidly taking place in Northern sentiment," the *Commonwealth* reported:

> The sympathizers with the mad act of John Brown and his deluded followers, though few in numbers, made a great deal of noise at first, and almost convinced some too credulous Southern men that their ravings were a fair reflection of Northern feeling. But now that the excitement of the moment has passed, the strong undercurrent of genuine Northern patriotism is beginning to be felt. Conservative Union meetings, at which resolutions condemnatory of the Virginia invasion and of all incendiary attempts to excite the slaves against their masters are passed, are being held throughout the entire North.[33]

The truthfulness of these reassuring reports may be in doubt. But there is no question that most conservative Unionist Kentuckians *hoped* they were true. As such, this editorial offers a rhetorical marker of conservative Unionism very much representative of the values of most white Kentuckians in 1860. John Brown's raid—and the sympathetic reaction to it across much of the North—was a key crystallizing moment for secessionists across the Lower South. As many southern editorialists queried, how could the South preserve its safety—not to mention its honor and power—if ordinary Yankees countenanced such fanatical treason? But Kentuckians, by and large, responded to the event with a solemn desire to preserve the Union and slavery. From then on, Kentucky conservatives would need to confront abolitionism as well as a very real secessionist threat coming from the Lower South.

From the "Cotton States," came the "fire-eaters," the "Yanceyites"

[33] Ibid., December 17, 1859.

and the "nullifiers" whose excessive zeal to protect the institution of slavery threatened both the Federal Union and, to conservatives, slavery itself. Slavery-based secession movements proliferated across the Lower South, dating from the Calhounite Nullification movement in 1832 but gaining momentum after Harpers Ferry. South Carolina always led the way, but secession drew its strongest adherents from the entire South, including Edmund Ruffin of Virginia, William Lowndes Yancey of Alabama, and Isham Harris of Tennessee. Secessionists failed to convince the southern states to leave the Union during the compromise crisis of 1850, but they gained considerable energy throughout the cotton-rich 1850s. Secessionists believed that the emergence of a dominant sectional party based on free-soil principles meant that the slaveholding South could no longer coexist in a Federal Union with its honor intact. Moreover, some secessionists longed for the expansion of slavery not only into the West, but into Central America, with Dixie serving as the capital of a hemispheric slave empire.[34]

The western territorial issue lay at the heart of southern expansionism, and the blockage of slaveholders' aspirations meant usurpation of their rightful power and the denial of their honor. But if the western territorial issue topped the list of secessionist grievances, Kentuckians who actually fought with abolitionists and freesoilers in the Kansas wars (most of the Missouri "border ruffians" had originally come from Kentucky) and with Ohio River abolitionists placed the western status lower down in their list of priorities. Nearly every mass meeting—pro-Union or prosecession—listed enforcement of the Fugitive Slave Act as the prime concern for Kentuckians.[35] For secessionists, the West signified honor and power—virtually no Alabamian or South Carolinian expressed any intention to carry his slave property into New Mexico or Colorado. For border conservatives,

[34] On Southerners who hoped to expand a southern slave empire into Central America, with filibusterers at the vanguard, see Robert May, *Manifest Destiny's Underworld: Filibustering in Antebellum America* (Chapel Hill, 2004); see also James McPherson, *Battle Cry of Freedom: The Civil War Era* (New York, 1988), 78-116.

[35] This was also true in the eastern border states like Maryland and Virginia.

such honor-laden language came across as haughty and impolitic in the extreme.

While conservatives in the border states recognized the dangers to slavery and the incendiary effect of abolitionism on northern politics, they viewed the entire crisis pragmatically. Most recognized the imminence of war if the South followed through on secession, and they feared the consequences for the border states. Richard Hanson of Bourbon County, speaking to a Union meeting in Lexington, warned that "slavery could not long exist in a State bordering upon a hostile nation at war with her about the subject of slavery."[36] Indeed, the prospect of "bringing the Canada line to the Ohio River" sobered even the most ardent border supporters of the southern cause.[37]

Though advocates of a new southern Confederacy regularly referred to themselves as secessionists, their opponents often described them as "nullifiers." This rhetoric clearly referenced the largely unpopular South Carolina nullification crisis in 1832-33. Since many of the secession sympathizers identified with the party of Andrew Jackson, the term "nullifier" carried significant pejorative weight. What is more, the locus of nullification, South Carolina, exacerbated border conservative doubts about secession. Kentucky conservatives repeatedly accused South Carolina secessionists of plotting to exploit the border states as a bloody battleground and buffer zone for the protection of the cotton states. As Richard Hanson commented, "There is a great prejudice in this section against South Carolina, and she deserves it all—she has by her rash and unprincipled course forfeited every claim to our sympathy and assistance. She has treated the border states with contemptuous scorn."[38] Since so few Kentuckians could trace their lineage to South Carolina, it is not surprising that they could use such vituperative language against a fellow slaveholding state. Kentuckians may have shared slaveholding status with the Palmetto State, but they shared little sympathy.

Perhaps the greatest fear of secession was the obvious conse-

[36] *Western Citizen* [Paris, Ky.], February 1, 1861.
[37] See speech by Garrett Davis, ibid., March 22, 1861.
[38] Ibid., February 1, 1861.

quence: civil war. Although many Deep South secessionists yearned to test their mettle on the battlefield, Kentuckians viewed the prospect of open warfare with considerably less enthusiasm. After all, Kentucky would serve as the front lines in a civil war with the North. To southern-rights advocates, the fears of the border placed the southern credentials of the region in doubt. In response, the *Western Citizen* noted, "According to them no man is a friend of the South who is not willing to risk civil war." Even if the South were to succeed in its fight for independence, a Bourbon County man noted, the separation into two republics would inevitably lead to "continual war" over "a thousand causes which now pass unnoticed," including navigation of the Mississippi River and continual raiding of Confederate slave property by hostile Northerners.[39] Inevitably, this perpetual war would destroy the very thing that secessionists claim to be defending. The Bourbon Countian presciently warned:

> When it is all over, and civil and servile war has done its work of desolation, and the bloody drama is closed—slavery is exterminated or driven to the rice fields of the extreme South as its last refuge—all prosperity utterly destroyed, and the people are impoverished and demoralised, by the terrible ordeal through which they have passed—who then will say that the slight and trivial evils that now exist justified the destruction of the government? Posterity will proclaim, with one voice, the ineffable folly and the eternal infamy of the act.[40]

At an ideological level, conservatives leveled most of their scorn at the radicalism of secession, which would thrust a peaceful society into the vortex of the unknown. Conservative Unionists regularly described secessionists as "fanatics" and "revolutionaries," as "violent and incendiary," as "disorganizers and disunionists."[41] Ironically, much of the same rhetoric conservatives used to describe secessionists they also applied to abolitionists, especially epithets like "fanatic" and

---

[39] Ibid.
[40] Ibid.
[41] Ibid.

"incendiary." Whatever the advocates of secession claimed about protecting slave society, they were dangerously not conservative.

Conservative Unionist rhetoric reflected more than mere rejection of the twin heresies of abolitionism and secession. Though it responded to a particular series of political crises that threatened the slave-based social order and the constitutional order that protected it, conservative Unionism drew from the great strength of the American Republic and the compromises that allowed the nation to grow to its prosperous status. The United States, as Bourbon Countian and future U.S. senator Garrett Davis proclaimed, was "the freest government on earth, one that was devised by the wisest and most virtuous men, and in the full development of a glory and grandeur which the most fertile imagination could not grasp, every citizen prosperous and blessed with the mildest, happiest, and most benignant institutions ever known."[42] The Union was not only wealthy and free, it was powerful. The bonds of Union "held us together for eighty years, as one of the noblest, one of the grandest and most potent confederacies upon the foot-stool of God."[43] Unionists at a mass meeting in Paris asserted that nobody had the right to "weaken or dissolve the relations which bind us to the Government of our Fathers; that we have an inheritance in that symbol of Union and Liberty—that old National Flag, the Star Spangled Banner—and, by the blessing of Heaven, we will not yield up."[44]

As Abraham Lincoln assumed the presidency over a fractured republic in March 1861, Kentucky conservative Unionists remained confident that his triumphant Republican Party posed no threat to their way of life. The *Nicholasville Democrat* in Jessamine County declared, "We do boldly assert that the Union party in Kentucky is as sound on the slavery question as the States Rights party can be. We believe that four-fifths of the slaves of the State are owned by Union men. Would it not be strange that the owners of this species of property should decide to deprive themselves of it to their own

[42] Ibid., March 22, 1861.
[43] Ibid.
[44] Ibid., June 7, 1861.

loss? There is no sort of affiliation whatever between Lincolnites and Unionists." To emphasize the distance between Lincolnian Republicanism and conservative Unionism, the editorial asserted, "The Union men love the Union for the sake of the Union and not for the man who may chance to be President at the time."[45] Conservative Unionists never adored President Lincoln, but they doubted secessionist claims that support for the Union was really support for an abolitionist regime. They remained loyal to the Federal government because they "love the Union for the sake of the Union," and nothing else.[46] The Union they knew and loved was the one in which the Constitution, southern representatives in Washington, and the great mass of antiabolitionist Northerners had protected the citadel of slavery for seventy years.

The Real Rebels on the Border

What historians have yet to appreciate is the threat to conservative Unionism from *within* Kentucky. The pressures from secession-sympathizers who rallied to the Confederate flag in the summer and fall of 1861 have long been acknowledged. In many ways, Kentucky Confederates like Henry Watterson, Basil Duke, Simon Bolivar Buckner, William Preston, and John C. Breckinridge were some of the first to ascribe a Confederate identity to the state just after the end of the war. But it was a different rebellion—from the slave population—that most seriously undermined the moderate political culture of conservative Unionism in Kentucky. And while the emancipation of Kentucky slaves—primarily through the enlistment of 57 percent of the male military-age slaves of Kentucky into the Union army—dealt the fatal blow to the old order, the seeds of this rebellion had long been present in the form of slave resistance.

Not subject to the Emancipation Proclamation, the slave population of Kentucky and that of the other border states and Tennessee launched one of the great social revolutions in modern history. First

[45] Quoted in ibid., June 28, 1861.
[46] See "The Black Military Experience, 1861-1867" in Ira Berlin et al., *Slaves No More: Three Essays on Emancipation and the Civil War* (New York, 1992), 203.

in a trickle, then in a flood, a sizable portion of the slave population of Kentucky escaped to Federal encampments, including, especially, Camp Nelson. Passing troop movements brought the Union army closer to the farms, and made running away much easier. Meanwhile, on the farms slave discipline virtually collapsed. Small slaveholders complained that Union army tactics "demoralized" their laborers, but, in reality, the slaves forced the hand of the Union army. Despite vigorous protests from conservative Unionist slaveholders and politicians, slaves read into Unionism a different cause: to wreak havoc on the system of bondage and use the war for Union as a struggle for emancipation. Conservative Union military officers feared that mass runaways would undermine the Kentucky economy, encourage a servile insurrection, and, more immediately, sap support for the Union war effort in the border. Yet, Kentucky slaves continually refused the entreaties of Union officers to go back to their masters. To slaves, their owners' loyalty to the Union or the South meant little in and of itself. Kentucky slaves recast the Union war effort as a fight for emancipation, regardless of the conservative claim that the Union cause was predicated on the *protection* of slavery.[47]

The social networks that tenuously connected the black community before the war facilitated the rapid transfer of news about troop movements and the degree of sympathy for slaves held by local Union military commanders. These networks also helped in the development and execution of mass runaway plots. As a result, slaves successfully exploited internal ties stretching over vast stretches of dispersed Kentucky land and external divisions within the white population over the future of the Union, in a bid for self-emancipation. For decades, slaves developed their own system of secretive communication and organization that would threaten Kentucky society at its core. "The negroes would talk among themselves, but never carried tales to the white folks," remembered Bert Mayfield, a former slave from Gar-

[47] Richard Sears, *Camp Nelson Kentucky: A Civil War History* (Lexington, Ky., 2002), xxxvii-xxxix; Dickson to Sidell, May 26, 1864, Letters Received, box 2, series 3967, Assistant Adjutant Provost Marshall General for Kentucky, RG 110, National Archives and Records Administration, Washington, D.C.

rard County, Kentucky. The "tales" Mayfield spoke of may have been religious in nature, about an afterlife free from bondage. "On Sundays we would hold prayer meetings among ourselves," he recalled. Or they may have been the whispers of rumor about life off the Stone farm near Bryantsville, like slaves passing along the road in shackles to the Deep South. Or about rumors of violence against their master or by other slaves against their masters, though Mayfield insisted that "there was no trouble between blacks and whites."[48] Or perhaps the tales related to the latest campaign by John Fee, whose abolitionist settlement at Berea lay a short distance away. Or perhaps the tales referenced free blacks or hired slaves traveling through Lexington, like Harriet Mason, who ran away back to Bryantsville to find her mother.[49] The tales may have even been about what lay across the Ohio River, only a hundred miles to the north, and the Underground Railroad of John Parker and Calvin Fairbank who carried dozens of slaves from central Kentucky to freedom.[50]

The possibilities are endless, which is precisely why they would have been threatening to Bert Mayfield's master. Indeed, any voluntary assemblage of slaves challenged the authority of the master, whose absolute domination demanded constant oversight. The confluence of small slaveholdings, slave hiring, and a sizable free-black population in Garrard County and elsewhere in Kentucky encouraged the creation and sustenance of extensive social and kinship networks. These networks, like the brush-arbor meetings where slaves kept their "tales" to themselves, gave meaning to community life and potency to the political aspirations of black Kentuckians. As the nation approached a simmering conflict in 1861, these relationships that flourished at the margins of the master's control positioned the black community to exploit the divisions within the white population

---

[48] George Rawick, ed., *Kansas, Kentucky, Maryland, Ohio, Virginia, and Tennessee Narratives*, vol. 16, series 1 of *The American Slave: A Composite Autobiography*, 24 vols. (Westport, Conn., 1972), 16, interview with Bert Mayfield.

[49] Ibid., 31, interview with Aunt Harriet Mason.

[50] On the Underground Railroad, see J. Blaine Hudson, *Fugitive Slaves and the Underground Railroad in the Kentucky Borderland* (Jefferson, N.C., 2002).

that ultimately manifested itself in an internal guerrilla war.

To be sure, the mostly enslaved blacks of Kentucky in 1860 had virtually no political power, their few legal and customary rights hanging by a thread in the increasingly hostile, late-antebellum period. In law and in custom, chattel slavery in Kentucky differed little from the institution thriving deep in the cotton belt. And consonant with the growing antiabolitionist militancy elsewhere in the South, the Kentucky legislature passed increasingly restrictive codes that both strengthened the master's total authority over the slave and pressured free blacks to leave the state.[51] Leading members of white society recognized the political threat of social and economic networks connecting slaves, hirees, free blacks, and poor whites to the overall system of personal domination necessary to sustain slavery. As slaves sought to defy their masters' power of individuation by creating an increasingly autonomous sphere of social, cultural, and economic life, the masters retaliated with renewed fervor.

Perhaps most pernicious aspect of Kentucky slavery was the massive slave trade funneling Kentucky slaves downriver to New Orleans or overland to Mississippi, Louisiana, and Texas. The extensive slave trade underscored the relative powerlessness of slaves to control their own future or their own communities. All told, approximately 77,000 slaves were sold to the Deep South from Kentucky during the antebellum era, with 3,400 a year sold in the 1850s.[52] Moreover, nearly a quarter of all Kentucky slave women in their twenties were sold away, thus permanently severing kinship bonds between women of childbearing age and their children.[53] Not all slaves sold went to the Deep South; in fact, the majority of private sales and sheriffs' auctions merely circulated the existing slave population within Kentucky itself.

Slaves did not go without a fight. Some slaves resisted sale

[51] The 1851 Constitution of Kentucky required free blacks to leave the state unless bonded by their former masters. See Richard H. Stanton, *Revised Statutes of Kentucky . . . 1851 and 1852* (Cincinnati, 1860).

[52] Marion B. Lucas, *From Slavery to Segregation, 1760–1891*, vol. 1 of *A History of Blacks in Kentucky*, 2 vols. (Frankfort, 1992), 99. Lucas notes that these figures are estimations, but they are the most commonly agreed-upon number for overall sale from Kentucky.

[53] Ibid.

to the Deep South by mutilating themselves, thus devaluing their own financial value as chattel. More commonly, slaves appealed to their master's sense of paternalism to keep families together. One Kentucky slave pleaded with his master not to be sold away from his wife. The master seriously considered the slave's feelings in the matter and even planned to change the prospects of sale if the slave absolutely refused to go. Writing to Calvin Morgan, John Hunt Morgan's brother, the owner wrote, "Aleck promised to think about it today and let me know this evening. He will try and make up his mind to go with Bryant in which event I think I can get 1900 for him, not more. Don't know positively yet."[54] The slave's protest clearly intervened in an otherwise cold business decision, thus hoping his master's paternalistic sympathies would trump market imperatives.

Like their compatriots in the Deep South, black Kentuckians employed a familiar array of tools to resist the total domination of slavery. At no point did slaves actually foment—or openly threaten— a large-scale insurrection against the master class and their white nonslaveholding allies who roamed the countryside as patrollers. But as elsewhere in the South, slaves whispered rumors of plots and rumors of rumors—enough to petrify the master class. One large slave "conspiracy" occurred in Hopkinsville, where a foiled Christmas insurrection in 1856 spurred panic and "excitement" throughout the entire state.[55] The largest plot in the slave-rich Bluegrass region occurred in the summer of 1848 which involved seventy-five slaves who escaped Fayette and Bourbon Counties with the help of a white abolitionist at Centre College in Danville and numerous free blacks. The slaves were all caught in Cynthiana, most likely on their way to the Ohio River; many had pistols and rifles with them. Lexingtonians were especially shocked because most of the participating slaves were "trusted house servants of Lexington's most socially prominent

[54] J. W. George to Calvin Morgan, January 11, 1861, New Orleans, La., box 15, folder 7, Hunt-Morgan Papers, special collections, UK.

[55] For local reaction to the Hopkinsville plot, see Wallace-Starling Family Diaries, KHS Collections. Ellen Kenton McGaughey Wallace reveals the terrified response of the community to the planned insurrection.

families."[56] Relationships connecting the white elites of Bluegrass society facilitated the creation of networks among their own servants. Meanwhile, slaveholders blamed white emancipationists who had been agitating for the gradual elimination of slavery in advance of a constitutional convention in the following year.[57] Whatever effect the white Danville abolitionist had, the plot would never have taken hold without well-established social and kinship bonds extending throughout the city.

Few actual runaway plots resembled the mass attempt of 1848 in Fayette County. When group runaways took place, they typically involved entire families. Thus, when eight Bourbon County slaves headed for Maysville on the Ohio River, five men and three women were among them.[58] Still, a sizable number of slaves made their way to the free states through Louisville and other river towns.[59] Runaways were a persistent form of slave resistance, made more available because of the geographic location of Kentucky. George Henderson, a former slave of the Cleveland family in Woodford County, Kentucky, recalled, "I have seen old covered wagons pulled by oxen travelling on the road going to Indianny and us children was whipped to keep us away from the road for fear they would steal us."[60] Children and other kin regularly faced the reality of sudden sale to the Deep South. But "theft" for the sake of emancipation was entirely different. Henderson was unclear in later life as to who might have threatened to steal the Cleveland slave children, as he certainly was unclear as a slave child. But the knowledge that some force outside the plantation—whether a white abolitionist or a free black—just might carry away the Cleveland family slaves to freedom nurtured the aspirations for freedom among the general slave population throughout the state. With Madison, Indiana, and its well-known

[56] J. Winston Coleman Jr., *Slavery Times in Kentucky* (Chapel Hill, 1940), 88-92; *Louisville Courier*, August 14, 1848, quoted in Hudson, *Fugitive Slaves*, 137.

[57] Tallant, *Evil Necessity*, 146.

[58] Hudson, *Fugitive Slaves*, 49.

[59] Ibid.; Harriet C. Frazier, *Runaway and Freed Missouri Slaves and Those Who Helped Them, 1763–1865* (Jefferson, N.C., 2004), 74-75.

[60] Rawick, ed., *Kansas, Kentucky*, 7, interview with George Henderson.

Antislavery League only eighty miles away, and wagon traffic regularly traversing the Bluegrass roads on their way to the Ohio River, "Marse Cleveland" understood the threat to his absolute domination over his slaves.[61] Severe whippings may have discouraged the slaves from gazing on the local highway to freedom, but the knowledge that an alternative to bondage lay such a short distance away undoubtedly weakened the slaves' conception of the master as absolute patriarch.

Overall, J. Blaine Hudson estimates that 1,200 Kentucky slaves ran away each year in the 1850s.[62] The limited scale of runaways from Kentucky to Ohio and Indiana, belies the extensive, informal set of relationships between fellow slaves, free blacks, and white abolitionists, upon which slaves could rely for their escape to freedom. Other than outright insurrection, running away was the slave's gravest political act of resistance. It directly usurped the master's authority and severed the vital master-slave relationship that lay at the heart of any slave-based society. To make this "quiet insurrection" possible, slaves had to rely on their "courage, patience, and, above all, incisive intelligence" as they "waged a continual war against slavery."[63] Without a subterranean network aware of the routes to freedom and the precise details of patrol activities, the deeply political act of running away would have been even less common.

Adding to slaveholders' anxiety, small-scale rumors of runaway and rebellion schemes simmered across state. In Frankfort, senior officers at the Kentucky Military Institute ordered the cadets to stand ready and armed in the event of a planned slave rebellion in April 1861.[64] No plot was discovered, but several blacks were arrested with "loaded guns and pistols." Undoubtedly, the national state of emergency that month accentuated the anxieties about slave intentions across central Kentucky. A rumored insurrection plot at

[61] On the Antislavery League, see Hudson, *Fugitive Slaves*, 25.

[62] Ibid., 62.

[63] Margaret O'Brien, "Slavery in Louisville during the Antebellum Period, 1820-1860" (MA thesis, University of Louisville, 1979), 130, quoted in Frazier, *Runaway and Freed Missouri Slaves*, 82.

[64] Thomas Morgan to Mother, April 29, 1861, box 15, folder 8, Hunt-Morgan Papers, special collections, UK.

Cynthiana, Kentucky, involving blacks and whites along the Lexington and Covington Railroad was "uncovered" shortly after John Brown's raid.[65] As usual, no actual plot existed, but the networks of slaves, free blacks, and white abolitionists meeting in "secret societies," as the local newspaper stated—most likely just for the purpose of absconding a handful of slaves to Ohio—did little to calm the nerves of an excited white population in the wake of Harpers Ferry. The appearance of slave conspiracies during seminal events—like John Brown's raid, the Christmas season, or the attack on Fort Sumter—underscores the latent political power vested in the "apolitical" slave population. Though the insurrectionary fears may have been imagined, slaveholders ironically imputed to their slaves the political savvy to exploit white moments of panic for their own ends.

In some cases, slaves did openly threaten violence when they believed that their masters usurped the prerogatives that the slaves had attained. In one case, slaves on a Woodford County, Kentucky, farm insinuated that they would destroy their master's home if he continued to interfere with their religious services. One of the former slaves there recalled, "We had our churches too. Sometimes the white folks would try to cause trouble when the negroes were holding their meetings, then at night the men of the church would place chunks and matches on the white folks gate post. In the morning the white folks would find them and know that it was a warning if they didn't quit causing trouble their buildings would be burned."[66] This kind of slave autonomy was the only sliver of political power the slaves had achieved, and the nightly church meetings served as the parliament halls of rural slave power. In the end, fear of insurrection was usually overblown; even the Woodford County case may have been more bark than bite. But the slaves knew that by harnessing their collective power outside the purview of the master, especially in the tense, late-antebellum days when rumors of Haiti-style uprisings abounded, the slaves dealt a serious psychological blow to the

---

[65] *Glasgow Weekly Times*, November 17, 1859.
[66] Rawick, ed., *Kansas, Kentucky*, 33, interview with Mary Belle Dempsey.

masters' sense of absolute political dominance.

Particular acts of violence and theft against the master provoked panic and outrage across the white community as well. In Bourbon County, Kentucky, a slave thief wrestled and ultimately killed an old white man who had apprehended him.[67] The appearance of white authority did little to prevent the thief in this case from fighting back. Numerous other cases appeared in Kentucky newspapers, though often presented carefully so as not to sow too much panic and concede to slaves the power of systemic threat.

A more serious social—and political—threat to the master class was the development of an underground economy through which slaves, hirees, free blacks, and poor whites traded goods at the margins of the master's domain. One of the most lucrative trades was "hemp tow." Slaves gathered the broken fibers of hemp throughout the Bluegrass region and sold them to paper- and rope-makers.[68] In other cases, hired slaves convinced hirers and owners to allot them some of the wages earned for service. The "problem" of the underground economy was widespread enough to encourage whites to petition for new laws banning any white person trading with slaves without their masters' permission. Because free-black communities developed in close proximity to slaves, especially in the towns like Danville and Nicholasville and in the larger cities like Lexington and Louisville, it was nearly impossible for masters to prevent the development of social and economic networks across status lines.

Considering the individuating effect of personal domination that the master held over slaves, the fields of resistance were broad.[69] Even acts not calibrated to resist the master's yoke, such as marriage or the creation of black religious organizations, had the effect of limiting the master's total dominance. These seemingly mundane moves to create social relationships outside the master's immediate control actually

---

[67] *Western Citizen*, September 1, 1860. The ultimate fate of the slave is unknown.

[68] Ebenezer Stedman, *Bluegrass Craftsman: Being the Reminiscences of Ebenezer Hiram Stedman, Papermaker, 1808-1885*, ed. Frances L. S. Dugan and Jacqueline P. Bull (Lexington, Ky., 1959). This practice is discussed in greater detail in Tallant, *Evil Necessity*, 65.

[69] Hahn, *A Nation Under Our Feet*, 16.

served as "the most basic and the most profound of political acts in which they engaged."[70] In addition to the bonds of marriage, the act of performing weddings enhanced the autonomy of the slave community, as slave ministers regularly performed wedding ceremonies, both under and outside the purview of the master.

Indeed, the most powerful institutions of slave autonomy in Kentucky were the churches—both formal structures and informal "brush arbor" meetings. Black churches thrived in both urban and rural settings along the border. Many of these churches, filled with free and enslaved African Americans, began as adjuncts to white churches and then split off. The First Colored Baptist Church of Danville broke away from the white First Baptist Church in 1846.[71] In mostly rural Jessamine County three separate black congregations—the African Methodist Episcopal Church, Colored Christian Church, and Colored Baptist Church, all in Nicholasville—were founded in the mid-1840s. All three churches primarily served the free-black population of Jessamine County, but each was open to slaves in Nicholasville as well.[72] One of the largest church buildings in antebellum Kentucky was the First African Church of Lexington. With the aid of small donations, the congregation built a meeting-house for two thousand people that cost eight thousand dollars.[73] By drawing small contributions from the slave and free communities of Lexington, the First African Church, whose roots dated back to 1786, established a bulwark of political power in a hostile environment.[74] Unlike the myriad brush-arbor meetings on rural farms, these large, permanent structures established within the public space the demand of the black community for humanity, respect, and autonomy.

Kentucky slave families persevered despite isolated settings and smallholdings that limited contacts with fellow African Americans.

[70] Ibid., 17.

[71] Mechal Sobel, *Trabelin' On: The Slave Journey to an Afro-Baptist Faith* (Westport, Conn., 1979), 333.

[72] Bennett H. Young, *A History of Jessamine County, Kentucky* (Louisville, 1898), 198-99.

[73] *Western Citizen*, April 6, 1860.

[74] Sobel, *Trabelin' On*, 335-36.

If the greatest bane of Upper South slavery was its isolation and circumscription of black social and family life, mobility—whether sanctioned through weekend familial visit passes or not sanctioned through running away—was the only tonic. Proximity to freedom was a two-edged sword. On the one hand, it underscored the cruelty of the slaves' present circumstances. That freedom was so near almost certainly made slavery even harder to bear. Stories of the free North trickled into Kentucky, making freedom a tantalizing, though unlikely, possibility for border slaves. Even a quick glance upon the teamsters headed for "Indianny" could result in a severe whipping. But the chance to steal away to free soil was, in fact, greater along the border than anywhere else, and an active Underground Railroad, staffed almost entirely by free blacks, ensured that slaves who decided to make the trek had a fighting chance of success. And because of the relatively high level of black mobility in Kentucky, along the carriageways, railroads, and rivers where hired slaves and free blacks routinely traveled between employers, the ability of the white population to prevent runaways was always in question.

Slaveholders were acutely aware of the risk of losing their slaves to free soil. In response, owners upped the reward payments if their slaves were caught outside the county, especially if in the free North. For example, Mrs. Thomas Reed of Danville, offered twenty-five dollars for the return of her male slave Isaiah if found within Boyle County, forty dollars if found in another county, and one hundred dollars if found outside the state.[75] The notice did not specify the state to which Isaiah was likely to run, but clearly Indiana and Ohio were real possibilities. Other slave notices specifically referenced the Ohio River. One broadside appearing in Lexington, in late 1859, described a runaway slave named Tom and offered twenty dollars if caught in Fayette County, fifty dollars if caught elsewhere in the Bluegrass, one hundred dollars if caught in a county bordering the Ohio River, and one hundred and fifty dollars if captured outside

[75] Broadside, December 26, 1861, Danville, Ky., property of Calvin Fackler, special collections, UK.

109

the state.[76] Running away to freedom was rare in the antebellum era, but it was not unheard of. Slaves undoubtedly knew of the various schemes and organizations that could facilitate such a brave gambit and would eventually exploit them when the surrounding white population was distracted by civil war.

What differentiates the Kentucky story from that occurring in the Deep South, then, was the structure of the African American community, which encouraged networks of resistance across the free–slave divide and over vast stretches of territory, and which carried powerful, though different, political possibilities. As Steven Hahn points out, the black politics of emancipation and Reconstruction emerged directly out of existing networks of slave politics.[77] This was true in Kentucky as well as in the Lower South. And the networks relied upon the movement of hired slaves, free blacks, and non-hired slaves living on small farms scattered throughout the Kentucky countryside. Various black-community actions in defense of social autonomy, familial solidarity, and economic self-determination formed the backdrop of later political agitation. The transfer of news and information in the antebellum era, whether rumored or confirmed, from one community to another, helped establish a larger black political network that transformed into an explicit and open emancipation force at the first sign of the Civil War. And as Stanley Harrold has argued, the tensions along the slave–free line—including the Ohio River—exacerbated sectional divisions that ultimately led to the Civil War.[78] With slaves as the primary agents of borderland agitation—as runaways, rebels, informants, and autonomous defenders of a slave culture—the political power of black rebels along the border becomes more apparent.

The Demise of Conservative Unionism

The crouching lion of conservative Unionism collapsed in the

---

[76] Broadsides, July 12, 1859, Lexington, Ky., J. Winston Coleman Papers, special collections, UK.

[77] Hahn, *A Nation Under Our Feet*, 1-10. This is one of the central themes of Hahn's book.

[78] Stanley Harrold, *Border Wars: Fighting Over Slavery before the Civil War* (Chapel Hill, 2010).

course of the Civil War. But timing and contingency are key to understanding the transformation of the Kentucky political culture. If not for the deep kinship-based, economic and social ties between Kentuckians and those living in the lower Midwest, Kentucky would likely have interpreted the threats to slavery in much the same way that those in central Virginia, North Carolina, and Tennessee did. Conservative Unionism ultimately collapsed as a national position, especially as the logic of war and the actions of slaves themselves undermined the traditional social order amidst civil war. But it persisted long enough within Kentucky itself to keep the Bluegrass State in the Union. It was the internal political culture—more than the careful machinations of the Lincoln administration—that preserved the Kentucky position in the Union during the critical spring and summer months of 1861. A rational calculation that slavery would be best preserved within the Union, coupled with a viable two-party system that tended to soften debate away from the maximalist positions of Radical Republicans in the North and fire-eaters of the Deep South, kept Kentucky in the Union. Without this political culture, Kentucky would likely have faced more internal pressure to secede or, at the very least, to set up a guerrilla-based insurgency such as appeared in Missouri. And with that, President Lincoln's famous warning—"To lose Kentucky is the same as to lose the whole game"—would likely have borne fruit.[79]

But it is equally significant that slaves—living on dispersed farms across Kentucky, and carrying news through slave hiring, slave trade, and Underground Railroad networks—understood the stakes of the war very differently than their masters. Their decades of resistance exacerbated tensions between Kentucky and the free states of the Old Northwest. And when war broke out—between Northerners and Southerners, and between Unionist and Confederate Kentuckians—slaves recast the Unionist cause from one based on the conservative defense of slavery to a radical struggle for freedom. When they joined

---

[79] Abraham Lincoln to Orville Browning, September 22, 1861, Roy P. Basler, ed., *The Collected Works of Abraham Lincoln*, 9 vols. (New Brunswick, N.J., 1953-55), 4:532.

the Federal army en masse in 1864 in defense of an emancipationist Union, it was too late for their demoralized masters to switch to the Confederacy. White Kentuckians would fashion a new postwar political culture of their own, defined by a belated Confederate regional identity, large-scale racial violence, and the emergence of one-party Democratic rule. But by then, the old conservative Unionist order was already dead.

NETHERWORLD OF WAR: THE DOMINION SYSTEM AND THE CONTOURS OF FEDERAL OCCUPATION IN KENTUCKY

By Christopher Phillips

From his home in Jefferson City in August 1861, Missouri attorney general J. Proctor Knott, grumbled to his mother at home in Lebanon, Kentucky, a more-than-rhetorical question. He wondered whether "Kentucky and Missouri [would] become parts of the great centralized despotism to which our government is so rapidly drifting, or whether they be destined to remain the cherished homes of Constitutional liberty after the present ravaging storm shall have passed by." Knott, well-versed in the law in both states and watching it suffer in each, in fact perceived the rapid wartime erosion of civil liberties that impinged upon residents of these loyal slave states and which resembled, even preceded, similar such intrusions on the populations of the occupied parts of the seceded states. Within months, he found himself removed from his position, disbarred, and imprisoned briefly for refusing to take the newly mandated oath of allegiance to the Missouri convention government. Two years later, he returned to his old Kentucky home, paroled by Federal officials, unemployed, and outraged.[1]

CHRISTOPHER PHILLIPS is the John and Dorothy Hermanies Professor of American History at the University of Cincinnati. He is the author of seven books, including *The Rivers Ran Backward: The Civil War and the Remaking of the American Middle Border* (New York: Oxford University Press, 2016).

[1] J. Proctor Knott to My Dear Mother, August 1, 1861, Knott Collection, ms. 53, box 1, folder 2, manuscripts & folklife archives, special collections, library, Western Kentucky University, Bowling Green, Kentucky (hereafter special collections, WKU); Lowell H. Harrison, ed., *Kentucky's Governors* (Lexington, Ky., 1985), 115.

What Knott saw in Missouri and Kentucky were measures by the Federal military that sharply categorized a deeply divided populace. Around him, he saw developing a dominion system of sorts, a knot of counterinsurgency measures initiated, although never routinized, by both state and Federal governments and implemented by low-level, often volunteer, post commanders. Together, they sought to establish control of a "chaos of incendiary elements," as Henry W. Halleck referred to the local, often-armed populations in border slave states whose true loyalties were often uncertain and ephemeral. Largely with Lincoln's assent, military leaders there often tolerated the subversion of civil liberties at the local level as part of the broader prosecution of the war. The official neutrality of Kentucky allowed secessionism to exist alongside Unionism, a situation made worse by there being no mechanisms for precise measurement of either. Federal commanders recognized almost immediately that their greatest challenge, as department commander Jeremiah T. Boyle put it, was to "sift" the mass of residents around their commands, determining their allegiances, and pressuring or punishing those who supported the Confederacy. If the price of liberty is eternal vigilance, the price of neutrality was even steeper. The calculus of loyalty and disloyalty would soon drive both armies and state governments beyond simply keeping the peace. It would require in these states "a stronger hand," as Halleck wrote—a hostile occupation of an ostensibly loyal state.[2]

With its purpose being the need to distinguish loyal from disloyal residents, the dominion system rested on six pillars. First, military districting at once focused and diffused military command, trying to

---

[2] Judkin Browning, "'I Am Not So Patriotic as I was Once': The Effects of Military Occupation on the Occupying Soldiers during the Civil War," *Civil War History* 55 (2009): 219-20; L. C. Turner to J[eremiah]. T. Boyle, November 2, 1862, Record Group 393: Records of the U.S. Army Continental Commands, 1821-1920 (hereafter USACC), part 1, series 2173: Letters Received, Department of Kentucky, 1862-69, box 1, National Archives and Records Administration, Washington, D.C. (hereafter NARA); Stephen V. Ash, *When the Yankees Came: Conflict and Chaos in the Occupied South, 1861-1865* (Chapel Hill, 1999), 44-45, 84; Henry W. Halleck to Hon. T[homas]. Ewing, January 1, 1862, and Halleck to George B. McClellan, December 19, 1861, both in *The War of the Rebellion: A Compilation of the Official Records of the Union and Confederate Armies*, 128 vols. (Washington D.C., 1880-1901) series 1, 8:475, 448-49 (hereafter *OR*), The term "dominion system" is the author's own construction.

regularize the myriad of orders and regulations that soon blanketed district commanders' offices while at once affording them latitude to implement policies. Each district would contain a series of garrisoned towns, occupied by squads of Federal troops, generally cavalry, who were themselves supported by the local Home Guards or state militia. Second, unconditional Unionist informants provided these Federal, state, and Home Guard commanders with names and often lists of known or suspected secessionists, compiled evidence against them, and led them to their homes, often miles from the towns through, in, or on woods, hills, and ridges, for investigation, questioning, or arrest. Third, provost marshals, generally civilians with and without military rank but not technically subordinate to the local garrison commander, had a wide range of powers and responsibilities by which to maintain order within the localities in which they served, including policing their town and its environs, issuing travel passes and various permits, fielding complaints and arbitrating disputes, and acting as liaison between the post and the municipal government. Fourth, oaths of allegiance and surety bonds, which provost marshals administered and cataloged, required civilians to attest both in writing and viva voce before witnesses that their loyalty either always had been or hitherto was to the state and Federal governments. If they refused, they were levied for guerrillas' damages to Unionists' property and deaths or banished to the Confederacy, their property often confiscated. Fifth, the Federal authorities assumed the right to impose, ad hoc, martial law over civilians, which mandated various restrictions of civil liberties and individual rights, including the suspension of habeas corpus and the creation of military tribunals (or commissions) to try civilians arrested by the Federal army despite the existence of civil authority in ostensibly loyal states. Finally, the Federal military regulated local trade, establishing a system by which, as treasury secretary Salmon P. Chase termed it, "commerce should follow the flag." Each of these planks of this dominion system were in place in parts of the border slave states like Kentucky by the summer of 1862; ad hoc measures, including oaths, began as early as a month after the war itself commenced.[3]

The dominion system had a brief Confederate complement, one that targeted Unionists and encouraged local secessionists and Confederate sympathizers to remain above ground. During the occupations of portions of the border states by Rebel armies, Confederate commanders created military districts, garrisoned towns behind the front lines, and sent squads into the countryside to roust local Unionists, confiscate horses and other supplies from their farms, and require oaths of allegiance. Beginning in southern Missouri, which Confederate troops occupied in the late summer of 1861, "peaceably-disposed citizens" who refused were often "driven from their homes because of their political opinions, or . . . left them from fear of force and violence." After the Confederate Congress allowed recruiting in the border slave states in early August 1861, squads circulated throughout the region behind Confederate lines, enlisting or impressing outliers of fighting age and levying local Unionists for arms, equipment, food, and forage. In late August, just before the Rebels occupied southern Kentucky, the Confederate Congress enacted a Sequestration Act that declared all property owned by persons not loyal to the Confederate government to be the property of that government. Rebel commanders could judge citizens who resided within the borders of the Confederacy as "alien enemies," subjecting their property to permanent, uncompensated seizure and sale for the benefit of Confederate citizens who had lost property to the Federal government.[4]

Confederate commanders in the border states were not limited by the congressional authority of such an act. Under the Sequestration Act, the confiscation of property owned by those deemed disloyal

---

[3] Report of Captain Nelson Cole, May 16, 1861, *OR*, series 1, 3:10-11; Martha M. Jones to My dear father [W. S. Buford], December 21, 1862, Jones Family Papers, folder 1, Filson Historical Society, Louisville, Kentucky (hereafter FHS); E. Merton Coulter, *The Civil War and Readjustment in Kentucky* (Chapel Hill, 1927), 80.

[4] Joint Proclamation of Sterling Price and John C. Frémont, November 1, 1861, *OR*, series 1, 3:563-64 (first and second quotes); An Act to authorize the President of the Confederate States to grant commissions to raise volunteer regiments and battalions composed of persons who are or have been residents of the States of Kentucky, Missouri, Maryland, and Delaware, August 8, 1861, ibid., series 4, 1:536 (third quote).

(meaning loyal to the Federal government) by the Confederate army could be enforced only within the boundaries of the Confederate nation. The Confederacy made no claim to dominion over the United States, and thus had no claim to property belonging to foreign citizens. That neither Missouri nor Kentucky had seceded—nor had the Confederate Congress yet admitted them—technically placed Unionist and secessionist civilians out of reach of the confiscatory authority of the Confederate government. (Although the law did not specifically so state, a Department of Justice circular instructed commanders to exempt residents of border slave states who did not "commit actual hostilities against the Confederate States.") But it did not put them out of reach of the Rebel army commanders who could, by a narrow definition of confiscation, determine the loyalty and disloyalty of local citizens and take their property for military necessity. Once the states had gained admission to the Confederacy at the onset of winter in 1861, they also fell under the terms of the act. The border slave states and their residents then found themselves in a perpetual "no man's land," as one historian has characterized the fringe of the Union-occupied Confederacy, squeezed between the competing legal, constitutional, and military claims of the belligerent nations.[5]

The presence of Confederate troops in southern and eastern

[5] Daniel W. Hamilton, "The Confederate Sequestration Act," *Civil War History* 52 (2006): 373-75, 383; Mark Grimsley, *The Hard Hand of War: Union Military Policy Toward Southern Civilians* (New York, 1995), 39, 42; Ash, *When the Yankees Came,* (quote) 45. With dubious legitimacy, the exiled legislature of Missouri passed an ordinance of secession in Neosho on October 30, 1861, and the Confederate Congress admitted it as its twelfth state on November 28. Despite the refusal of the legislature of Kentucky to call a secession convention and its official vote for neutrality and for remaining in the Union if its neutrality were to be violated, a convention representing sixty-eight Kentucky counties met at Russellville and passed a declaration of independence on November 20, 1861. On December 10, the Confederate Congress admitted it. For the most recent analysis of the complicated history of secession in the border slave states (Delaware, Maryland, Kentucky, and Missouri) and the equally complicated claims of secession for Kentucky and Missouri, see William C. Harris, *Lincoln and the Border States: Preserving the Union* (Lawrence, Kans., 2011), esp. chaps. 1-4. The Sequestration Act empowered legislative confiscation and property transfer authorized by law. Military confiscation is generally ad hoc and temporary, imposed according to the strategic needs of the military. See Daniel W. Hamilton, *The Limits of Sovereignty: Property Confiscation in the Union and Confederacy during the Civil War* (Chicago, 2007), 12.

Kentucky and the relative absence of Federal troops outside Louisville, Lexington, the Bluegrass counties, and those counties adjacent to the Ohio River kept many secessionists in place for much
of the winter of 1861-62. They found their commitment tested as
spring approached and their families at home were pressed to provide for themselves. As the Confederate Congress began debate
over a conscription bill, which it would pass in March 1862, many
Confederate-leaning residents in the Confederate areas of occupation found reason to oppose the presence of those they had once
considered their protectors against Federal invaders. The rumor of
a Confederate draft sent many would-be Rebels behind Federal lines,
willingly taking the detested Federal oath rather than serve in the
Rebel ranks. Their families quickly supported their decision. In the
summer of 1862, one Unionist woman in southeastern Kentucky,
convinced by the Confederates that the Yankees would "come there
to Kill the women and children," was nonetheless relieved to find
blueclad troops at last in her midst. "[T]he woman come runing out,"
wrote a Kentucky soldier, "and said that they thanked God that we
had come in the country for we looked like white men to the nasty
lousy raged set of [Rebel] rascals that they had been use to seeing."[6]

The withdrawal of the Rebel armies in the spring of 1862 not
only ended the brief Confederate dominion system but ushered in
a wave of refugees heading to the Confederacy, accompanying the
Rebel army rather than face the Federal occupation of their own
states. Many, like Anna Hunt of Kentucky, who after an extended
search for affordable lodging settled her family in north Georgia,
found the area foreign. "We are boarding at Mr Satlers and it is very
lonely hear," she wrote to her aunt, "and I dont like Dixies land half
as well as Kentucky." A few who held slaves "fled at the approach
of our [Union] troops, going south, because 'Lincoln wanted their
niggers.'" In wagons loaded with "trunks [filled with] little articles
such as books, dagueratypes, mantel ornaments," Bluegrass residents
William and Mary Van Meter and their slaves left their "home, friends,

---

[6] W[illiam]. F. Wickersham to Dear Brother and Father and Mother, July 7, 1862 (typescript,
11-12), Wickersham Family Papers, 1861-1877, special collections, WKU.

country, all behind to fall into the hands of an enemy who knows not how to exercise mercy towards friend or foe." After briefly finding refuge with another displaced Kentucky family in Tuscumbia, Alabama, they moved on to northern Mississippi. The war often found them, despite their best efforts to avoid it, and many returned to their border-state homes. Rather than face the Yankees in an adopted land, Mary decided painfully that she "must go home" to Kentucky, leaving her husband to tend their leased farm. After three long months of travel, she arrived in occupied Bowling Green, located in a part of the state which she found (but for her father's household) largely unfamiliar. "I now sit by the window all day, and scarcely recognize a familiar face," she wrote dejectedly. "Where oh where are the dear friends who used to meet me on the wharf to welcome me home[?], Alas, I know too well they are exiles far from home."[7]

Administering the Federal dominion system, which began in parts of the border states even before the Confederate withdrawal and would ultimately spread throughout them and last virtually through the war, required interaction between Federal troops, Unionist militia or Home Guard, and Unionist citizens. It also placed real impositions on local populations. Garrisoning towns, especially small ones, often required the commandeering of many if not most of the buildings and private homes of these communities for army use. As one soldier stationed in west-central Kentucky wrote home to his sister, "Calhoun . . . might be called an hospital, or army store house, a large part of the houses being occupied by the sick, the Quartermaster's stores, and factors Stores. Then there is two or three taverns which are now Soldier's Eating houses, and nothing else." Damage or destruction often followed, as did the confiscation of private property. Once the towns had been garrisoned, ferreting out and suppressing

[7] Anna Hunt to Henrietta H. Morgan, undated, Hunt-Morgan Family Papers, box 15, folder 10, special collections, University of Kentucky Libraries, University of Kentucky, Lexington, Kentucky (hereafter special collections, UK); Civil War Diary of John Preston Mann (transcription, 6), March 26, 1862, entry, Mann Family Papers, special collections and archives, Southern Illinois University, Carbondale, Illinois; Mary E. Van Meter diary (microfilm), February 10, 1862–February 25, 1863, special collections, UK; 1860 U.S. census, Population Schedule, Warren County, Kentucky.

disloyalists—their primary task—required search patrols, small and large, whose soldiers performed professionally under the best of circumstances and overzealously, even murderously, under the worst. In either case, cavalry patrols regularly roamed the countryside on "scouts," as these patrols were termed, looking for disloyalists, saboteurs, and guerrilla bands, the latter of whom had operated strictly on their own until April 1862 when the Confederacy passed its Partisan Ranger Act, commissioning officers to organize bands of partisans that were already in operation as well as those that would form.[8]

The squad-based actions of Federal troops under Colonel Charles Whittlesey in the northern Kentucky counties of Gallatin, Grant, and Owen over the winter of 1861-62 are representative of the early and daily implementation of the dominion system. Whittlesey, a New England-born, West Point-trained lawyer and newspaper editor in Cleveland, Ohio, commanded the Twentieth Ohio Volunteers and, as chief engineer for the Department of the Ohio, planned and constructed the defenses across the river from Cincinnati. In December 1861, in order to implement military order in those counties and locate arms that were fueling the growing insurgency, he ordered squads to search the properties of named Confederate sympathizers. "Still continue to search the premises of those quiet and inoffensive sympathizers with the south," reported the captain who commanded a scout. "The *Union Men* discourage this—in case we are successful in recovering the arms without—We have a plan that will bring the arms without further search." Between December 28, 1861, and January 14, 1862, Whittlesey received nine written tips from local Unionists about disloyal actions by residents in three communities, ranging from holding weapons to harboring or aiding known guerrillas or guerrilla bands to firing a gun in anger across the Ohio River to threatening Unionists, including one who vowed to "kill his brother

[8] Robert Winn to Dear Sister, December 31, 1861, Winn-Cook Family Papers, box 1, folder 1, FHS; David T. Statham to Dear Brother, November 16, 1861, David T. Statham Papers, Manuscripts Division, Ohio Historical Society, Columbus, Ohio; Michael Fellman, *Inside War: The Guerrilla Conflict in Missouri During the American Civil War* (New York, 1991), 76-77, 98-99, 281n108. On April 28, 1862, Jefferson Davis reluctantly signed the Partisan Ranger Act, authorizing the organization and military structuring of irregular partisan bands.

Dick for joining the Union army to cut his heart out, boil and eat it." Whittlesey ordered two raids of two companies each, conducted by different commanders, to investigate the reports. One rode first to a mill of a known secessionist, looking unsuccessfully for a guerrilla, and then on to New Liberty, where they occupied public buildings on either end of the main street and declared martial law while they searched for arms and ammunition. The other, which went to the hilltop hamlet of Mount Zion, resulted in the arrest of twelve suspected guerrillas, parole violators, or aggressive pro-Confederates. All told, some fifteen men were arrested during the period. Whittlesey paroled several with stipulations, and others he held indefinitely for their alleged disloyal behavior.[9]

The success of patrols relied on a foundation of information gained from local Unionists. They provided tips on known secessionists and their gathering points, and the bolder ones even accompanied the horsemen as guides. Some, like those in Hancock County, drew detailed maps of roads, heavy woods, and the residences of known and suspected secessionists and Unionists in the county, complete with locations where guerrillas hid out. But the report also reflects the large expanse of territory that garrisoned troops were required to traverse and the limits to their authority placed on them by it. Smaller patrols were far more common, but as the number of guerrillas and partisans increased and they became real dangers rather than mere annoyances, the patrols became less effective. Unionists, recognizing the inability of Federals to be everywhere, were less likely to assist for fear of their own lives.[10]

The dominion system, of course, had flaws—the expanse of territory to control only heading a long list. However patriotic were

[9] E. Hyatt to Whittlesey, December 30, 31, 1861; C. H. McElroy to Whittlesey, January 2, 1862; John N. Cossells to Whittlesey, January 14, 1862, and various notes on arrests, December 28, 1861–January 1, 1862, all in Charles Whittlesey Papers (microfilm), Western Reserve Historical Society, Cleveland, Ohio (hereafter WRHS).

[10] Map of Country Near Hawesville, Ky., undated (1863-64), USACC, part 1, series 3349: Letters Received, Northern Department, box 3, NARA; Gordon Granger to [Jeremiah T.] Boyle, November 28, 1862, USACC, part 1, series 2173: Letters Received, Department of Kentucky, 1862-69, box 1, ibid.

the motives of soldiers and officers nationwide, many in the Federal ranks who hailed from free western states, especially from their northernmost sections, arrived with preconceived notions not only of the border region but of its inhabitants as uniformly wealthy, pro-slavery, disloyal Southerners. Such prejudice caused all distinctions between loyal and disloyal property owners to evaporate in the minds of occupying troops. Many thus evinced distrust, even disdain, for the mass of residents, especially slaveholders. Williamson D. Ward wrote to his family at home that he and his Indiana comrades at Camp Rousseau outside Louisville paid five cents to one farmer for all the apples and peaches they "could eat and carry off." He then added, "I believe the old chap is a Secessionist he said he was union. He owned several Slaves and a farm of 600 acres I asked him if that was not too much for one man to have he said no I told him if a man in Indiana had a farm of 160 acres he had all he wanted to take care of." Norman G. Markham, who served in the Eighteenth Michigan, was surprised when his regiment entered Lexington to find that residents "had flags strung across the street and they cheered us and hurrahed for the Yankees. . . . [S]o you see there is some good union folks in Kentucky." But he found it difficult to separate his conceptions about the slaveholding society he saw from those of the South he had expected to find, and change. "This is the only place we have been in since we came into Kentucky where the folks act as if they were glad to see us," he grumbled. "The farmers are very wealthy. They own large plantations and lots of niggers. They have the finest buildings that I ever saw, have nice horses and carriages and nigger drivers. . . . I think when this war ends these big plantations will be cut up some."[11]

Beyond the bias that many free-state troops packed along, personal disputes, feuds, slights, and political differences lurked beneath this war raging among the residents of these states. After having festered for years, these old wounds were broken open by the war and

[11] Williamson Dixon Ward Civil War Journal, October 25, 1861, special collections, WKU; Norman G. Markham to My Dear Eunice, October 25, 1862, and Markham to Dear Wife and Boy, February 3, March 20, 1863, N. G. Markham Papers, folder 1, FHS.

its resultant societal divisions as scores to be settled by accusations and arrests. One Kentuckian lamented that a Unionist neighbor "has made it his business to arrest all his Rebel friends that he has a spite against," while an Indiana soldier wrote in his journal that the provost guard of his regiment arrested a Baptist minister near Louisville in mid-October 1861 for being a secessionist with no more evidence than an elder's claim that "while in church he took out a Rope and threatened to hang the union men with it." The morass caused one Federal captain, Indianian James H. Goodnow, to grumble to his wife in August 1862 that "[o]ur Regiment curses Kentucky daily and hourly." Class resentments certainly drove many such complaints against prominent landowners. The Home Guard and state militia who supported or replaced the garrisoning Federal troops were as much contributors to this private war as caught in its crossfire. War offered what one Kentuckian called an "evening-up time . . . [when] many a man became a violent Unionist because the ancient enemies of his house were Southern sympathizers." Another complained similarly of the elevation of her local Home Guard of personal motivations over others, arresting "such citizens as had displeased them" rather than conspicuous Confederate sympathizers. "The Secessionists said the secret clue to this seeming capriciousness was the private business affairs of the two parties," she wrote. "If a Southerner held the note of a Union man and the day for payment approached nothing would save the best government the world ever saw but the transfer of the Southerner to Camp Chase." Lincoln himself heard similar complaints in the border region "that arrests, banishments, and assessments are made more for private malice, revenge, and pecuniary interest than for the public good."[12]

[12] James M. McPherson, *For Cause and Comrades: Why Men Fought in the Civil War* (New York, 1998), 3-13, and passim; Ettie Scott to Susan Grigsby, August 3, 1862, Grigsby Family Papers, folder 173, FHS; Williamson Dixon Ward Civil War Journal, October 12, 1861, special collections, WKU; James H. Goodnow to Nancy Goodnow, August 29, 1862, James H. Goodnow Papers, Library of Congress, Washington, D.C. (hereafter LC); Edward C. Smith, *The Borderland in the Civil War* (New York, 1936), 367-68; William Crawford to H[enry]. W. Halleck, January 5, 1862, USACC, part 1, series 2593: Letters Received, Department of the

Widespread military arrests, often made "on the slightest and most trivial grounds," including writing to those in the Confederate army or states, occurred throughout the border slave states. (Robert Anderson, placed in command of state volunteers after the Kentucky legislature ended its neutrality in September 1861, in fact tried to rein in the arrests in and around Louisville, perhaps contributing to his resignation as much as did his ailing health. His successor, William T. Sherman, soon left his command from nervous exhaustion for the same reason.) Without oversight, prisoners jammed courthouse jails and other places of confinement. Neither Henry Clay's son James nor the former governor of Kentucky, Charles S. Morehead, a Whig member of the Peace and Border State Conventions who was well known for his humanitarian reform of the state prison system, evaded arrest or even imprisonment for strong criticisms of the Lincoln administration. The number of arrests made of suspected secessionists, especially prominent ones, because of flimsy or circumstantial evidence troubled even Sherman, while yet in command in Louisville. "We cannot imprison and keep in custody all suspected persons," he rebuked one subordinate in central Kentucky, "[lest] we would soon fill all the places of confinement in Louisville . . . . So many improper arrests were made by self-constituted authorities that there was a physical impossibility of keeping them." The concerned Sherman instituted a policy by which commissioners, generally prominent Unionist county judges or justices of the peace selected by a trusted U.S. Supreme Court justice (with jurisdiction over the Kentucky and Missouri circuit), would be stationed in garrisoned towns in the various subregions of his command. Evidence brought before them prior to ordering incarceration would "obviate our hitherto trouble of judging cases from mere letters and the explanations of the accused." Mark E. Neely, closely examining the Federal government arrest records during the war, has concluded

Missouri, 1862-67, box 2, NARA; Abraham Lincoln to Samuel R. Curtis, January 5, 1863, *OR*, series 1, 22, part 2, 17-18. Camp Chase was the Federal military prison at Columbus, Ohio.

124

that some thirteen thousand civilians were arrested throughout the nation, the largest portion in these border slave states. Yet Neely acknowledges that poor record-keeping and fragmentary evidence would likely ratchet up this estimate, especially in the West and most particularly in the first year of the war.[13]

Following on the heels of the widespread arrests, formalized oaths of allegiance became at once the most ubiquitous symbols and tools, even weapons, of Federal authority in the border slave states. Although most residents in the occupied areas of the seceded states found Federal oaths repugnant, none were more opposed than those living in the border states. The assumption that disloyal majorities of secessionists and neutralists were cowing loyalist minorities in the border states inverted the Federal war-makers' collective view of the populations of the Confederate states. Certainly, Confederates used the Federal occupation to portray border staters generally as victims of Yankee oppression. "They are being forced in Cumberland, Clinton, Russell, Wayne, and Pulaski Counties to take the oath of allegiance at the point of the bayonet by the Federal forces and Home Guards," wrote an angry Kentuckian to Albert Sidney Johnston in October 1861. Printed on blanks and administered at provost marshals' offices or in courthouses, a signed copy of the sworn oath was required to be carried on their person by those judged as disloyalists, much like free blacks, a detestable come-uppance for white men in slaveholding societies. As Bettie Terrell, a student at Midway College, prepared for her senior year at home near Versailles in the summer of 1862, she was fearful of a war-imposed interruption, especially that one of her professors should be arrested for disloyalty. "I saw in the paper a few days since that no one would be permitted to teach

[13] General Order No. 5, October 7, 1861, *OR*, series 1, 4:296 (first quote); Harrison, ed., *Kentucky's Governors*, 75-77; Coulter, *Civil War and Readjustment*, 148; Smith, *Borderland in the Civil War*, 372; William T. Sherman to W. T. Ward, November 2, 1861, *OR*, series 1, 4:327 (second and third quotes); R. A. Curd to Cal Morgan, June 22, 1862, Hunt-Morgan Family Papers, box 15, folder 9, special collections, UK. The Supreme Court justice was John Catron, a Tennessean. Charles Morehead was held four months in Fort Lafayette in New York before gaining his release in January 1862.

unless they took the oath," she related to her aunt, and she claimed that one of her teachers "says he will go to Camp Chase first." With the pervasive Victorian ideals upholding women as exemplars of domestic virtue, including honesty, Federal troops initially did not require Terrell and other women to take the oath. But commencing in many places in 1863, and adding to the repugnance they felt for what they considered coercive authority, women who demonstrated hostility toward occupying troops often found themselves before a swearing officer, threatened with expulsion for refusing to take it.[14]

Even Unionists objected to being forced to take the Federal oath. A soldier stationed at Columbia wrote home to his aunt about administering the oath that, "It just sutes me to hear [disloyalists] grumble," but the many Unionists' objections surprised him. "It dont hurt a union man to take the Oath," he admitted, "but we find once in a while one that hates to take the Oath but durst not say anything Once in a grate while they are catched by some of us that over hear their conversation and then put them under an arrest." One woman complained that "every one has been required to take the oath—they are then called Loyal—What a mockery." Many residents objected to the oath as "simply a test of adherence or submission to party, a most false test of loyalty in any true sense." One angry Kentuckian, who signed an oath of allegiance in front of the provost marshal at Smithland, could not have helped noticing the last line: "The penalty for a violation of this oath is Death." Public officials, who condemned such oaths as extralegal, having taken one already when assuming their positions, and who refused to take the oath, were judged to be guilty of disloyalty.[15]

This was, of course, exactly the point. Those who balked implic-

---

[14] James W. McHenry to Albert Sidney Johnston, October 10, 1861, *OR*, series 1, 4:442-43; Bettie Terrell to Susan Grigsby, July 29, 1862, Grigsby Family Papers, folder 173, FHS.

[15] F. D. Dickinson to Dear Aunt, May 15, 1863, F. D. Dickinson letter, FHS; Oath of Allegiance, May 19, 1862, William Johnson Stone Papers (microfilm), special collections, UK; J. Howard McHenry to Lt. Col. Chesebrough, February 21, 1863, Hunt-Morgan Family Papers, box 16, folder 9, ibid.; M. A. Shelby to Susan Grigsby, July 26, [1863], Grigsby Family Papers, folder 179, FHS.

itly rejected either the legitimacy of their state governments, whether elected or provisional, or that of a Federal government headed by Republicans. Residents' refusal to take either the Federal or state oath thus smoked them out, as it were, especially the final words by which they swore: "So Help Me God." One resident knew well the ideological dimensions of many of his neighbors' feigned neutrality, which taking the oath would unmask. "They believe this war is waged against slavery," wrote Joseph C. Maple, an Ohio-born Baptist minister who shared his neighbors' anger at the dominion system. He condemned "the Republican mode of carrying on war. . . . [T]he one side is abolition and the other side proslavery, they are determined if they fight to fight for the South. Hence they do not wish to take an oath which will cut them off from giving aid to the South." The oath sharpened blurred lines, to the great advantage for the government. Indeed, those so exposed were arrested, publicly listed, and required to post bond in order to gain their release. Unionists alone could guarantee their neighbors' sureties, from a few hundred to many thousands of dollars, put up for future good behavior.[16]

However unpopular they were, oaths and bonds had an obvious practical value. Identifying known, much less unknown, secessionists was a challenge, perhaps *the* challenge for Federal authorities. Putting the oath before residents would, if imperfectly, verify their base loyalty either by taking or refusing it, and the lists generated were essential identification tools for Federal commanders in local areas. Frances Dallam Peter of Lexington noted seeing a Federal commander with "a black book that he (Col Gracie) kept in which were marked down the names of everybody, whether they were union or secesh, and what they had been doing for the last 9 months back against the Confederacy and even the division in families." The terms of western Kentuckian R. B. Steele's bond of six thousand dollars in November 1862 included not only that he remain in his home county through-

[16] Printed Oath of Allegiance, August 16, 1864, Thomas S. Crutcher file, FHS; Oath of Allegiance of Samuel Jones Denton, ibid.; Bettie Morton to Pat [Joyes], July 21, 1862, Joyes Family Papers, folder 18, ibid.; Coulter, *Civil War and Readjustment*, 151; Grimsley, *Hard Hand of War*, 38.

out the war but that he "provide information of hostile movements, conspiracies, &c." (Federals there had identified his son, Leon, as a guerrilla.) Many, especially neutralists, did not want the consequences of being labeled disloyal. As Fanny Gunn wrote to her sons in the Federal army of their Lexington neighborhood, "A large number of them have taken the oath voted the Union Ticket and declare if any one says they ever were secessionist they will sue them for slander." Others adhered to their oaths, even enlisting and serving dutifully in the militia. But taking such an oath presented a crisis of both honor and conscience for many citizens, even neutralists, it being the most visible symbol of personal coercion.

For many white Kentuckians and Missourians, these oaths were at best superfluous, since those targeted were residents of loyal states and the measures were, at worst, unconstitutional, assuming citizens' guilt before their innocence and abrogating their First Amendment rights. They resented that local commanders and provost marshals forced them on residents who did nothing more than speak out in favor of southern rights. "There are a number of influential citizens in this vicinity of Rebel proclivities," wrote one cavalry colonel in southern Kentucky, "who although they have not committed any overt act . . . in conversation they have defended the cause of the South in a very noisy and offensive manner. Some of these, I have placed under bonds and obliged them to take the Oath of Allegiance." Worse, once they had taken the oath or posted bond, or both, they lived in fear of visits from known disloyalists that might bring armed Federals to their door. Despite reports of capricious and even corrupt determinations of loyalty and disloyalty, Lincoln left to local commanders the discretion to make such decisions. As he wrote to the department commander in Missouri, assessing the loyalty of residents "must be left to you who are on the spot."[17]

[17] Fanny Gunn to John and Thomas Gunn, August 16, 1862, Gunn Family Papers, special collections, UK; John David Smith and William Cooper Jr., eds., *A Union Woman in Civil War Kentucky: The Diary of Frances Peter* (Lexington, Ky., 2000), 65; Bond of R. B. Steele, November 15, 1862, and W. L. Gibson to S. G. Hicks, November 19, 1863, both in USACC, part 1, series 2173: Letters Received, Department of Kentucky, 1862-69, box 1, NARA; O.

Such a strategy assumed risk. The reliance of the dominion system on oaths and lists to suppress disloyalists spread throughout their districts stemmed in part from vulnerability. Their small, town-based garrisons were hard-pressed to keep order so far from the army. Moreover, residents frequently manipulated the oath, taking it disingenuously to retain a semblance of normalcy in their daily lives. However "loyal" their taking of the oath made them officially, their true loyalties often lay hidden. A Kentuckian wrote that some of the residents around him "say that they did not mind taking the oath as they did not consider it binding on them, in fact they would rather take the oath than not as it gives them protection and they can get passes to go where they please." Another argued, given that disloyalists were "doubtless willing to take the oath prescribed with a mental reservation as heretofore expressed by many to disavow its obligations," he believed it "proper therefore that the State authorities should be advised of the proclivities of the applicants."

As such, department commanders and provost marshals routinely required accompanying verification of letter writers' own loyalty in order to solicit a response to their claims or grievances. Mistakes occurred frequently, eliciting remonstrances that required commanders to discern whether names on lists were legitimate or not and whether the information they had received on such persons was accurate or politically contrived. "Sir, you have the name of Hansbrough of Downingsville on your list as a Rebel," wrote C. H. McElroy to Charles Whittlesey at his headquarters in Warsaw, Kentucky. "[T]he parties who furnished you with his name say that it is an error; that he has always been an active union man—The error probably occurred from having used his name as a reference in regard to some traitors."[18]

D. Williams to Samuel R. Curtis, December 4, 1862, USACC, part 1, series 2593: Letters Received, Department of the Missouri, 1862-67, box 7, ibid.; Isaac R. Gray to J[eremiah]. T. Boyle, November 17, 1862, USACC, part 1, series 2173: Letters Received, Department of Kentucky, 1862-69, box 1, ibid.; Abraham Lincoln to Samuel R. Curtis, January 2, 1863, Roy P. Basler, ed., *The Collected Works of Abraham Lincoln*, 11 vols. (Springfield, Ill., 1953), 6:33-34.

[18] John S. Morton to Pat [Joyes], July 26, 1862, Joyes Family Papers, folder 18, FHS; Samuel W. Pruitt to Dear Bettie, April 20, 1863, Samuel W. Pruitt Letters, ibid.; James Prentiss to

Oaths, the most visible imposition of the dominion system, visibly divided communities. As one resident groused, "This new development makes some people very uncomfortable about both themselves and their friends." It drove Confederate sympathizers underground, many of whom then only affected loyalty, even displaying the national colors at their homes despite their private hatred of Federal authority. Passes for travel placed white residents in the exact place traditionally reserved for slaves, a fact not lost on the Harrodsburg Board of Trustees. At its October 1861 monthly meeting, the board appointed a committee to "wait on the military authorities at the Camp and request them not to allow the travel along the public roads to be interfered with by the Soldiers under this command." Two months later, having gained no satisfaction from the garrison commander, the members doubled the town police force to "keep the slaves off the streets and in subjection" and forbade night meetings "at any African Church" over the Christmas holiday. Verification of disloyalty often required the testimonial of Unionist neighbors, some of whom were happy, perhaps too happy, to provide it. In February 1862, David Daniel and Mathew Morris appeared before the justice of the peace in Johnson County "and made oath as follows, they state that they believe the said William Carter to be a sesesion in pricipal, we do not know of him doing any thing untill about the 20th of December 1861, when he went into the army, they futher state that said Carter told them he would not go into camp unless he was forsed to."[19]

Reprisals often followed, resulting in societal divisions that in some cases worked to the advantage of the government. Just as Unionists, government troops, and the Home Guard used the oaths against neutralists, Confederate sympathizers, and secessionists

John B. Bruner, September 12, 1861, John B. Bruner Papers, folder 17, ibid.; C. H. McElroy to Charles Whittlesey, January 2, 1862, Charles Whittlesey Papers, WRHS.

[19] Ash, *When the Yankees Came*, 122-23; Minutes of the Harrodsburg Trustees, 1786-1875 (microfilm), October 2, December 9, 1861, special collections, UK; Deposition of David Daniel, M. Morris, February 21, 1862, USACC, part 1, series 2173: Letters Received, Department of Kentucky, 1862-69, box 3, NARA.

who refused to take them, residents often chastised those neighbors who did take or support it, whether feigned or not, as cowards or disloyalists to the Confederate cause. Samuel Haycraft, a Unionist state senator at home in Elizabethtown, wrote in his journal in the early summer of 1862 of an ominous visit paid by one of his neighbors under the cover of night. "[S]ome unknown person cal[l]ed at my gate and in a strange voice asked me to come there," wrote the alarmed Haycraft. "I asked his name twice. He refused to give it but still insisted on my coming. I refused to do it as it was dark he then cursed me for a black hearted rascal and said he would shoot me." Ettie Scott complained that a spiteful neighbor plied a young man with whiskey "but did not drink himself—heard all he had to say—came back the next evening with a posse of soldiers, took young [name scratched out] prisoner: his brother got him to take the oath which he does not consider binding—but so it is Young B____ is branded by his former associates as a spy—and they shun him at every corner." Shunning was only the most benign form of retribution made against oath-takers; many others were insulted, threatened, and even attacked for their capitulation to Yankee aggression. Or worse, these closeted secessionists turned them in to garrison commanders as disloyalists.[20]

Small wonder that so many who objected to the prescribed oaths recognized that they had little choice but to take them. Some men with legal training saw an opportunity to alter the oath taken to conform to their personal notions of sovereignty and especially loyalty. Thomas B. Gordon, a Georgia-born attorney living in Bath County, presented a reworded oath to the deputy provost marshal "with that construction I would take *it* to avoid going to prison, but under no circumstances could I take the other . . . objectionable oath." After paying a twenty-dollar fee, he considered extortive, Gordon was sub-

---

[20] Samuel Haycraft Journal, 1849-1873, June 17, 1862, FHS; R. A. Curd to Cal Morgan, June 22, 1862, Hunt-Morgan Family Papers, box 15, folder 9, special collections, UK; Thomas B. Gordon to Neal M. Gordon, August 12, 1862, Gordon Family Papers, ms. 51M40, box 4, ibid.; Ettie Scott to Susan Grigsby, August 3, 1862, Grigsby Family Papers, folder 173, FHS.

sequently imprisoned and required to take the prescribed oath and present a three-thousand-dollar bond. "I have suffered oppression of one kind rather than of another," he wrote after his release, still troubled by his decision to submit. "That I have chosen the lighter [path], rather than suffer the more severe but certainly more honorable—The issue above will be whether I did right."[21]

While oaths were the most visible symbol of Federal authority, assessments were the most reviled. A revision of the eighteenth-century practice of forced contributions, assessments allowed Federal authorities to levy the property of disloyalists to compensate Unionists for guerrillas' damage to their property. Entwined with oaths and bonds, they provided an essential informational corpus for Federal commanders. The controversial policy, begun by John Pope in northern Missouri, gave teeth to the oath requirements and soon became policy throughout the border states. Subsequent commanders authorized boards of assessment, comprising both military and local prominent Unionist civilians, who would compile lists and levy fines against registered disloyalists to compensate "undoubted Union men" for damages that guerrillas committed to personal and even public property in local areas. As one commander in Kentucky noted, levies drove home the point that "it costs something to be disloyal." The policy met with stiff resistance from Confederate sympathizers and even some Unionists, who complained that it was unconstitutional and arbitrary. Those who refused such levies had their property confiscated, regardless of loyalty. Many thus judged assessments as little more than government-sponsored robbery. On occasion, secessionists managed to infiltrate the assessment boards in order to levy Unionists, who in turn begged that the assessments be suspended. The new secretary of war, Edwin M. Stanton, praised the success of assessments, even as Kentucky congressman Lazarus Powell asked the president to intervene to stop them. Lincoln refused, but he cautioned that they not be abused.[22]

[21] Thomas B. Gordon to Neal M. Gordon, August 12, 1862, November 24, 1863, both in Gordon Family Papers, box 4, special collections, UK.

[22] W. Wayne Smith, "An Experiment in Counterinsurgency: The Assessment of Confederate

In 1862, after John Hunt Morgan's first major cavalry raid into their state, unconditional Unionists in Kentucky convinced Jeremiah T. Boyle—despite the strong objections of the new governor, James F. Robinson—to initiate similar measures to punish secessionists and Confederate sympathizers. "I shall levy heavy contributions on his uncles and other secessionists," Boyle vowed, "it is the only way to prevent a repetition of his raids." But the levies also were intended to pay for the government occupation and to assist the oppressed families of Federal enlistees. And they were weapons by which to attack neutralism. As in Missouri, Federal commanders in Kentucky recognized that the county Home Guards were woefully underfunded, and Boyle soon allowed provost marshals to assess "the weak-back Union men" for their support. (Boyle would become creative in his assessments, forcing "secessionists and domestick Rebels . . . to furnish timber and their wagons to aid in the work" of rebuilding a railroad trestle near Bardstown destroyed by Morgan's retreating Confederates.) In December 1862, the commander in Hopkins County in western Kentucky empowered a civilian board which levied and collected $13,335 in seven counties; farther south in Russellville, James M. Bell and his neighbor were levied five hundred and three hundred dollars, respectively, for witnessing guerrilla depredations and not resisting or reporting them. (The latter swapped a set of boots to a Rebel so he would not take his horse, only to lose the horse to Boyle's assessment penalty.) Many disloyalists liquidated their assets, especially livestock, to avoid having them confiscated. Boyle soon encountered resistance from his superior officer in Cincinnati, who questioned the authority of "a department commander to levy contributions on disloyal persons in a loyal State for the purpose of

Sympathizers in Missouri," *Journal of Southern History* 35 (1969): 361-67; Notice and General Order No. 3, both dated July 31, 1861, and John Pope to Stephen Hurlbut, August 17, 1861, all in *OR*, series 2, 1:189-90, 195-96, 211-12; John W. Foster to J[eremiah] T. Boyle, January 6, 1863, USACC, part 1, series 3514: Letters Received, Department of the Ohio, box 3, NARA; Louis S. Gerteis, *Civil War St. Louis* (Lawrence, Kans., 2001), 174-77; Grimsley, *Hard Hand of War*, 38.

reimbursing losses suffered by loyal citizens from the Rebels" and ordered a temporary suspension of the policy.[23]

Assessments, as was true with oaths, revealed the limits as much as the strengths of the power of the government over both combatants and civilians in wartime. Branding levied residents with the stigma of being disloyal often seemed as much the goal as raising revenue. Complaints against assessments by prominent Unionists in both states were plentiful, questioning the severity of the policy as well as the capriciousness and, especially, the corruption it spawned. Even Lincoln heard that two-thirds or more of the assessment of one Kentucky county was siphoned off before auction. Most important, assessments seemed to be fueling the insurgency, especially in western Kentucky and Missouri. Beyond its limitations, assessment also revealed the discretionary power of a wartime administration to implement policies that eroded civil liberties. Where in some assessment practices Lincoln might have agreed with these opponents, he did not oppose levies in theory, seeing their benefit as a social-control measure. Only when the president learned from outraged Missouri Unionists, including some officers, that John M. Schofield had assessed the residents of St. Louis County half a million dollars to "be used in subsisting, clothing, and arming the enrolled militia while in active service, and in providing for the support of such families of militiamen and U.S. volunteers as may be left destitute" did he take assessment policies under advisement. In January 1863, Lincoln quietly suspended assessments in both Missouri and Kentucky. He did not, however, countermand current assessment orders (other than Schofield's), heeding the complaints of militia commanders and recognizing the value of their remaining on the books. He continued to endorse assessments in spirit and practice and allowed discretion to commanders to implement them "sparingly," arguing later that

[23] James F. Robinson to Dear Sir, October 8, 1862; W. A. Allbrecht to J. A. Duble, September 27, 1862; William B. Sipes to Gordon Granger, October 17, 1862; and John W. Foster to J[eremiah] T. Boyle, January 6, 1863, all in USACC, part 1, series 3514: Letters Received, Department of the Ohio, boxes 1-3, NARA.

"experience has already taught us in this war that holding these smoky localities responsible for the conflagrations within them has a very salutary effect." Assessments continued sporadically for the duration of the war, and local commanders used them as political weapons to intimidate local residents who opposed the Lincoln administration. They thus deepened the strife overspreading these states.[24]

If oaths and assessments were respectively the most visible and loathed aspects of the dominion system, martial law (the suspension of civil authority in favor of military rule) and trade restrictions were the most widely felt, and they frequently carried over the rivers into the lower portions of the free states. Martial law was most often declared ad hoc in local areas rather than for an entire state, generally coincident to a perceived threat from guerrillas or Confederate troops. Consequently, secessionist or Confederate-sympathizing citizens, men or women, quickly became targets. Banishment, curfews, and even occupation of the homes of known secessionists were common, often imposed under the pretext of the inability of the garrison to protect them from local Unionists and even troops. When rumors reached one Federal commander, William T. Ward, that John Hunt Morgan's Rebel cavalry was approaching Lexington in the summer of 1862, he declared martial law and sent most of his troops, including both Home Guards and Provost Guards, to man the earthworks outside the city. He then ordered saloons closed and those on the disloyal

---

[24] J[eremiah] T. Boyle to H[oratio] G. Wright, November 14, 1862, and Henry Dent to Boyle, November 14, 1862, and responses, November 19-20, 1862, all in OR, series 1, 30, part 2, 51, 95-96; Boyle to Capart King, November 14, 1862; Leonidas Metcalfe to Boyle, December 14, 1862; B[enjamin]. H. Bristow to S. D. Bruce, December 21, 1864, all in USACC, part 1, series 2173: Letters Received, Department of Kentucky, box 1, NARA; Gerteis, *Civil War St. Louis*, 90-91, 177, 358n21; Abraham Lincoln to Jeremiah T. Boyle, February 1, 1863, Basler, ed., *Collected Works*, 6:87; Lincoln to John R. Underwood and Henry Grider, October 26, 1864, and to Stephen G. Burbridge, October 27, 1864, both in ibid., 8:77-78; Thomas B. Fairleigh to A. C. Semple, August 26, 1863, with endorsements and enclosures, OR, series 1, 30, part 3, 180-83; Edward R. S. Canby to Ambrose E. Burnside, November 21, 1863, ibid., series 1, 31, part 3, 221; E. D. Townsend to S[tephen]. G. Burbridge, November 26, 1864, and endorsement, ibid., series 1, 52, part 1, 663-64; J. Bates Dickson to Daniel J. Dill, and Dickson to Samuel Matlack, both February 16, 1865, in ibid., series 1, 49, part 1, 733-34; Smith, "Experiment in Counterinsurgency," 363, 373-75; Fellman, *Inside War*, 95.

list to remain inside their homes. Morgan's mother, Henrietta, and her sister, once Unionists but now perhaps the city's most prominent secessionists, "were sent out of town as the people threatened to level their houses with the ground, and Major [F. G.] Bracht said he could protect them no longer." The city council then issued an order that all other secessionists shoulder muskets to defend the city; those who refused were jailed. As one resident saw it, the order was retaliatory, a response to pro-Confederate residents' verbal abuse of the Home Guard and "only done to scare them a little . . . and the soldiers took their revenge by that order."[25]

In many ways, martial law gave fangs to the dominion system. Civilians could be arrested, or worse, simply for being citizens. Soldiers suppressed seditious discourse—sermonized, written, printed, or spoken. Young men whose tongues were loosed by strong drink often brought on retribution that their families were forced to suffer. "Edd Hensley of our town—but the truth was the young man drinks too much whiskey—and talked too much himself," wrote one Kentucky woman, "and so his family are blamed." Insults hurled at Federal troops evoked particularly hard responses. Jeremiah T. Boyle issued a circular in June 1862 requiring the arrest of citizens who would not "refrain from language and conduct that excites to Rebellion," and rumors circulated that those who "hurrah[ed] for Jeff Davis on the street [would] be shot down." A rumor common to the border region held that "if one Secessionist wanted to speak to another he [or she] had to go into a cornfield and put out pickets." Newspaper editors, such those of the *Kentucky State Flag*, the *Louisville Courier*, the *Presbyterian Herald*, and the *Paducah Daily Herald*, learned the lesson painfully. Vigilance committees, with assistance from Federal troops, banned their papers in garrisoned cities, or worse. Editor-proprietors of dissenting newspapers who did not choose to flee arrest warrants often found themselves shackled in front of

---

[25] Mark E. Neely Jr., *The Fate of Liberty: Abraham Lincoln and Civil Liberties* (New York, 1992), 32-39; Gerteis, *Civil War St. Louis*, 131-34, 174-75; Smith and Cooper, eds., *Union Woman in Civil War Kentucky*, 4-5, 21-29.

military commissions.

Walter N. Haldeman, owner-editor of the *Louisville Courier*, had his paper suppressed; as the U.S. surveyor of customs in Louisville, he was accused of ignoring trade restrictions with the Confederacy. He left Louisville in September 1861 first for Russellville then into peripatetic exile in the Confederacy. He continued to print a version of his paper that his competitor, George D. Prentice, sneeringly referred to as the "Nashville-Bowling Green-Louisville Courier," until Federal forces captured Nashville. His former partner, Reuben T. Durrett, was arrested and imprisoned for treasonable language published in his paper. Released later that year after taking the oath, Durrett was the only one of the suppressed editors of Louisville to return to his home city before the end of the war. Irish-born Presbyterian minister Stuart Robinson began editing the *True Presbyterian* in Louisville in April 1862. His nonsectarian paper preached strict spiritual and political neutralism—with the exception of abolition, which his consistently proslavery columns condemned. "[T]he agitation in favor of emancipation . . . [would] distract and divide the Churches, and lead to the ruin of the country," he claimed. His stance made him a contrarian in his Kentucky synod, yet critics condemned him as a secessionist (although he had never supported the Confederacy in print) and his paper was twice suppressed. In the fall of 1862, under threat of arrest for disloyalty, he quietly removed to Canada, where he continued to publish his paper intermittently and to preach to large audiences. Although larger urban opposition papers more often walked the line in efforts to stave off suppression, to keep readers they found ways to be critical of the war and the Lincoln administration. Indeed, one resident recalled that "[t]he *Cincinnati Enquirer* [was] the paper universally taken by the Secessionists of Kentucky." Historian George Vander Velde has claimed that suppressions of newspapers during the war, either by military authority or civilian mobs, exceeded all others in American history.[26]

[26] Gerteis, *Civil War St. Louis*, 131-32, 169-70, 173-74; Ettie Scott to Susan Preston Shelby Grigsby, May [1862], Grigsby Family Papers, folder 172, FHS; *Gallipolis (Ohio) Journal*, August

Of the various mandates of the dominion system, trade restrictions were the most overtly political. They were also perhaps the most universally hated. Access to or control of the navigable interior rivers underlay both Federal and Confederate military strategy in the western region just as it drove the fateful decision of Kentucky for neutrality. Trade between Kentucky cities and the South actually thrived during the first months of war. At its political heart, neutrality meant unregulated trade with both belligerents, and cities like Louisville, connected not only by river but by rail, took full advantage when conditions allowed. Many free-state politicians were not willing to risk, as Ohio governor, William Dennison, argued, "a rupture with any State which has not declared itself already out of the Union." On May 2, the War Department instructed the commander of troops at Cairo not to block southbound river shipments so "irritating to Kentucky and other States bordering on the Ohio . . . [t]hat this may not be used as a means for extending the spirit of secession." If neutrality worked in any way to the advantage of the middle-border slave states, however temporarily, it was in the matter of trade. This conciliation, too, would not long last. In fact, it would not survive the day of May 2, 1861.[27]

29, 1861; George Quigley Langstaff Jr., ed., *The Life and Times of Quintus Quincy Quigley, 1828-1910: His Personal Journal, 1859-1908* (Paducah, Ky., 1999), 81; G. Glenn Clift, ed., *The Private War of Lizzie Hardin* (Frankfort, Ky., 1963), 66, 74; Neely, *Fate of Liberty*, 44; Lowell H. Harrison and James C. Klotter, *A New History of Kentucky* (Lexington, Ky., 1997), 206; *True Kentuckian* [Paris, Ky.], November 10, 1869; Alexander I. Burckin, "The Formation and Growth of an Urban Middle Class: Power and Conflict in Louisville, Kentucky, 1828-1861" (PhD dissertation, University of California, Irvine, 1993), 525; E. Polk Johnson, *A History of Kentucky and Kentuckians*, 3 vols. (Louisville, 1912), 2:848-49; *Louisville Past and Present* (Louisville, 1875), 263; Preston D. Graham Jr., *A Kingdom Not of This World: Stuart Robinson's Struggle to Distinguish the Sacred from the Secular during the Civil War* (Macon, Ga., 2002), 6 and passim; *True Presbyterian* [Louisville, Ky.], April 17, 1862; A. C. Semper to [Stephen G.] Burbridge, August 9, 1864, USACC, part 1, series 2173: Letters Received, Department of Kentucky, box 4, NARA; Lewis George Vander Velde, *The Presbyterian Churches and the Federal Union, 1861-1869* (Cambridge, Mass., 1932), 167-77; *The Kentucky Loyalist* [Lexington, Ky.], July 11, 1863.

[27] Coulter, *Civil War and Readjustment in Kentucky*, 57-68 (quote, 68), 71-78 (quote, 71); Gerteis, *Civil War St. Louis*, 236-42. Whitelaw Reid, *Ohio in the War*, 2 vols. (New York, 1868), 1:39-40; E. D. Townsend to Commanding Officer Illinois Volunteers, May 2, 1861, *OR*, series 1, 52, part 1 (quote, 137). The Illinois Central Railroad terminated at Cairo, where

By way of the Louisville & Nashville Railroad, the only true north-south line west of the Appalachians completed before the war, increasingly heavier amounts of freight went by rail through Kentucky, and often on to Nashville, Memphis, Chattanooga, and as far as New Orleans. Even arms went southward after Fort Sumter. Pressed by the unconditional Unionists of Cincinnati, who were fearful that the merchant class of their own and other cities were putting business ahead of the Union, on May 2 Secretary of the Treasury Salmon P. Chase issued a circular to all custom port officers in western river cities, requiring examinations of all manifests and searches of "all steamers, flatboats and other water crafts . . . railroad cars and other vehicles . . . laden with merchandise . . . and all other goods and commodities which might be useful to the enemy in time of war" and destined for "any port or place under insurrectionary control." Chase left unspecified whether neutral Kentucky was, in fact, controlled by loyal or disloyal leadership, and subsequent inquiries brought only muddy clarifications, giving latitude to commercial interdiction. Agents on the ground agreed that Kentucky, especially Louisville, was the weak link. The state's "'neutrality'," as one Cincinnati editor fumed, "seems to consist in perfect freedom to furnish our enemies the wherewith to make war upon us."

When Lincoln refined the interior-trade policy in June, similar to his recent relaxation of the blockade for select coastal cities and New Orleans, he left plenty of room for smuggling not only from Kentucky but from all of the border states by boat and rail. Congress thought the president needed to take a sterner approach and authorized him to prohibit all commercial intercourse with states "under insurrectionary control." In August, Lincoln did just that for shipments he and his treasury secretary had not approved. In September, the administration stopped trade altogether with western

some train freight was transshipped to Columbus or Hickman, Kentucky, terminuses for two Gulf-bound railroad lines. For the most thorough assessment of the Federal naval blockade and its effects on the Confederate war effort, see David G. Surdam, *Northern Naval Superiority and the Economics of the American Civil War* (Columbia, Mo., 2001).

Kentucky, and Grant applied the ban to southbound boats passing by Cairo, stopping and confiscating them despite "hav[ing] my serious doubts whether there is any law authorizing this seizure." Similarly, the Confederate Congress banned key exports to the Union states, including Kentucky and Missouri, and Confederates at Columbus interdicted shipments upriver while they occupied the city. By the summer of 1862, all southbound trade on the Ohio below Wheeling and on the Mississippi below the northern border of Missouri required permits.[28]

Just as troops on the ground recognized the difficulty of discerning the intentions of the local populations, so also did "aids to the revenue" (special agents), treasury officials, and army officers. War Department policy required them to regulate trade, and they were charged with judging the loyalty of those who sought to ship or receive trading goods. The policy extended not only into seceded states but to those "occupied by the military forces of the United States," leaving no doubt as to the status of border states like Kentucky. Only persons "strictly loyal" were to receive permits and licenses for trade; all others were required to post bonds. As early as May 1861, Thomas E. Wilson, operator of the Louisville Chemical Works, was less angry that his government might soon deny him substances commonly received by rail from Tennessee that he used to make medicines—nitric acid and mercury leading a long list—than that his patriotism was questioned simply by his living in a slave state. "I must bow to the orders of my govt in every thing *save one*, that is to go out side of my state to aim a rifle at a brother on either side of the line," he complained, "and this in the estimation of many of my

---

[28] Proclamation, April 19, 1861, *OR*, series 3, 2:31 (quote); Neely, *Fate of Liberty*, 33-34; U[lysses]. S. Grant to Chauncey McKeever, October 1, 1861, *OR*, series 1, 3:511 (quote); E. M[erton]. Coulter, "Commercial Intercourse with the Confederacy in the Mississippi Valley, 1861-1865," *Mississippi Valley Historical Review* 4 (1919): 381-82. Coulter contends that inconsistent application of trade restrictions in the border slave states made them ineffective. He presumes that the administration strictly interpreted the nonintercourse policy, while agents played "fast and loose in its policy of trading" with them.

northern friends, makes me a Rebel." Wilson knew that his business would soon suffer for it.[29]

Recognizing that compiling loyalty identifications would tax an already overburdened army, especially in large cities with concentrated populations, the War Department order authorized local treasury agents, many of whom had military rank and with guidance from commanders, to appoint boards of trade. These boards would be constituted of unquestionably loyal civilians "by whose approval and permission only . . . goods, wares, or merchandise . . . shall be unloaded or disposed of." In effect, the boards determined not only who could, and more importantly who could not, conduct trade, perhaps the most potent weapon wielded by the Federal authorities against civilians short of arrest and punishment for treasonable activities. Moreover, they also affixed the names of those determined to have engaged in contraband trade to disloyalty lists. By March 1862, boards of trade operated in most of the border cities lying on navigable rivers as well as in many interior towns, and would continue to do so until early 1865.[30]

"There seems to be an abiding confidence in the minds of busi-

[29] Coulter, "Commercial Intercourse with the Confederacy," 377-82; Thomas E. Wilson to Joseph Holt, May 5, 1861, General Correspondence and Related Material (Bound), 1817-1894, book 27, Joseph Holt Papers, LC

[30] General Order No. 5, October 1, 1862, OR, series 1, 13:698-700; General Order No. 10, March 28, 1862, ibid., series 1, 8:834; Coulter, "Commercial Intercourse," 382n15; E. W. Bradley to Gen. [J. M.] Judah, April 13, 1863, USACC, part 1, series 2173: Letters Received, Department of Kentucky, 1862-69, box 1, NARA. Western cities with boards of trade operating in them included Pittsburgh, Pennsylvania; Wheeling, Virginia; Cincinnati, Ohio; Madison, Lawrenceburg, New Albany, and Evansville, Indiana; Cairo and Quincy, Illinois; Maysville, Louisville, Paducah, Hickman, Cadiz, Hopkinsville, Bowling Green, and Catlettsburg, Kentucky; St. Louis and Rolla, Missouri. See Salmon P. Chase to William P. Mellen, July 4, 1863, Record Group 56: Department of the Treasury Records, part 56, series 40: Letters Sent Related to Restricted Commercial Intercourse (hereafter DOTR), box 60, book 13, entry 3/6, 321, 362-64, NARA. By August 2, 1861, the Confederacy had banned the trade of cotton, tobacco, sugar, rice, molasses, and naval stores with the United States. On January 5, 1865, Stephen G. Burbridge, then commander of the Department of Kentucky, banned boards of trade in his department owing to corruption. Thomas M. Redd to D. G. Barnitz, January 25, 1865, USACC, part 1, series 2173: Letters Received, Department of Kentucky, 1862-69, box 5, ibid.

ness men that trade will soon be restored between the two sections of the Union" wrote the editor of *The Western Citizen* in March 1862 from Paris, Kentucky. As the Federal armies drove southward, the hope that sprang eternal among the Unionist business class of the region (of which this editor was one) might well have spoken to the means and measures of the local boards of trade. In effect, these boards quickly became as or even more important to establishing loyalty and disloyalty as the provost marshals who had official charge of making such determinations. (Often, the provost marshals were themselves members of these boards.) Although the baseline criteria for the selection of board members was their reputation for unconditional Unionism regardless of political party affiliation, they were nearly all prominent businessmen, editors, manufacturers, or public officials, or all at once. And they, in turn, often selected their local provost marshals, suggesting the prominence of business interests and influence in the emerging calculus of loyalty and order on the home front. Their ostensible willingness to forego personal gain or to put aside business or private relationships in order to stop illicit trade with the Confederacy, as well as connections with the administration, got them their positions.[31]

Because patriotism and profit were not mutually exclusive impulses, many such safeguards were ineffective. The trade restrictions imposed by both governments gave license to many opposed to them and to the occupation to smuggle. Mismarking barrels and boxes and bribing treasury agents and inspectors was standard practice, and many agents fell prey to wily shippers or to graft. Contraband thus continued southward on rail cars and steamboats. Overburdened army officials, however much they believed in the mission of stopping this trade, soon recognized the impracticality of trade

---

[31] *Western Citizen* [Paris, Ky.], March 7, 1862; J. M. Judah to A. C. Semple, April 18, 1863; Charles B. Colton to J[eremiah]. T. Boyle, December 22, 1862; Thomas M. Redd to William P. Mellen, October 3, 1864; Redd to Stephen G. Burbridge, October 27, 1864; S. Meredith to J. Bates Dickson, February 7, 1865; all in USACC, part 1, series 2173: Letters Received, Department of Kentucky, 1862-69, boxes 1, 4, 5, NARA.

regulations. More than Federal marshals and deputies who directly enforced the trade restrictions, they soon criticized local boards of trade, especially in border slave states like Kentucky, for suspect ethics and even disloyalty. "These Boards cannot possibly fulfill the purposes for which they were created," wrote an exasperated commander in Bowling Green, Kentucky. "Supposing it possible to find three unconditional Union men so to act (a fact I am not disposed to admit as far as some towns are concerned)—their very isolation places them at the mercy, and under the control, of the disloyal population around them." He was not off the mark; guerrillas targeted board members, forcing some to flee upon rumors of the approach of horsemen. "Add to this family and social ties, and the chances of protection for the Government against the abuses they were appointed to correct, amount to nothing." Commanders thus devised other means to reduce the illegal trade, including the discretion to enforce prohibitions against traffic in contraband goods in the hopes that it would encourage compliance with restrictions. In August 1864, the army halted all trade in and out of Kentucky by known disloyalists. Loyalists were soon caught in the snare, often detained hours or even overnight as they waited for passes, which resulted in "most unfriendly comment and acrimonious feeling." An exasperated Ulysses S. Grant issued an order expelling Jewish traders from Paducah and his department owing to beliefs about their illicit pursuit of profit over patriotism. (Embarrassed, Lincoln would soon rescind the notorious expulsion order, as well as the prohibitions against trade into the border states.)[32]

The same political motives that influenced agents and boards

---

[32] J. M. Judah to A. C. Semple, April 18, 1863, and enclosures; J. P. Jackson to J. Bates Dickson, August 20, 1864; Thomas M. Redd to William P. Mellen, October 3, 1864 (first and second quotes), all in USACC, part 1, series 2173: Letters Received, Department of Kentucky, 1862-69, boxes 1, 4, NARA; *Cincinnati Daily Enquirer*, September 4, 1861; Lloyd W. Franks, ed., *The Journal of Elder William Conrad: Pioneer Preacher* (Lexington, Ky., 1976), 81-82 (third quote); Steven V. Ash, "Civil War Exodus: The Jews and Grant's General Orders 11," in *American Jewish History: Anti-Semitism in America*, ed. Jeffery S. Gurock (New York, 1998), 135-55; Coulter, "Commercial Intercourse with the Confederacy," 381n10.

of trade to overlook illicit trade also drove the implementation of trade policies. "Let commerce follow the flag," Salmon P. Chase enjoined famously. In his latest incarnation as a faithful Republican, the treasury secretary spoke not purely of national patriotism. He demarcated something of an ideological and political loyalty test. In the border states, changing circumstances among a divided populace made loyalty and disloyalty essential identifiers, but they also made them uncertain and fluid. Unconditional Unionism was the benchmark in the cities and states where boards of trade operated, and army officers wielded a heavy club by manipulating such distinctions as they saw fit. Beyond any simple taking of the oath, in the fall of 1862 Jeremiah T. Boyle ordered in much of central Kentucky that persons could not "engage in the buying, selling, or shipping of merchandise or groceries without having first obtained a certificate signed by six Unconditional Union men of good standing that said person himself is an Unconditional Union man." Widespread abuses of the permit system compelled the last wartime governor of Kentucky, Thomas E. Bramlette, a Union Democrat, to complain to Lincoln that "many *loyal men* are driven out of business . . . for no other reason than their political preferences." When the army refused to honor the rescissions of trade restrictions in Kentucky in early 1864 by the Treasury Department, the governor condemned the permit system as "a most shameful and corrupt system of political partisan corruption and oppression."[33]

In fact, the responsibilities and criteria of the boards of trade had transcended a simple oath to stop trade with the enemy. By the summer of 1862, political patronage (namely Republican bona fides) became not just *a*, but *the*, litmus test for the granting of trade permits, just as it was for the awarding of military contracts and appointments by the War Department to the boards of trade. Boards

---

[33] Salmon P. Chase to William P. Mellen, May 29, 1861, DOTR, box 60, book 11, 16-17, NARA; Franks, ed., *Journal of Elder William Conrad*, 81; Lowell H. Harrison, *The Civil War in Kentucky* (Lexington, Ky., 1975), 99-100; J. H. Hammond to J. Bates Dickson, September 3, 1864, USACC, part 1, series 2173: Letters Received, Department of Kentucky, 1862-69, box 4, NARA.

put traders on notice that opposing the administration, not simply the war, would hurt them significantly. A potent stew of trade, politics, and definitions of loyalty soon boiled over in the western river states, enough to cause many western businesspeople to complain about flagrant patronage in trade decisions. When John Skiff, a Cincinnati merchandiser, admitted to attempting to smuggle south through Kentucky a load of butter marked as ale in May 1861, he claimed that he "had done no worse than others" and grumbled that his greatest crime was to have voted for John Bell in 1860. Skiff recognized things on the ground for what they were, just as did army and treasury officials who wielded Chase's slogan as a shibboleth.[34]

The effects cascaded down through the population. Businessmen who could not do business could not then pay workers, who in turn could not pay their bills. Many were left destitute, forced out of their lodgings and into those of friends, neighbors, and relatives, or they relocated to where they could find work. Some moved into abandoned homes and buildings or became vagabonds. One visitor to Louisville, the Federal supply center, in May 1862 remarked that the city had "suffered terribly" from a year of conflict, its nonmilitary economy stagnant, its storefronts boarded, factories silent, giving it a "sleepy, drowsy look." Even the affluent, such as the Jeffrey family, fell prey to the various layers of entrapment of the dominion system. Alexander Jeffrey of Louisville owned and managed a number of gasworks in the region and in Mississippi. He fell afoul of Federal authorities in the city because of his outspokenness against partisanship in the granting of trade permits. Placed on the disloyal list, his

---

[34] Joseph C. Butler, W[illia]m. McCreary, and Geo[rge]. H. Thurston to Edwin M. Stanton, March 26, 1862, in *OR*, series 3, 1:950-51; Patricia Ann Hoskins, "'The Old First is with the South': The Civil War, Reconstruction, and Memory in the Jackson Purchase Region of Kentucky" (PhD dissertation, Auburn University, 2008), 150-54; Clinton W. Terry, "'Let Commerce Follow the Flag': Trade and Loyalty to the Union in the Ohio Valley," *Ohio Valley History* 1 (2001): 1-3, 7-9; Charles B. Colton to J[eremiah]. T. Boyle, December 22, 1862, USACC, part 1, series 2173: Letters Received, Department of Kentucky, 1862-69, box 1, NARA. Coulter employs a version of this phrase that Chase himself included in his 1861 annual report on government finances; see Coulter, *Civil War and Readjustment*, 80n142.

businesses were ordered closed, and he left the city for Lexington, leaving his family behind to prevent their home from being vandalized. Without income while he tried to obtain clemency from the district commander, Jeffrey took several of his male slaves and hired them out or tried to sell them, but he soon found both employers and buyers unreliable. One prospective hirer, prohibited by the local board of trade from conducting business and unable to pay wages, offered to house a male slave, Dan, and provide his upkeep until his firm regained its trade permit. Federal troops were even more intrusive—Dan soon ran off, and they impeded police efforts to find him. A frustrated Jeffrey wrote to his wife, "I really think it is better to live any where than here the people are perfectly down trodden . . . Ky is a subject province under the most arbitrary military despotism. . . . I did not think such heart burning and bitter feeling could have been roused in me again, but I do find myself getting very savage." The dominion system by then firmly entrenched, the neutrality of Jeffrey and others, like that of their state, was dead and buried.[35]

******

On a bleak, rainy February evening in 1863, Mary E. Van Meter sat writing in her journal at the parlor table beneath a street-facing window from her father's home in Bowling Green, Kentucky. The twenty-six-year-old native Virginian had many lonely moments to reflect upon during these past months. She had no children and her husband was still in Mississippi, less from his unwillingness to abandon his farm there, beyond Federal lines, than his refusal to submit to the Yankees, take the oath, and return home. She had been forced to take the oath in order to get passes and permits for her crates and slaves to travel to Kentucky. The words that this Confederate sympathizer scratched came hard, tinged with pain and bitterness. "How have we been deceived in regard to civil liberty in Kentucky,"

---

[35] Edward Dicey, *Spectator of America*, ed. Herbert Mitgang (1971; repr., Athens, Ga., 1989), 175-81; Contract from Rule and Bro. to Alexander Jeffrey, July 21, 1862, and Jeffrey to Rosa V. J. Jeffrey, January 6, 7, 1863, Rosa V. J. Jeffrey Papers, folder 83, FHS.

she lamented. "I came back to the state of my adoption believing civil law reigned supreme, but alas it is not so. Military despotism rules with its rod of iron, and woe to those who dare question the justice of this tyrannical enemy." Her anger was directed less at the conventional war that separated her from her husband than at the dominion system of the Federal military, one by then well entrenched around her and which, in her opinion, held her home and occupied state deep in the netherworld of war.[36]

[36] Mary E. Van Meter diary [microfilm], December 2, 1862–February 25, 1863, special collections, UK.

GARRETT DAVIS AND THE PROBLEM OF DEMOCRACY AND EMANCIPATION

By Christopher Waldrep

It should come as no surprise that two Civil War–era political leaders born in Kentucky would hold similar constitutional understandings. President Abraham Lincoln (1809-65) and Senator Garrett Davis (1801-72) shared a common biography; both were natives of Kentucky and both followed Henry Clay to oppose slavery and favor democratic values. Both revered the founding principles of the U.S. Constitution as binding. Both served as Whigs in Congress, Lincoln

CHRISTOPHER R. WALDREP was the Jamie and Phyllis Pasker Professor of History at San Francisco State University in San Francisco, California, from 2000 to 2013. He is the author of many books, articles, and reviews. His most recent book is *Jury Discrimination: The Supreme Court, Public Opinion, and a Grassroots Fight for Racial Equality in Mississippi* (2010). His article "Joseph P. Bradley's Journey: The Meaning of Privileges and Immunities," published in the *Journal of Supreme Court History*, won the 2010 Supreme Court History Society's Hughes-Gossett Award for the best article. Prof. Waldrep's first journal article was "Mathew Lyons Comes to Frontier Kentucky," which was published in the *Register* 77 (1979): 201-6.

The Kentucky Historical Society helped immeasurably in locating and copying key documents necessary for this article. I also appreciate the help I got from the Filson Historical Society, especially Jim Holmberg. Librarians and archivists at the Historical Society of Pennsylvania, Butler Library at Columbia University, the National Archives, the Detroit Public Library, and the State Historical Society of Wisconsin all provided valuable assistance. Janelle Waldrep assisted with the research for this article. Les Benedict, Tom Appleton, and Mike Fitzgerald read an earlier and different version of this essay and kindly offered useful commentary. I also benefited from conversations with Bill Carrigan and Mike Caires. Many thanks to Prof. Barbara Loomis of the history department at San Francisco State University for her help with the final stages of manuscript preparation.

for one term, 1847-48, and Davis for four terms, 1839-46, where both opposed the Mexican War for similar reasons: they opposed the expansion of slavery. In the secession crisis, the two worked together as a team to keep Kentucky in the Union and crush the Confederacy.[1] They fell out after 1863, ultimately because they disagreed not just over slavery but over the nature and meaning of self-government.

Elected to the Senate in 1861, Davis came to Washington echoing key points Lincoln had made in his first inaugural address, especially the idea that "mystic chords" bound the American people together, committing ordinary citizens to their nation and its founding principles. To Davis the "mystic chords" were a "golden cord" or a "magic chain," but the idea was obviously the same.[2] Lincoln and Davis both recognized that the power to interpret constitutional law ultimately resided in the people, but at the same time they saw that power was limited by organic law. Before the Civil War, many or most white Americans shared the idea that a static, unchanging Constitution constrained politics.[3]

The rub came when Lincoln attacked the idea that slavery could be a local matter, left to local elections; slavery, he said, was a moral wrong, an affront to the "leading principle—the sheet anchor of American republicanism" as articulated in the Declaration of Independence. He said that the entire nation had an interest in whether

---

[1] Lincoln biographies are legion, but I found the following particularly useful: Robert Carwardine, *Lincoln: A Life of Purpose and Power* (New York, 2003); Eric Foner, *The Fiery Trial: Abraham Lincoln and American Slavery* (New York, 2010); Orville Vernon Burton, *The Age of Lincoln* (New York, 2007); Michael Burlingame, *Abraham Lincoln: A Life*, 2 vols. (Baltimore, 2008); David Herbert Donald, *Lincoln* (New York, 1995). Garrett Davis has no biographer, but his discursive Senate speeches provide a useful autobiography, as the following notes reveal.

[2] Lincoln, "First Inaugural Address," March 4, 1861, Roy P. Basler, ed., *The Collected Works of Abraham Lincoln*, 9 vols. (New Brunswick, N.J., 1953-55), 4:271; Congress, Senate, Senator Davis of Kentucky speaking on Proposed Expulsion of Mr. Powell, 37th Cong., 2nd sess., Congressional Globe (hereafter Cong. Globe) (March 13, 1862), 1216 ("golden cord"); Congress, Senate, Senator Davis of Kentucky speaking on Punishment of Treason and Rebellion, 37th Cong., 2nd sess., ibid. (May 20, 1862), 2221 ("magic chain"). This paraphrases John Marshall in *Cohens v. Virginia*, 19 U.S. 264, 389 (1821): "The people made the constitution, and the people can unmake it. It is the creature of their will, and lives only by their will."

[3] Michael Vorenberg, *Final Freedom: The Civil War, the Abolition of Slavery, and the Thirteenth Amendment* (Cambridge, Mass., 2001), 8-35; Silvana R. Siddali, *From Property to Person: Slavery and the Confiscation Acts, 1861-1862* (Baton Rouge, 2005), 6-10.

the states had slavery or not.[4] To Davis, such thinking violated democratic principles. He thought that the Founders had limited popular authority by channeling it through the state governments. The people could end slavery but only through their state political systems, not through the apparatus of the national government, so long as they stayed in the Union. Such state-centered constitutionalism could encourage sectional agitation, as Davis fully understood.

Davis saw two features in the "social system" of American constitutionalism that strengthened its force and tended the Union toward permanency.[5] The Framers, rather than challenging nature, which would have made the document seem unnatural and contrived and therefore vulnerable to criticism, had instead adapted fundamental rights universally found in natural law. The most important of these, in Davis's mind, protected private property with due process of law. Natural law did not *dictate* property rights: "The natural law gives no right of property to a man in anything," Davis said. Through a political process the American people chose to put naturally occurring property rights in their constitution. He called it "public national law, growing out of the practice, usages, and uniform customs of the civilized world."[6] So long as they remained in the Union, property owners need not fear government confiscation of their property outside legal processes. Basing the Union on natural law, and not just political bargaining, made any agitation against it seem less legitimate, Davis thought. For Davis, though, the naturalness of the Constitution went beyond such bedrock principles, no matter how important they might be. He also thought the Constitution incorporated a way

[4] Lincoln, "Speech at Springfield, Illinois," October 4, 1854, Basler, ed., *Collected Works*, 2:266.

[5] For the Union as a social system and not merely a compact or a league, see Congress, Senate, Senator Davis of Kentucky speaking on Proposed Expulsion of Mr. Bright, 37th Cong., 2nd sess., Cong. Globe (January 22, 1862), 431.

[6] Congress, Senate, Senator Davis of Kentucky speaking on Aid to the States in Emancipation, 37th Cong., 2nd sess., ibid. (March 24, 1862), 1334. Many Americans shared this view. William W. Fisher III, "Ideology, Religion, and the Constitutional Protection of Private Property, 1760-1860," *Emory Law Journal* 39 (1990): 65-134, argues that ideology and religion encouraged constitutional thought that discouraged uncompensated expropriation of private property as illegitimate. Siddali, *From Property to Person*, has also argued for the centrality of property rights as an issue in the Civil War.

of thinking about race consistent with the best scientific knowledge available.

Primarily by their silences, many historians have argued for Davis's irrelevance.[7] Davis's frequent absences from the secondary sources, when he is so prominent in the primary sources, silently argues that most Civil War–era white Americans did not share his ideology or his continued commitment to antebellum constitutionalism in the postbellum era. "Racism had been rampant" before the Civil War, one scholar recently wrote about Northerners before continuing, "[b]ut the war years changed those attitudes." Racial prejudice endured at the end of the war, another scholar acknowledges, yet "it was not the overpowering force that it had been." Emancipation "pushed whites" to transform their thinking about themselves and their nation. "No one here talks conservatism any longer, or speaks of the old Constitution," Eric Foner quotes one New Yorker after the Emancipation Proclamation. According to this story, Northerners did not revert to their old racism until the end of the nineteenth century when they could watch lynching "complacently."[8] Although scholars sometimes do complain that the narrow language Congress wrote into the Civil War amendments hamstrung Reconstruction, more commonly they absolve the Civil War–era public from culpability for the failure of the North to thoroughly reform postwar southern society.

---

[7] The current generation of historians has scarcely taken note of Garrett Davis. Eric Foner, *Reconstruction: America's Unfinished Revolution* (New York, 1988), 392, mentions Davis one time. Michael Les Benedict, *A Compromise of Principle: Congressional Republicans and Reconstruction, 1863-1869* (New York, 1974), 165, 203, scarcely mentions Davis. Vorenberg, *Final Freedom*, 95-97, (quote, 106), 110, 113n, gives Davis more attention but observes that Republicans "easily fended off his jabs." Earlier historians thought Davis mattered more. See Horace Edgar Flack, *The Adoption of the Fourteenth Amendment* (Baltimore, 1908); David Herbert Donald, *Charles Sumner and the Rights of Man* (New York, 1970); Charles Fairman, *Reconstruction and Reunion, 1864-88* (New York, 1971); E. Merton Coulter, *The Civil War and Readjustment in Kentucky* (1926; repr., Gloucester, Mass., 1966), 27, 54, 142, 208-9, 268, 330-35. J. G. Randall treated Davis as an entirely reasonable opponent of excessive government power; see J. G. Randall and David Donald, *The Union Divided* (Boston, 1961), 285, and J. G. Randall, *Constitutional Problems under Lincoln* (Urbana, Ill., 1951), 81, 350.

[8] Heather Cox Richardson, *The Death of Reconstruction: Race, Labor, and Politics in the Post-Civil War North, 1865-1901* (Cambridge, Mass., 2001), ix; Phillip Shaw Paludan, *"A People's Contest": The Union and Civil War, 1861-1865* (New York, 1988), 198, 222; Foner, *Fiery Trial*, 231.

The people and their elected representatives, Michael Vorenberg has written, deserve no blame for the failure of the government to forestall later racial horrors.[9] Only by excising Garrett Davis from Reconstruction and Gilded Age history can the postbellum period be understood as a time when white Americans first embraced and then spurned black Americans. In his mind, momentary changes in the popular mood should not, ultimately could not, contradict the deeper and more permanent understandings of race entrenched in scientific fact.[10] The violent, brutal racism that characterized the American Gilded Age did not spring forth full-grown, like the unlikely birth of Venus in Botticelli's famous painting but rather had roots deep in American life, embedded in the foundational principles many

[9] Michael Vorenberg, "Imagining a Different Reconstruction Constitution," *Civil War History* 51 (2005): 425.

[10] For popular constitutionalism, the key work is Larry D. Kramer, *The People Themselves: Popular Constitutionalism and Judicial Review* (New York, 2004). This work must be supplemented with Kramer, "'The Interest of the Man': James Madison, Popular Constitutionalism and the theory of Deliberative Democracy," *Valparaiso University Law Review* 41 (2006): 697-754. For slavery and the Constitution, John Hope Franklin wrote, in 1975, that by refusing to end slavery, the founding generation did not bestow the blessings of liberty on its posterity. More tellingly, in 1977, Herbert Storing described as "common" the view that by failing to end slavery, the founders left an example to be "lived down rather than lived up to." John Hope Franklin quoted in Herbert J. Storing, "Slavery and the Moral Foundations of the American Republic," in *The Moral Foundations of the American Republic*, ed. Robert H. Horwitz, 2nd ed. (Charlottesville, Va., 1979), 314-15. In a collection of essays in 1989 on southern constitutionalism, Herman Belz wrote that "protection of slavery was a leading motive and object of southern delegates to the Constitutional Convention" and northern delegates were prepared to go along with the demands of the South. Herman Belz, "The South and the American Constitutional Tradition at the Bicentennial," in *An Uncertain Tradition: Constitutionalism and the History of the South*, ed. Kermit L. Hall and James W. Ely Jr. (Athens, Ga., 1989), 22. Paul Finkelman has strongly argued for the role of slavery at the founding, see Paul Finkelman, "A Covenant with Death: Slavery and the U.S. Constitution," *American Visions* 1 (1986): 21-27; Finkelman, "Slavery and the Constitutional Convention: Making a Covenant With Death," in *Beyond Confederation: Origins of the Constitution and American National Identity*, ed. Richard Beeman, Stephen Botein, and Edward C. Carter II (Chapel Hill, 1987), 188-225; Finkelman, "The Constitution and the Intentions of the Framers: The Limits of Historical Analysis," *University of Pittsburgh Law Review* 50 (1989): 349-97. More recently, see David Waldstreicher, *Slavery's Constitution: From Revolution to Ratification* (New York, 2009); George William Van Cleve, *A Slaveholders' Union: Slavery, Politics, and the Constitution in the Early American Republic* (Chicago, 2010); Robin L. Einhorn, *American Taxation, American Slavery* (Chicago, 2006). For an older but more nuanced view, see Jack N. Rakove, *Original Meanings: Politics and Ideas in the Making of the Constitution* (New York, 1996).

Americans identified with their Constitution and refused to abandon even in the so-called revolutionary moment of Reconstruction.[11]

According to the view favored by many historians, Representative James M. Ashley of Ohio represented the impact of the Civil War on public opinion better than Davis, when he enthused in 1866 that America had turned a corner racially. To Ashley the question came down to whether Congress would follow the will of a people energized to battle slavery and all its accoutrements. He framed his criticism of the congressional committee charged with drafting Reconstruction legislation by saying "the loyal men of the South" required justice and, in fact, "all over the land, North and South, a cry is raised" calling on Congress to write egalitarian values into law. There had been such a sea change in public opinion toward racial egalitarianism, Ashley declared, that politicians and government leaders could only get out of the way. "I am desirous to know whether this Congress is going to attempt the work of staying the great anti-slavery revolution which has swept over the country," he demanded. Ashley wondered whether the institutions of government would dare obstruct the mighty wave of popular sentiment sweeping the nation against racism with their "puny" powers.[12]

That was one view Davis encountered in Washington but not the only one.[13] Other Republicans based their commitment to freedom not on a revolution in public sentiment but on the founding principles

---

[11] The supposed revolutionary nature of the Civil War and Reconstruction has long been a matter of historical debate. Viewing the question socially rather than constitutionally, Eric Foner very famously characterized Reconstruction as "America's Unfinished Revolution" in his *Reconstruction: America's Unfinished Revolution, 1863-1877* (New York, 1988). Constitutional historians Michael Les Benedict and Robert Kaczorowski have come down squarely on opposite sides. See Benedict, "Preserving the Constitution: The Conservative Basis of Radical Reconstruction," *Journal of American History* 61 (1974): 65-90; Kaczorowski, "To Begin the Nation Anew: Congress, Citizenship, and Civil Rights after the Civil War," *American Historical Review* 92 (1987): 45-68. Both authors focus on the constitutionalism of Republican reformers more than on conservatives like Garrett Davis.

[12] Congress, House, Representative Ashley of Ohio speaking on Reconstruction, 39th Cong., 2nd sess., Cong. Globe (May 29, 1866), 2879 (first quote), 2880 (second quote), 2882 (third quote).

[13] For a recent version of this duality in American thought generally, see Aziz Rana, *The Two Faces of American Freedom* (Cambridge, Mass., 2010).

of the nation. Publicly stated, such pronouncements can seem like saccharine banalities for the masses, nothing more than Fourth of July rhetoric, but many Republicans expressed these beliefs in their most private communications. In 1861, James W. Nye, a Republican and early member of the Free-Soil Party, privately wrote that the question of "whether liberty to man is worth fighting for" had been settled by the founding generation. In the midst of secession, Nye grumbled, the Buchanan administration could only lie down supinely in the face of its foes. "Our fathers thought differently & laid down their lives upon the opposite theory," Nye observed. Wishing for a Moses to lead the country out of its wilderness, he regretted that he lacked the "power to call up the spirit of our Revolutionary fathers." For Republicans like Nye, the Founders had set freedom as the prime American principle and slavery had simply been a long distraction from that lodestar. Secession was an opportunity to get back on track, and in the weeks before Lincoln's inauguration Nye waited impatiently for the right leadership to take charge.[14] The problem, of course, was that other Americans, while sharing Nye's confidence in the force and permanency of constitutional thought, had very different ideas about the nature of those principles. This disagreement split families. The Republican senator from Maine, William Pitt Fessenden, told his father that the idea that slavery could not be reconciled with natural law was "absurd." The older Fessenden did not agree. Samuel Fessenden had such a passionate commitment to abolitionist principles that he had once jettisoned a promising political career rather than compromise. With a trembling hand, the old man picked up a pen to tell his son that, "I have no doubt that Slavery cannot and does not exist in the U States under or by the Power of the Constitution of the U.S." Every slave in the United States, he declared, "ought to be discharged on Habeas Corpus."[15] It was to guard against such

[14] James W. Nye to Jacob M. Howard, January 15, 1861, box 5, Jacob M. Howard Papers, Burton Collection, Detroit Public Library, Detroit, Michigan (hereafter Howard Papers, Detroit Public Library).

[15] Samuel Fessenden to William Pitt Fessenden, May 9, 1862, folder 2, box 10, Fessenden Collection, George J. Mitchell Department of Special Collections and Archives, Bowdoin College, Brunswick, Maine; William Pitt Fessenden to Samuel Fessenden, May 19, 1862,

idealistic claptrap, Garrett Davis felt, that the Founders had written enduring principles into the Constitution.

Confidence in the force of constitutional principle led some Congressional Republicans in a different direction than either Ashley or Nye. No less than his fellow Ohioan, Representative John Bingham favored equal rights for all Americans. Bingham, though, doubted that the public had so easily shifted its thinking about race and the Constitution. In his mind, the Civil War had not so much revolutionized thinking about race as it had cast doubts on the antebellum theory that the states could be trusted to protect rights without federal supervision. The war had opened an opportunity for Congress to amend the Constitution to allow citizens to defend their rights in federal court. Under this theory, the war had created no new rights, but Bingham expected it could be used to pump new life and meaning into the existing Bill of Rights. From the first days of the 1866 Congress, Bingham pressed to clothe the federal judiciary with power to protect citizens' rights.[16] For that reason, he carefully constructed section one of the Fourteenth Amendment from found materials, drafting the amendment so that it would "stand in the very words of the Constitution." From the high ground the original 1787 Constitution offered, Bingham could ridicule his opponents as not daring to directly criticize or oppose the Bill of Rights while quibbling that its provisions should not be enforced in federal courts.[17] Bingham has always done better with historians than Davis; he, at least, is not ignored. Nonetheless, a generation of historians criticized Bingham for his "peculiar mode of thought" and "confused discourse." In 1971, Charles Fairman pronounced himself disconcerted by Bingham's

---

folder 3, box 10, ibid.

[16] Congress, House, Representative Bingham of Ohio speaking on the Policy of the President—Again, 39th Cong., 2nd sess., Cong. Globe (January 9, 1866), 158. Daniel W. Hamilton, *The Limits of Sovereignty: Property Confiscation in the Union and the Confederacy during the Civil War* (Chicago, 2007), calls Bingham a "Radical." Michael Les Benedict, *A Compromise of Principle: Congressional Republicans and Reconstruction, 1863-1869* (New York, 1974), 27, calls him a "consistent conservative."

[17] Congress, House, Representative Bingham of Ohio speaking on the Rights of Citizens, H. R. No. 63, 39th Cong., 2nd sess., Cong. Globe (February 28, 1866), 1089.

use of existing constitutional language to achieve egalitarian ends.[18]

Bingham understood that Garrett Davis's commitment to an unchanging Constitution represented a real threat to the rights and safety of African Americans. In contrast to Ashley, Bingham considered public opinion at the moment of emancipation too weak a reed to rely on for the permanent protection of rights. He feared that there might be some truth in Davis's speeches. Better to use the existing Bill of Rights as a foundation for change. Bingham crafted the Fourteenth Amendment with exactly the kind of arguments Davis made in mind. The existing Constitution, Bingham said, as did Davis, did not protect black rights and could not be made to protect black rights. Only by amending the Constitution, and placing the Bill of Rights under the care and protection of the judiciary, could Republicans thwart Davis's constitutionalism—or so thought the author of the Fourteenth Amendment.

Davis's origins help explain the nature of his constitutional thinking. Born and raised one hundred fifty miles from Lincoln's birthplace, he absorbed the ambivalence about slavery common among Bourbon County Whigs. By 1850, Bourbon County had the fourth-largest concentration of slaves in Kentucky (after Christian, Fayette, and Jefferson Counties) but that concentration did not mean that slaveholders held their property untroubled by guilt or doubt. In the 1820s and 1830s, numerous Bourbon County slaveholders manumitted their slaves, filing their documents in the county courthouse. One historian claims to have found the courthouse files "teeming" with these records, and in 1850 the census recorded 245 "Free Colored" persons still living in Bourbon County, not the heaviest concentration in the state but a substantial legacy from that earlier era nonetheless. Only six Kentucky counties had more. The local newspaper got in the swing of things, condemning the "diabolical damning practice of soul-peddling." This swiftly changed when abolitionists shifted their focus from colonizing freed slaves to Africa to immediate emancipation. In the 1840s, the ranks of Bourbon County emancipators

---

[18] Fairman, *Reconstruction and Reunion*, 1270, 1288-89; Pamela Brandwein, *Reconstructing Reconstruction: The Supreme Court and the Production of Historical Truth* (Durham, N.C., 1999).

dwindled to a few dozen and the local newspaper suddenly changed its tune, urging stern discipline against recalcitrant slaves. It was in the midst of this transition that Garrett Davis began his public career, coming on the stage as a dynamic Whig orator campaigning against Texas annexation. When his enemies responded by calling him an abolitionist, Davis denied the label but would not temper his criticism of slavery. Davis, though, struggled to reconcile his doubts about slavery with his faith in property as a constitutional right, and he sometimes questioned slavery and defended property rights in the same speech.[19] At the Kentucky 1849 constitutional convention, Davis advocated emancipation, albeit gradual and compensated.[20]

Despite his speeches criticizing slavery, Davis, like nearly all nineteenth-century white Americans, had racist beliefs which he could never shed and which robbed his emancipationist vision of any practical effect. God, Davis believed, had decreed that black and white people must remain forever separate and never "amalgamate" either socially or politically. To Davis, such beliefs reflected his personal experiences with slavery and very conveniently justified his economic stake in the institution, though many Americans harbored the same prejudices without owning slaves. In 1860, Davis owned fifteen slaves, a fact documented by the census slave schedule which listed his slaves only by their age, gender, and color. Nonetheless, this dry bureaucratic document does allow a glimpse into the humanity of the Davis slaves, as the enumerator's arrangement of their ages suggested that Davis owned three families, ranging in age from six months to seventy-five. At least in public, Davis viewed his slaves sentimentally: "I have played with them. They have shared with me my joys and my sorrows." Davis insisted that he held such a familial attachment to his human property that he would never sell a slave and had not punished one in twenty years. He fed them well and provided good housing; they got their health care from the best physi-

---

[19] H. E. Everman, *The History of Bourbon County, 1785-1865* (Paris, Ky., 1977), 85-91; "Statistics of Kentucky" in J. D. B. DeBow, comp., *Statistical View of the United States . . . Being a Compendium of the Seventh Census* (Washington, D.C., 1854), 236, 242.
[20] Everman, *History of Bourbon County*, 94.

cians available. Davis imagined his slaves as faithful and contented, "so far as I know."[21] From our vantage point, it is hard to calculate just how thoroughly Davis had tied his personal fortune, much less his personal thinking, to his slaves. While Davis had an investment in slavery that reached thousands of dollars, emancipation did not devastate him financially. For most slaveholders, human property accounted for the bulk of their personal estate. Davis owned $34,500 in personal property in 1860, and $20,000 in 1870, a loss to be sure, but the value of his real estate grew steadily from $10,500 in 1850 to $17,000 in 1860 and to $56,500 in 1870 (nearly a million dollars in today's dollars).[22] These numbers have to be taken with a very large grain of salt as census enumerators often guessed at the values they recorded in their books and the persons being enumerated sometimes exaggerated their holdings once confident that the inquiring official was not a tax collector. The census figures nonetheless make it highly unlikely that Davis lived in poverty after losing his slaves. He was still a wealthy man in 1870.

Some Northerners blamed the Civil War on southern politicians' lust for power, the "unreasoning vanity and dashing ambition so peculiar to them," as Jacob Howard of Michigan put it in a letter to his brother.[23] Though he avoided criticizing southern culture, Davis said much the same thing. Like a majority of Kentucky voters, Davis had supported Bell in 1860. But while he told followers that he distrusted Lincoln, he did not see the defeat of his candidate as a reason to break up the Union. Nor did he blame Republicans for the outcome of the election. Davis alleged that demagogic, white southern extremists had deliberately engineered the election of Lincoln

---

[21] Davis, Proposed Expulsion of Mr. Bright, 452.

[22] Congress, Senate, Senator Davis of Kentucky speaking on Slavery in the District, S. No. 108, 37th Cong., 2nd sess., Cong. Globe (March 24, 1862), 1338; 1850 U.S. census, District No. 1, Bourbon County, Kentucky, microfilm M432, 290; 1860 U.S. census, Eastern District, Bourbon County, Kentucky, microfilm M653, 683; ibid., Eastern District, Bourbon County, Kentucky, Slave Schedule microfilm M653; 1870 U.S census, Second Ward, Paris, Bourbon County, Kentucky, microfilm M593.

[23] Jacob M. Howard to brother, June 5, 1861, letter book 26, Howard Papers, Detroit Public Library.

to provoke a war so they could secede from the Union. According to Davis, they had nominated John C. Breckinridge knowing that he could not win but knowing also that he would split the Democratic vote so that a Republican could become president and thereby spark secession.[24] In Davis's telling of the story, he and other slaveholding Unionists battled to "instruct the public mind": "we reasoned with them; we reminded them of our past history, of the unbroken and unsullied fidelity of Kentucky to her allegiance."[25] He would later change his mind, but at least in 1862, Davis saw the southern secessionists as a greater threat to constitutionally protected slavery than the Northerners. On March 13, 1862, Davis told the Senate that Confederates controlled a quarter of Kentucky, waging a vandal war, outraging humanity, insulting womanhood, and carrying away $300,000 in slaves. Those Kentuckians sympathetic to the South organized "peace meetings" across the commonwealth, scattering themselves all over Kentucky, "on plain and on mountain, in city and hamlet and field and everywhere."[26]

In the North, Republicans saw Davis's work to keep Kentucky loyal as vital to their efforts to save the country. Lincoln's biographers seldom fail to quote his observation that "to lose Kentucky is nearly the same as to lose the whole game."[27] Lincoln hardly stood alone in such beliefs. To understand the significance of that quote, there is no better place to go than Michigan, where Republican Jacob M. Howard doubted that the government should "indulge" abolitionists' "impatience" at the cost of stripping the Union men in the border states of all hope by "adopting a policy in which they cannot—cannot sympathize." Even as Howard wrote those words, and even as he publicly assured friends that the Republican Party had no formal plan to abolish slavery, he secretly envisioned the end of slavery.

[24] Davis, Proposed Expulsion of Mr. Bright, 433.

[25] Davis, Proposed Expulsion of Mr. Powell, 1213.

[26] Ibid., 1215, 1214.

[27] Abraham Lincoln to Orville H. Browning, Septembeer 22, 1861, Basler, ed., *Collected Works*, 4:533; Carwardine, *Lincoln: A Life of Purpose and Power*, 176; Foner, *Fiery Trial*, 179; Donald, *Lincoln*, 317.

Slavery had little chance on the slippery slope of military occupation he observed, asking "who cannot see the final results of such a policy?"[28] The answer, of course, was Garrett Davis.

Though he had opposed Lincoln's election, Davis did not hesitate to work with the new administration to secure the Union, urging that it deliver a quick knockout blow to the Confederacy. "My hopes," he explained "are for the triumphant movement of the armies of the U.S., the restoration of the union." Davis condemned the "Virginia heresy" of states' rights which he hoped to eradicate forever. Given a choice between the Union and slavery, Davis told Lincoln, "another fibre of cotton should never grow in our country."[29] By May 1861, Davis had joined a private committee coordinating with Lincoln to funnel arms into the hands of Kentucky Unionists eager to "sustain the State to her union & constitutional moorings."[30] In the summer, Davis contacted Lincoln's secretary of war, collaborating on plans to organize a Unionist militia and win enough seats in the Kentucky Senate to impeach the pro-Confederate governor, Beriah Magoffin. Davis pushed the Lincoln administration to march three columns of troops through Kentucky to secure Tennessee for a strike into the Deep South. One column could go through the Cumberland Gap, he urged, one could march out of Louisville, and the third could hit Memphis from Paducah or Columbus.[31] When Kentucky's southern-leaning legislature questioned his arms-trafficking, Davis unflinchingly went to Frankfort to confront his critics, characteristically appealing to the Constitution for his rights, in this case the Second Amendment right to bear arms. Impressed, the *Daily National Intelligencer* praised Davis for his "vigor, boldness, and directness."[32] When the Kentucky

---

[28] Jacob M. Howard to Charles Newett Niles, December 23, 1861, box 5, Howard Papers, Detroit Public Library.

[29] Davis to Abraham Lincoln, August 4, 1861, series 1, general correspondence, 1833-1916, Abraham Lincoln Papers at the Library of Congress, Washington, D.C. (hereafter Lincoln Papers, LC).

[30] Charles A. Wickliffe et al. to Abraham Lincoln, May 28, 1861, ibid.

[31] Davis to Simon Cameron, July 15, 1861, box 1, Thomas-Metcalfe Collection, Kentucky Historical Society Collections, Kentucky Historical Society, Frankfort, Kentucky.

[32] "Arming Unionists in Kentucky," *Daily National Intelligencer* [Washington, D.C.], June

legislative elections rolled around in August, Davis cheered when his fellow Unionists won control of both houses.[33]

That election put the Unionists solidly in control of the state legislature, but left two pro-Confederate senators. The Unionist legislature speedily voted to instruct John C. Breckinridge and Lazarus W. Powell to resign their seats. For Breckinridge, this was no problem. He had quickly abandoned the Senate to command the Kentucky Brigade in the Confederate army, but Powell stubbornly stayed on. Elected to replace Breckinridge, Davis went to Washington determined to oust Powell from his seat as a traitor. On December 23, 1861, when Davis joined the Senate eager to set battle against Powell in motion, the Congress was about to commence its second session. In the first session, members had debated legislation as Confederate and Union troops battled over Manassas, just twenty-five miles away. Nervous congressmen could hear artillery fire from their boardinghouses; to hear it more clearly, they had only to scale the Capitol dome. "Hour after hour the deadly roar beat the air," one distracted senator wrote. Intense excitement seized the city as Congress wondered whether the Confederate army might overrun the capital.[34] By the time Davis arrived, the battle of Bull Run had concluded, but fear and trembling still gripped Capitol Hill. "The very foundations of the Government are rocking," Wisconsin senator Timothy Howe wrote his niece that December, adding, "God only knows what sort of landscape will be exhibited when the convulsion is over."[35]

By the end of 1861, when Davis came to Washington, some already doubted that the new landscape Howe envisioned would have any slaves in it. Davis plunged into the Senate trumpeting his hatred for secession, delivering patriotic speeches that thoroughly blasted disunion but also defended slavery. "I was born under the

13, 1861.

[33] Davis, Proposed Expulsion of Mr. Powell, 37th Cong., 2nd sess., Cong. Globe (March 13, 1862), 1214.

[34] Timothy Howe to Grace T. Howe, July 21, 1861, box 1, Timothy O. Howe Papers, State Historical Society of Wisconsin, Madison, Wisconsin (hereafter Howe Papers, State Historical Society of Wisconsin).

[35] Timothy Howe to Grace T. Howe, December 30, 1861, box 1, ibid.

stars and stripes," he told the Senate in 1862, "within the ark of the Union, educated religiously to maintain and support the principles of that immortal system of government."[36] When Massachusetts senator Charles Sumner said he always sympathized with slaves, Davis thanked Sumner for his candor and accused him of treason.[37] The world would change around Davis, but he remained true to this sentiment for the rest of his life. The Union was an "ark" and Davis maintained a religious devotion to the unchanging principles of the Constitution, an "immortal system of government." Davis's Unionism won him admirers. Far from condemning his speeches as rambling or disjointed, the *New York Times* in 1861 praised his forcefulness and cogency. His speeches were not graceful but were nonetheless "relentless and unsparing" the *Times* reported, calling him a "master of sarcasm" with "great power over the masses."[38] The Virginia Unionist John B. Baldwin thought Davis's "high character" and integrity noteworthy.[39]

So did Abraham Lincoln. In late April 1861, as Lincoln considered the thorny problem of Fort Sumter, he turned to Davis for advice, assuring him that his administration had no aggressive designs against the South there. A year later, one of Lincoln's secretaries, John Hay, published an anonymous article praising Davis as a "wise, sagacious and incorruptible" man, "quiet, grave" with "a complexion untarnished by dissipation, and an expression of feature honest and steadfast, without concealments and fear." Scholars have concluded that Hay's writings "came direct from Lincoln's office" and were "inspired by Lincoln."[40] Davis seems to have persuaded Lincoln to temper his emancipationist tendencies as the price for his well-known goal of keeping Kentucky in the Union. When Davis

---

[36] Davis, Proposed Expulsion of Mr. Powell, 1211.

[37] Congress, Senate, Senator Davis of Kentucky speaking on Punishment of Treason and Rebellion, 37th Cong., 2nd sess., Cong. Globe (May 20, 1862), 2223.

[38] "The New Senator from Kentucky," *New York Times*, December 11, 1861.

[39] Burlingame, *Abraham Lincoln*, 2:122.

[40] Michael Burlingame, ed., *Lincoln's Journalist: John Hay's Anonymous Writings for the Press, 1860-1864* (Carbondale, Ill., 1998), xxii (first and second quotations), 190-91 (third, fourth, and fifth quotations).

told Lincoln that loyal Kentuckians "would not resist his gradual emancipation scheme if he would only conjoin with it his colonization plan," Lincoln evidently took this to heart. Soon after talking to Davis, Lincoln biographer Michael Burlingame writes, "Lincoln was singing that necessary tune." According to Kansas senator Samuel S. Pomeroy, Lincoln "is always quoting" Garrett Davis as evidence of what he must do to keep Kentucky in the Union.[41]

Davis certainly seemed just as steadfast and fearless as Lincoln's secretary said, when, in the early months of the war, he first joined an attack on two senators unwilling to "coerce" the rebelling states back into the Union and then accused former president James Buchanan of harboring Rebel sympathies. Favoring the expulsion of Indiana Democrat Jesse Bright, Davis alleged that "the gentleman has never, in a solitary measure, shown any sympathy with the Government in its life and death struggle."[42] Most senators agreed with Davis on Bright and they expelled him. When they next considered Kentucky senator Lazarus Powell, Davis urged them on, saying that he came to Washington unalterably convinced that duty and honor required him to oust his fellow Kentuckian from Congress. On March 13, Davis listed eight measures necessary for fighting the war, including tax increases, an authorization to employ volunteers against the rebellion, and a reorganization of the military establishment, all measures opposed by Powell. Davis told the Senate that in the great fight for Kentucky in 1861, he had led the Union side only to find Powell lined up with the secessionists. In the midst of this debate, Davis accused Powell of advocating a "separate existence" for the states, a sentiment he labeled treasonous. Not only did the Senate not expel Powell, but ultimately the two Kentucky senators became allies after Davis decided that states could have a separate sovereignty after all, if not a separate existence.[43]

[41] Burlingame, *Abraham Lincoln*, 2:154, 236, 383; Adams S. Hill to Sydney Howard Gay, August 25, 1862, box 38, Sydney Howard Gay Collection, Manuscript Collections, Columbia University Libraries, New York, New York (hereafter, Gay Collection, Columbia University).

[42] Davis, Proposed Expulsion of Mr. Bright, 432.

[43] Davis, Proposed Expulsion of Mr. Powell, 1209-12 (quote, 1211).

On December 15, Davis proposed censuring James Buchanan for failing to prevent secession. As president, Buchanan set silencing northern agitation against slavery as his goal, one necessary to preserve the Constitution and the Union. In his zeal to save the Union, Buchanan could not help but despise what he saw as the greatest threat to its survival, the Black Republican Party, as he consistently called it in his private writings.[44] Davis certainly concurred with Buchanan's goal of ending agitation over slavery and entirely agreed that slavery had to be left to the states, but more than his fellow senators, he could not forgive Buchanan's failure to achieve that goal. He disparaged Buchanan's masculinity, calling him "feeble," an "imbecile," "effete," and "driveling."[45] The Senate only briefly discussed the resolution before voting by a wide margin to table it, with just two Republican senators joining Davis to support it. When word reached the former president that Davis wanted to censure him, he could hardly contain his indignation. From his retirement home outside Lancaster, Pennsylvania, Buchanan wrote that he saw the attempted resolution as evidence that "the spirit to do me injustice still prevails in the Republican Party," apparently forgetting that Davis was no Republican and that all Republicans but two voted to table the resolution. Buchanan dismissed Davis's efforts as "infamous" and "ridiculous," but he clearly could not ignore them either, taking time in a letter to his nephew and ward to denounce Davis.[46]

Davis explained his determined Unionism and hatred for the treason of rebellion in long speeches that sometimes resembled American history lectures or unguided reminiscences, hours spent on general

[44] James Buchanan to Malcolm Ives, September 10, 1856, box 51, James Buchanan Papers, collection 91, Historical Society of Pennsylvania, Philadelphia, Pennsylvania; James Buchanan to William B. Reed, September 14, 1856, ibid.; James Buchanan to John Y. Mason, December 27, 1856, ibid.; James Buchanan to Arnold Plumer, February 14, 1858, ibid.

[45] Davis, Proposed Expulsion of Mr. Bright, 432 (feeble, imbecile); Davis Proposed Expulsion of Mr. Powell, 1210 (effete, driveling).

[46] James Buchanan to James Buchanan Henry, December 19, 1862, box 52, James Buchanan Papers, Historical Society of Pennsylvania; Congress, Senate, Senator Davis speaking on the Censure of President Buchanan, 37th Cong., 3rd sess., Cong. Globe (December 15, 1862), 83; ibid. (December 16, 1862), 101-2. Two Republicans joined Davis to favor the motion: Timothy Howe of Wisconsin and Morton Wilkinson of Minnesota.

topics, as one senator complained. The Kentucky senator delivered these speeches with apparent sincerity and, indeed, his private writings matched his public declarations. He claimed to his friends that he had learned American constitutionalism from the writings of Washington, Marshall, Webster, and Clay, just as he said in his speeches. Our fathers, he said, led by "that godlike man" George Washington, repudiated the Articles of Confederation to create a Constitution that became the government of the people and not the states. The new government would not operate through the states but directly upon the people, he explained. Seven years of experience with the Articles, Davis said, had exposed the folly of state sovereignty.[47] The Founders taught that sovereignty existed only in the people, Davis said. His doubts about state sovereignty did not mean that he did not see the Constitution as a bargain between southern and northern interests. The delegates to the Constitutional Convention met in "a spirit of concession and compromise," Davis said in 1862, adding, "In no other spirit could the Constitution ever have been adopted or ratified."[48] The Founders made the Constitution synonymous with slavery, Davis proclaimed. In this, Davis parted company with the Republicans, but he understood and enjoyed the fact that leading abolitionists had said the same thing. No doubt he delighted in citing Wendell Phillips as making the same argument he made: the Constitution supported slavery, demonstrating the skill at sarcasm so admired by the *New York Times*. The constitutional guarantee of property rights meant that the Congress could not abolish slavery anywhere, not in any state, not even in the District of Columbia, Davis declared. The Founders had made slavery so fundamental to the Union that it could not be overturned even in the district, where Congress exercised unquestioned sovereignty. He understood that the District of Columbia was not a state and Congress ruled it

[47] Davis to B. Bruner, September 16, 1865, folder 22, Thomas Bruner Papers, Filson Historical Society, Louisville, Kentucky (hereafter Bruner Papers, Filson Historical Society); Davis, Proposed Expulsion of Mr. Powell, 1211.

[48] Congress, Senate, Senator Davis of Kentucky speaking on the Confiscation of Property, S. No. 151, 37th Cong., 2nd sess., Cong. Globe (April 23, 1862), 1779.

directly, but that did not matter because, he insisted, slavery was a fundamental national right. At the same time, he did believe that the people, working through their states, could abolish slavery in their neighborhoods and communities. In 1855, he wrote a friend that if the state government of "Kanzas" [*sic*] voted to become a slave state, "no power but the people of the state can nullify it." But while he respected democratic localism, he saw property rights as the greatest of all constitutional rights. The Constitution, Davis orated, "adopts certain great principles, and secures certain great rights." One great right is the right to property and no citizen can be deprived of his property except through due process, judicial procedure authorized by the Constitution.[49] On this point, Davis clashed with the Republicans. For Republicans the struggle between slavery and freedom was foundationally no political question at all but rather a moral question, the "eternal struggle between right and wrong." National principles should not be abrogated to local politics, Lincoln had said, and congressional Republicans agreed.[50]

Davis understood that even great constitutional principles had to be defended against popular insurgencies and he kept a weather eye out for treasonous threats from either the North or the South. Even in the midst of a civil war sparked by southern secession, Davis complained that the North had a history of criticism of the Union that easily matched that of the South. At various times throughout the Civil War, Davis needled Northerners by reminding them that Bostonian abolitionists had threatened the Union when they tried to rescue Anthony Burns in 1854, an act of treason that most Northerners ignored if they did not actively promote. When it came to fighting treason, Davis boasted, no Northerner could match his own patriotic consistency.[51]

[49] Davis to Adam Beatty, August 9, 1855, folder 42, Beatty-Quisenberry Family Papers, Filson Historical Society; Davis, Slavery in the District, S. No. 108, 1335; Davis to B. Bruner, September 16, 1865, folder 22, John B. Bruner Papers, Filson Historical Society.

[50] Congress, Senate, Senator Seward of New York speaking on Freedom and Public Faith, 33rd Cong., 1st sess., Cong. Globe (May 25, 1854), app., 155; Abraham Lincoln, Speech at Bloomington, Illinois, September 26, 1854, Basler, ed., *Collected Works*, 2:239

[51] Davis, Confiscation of Property, 1778, 1777; Congress, Senate, Senator Davis of

Every white American owed his nation such patriotic fealty, Davis urged. Although Davis so closely associated himself with Henry Clay that virtually every biographical sketch of his life describes him as a friend of the Great Compromiser, he nonetheless remembered the 1832 nullification crisis with regret because his hero had opposed Andrew Jackson's plan to march the army into South Carolina and crush the whole idea of nullification and secession once and for all. Jackson's unique popularity with the public had been an opportunity to save the nation from civil war forever. "It would have been better—oh! How much better—that the issue had been met under that great chief," Davis declared. Jackson had the confidence of the American people, Davis recollected, and the people would have supported "the hero of Orleans" had he crushed secession in 1832. That he did not do so was an opportunity tragically lost, a loss that led to civil war and emancipation, Davis said. Later he lamented that if only Jackson had been president instead of Buchanan, he would have nipped the Civil War in the bud.[52]

Davis insisted that he did not support slavery but rather favored gradual and compensated emancipation, very gradual indeed as Davis expected the process would stretch over one hundred years. Owners in loyal states would be compensated, under the Davis plan, according to values set individually, case by case, in courts after jury trials.[53] The senator spent a lot of his time battling for the "just compensation" he thought the government owed Kentucky slaveholders. Davis was no eccentric in making this argument. In the 1862 debate over the Second Confiscation Act, he joined a conservative coalition that made up about a third of the House and Senate, all in agreement that confiscation was constitutionally impossible outside the judicial process. Orville Browning of Illinois, a friend of Lincoln, joined

Kentucky speaking on the Proposed Expulsion of Mr. Davis, 38th Cong., 1st sess., Cong. Globe (January 13, 1864), 179, 181.

[52] Davis, Proposed Expulsion of Mr. Bright, 433. In the antebellum era, Lincoln also closely associated himself with Clay and like Davis favored only gradual emancipation. Foner, *Fiery Trial*, 18-19.

[53] Davis, Slavery in the District, 1339.

with Jacob Collamer of Vermont to lead this faction.[54] They found their enemy in Lyman Trumbull of Illinois, who campaigned for confiscation, urging international law as a justification for seizing the property of Rebels in the Confederate states without trial and by legal process in places where the courts were open and functioning. Some of his allies disliked this last concession, wanting to dispense with due process for any disloyal person anywhere. One senator, averring that he would not pull out his Blackstone when attacked by an assassin, said that in the emergency of secession he saw no reason to follow due process of law. Even many Republicans blanched at such declarations, remembering that the great John Marshall had championed "vested rights" as a constitutional doctrine.[55]

Much of this debate turned on the respective powers of Congress and the president. Davis joined with those senators favoring the most dramatic use of presidential power to put down the rebellion. This even extended to seizure of private property by the army in battle. In wartime, Davis said, "irregular power must necessarily be sometimes assumed." When the president and the Union armies marched into the South, Davis said, the Constitution allowed them "discretionary" powers but, he added, those powers belong only to the president and his generals, not to Congress. Davis thus defended the seizure of property in wartime, saying that "modern international law" protected private property from confiscation, but international law did not apply to the South and could not until and unless the South achieved sovereignty and independence, something he did not expect to see. "I want the property of incorrigible traitors forfeited," he declared, recognizing that "This forfeiture may operate to the disenthralling of 3,500,000 negroes." But he doubted that freed slaves would live alongside their former masters; that would be "utterly impossible," he observed. To escape the conundrum, Davis favored trying "the

---

[54] Hamilton, *The Limits of Sovereignty*, 47-48; Siddali, *From Property to Person*, 140-41.

[55] Congress, Senate, Senator Wright of Indiana speaking on Confiscation of Property, S. No. 151, 37th Cong., 2nd sess., Cong. Globe (April 30, 1862), 1878; Hamilton, *Limits of Sovereignty*, 45.

experiment" of colonization.[56] Here, too, Garrett Davis occupied no eccentric position but rather one also occupied by the president, and he joined with Lincoln to say that in wartime the army could take private property from citizens in the seceded states to win the war. At this point, in 1862, leading Republicans did not shun Davis or think his speeches particularly tedious or unreasonable. Republican senator John Sherman of Ohio cited Davis as an ally on this narrow point, noting that "even my friend from Kentucky" had not questioned the right of the military to seize property in wartime.[57]

Like several senators, Davis proposed an alternative to Trumbull's bill, one guaranteeing a jury trial before the government could seize property outside the war zone (in places like Kentucky, for example). Some Republicans agreed with Davis and proposed similar bills that attracted enough support to split their party into warring factions. Moderate and conservative opponents of Trumbull's version of confiscation won the battle by referring the matter to committee. Trumbull and his faction voted against this, but they went down to defeat. Trumbull's Republican opponents wrote their own bill in committee, one that made confiscation very nearly a criminal statute, calling for trials, just as Davis advocated. The new bill denied that Congress could emancipate slaves. Not only did Congress largely follow Davis's logic, so did the president. Lincoln followed the conservatives' leading tenets to argue that the government could take property only after a trial and conviction.[58]

The first signs of real trouble in Davis's friendly relations with Lincoln came in March 1862. On March 6, Lincoln formally proposed to Congress what he must have thought was the Garrett Davis plan for emancipation: compensated emancipation followed by colonization with the federal government picking up the tab as the states paid

---

[56] Congress, Senate, Senator Davis of Kentucky speaking on Amendments to the Constitution, S. No. 16, 38th Cong., 1st sess., Cong. Globe (March 30, 1864), 107.

[57] Congress, Senate, Senator Sherman of Ohio speaking on Confiscation of Property, S. No. 151, 37th Cong., 2d sess., Cong. Globe (April 23, 1862), 1783-4.

[58] Hamilton, *Limits of Sovereignty*, 75-76.

slaveholders. It may be a measure of Davis's influence on Lincoln that in the space of three days, between March 6 and March 9, the senator visited Lincoln three times. On each occasion the president eagerly looked for signs of approval. Davis had been "very cordial," a frustrated Lincoln wrote Frank Blair, but "he has never yet opened his mouth on the subject."[59] Davis agreed with the basic outline of Lincoln's proposal, but he wanted more specific protections for states' rights over slavery. He wanted a more explicit guarantee that the national government would carry the cost of compensating slaveholders and colonization. Some senators could hardly tell the difference between Lincoln's proposal and Davis's alternative version, but Davis somehow could not bring himself to support Lincoln's version of his own plan.[60] On July 12, the president could stand the suspense no longer and invited two dozen border-state congressmen, including Davis, to the Executive Mansion. Lincoln's visitors were not in the best of spirits; Congress had reached the end of its session "jaded, worn out, tired, and *cross*," according to Senator Timothy Howe of Wisconsin.[61] At this meeting, Lincoln made his pitch for gradual and compensated emancipation followed by colonization. "I do not speak of emancipation *at once*," Lincoln pleaded, "but of a *decision* at once to emancipate gradually." The president added that blacks could be cheaply relocated to South America and predicted that "the freed people will not be reluctant to go." At this point, Lincoln's attitude toward colonization closely matched the feelings of Davis and his fellows. In August, Lincoln would tell a delegation of blacks that race relations in America were so hopeless that their only chance was to migrate. "It is better for us both . . . to be separated," Lincoln told a group of black ministers visiting him. In this, he may very well have been influenced by Davis. According to a journalist,

[59] "Message to Congress," March 6, 1862, Basler, ed., *Collected Works*, 5:144-6; Burlingame, *Abraham Lincoln*, 2:340-41.

[60] Congress, Senate, Senator Davis of Kentucky speaking on Aid to the States in Emancipation, 37th Cong., 2nd sess., Cong. Globe (March 26, 1862), 1371.

[61] Timothy Howe to Grace Howe, July 2, 1862, box 1, Howe Papers, State Historical Society of Wisconsin.

Lincoln frequently quoted Davis as calling emancipation impossible without colonization.[62]

The congressmen heard the president out and then retired to debate their response. On July 14, Davis joined with nineteen other congressmen to reject Lincoln's proposal in extremely careful and diplomatic language: "We have not been wanting Mr. President, in respect to you and in devotion to the Constitution and the Union." Davis and his fellows pointed out that they had sacrificed much for the Union, voting all the men and money requisitioned, only to have "a radical change in our social system" thrust upon them. The congressmen first claimed that the nation could not afford the cost of purchasing and colonizing the slaves living in the border states, over a million persons. They estimated the cost to relocate so many people would come to nearly five million dollars. "We did not feel that we should be justified in voting for a measure which . . . would add this vast amount to our public debt."[63]

The congressmen then warned that Lincoln's plan would actually strengthen the Confederacy. The Confederates, they wrote, fell into two groups. One group, once known as the states'-rights party, "seek to break down national independence, and set up State denomination." While Davis's name came second on the list of twenty signatories, not first, this sentence sounds like his position, articulated throughout 1861 and into 1862. Unscrupulous politicians, Davis alleged, had schemed against the Union to aggrandize power to themselves in their states. Seeing the Confederacy this way helps explain why Davis had so vigorously attacked states'-rights arguments. The second group, according to the border-state congressmen, fought "to maintain and preserve its rights of property and domestic Safety." This group "has been made to believe" that

[62] "Appeal to Border State Representatives to Favor Compensated Emancipation," July 12, 1862, Basler, ed., *Collected Works*, 5:317-19; "Address on Colonization," August 14, 1862, ibid., 370-75; Foner, *Fiery Trial*, 221.

[63] Border State Congressmen to Abraham Lincoln, July 14, 1862, series 1, general correspondence, 1833-1916, Lincoln Papers, Library of Congress. The *New York Times* initially took the same position. Lincoln to Henry J. Raymond, March 9, 1862, ibid.

its rights "are assailed by this government." One can see elements of Davis's thinking here too, though Davis certainly identified with Southerners seeking to preserve property rights. But he had said, several times, that he did not believe Lincoln "assailed" property rights more than the Confederates.[64]

Davis and his fellow congressmen thought the nature of southern society should dictate the correct strategy for defeating the Confederates. Southern politicians fell into two groups. One faction, which schemed to divide the Union for personal gain, could only be written off as hopeless. Such unscrupulous and devious politicians would never be brought back into the fold. But the second group, made up of people innocently committed to their property rights, could be readily reconciled with the Union again, Davis and his fellows argued. They stayed in the Confederacy only through force of southern arms and because they feared the North. "Remove their apprehensions," the congressmen urged, satisfy them that no harm will come to their institutions, and they will return to the Union just as soon as the Union freed them from Confederate "military dominion." This explains why Davis pressed Lincoln so hard to send columns of troops through Kentucky to crush the rebellion at its outset. The greatest threat to slavery in the border states, he thought, was the disloyalty to the Union, something promoted by Confederate military occupation.[65]

Davis and his fellow border staters thus discarded the only chance they had to recoup some return on their slave property. For a year, some senators had been predicting that "the end of the slave power draws near."[66] Shortly after Lincoln's ill-fated encounter with the border-state congressmen, the moderately Republican *New York Times* predicted that "harsher, severer measures" against slavery might become necessary if the war continued and that such measures would likely forestall the only chance the Confederates had of winning, that

[64] Border State Congressmen to Abraham Lincoln, July 14, 1862, ibid.

[65] Ibid.

[66] Timothy Howe to James, April 20, 1861, box 1, Howe Papers, State Historical Society of Wisconsin.

is, foreign intervention. Frustrated by the border-state response to his colonization plan, Lincoln moved closer to issuing his Emancipation Proclamation. One day after his meeting with the congressmen, Lincoln confided to Gideon Welles and William H. Seward his plans to emancipate the slaves through a presidential proclamation. "It was a new departure for the president," Welles believed. At the end of July, Lincoln shared with his cabinet drafts of military orders calling on the army to more aggressively confiscate the property of unrepentant Confederates, including slaves. He also stunned his cabinet with a draft proclamation freeing the slaves.[67] The public knew none of this. In August, the *New York World* Washington correspondent, informed by his excellent sources inside the Lincoln administration, wrote his managing editor, the abolitionist Sydney Howard Gay, that the president would emancipate upon assurance that colonization would "stand." Thus it still "may be necessary to ride this hobby" of colonization "to achieve the great result," Adams Hill concluded. But Davis apparently already knew better; he said later that he went home at the end of the congressional session feeling "despondent." In the nineteenth century, politicians called the popular issues they used to get elected "hobbies," which they sometimes distinguished from the real questions they had to confront when governing. At this point, while Davis feared the president had moved away from compensation and colonization, he had no solid evidence and kept his cordial relations with Lincoln. In September, he applauded the president for his "force, clearness, truth and *earnestness.*"[68] Davis still felt comfortable enough with Lincoln and committed to his success that he shared his concerns that the president had "a very discordant cabinet." In prosecuting the war, Davis urged, the cabinet must be a

[67] "The President and Slavery," *New York Times,* July 17, 1862; Howard K. Beale, ed., *Dairy of Gideon Welles, Secretary of the Navy under Lincoln and Johnson,* 3 vols. (New York, 1960), 1:70-71; Foner, *Fiery Trial,* 217-19; Vorenberg, *Final Freedom.*

[68] Garrett Davis and others to Abraham Lincoln, September 6, 1862, series 1, general correspondence, 1833-1916, Lincoln Papers, LC; Adams S. Hill to Sydney Howard Gay, August 25, 1862, box 38, Sydney Howard Gay Collection, Columbia University. For the term "hobby," see J. Mills Thornton, *Politics and Power in a Slave Society: Alabama, 1800-1860* (Baton Rouge, 1978), 71.

unit. Historians have sometimes made the same point.[69] Davis wrote those friendly letters on September 6 and 7, 1862.

Those would, however, be the last amicable letters Davis sent Lincoln. On September 12, reports leaked that Lincoln intended to enlist and arm black soldiers.[70] Ten days later, Lincoln issued the preliminary Emancipation Proclamation. Lincoln always tried to balance public opinion against Divine Will, but on this question he apparently tipped the scales away from politics. It struck the secretary of the navy forcefully that Lincoln saw freeing the slaves as consistent with Divine Will. While Lincoln did not indulge religious sentiment loosely, he sheltered himself from the slings and arrows of his critics through his belief in predestination. In 1861, as he journeyed to Washington to become president, making numerous speeches along the way, Lincoln had pronounced himself "exceedingly anxious" to preserve the Union, the Constitution, and liberty in accordance with the original idea behind the American Revolution, "and I shall be most happy indeed if I shall be an humble instrument in the hands of the Almighty."[71] "His mind was fixed," Welles observed on September 22 after hearing Lincoln unveil his emancipation plans to the cabinet. Such confidence might seem surprising in a politician turning against public opinion but not so surprising for a morally certain believer in universal principles. When one of his assistants tried to bring him up to speed on newspaper reaction, the president impatiently dismissed him, saying he had studied the matter and knew more about it than the journalists.[72]

[69] Garrett Davis to Abraham Lincoln, September 7, 1862, series 1, general correspondence, 1833-1916, Lincoln Papers, LC.

[70] "What the Cry for Emancipation Means," *New York Times*, September 12, 1862.

[71] "Address to the New Jersey Senate at Trenton, New Jersey," February 21, 1861, Basler, ed., *Collected Works*, 4:236; Don E. Fehrenbacher, *The Slaveholding Republic: An Account of the United States Government's Relations to Slavery* (New York, 2001), 309; Abraham Lincoln, Proclamation, September 22, 1862, 12 *U.S. Statutes at Large*, 12, No. 16, 1267 (1862). For Lincoln's religion, the best sources are, in addition to Fehrenbacher, Burton, *The Age of Lincoln*, 114-16, and Carwardine, *Lincoln: A Life of Purpose and Power*, 32-44.

[72] Beale, ed., *Diary of Gideon Welles*, 1:142-43; Michael Burlingame and John R. Turner Ettlinger, eds., *Inside Lincoln's White House: The Complete Civil War Diary of John Hay* (Carbondale, Ill., 1997), 41.

Public reaction mattered much more to the junior senator from Kentucky. Davis received what he saw as the bad news of emancipation in Kentucky, where he had journeyed after Congress closed its session. His heart sank at the news of Lincoln's "extraordinary" proclamation not because he feared the public might side with Lincoln—he saw no danger of that—but to the contrary because the proclamation so blatantly contradicted popular will, leaving Davis with only "a feeble, palpitating hope for my country." By repudiating public opinion, the president, Davis concluded, threatened constitutional liberty.[73] But all was not hopeless. Davis reassured himself that the people could strike back at the ballot box in the 1862 off-year elections. They did. The Democrats eagerly made the most of Lincoln's proclamation, blasting the Republicans as "Nigger worshippers." Such racist appeals "paid electoral dividends," historian Foner has observed. In New York, for example, the Democrats' racist appeal triumphed, leaving Republicans mortified and the Democrats celebrating with "a grand jollification." To Davis these dividends confirmed his confidence in the people and his heart soared to see "the sane, loyal, and conservative freemen of the North" rising against the president and his policies. "My heart and my hope loomed up again," he said later.[74]

Davis went back to work emboldened to sharpen his criticism of Lincoln, telling his fellow senators in February that he had lost confidence in the administration and criticizing Lincoln's policies as "mischievous and revolutionary." The large majority of the Union people of America, he declared, "are at a loss to determine which threatens the greatest evil, the administration of Jeff Davis or Abraham Lincoln." Davis said that the policies and principles Lincoln had followed at the outset of the war inspired "the people of the United States" to the flag, suggesting that Lincoln now imperiled that

[73] Congress, Senate, Senator Davis of Kentucky speaking on Arrests of Citizens in Delaware, 37th Cong., 3rd sess., Cong. Globe (December 15, 1863), 90.
[74] Foner, *Fiery Trial*, 234-35; "The Election," *New York Times*, November 8, 1862; "Democratic Peace Plans," ibid., November 11, 1862; Davis, Arrests of Citizens in Delaware, 90.

patriotism.[75] Dissatisfaction over emancipation had already surged through parts of the Union army, he warned.[76] Certainly, Lincoln had stripped Kentucky troops of their "heart and enthusiasm" for the fight.[77] Though Davis sharply criticized the president, his rhetoric after the Emancipation Proclamation still remained within the bounds of a loyal opposition. At least some senators still laughed at his jokes; they took his criticisms seriously enough to hear him out and then answer. That they did not flee the hall when he spoke is evident in the published transcripts of his speeches, recording the interruptions to his speeches as his fellow senators posed questions.

When the Thirty-Seventh Congress adjourned on March 3, 1863, Davis again went back to Kentucky for the August election for members of Congress and state offices. He and everyone else in Kentucky saw this election as crucial for deciding the fate of the commonwealth. Union army officers feared the Confederates might try to win victories at the ballot box they could not win on the battlefield. Reports circulated that to influence the election, the Confederate army had decided to send home the Kentuckians in its ranks. To better ensure Unionist success at the polls, the Kentucky legislature enacted a law intended to deny Confederate-sympathizing citizens the right to vote in Kentucky. In May 1862, Davis had tried unsuccessfully to persuade Congress to pass a federal law along similar lines because he feared Confederate soldiers and sympathizers would return to Kentucky and vote.[78] In 1863, some Unionists believed the law could be enforced only by the Union army. Lucian Anderson, a Unionist candidate for Congress, asked the army to station cavalry units at the voting precincts. "Traitors are active," he said.[79] The election probably influenced the Union army commander

<hr />

[75] Congress, Senate, Senator Davis of Kentucky speaking on Conscription Bill, S. No. 511, 37th Cong., 3rd sess., Cong. Globe (February 28, 1863), 1377-78.

[76] Ibid., 1387.

[77] Ibid.

[78] Congress, Senate, Senator Davis of Kentucky speaking on Punishment of Crime and Rebellion, 37th Cong., 2nd sess., Cong. Globe (May 19, 1862), 2196-97. Other senators condemned the proposal as an unconstitutional interference in states' rights.

[79] An Act to Amend Chapter 15 of the Revised Statutes, entitled "Citizens, Expatriation,

at Paducah to order his troops to stop "aiding and abetting" escaping slaves, thus interfering with loyal slave owners' property rights. "Kentucky having been declared a loyal state, the rights of citizens within this command must be respected," Colonel James S. Martin insisted on May 4.[80]

Unionists like Lucian Anderson had good reason to fear the election. "No administration man can be elected in Kentucky," one newspaper said on April 1, 1863. The Union army high command harbored a similar apprehension. On April 11, U.S. Army General-in-Chief Henry W. Halleck instructed the commander of the Department of the Ohio, which included Kentucky, to closely observe one potential Democratic candidate for governor, U.S. Senator Lazarus Powell. Burnside's biographer suggests that Powell served the Confederate cause in Kentucky, since "Confederate operatives looked upon him as a valuable friend." Had Burnside arrested Powell, the Kentuckian would today be as well known as Clement Vallandigham, the Ohio political leader Burnside did arrest and try before a military commission. To guard against voting by anyone sympathizing with the South, Burnside decided to screen potential voters and candidates in a manner without parallel in American history. Army officers issued orders forbidding anyone not "avowedly and unconditionally for the Union" from running for office or voting. Even that was not enough and, at the end of July, Burnside's subordinates enlarged on their original order by forbidding anyone guilty of "uttering disloyal language" from voting or standing for office. Many potential voters lost their right to vote because the army required that they swear an oath not only to unconditionally favor the Union but also to furnish the Union army men and money.[81] The army intended to use such

and Aliens," reprinted in Edward McPherson, *The Political History of the United States of America during the Great Rebellion* (Washington, D.C., 1882), 312; J. T. Bolinger to Ulysses S. Grant, April 29, 1863, box 1, U.S. Army Continental Commands, part 2, RG 393, National Archives and Records Service, Washington, D.C. (hereafter U.S. Army Continental Commands, NARA, Washington, D.C.); J. D. Landrum and others to Alexander Asboth, July 30, 1863, ibid.; Lucian Anderson to Alexander Asboth, July 30, 1863, ibid.

[80] James S. Martin, General Order No. 4, May 4, 1863, box 1, ibid.

[81] H. W. Halleck to Ambrose Burnside, April 11, 1863, in U.S. War Department, *The*

oaths to prevent traitors or Confederate infiltrators from voting, but they could also be seen as insulting Americans' rights to free speech and open elections. In the days before the election, the Hungarian-born general Alexander Asboth, commander of the Union army in western Kentucky, specified particular counties where he wanted his men to "watch over and control" voting. Union army officers not only forbade disloyal men from running for office, they also gave political advice to Unionists, devising strategies for electoral success. Asboth urged one Unionist candidate for Congress to withdraw from the race "for the benefit of our common cause." The night before the election, the army perfected its plans, dispatching cavalry and infantry to polling places with strict instructions to arrive no later than six o'clock in the morning.[82]

Some Kentucky voters saw the presence of the military as heavy-handed and intrusive. "People had to vote just as the military saw fit," one observer grumbled. The Union side won in Kentucky. A former Union army officer became governor, but Davis had no doubt whatsoever that most voters actually opposed Lincoln. The manner in which the army controlled the election very likely increased hostility to the Republicans. Burnside found it increasingly difficult, in fact nearly impossible, to recruit soldiers in Kentucky. In 1864, Kentucky voters erased any lingering doubts about their hostility to Lincoln when they chose George McClellan over Lincoln nearly three to one.[83]

War of the Rebellion: A Compilation of the Official Records of the Union and Confederate Armies, 128 vols. (Washington, D.C., 1880-1901), series 1, vol. 23, part 2, 230; Alexander Asboth to Stephen Hurlbut, July 30, 1863, ibid., 568-69; Special Order No. 159, July 14, 1863, ibid., 570; General Order No. 47, July 29, 1863, ibid., 570-71; General Order No. 120, July 31, 1863, ibid., 572; McPherson, *Political History of the United* States, 313-14; William Marvel, *Burnside* (Chapel Hill, 1991), 234-35.

[82] Alexander Asboth to Major W. R. Rowley, July 31, 1863, 121, vol. 93, Letters Sent, e. 986, U.S. Army Continental Commands, part 2, RG 393, NARA, Washington, D.C.; Alexander Asboth to Thomas H. Owens, July 31, 1863, 122, ibid.; T. H. Harris to Brig. Genl. N. B. Buford, August 2, 1863, 123-24, ibid.; T. H. Harris to Major W. R. Rowley, August 2, 1863, 127-28, ibid.

[83] "Kentucky Election," *Louisville Journal,* July 25, 1863, reprinted in *Boston Daily Advertiser,* July 30, 1863; Marvel, *Burnside,* 246; Lowell H. Harrison, *The Civil War in Kentucky* (Lexington, Ky., 1975), 84-85. It may be worth noting that Lincoln's showing in 1864, though very poor

White Kentuckians' increasing hostility to Lincoln widened the wedge between Davis and the president. Davis journeyed back to Washington where, on January 5, 1864, he introduced resolutions calling on northern voters to "revolt" against their war leaders "and take this great matter into their own hands." He accused Lincoln of subverting free speech, freedom of the press, free suffrage, and the constitutions of the states and the United States. He charged Lincoln with double-dealing, professing to vindicate the law, when in reality he plotted the unconstitutional and total subversion of slavery. Davis's intemperate language so infuriated Senator Henry Wilson of Massachusetts that he tried unsuccessfully to have the Kentucky senator expelled as a traitor.[84] Davis wrote his resolutions at a time when members of Congress increasingly saw not just secession but the persistent commitment to white supremacy as treasonous. A year later, Timothy Howe wrote that the rebellion had not just been against the Constitution but "upon the great law of human right" as well, "an assault not merely upon the divine idea of equal rights of all men . . . but upon the American idea."[85]

Davis devoted the larger portion of his resolutions to denouncing Lincoln's interference with the 1863 elections, putting himself on the side of free speech and fair elections, suggesting that the elections more than emancipation had triggered his break with Lincoln. It is more likely that the increasing hostility of Kentucky voters, his constituents, toward the president influenced Davis. His constituents' "extreme revulsion" against Lincoln after the proclamation left Davis "a changed man," historian E. Merton Coulter wrote.[86] Believing in popular constitutionalism as expressed through the states, Davis no doubt felt compelled to escalate his own rhetoric against the president if that was what the white voters of Kentucky wanted.

at 30 percent, actually improved on his vote in 1860 of 0.93 percent.

[84] Congress, Senate, Senator Davis of Kentucky speaking on Presidential Power, 38th Cong., 1st sess., Cong. Globe (January 5, 1864), 96; Congress, Senate, Senator Wilson of Massachusetts speaking on the Proposed Expulsion of Mr. Davis, ibid. (January 13, 1864), 174.

[85] Timothy Howe to E. G. Ryan, January 1865, box 1, Howe Papers, State Historical Society of Wisconsin.

[86] Coulter, *Civil War and Readjustment in Kentucky*, 208.

And escalate he did. He charged Lincoln with perpetuating a crime so great that it unmasked his pretense as a statesman, revealing a "mere political charlatan," a "consummate dissembler," and a "sagacious demagogue." Returning obsessively to the 1863 elections, Davis accused the Republicans of using military power to steal the elections in the border states. Through the spring of 1864, Davis continued to criticize Burnside's declaration of martial law the previous August. He complained that candidates had gone to prison and soldiers had bullied the voters in an "armed overthrow of the laws of those [Border] States." Davis linked the 1863 election irregularities with Lincoln's moves toward emancipation; in essence, he charged Lincoln with violating the will of the people not only by freeing the slaves but by stealing the election as well. To see the democratic process subverted and slavery illegitimately abolished were but two sides of the same tyrannical coin, Davis orated in speeches delivered through the spring of 1864.[87]

In such speeches, Davis echoed what many of his constituents said. In 1864, the county judge in Morgantown warned James Speed that Kentucky voters had "one very serious objection" to the Republican Party, "and that is its manifest tendency to negro equality."[88] That critic went with the Democrats, but by that year, if not sooner, Lincoln's policies discomfited even Kentucky Republicans. Party stalwart Benjamin Bristow had been so outraged by secession that he personally raised, armed, and led a regiment against the Confederate invasion of Kentucky. As U.S. attorney he would later enforce the Civil Rights Act in Kentucky so vigorously that his biographer titled that chapter of his life "A Champion of Civil Rights." But now, in June, he said that while he fully expected to campaign for the Republicans that summer, he dreaded confronting "at every point" complaints that the Lincoln administration used force to illegally

[87] Davis, Amendments to the Constitution, S. No. 16, 107; "Kentucky State Election," *Daily Cleveland Herald*, August 2, 1863; "The Kentucky Election," *Boston Daily Advertiser*, August 6, 1863; "The Kentucky Election," *Boston Liberator*, August 21, 1863.

[88] B. F. O. Guffy to James Speed Morgantown Ky., March 19, 1864, folder 37, Speed Family Papers, 1813-1981, Filson Historical Society.

emancipate Kentucky slaves. Union soldiers sometimes invaded Kentucky plantations to take "*by force*" all the blacks, he complained and blasted such "outrages" as indefensible.[89] A year later, Joshua Speed, James's brother, called extending the vote to former slaves a "blunder" no less absurd than secession. The federal government had no more business intruding into voting than it had interfering with local dog laws, Joshua Speed fumed.[90] To white Kentucky Republicans, the high-handed tactics of the army won recruits for the pro-Confederate side at an alarming rate. In 1866, Bristow warned that disloyalty to the federal government raged stronger in Kentucky than at any time since 1860.[91]

While Davis accurately reflected the views of many Kentuckians, Washington was a different story. Davis's fellow senators increasingly dismissed him as a disagreeable old nag. Instead of laughing at his witticisms, they made him the butt of their jokes. To them, his positions had become outrageous. Davis still believed that the Union army could rightly seize property in the seceded states, but he denied that the national government could emancipate slaves in states that had not seceded from the Union. He battled against the proposed Thirteenth Amendment by arguing that, "The power to amend is but the power to improve." Ending slavery, he said, so contradicted the Founders' original intent that it threatened free and popular government. If such a revolutionary act had to be taken, he pleaded, it should not be done in the heat of the moment, in the midst of war but only in "settled and stable repose" after sectional passions had abated. To many Kentuckians, this seemed a reasonable position; some dared hope that slavery might be resurrected, but even those willing to acknowledge the demise of slavery did not like to think that the Federal government could constitutionally impose

[89] Ben Bristow to James Speed, June 13, 1864, folder 40, ibid.; Ross A. Webb, *Benjamin Helm Bristow: Border State Politician* (Lexington, Ky., 1969), 23, 50-70.

[90] J. F. Speed to James, September 15, 1865, folder 11, Speed Family Papers, 1813-1981, Filson Historical Society.

[91] B. H. Bristow to James Speed, July 11, 1866, folder 15, ibid.

abolition on the states.[92]

In April, Reverdy Johnson of Maryland patiently answered Davis. Like Davis, Johnson had been a border-state Unionist and a Whig, but more than Davis he had carved out a reputation as a respected constitutionalist, regularly arguing cases before the Supreme Court. He agreed that the states were sovereign, "in a certain sense," but he denied that the United States was not equally sovereign. The next portion of Johnson's speech closely resembled what Davis himself had said before 1863. The Founders had tried exclusive state sovereignty with the Articles of Confederation but had been forced to reject that formula in favor of national sovereignty in the people. No one would deny, he asserted, that had the Founders wanted to end slavery in the name of the people, they could have done so at the founding. Acknowledging that obvious truth, he continued, "why is it that it cannot be done by them now?" He then went on to deny that the Founders looked at African Americans as not entitled to the rights they called inalienable, "merely because they differed in color from themselves."[93]

The 1864 presidential election rendered Davis's opposition to the Thirteenth Amendment untenable. Though Lincoln did poorly in Kentucky, he decisively won nationally with 55 percent of the vote. This victory electrified opponents of slavery as it allowed them to argue that the public supported ending slavery through a constitutional amendment. One Republican wrote that "there ought to be no difficulty" now in passing such an amendment, "in view of the popular approval of the anti-slavery policy in the Presidential vote." This observer believed that a constitutional amendment would make the country safe from weak-kneed Northerners seeking to accommodate returning southern states by allowing them to continue slavery

---

[92] Davis, Amendments to the Constitution, S. No. 16, 105 (first and second quotations), 106 (third and fourth quotations); Davis, Presidential Power, 96; Wilson, Proposed Expulsion of Mr. Davis, 174; B. H. Bristow to James Speed, July 11, 1866, folder 15, Speed Family Papers, 1813-1981, Filson Historical Society; W. D. Black to James Speed, March 7, 1864, folder 37, ibid.

[93] Congress, Senate, Senator Johnson of Maryland speaking on the Amendment of the Constitution, S. No. 16, 38th Cong., 1st sess., Cong. Globe (April 5, 1864), 1422-23.

under the name of "magnanimity & generosity."[94] The Thirteenth Amendment had an even greater significance for Kentucky than for the seceded states as it upended Garrett Davis's constitutional argument against abolishing slavery in the loyal states. To Davis, the fact that his enemies had the power to graft their emancipationist vision onto the Constitution in defiance of the Founders' original intent did not legitimize their efforts or make them less insane.

Unable to derail the Thirteenth Amendment from congressional approval, Davis attacked it with racist appeals. He proposed changing the proposed Thirteenth Amendment by adding: "But no negro, or person whose mother or grandmother is or was a negro, shall be a citizen of the United States." Both Kentucky senators voted for this, but it failed miserably and quickly, gaining only five votes. Failing in that, Davis tried again, proposing an amendment that would have resettled the freed slaves "among the several States and Territories thereof in proportion to the white population of each State and Territory to the aggregate population of those of African descent."[95] This could not have been a serious proposal; Davis sought only to expose what he saw as northern hypocrisy. Perhaps he thought that he had made a joke, but the *Congressional Globe* reporter recorded no laughter, and the Senate immediately voted it down.

With slavery constitutionally dead, Davis shifted his focus to compensation, once again making a constitutional argument. His long battle to compensate slaveholders for their slaves lost to the Union army continued his lifelong commitment to property rights but as a bonus also reflected the views of his constituents. In 1864, Congress passed a law requiring the secretary of war to appoint commissioners in each of the slave states represented in Congress to award loyal owners of slaves a compensation, not exceeding three hundred dollars, for each slave mustered into military service.[96] Davis denounced

---

[94] John Jay to William D. Kelley, November 21, 1864, box 1, Kelley Family Collection, Butler Library, Columbia University, New York.

[95] Davis, Amendment of the Constitution, 1425.

[96] An Act to Amend the Act Entitled An Act for Enrolling and Calling out the National Forces, and for Other Purposes, *U.S. Statutes at Large*, 13, sec. 24, 11 (1864).

this law as inadequate, three hundred dollars was too low in his estimation, and he argued that the Constitution required that any figure
come from courts and juries, the judicial process, and due process of
law, not by legislative fiat. Davis tilted at that windmill for hours at
a time, but, in fact, just getting the three hundred dollars proved no
easy feat. He wrote later that members of the Kentucky congressional
delegation repeatedly called on Lincoln and Secretary of War Edwin
M. Stanton but could not get the commissioners appointed. Davis
blamed "the malign influence of the Secretary over the President"
for his failure to get Kentucky slaveholders their money.[97]

In 1865, in the waning days of the Thirty-eighth Congress, the
entire Kentucky delegation met to plot what they could do for their
slaveholding constituents. Davis wrote that they agreed that so long
as that "bad man" Stanton remained secretary of war, their cause
was hopeless. So, when Stanton did finally appoint the commissioners, his move surprised Davis. But surprise quickly turned to dis-
pleasure when Davis realized that Stanton had found three "Radical
Abolitionists" to fill the slots. Davis fumed that the secretary of war
had concocted yet another scheme to "visit Kentucky with injustice
and oppression." Davis took his complaint to President Andrew
Johnson, demanding that he forestall the appointments. Johnson
answered that he would take the matter to his cabinet, which he did.
Johnson overruled Stanton and put the appointments on hold. In a
public letter, Davis expressed confidence that Johnson would see to
it that that only "honest men" became commissioners. That hope
ended on March 30, 1867, when Congress enacted a joint resolution
suspending the bill and directing the secretary of war to dissolve the
commission.[98]

Garrett Davis and many white Kentucky slaveholders believed

[97] Garrett Davis, "Letter from Hon. Garrett Davis to the People of Kentucky," *New
York Times*, October 15, 1866.
[98] Ibid.; Davis to Andrew Johnson, August 20, 1866, Paul H. Bergeron et al., eds., *The
Papers of Andrew Johnson*, 16 vols. (Knoxville, 1967-2000), vol. 11, *August 1866–January 1867*
(Knoxville, 1994), 99; Joint Resolution Suspending all Proceedings in Relation to Payment
for Slaves Drafted or Received as Volunteers in the Military Service of the United States,
U.S. Statutes at Large, 15, No. 31, 29 (1867).

that Lincoln's administration betrayed the Constitution when it interfered with the 1863 Kentucky state election and emancipated the
slaves. They believed that both acts lacked public support and therefore abused popular constitutionalism. On this point, Davis took a
position not so different from that of some leading Republicans in
1861. Military occupation ended slavery, Jacob M. Howard wrote,
and Davis heartily agreed. But Howard saw emancipation in the
seceded states as a gateway to total emancipation. "Man proposes,
God disposes," Howard wrote, recognizing a higher power at work
undermining politicians' need to protect slavery.[99] That was not how
Davis read the Constitution. States that had not broken the original
covenant establishing the Union had a continuing constitutional right
to their slaves. They had not violated the original bargain, why should
they pay the price of emancipation?

For Garrett Davis the Constitution did not change during the
Civil War, but Congress had. When he took the floor to speak, his
desk covered with reference books and notes, senators reported that
their "hearts sank within us," knowing he would drone on for hours
following lines of argument most in Congress had long abandoned.[100]
In one speech, Davis tried to take the president's side but senators
strained to grasp his point, one senator writing that "I *suppose*" he
defended the president's veto.[101] When he outlined his objections
to Trumbull's bill, he met the kind of sarcasm he himself had once
mastered. Trumbull used language he would not have dared in 1862,
calling Davis's objections "absurd" and "preposterous." When he
mistakenly called Davis a "long gentleman," several senators immediately understood the joke and quickly interjected a correction:
"You mean the short gentleman's long speech." As laughter swept
through the hall, Trumbull smilingly corrected himself. The tide
had turned. Trumbull was no longer in the beleaguered minority,

[99] Howard to Charles Newett Niles, December 23, 1861, box 5, Jacob M. Howard Papers,
Detroit Public Library.
[100] Timothy Howe to Grace Howe, April 7, 1866, box 1, Howe Papers, State Historical
Society of Wisconsin.
[101] Timothy Howe to Grace Howe, February 21, 1866, box 1, ibid.

but Davis was and in a minority so small it sometimes included only himself and Powell.[102]

Garrett Davis's journey from a respected and influential states-man to a pathetic object of ridicule is a part of our Civil War history, though a part not yet carefully analyzed by historians. He believed in a kind of constitutionalism both static and popular before the war and could not adjust to the new ideas Republicans promoted during and after the conflict. Many people, in and out of Congress, agreed with Davis before the war. During the war, and after emancipation, most congressional Republicans reached a different conclusion even as Davis clung to his antebellum notions. Polling data does not exist, but election results and the kind of qualitative evidence historians often use strongly suggests that Davis accurately represented the thinking of most white Kentuckians. Even such a progressive figure as Benjamin Bristow could not credibly defend military emancipation in a state that had not seceded from the Union; he realized that the people would shun him if he tried. To Davis such a popular com-mitment to a constitutional question could not be ignored. Davis, then, followed the kind of popular constitutionalism some scholars have recently argued that gave the power to interpret constitutional law to the people. "It was the community at large . . . that controlled the meaning of the Constitution," Larry D. Kramer has written.[103] Davis's kind of constitutionalism held that the public had to express its power through their states rather than Congress, but it seems at least plausible that most Americans also agreed with that. But not Lincoln. To Lincoln, Divine Will predestined events, and as president he had to steer public opinion toward that Will.

Davis died in 1872, railing against civil rights laws to the end, but his idea of a static constitution not only survived the Civil War intact but did so with such robust strength that some white people would not accept even the Civil War amendments as truly legitimate. In 1871, Lincoln's former secretary of the navy grumbled that the Four-

---

[102] Congress, Senate, Senator Trumbull of Illinois speaking on Freedmen's Bureau, S.B. No. 60, 39th Cong., 1st sess., Cong. Globe (January 25, 1866), 420.

[103] Kramer, "The Interest of the Man," 698.

teenth and Fifteenth Amendments merely followed "the superficial forms" the Constitution prescribed for the amending process, but, Gideon Welles continued, "in their very inceptions they are usurpations." Congress drafted them at a time when not all the states had been represented in Congress "as they should have been." Had the South been represented, "those amendments, as they are called, could never have got through congress in the first instance." While Welles recognized that he had no choice but to "submit" to them, he could not "adopt or sanction them" because they did not truly have the support of all white Americans and contradicted the original intent of the framers.[104] In 1866, white Northerners still worried about "interfering with the internal relations of the states any further than the war has compelled and made necessary." A continued commitment to white supremacy lay behind many fears of "centralization." As one northern voter wrote, "Without disparaging the African, it is nevertheless incontrovertible [that] we and the world must look to the whites of that region" for leadership.[105] Such attitudes foreshadowed what was to come. The violent eruption of racial violence after Reconstruction seems more explicable when the doubts of Garrett Davis and others of like mind about Republicans' Reconstruction constitutionalism are taken into account. That violence grew out of a continuing constitutional commitment to the Framers' original intent as perceived by many white Americans.

[104] Gideon Welles to James Doolittle, August 29, 1871, folder 3, box 3, James Rood Doolittle Papers, State Historical Society of Wisconsin, Madison, Wisconsin.

[105] C. S. Sholes to James Doolittle, January 1, 1866, folder 6, box 2, ibid.

LINCOLN'S JUDGE ADVOCATE GENERAL: JOSEPH HOLT OF KENTUCKY

By Elizabeth D. Leonard

Born in Stephensport, Kentucky, in January 1807, Joseph Holt was not the first judge advocate general of the army, but the post he assumed on September 3, 1862, had changed dramatically since the war began, not unlike the Federal army itself, which had grown from a small force of about sixteen thousand regular soldiers into a massive conglomerate of regular and volunteer regiments in which more than 2.2 million men served before the war came to a close. Prior to the Civil War, the Federal government "agency" assigned to monitor the application of military law had consisted of a single bureaucrat, whose responsibilities had been limited to maintaining the army court-martial records. On July 17, 1862, however, the U.S. Congress substantially expanded the size and purview of the judge advocate general's office, assigning to its head the rank, pay, and al-

ELIZABETH D. LEONARD is the John J. and Cornelia V. Gibson Professor of History, Emerita, at Colby College in Waterville, Maine. She earned her PhD in U.S. history from the University of California, Riverside, in 1992, and is the author of a number of articles and seven books on the Civil War era, including: *Yankee Women: Gender Battles in the Civil War* (1994); *All the Daring of the Soldier: Women of the Civil War Armies* (1999); *Lincoln's Avengers: Justice, Revenge, and Reunion after the Civil War* (2004); *Men of Color to Arms! Black Soldiers, Indian Wars, and the Quest for Equality* (2010); *Lincoln's Forgotten Ally: Judge Advocate General Joseph Holt of Kentucky* (2011), which was co-winner of the 2012 Gilder Lehrman Lincoln Prize; and *Benjamin Franklin Butler: A Noisy, Fearless Life* (2022). She is also the proud mother of two wonderful sons, Anthony and Joseph.

This article is adapted from *Lincoln's Forgotten Ally: Judge Advocate General Joseph Holt of Kentucky* (pages 158-99), published by the University of North Carolina Press. I thank the press for giving permission to republish this material.

189

lowance of a colonel of cavalry and authorizing him to appoint a team of assistant judge advocates, each of whom served with the rank and pay of a major. The tasks assigned to the office also multiplied. Henceforth, the tasks included (but were not limited to) receiving, revising, and recording the proceedings of all courts-martial, courts of inquiry, and military commissions conducted by the army; providing reports to the secretary of war in connection with those cases that required the action of the president; dealing with applications for clemency received either by the president or the secretary of war; overseeing—and in many cases personally preparing—the charges against persons being brought to trial; rendering opinions on any and all questions of military law (or on the internal legal workings of the War Department), as requested by the president, the secretary of war, or the commanding general of the army; and assisting in the review of cases brought for appeal. In sum, the judge advocate general of the army became the primary adjudicator of military law in much the same way that the attorney general was the primary arbiter of the law in the civil realm.[1]

A lifelong Democrat and an unshakeable Unionist who had served as President James Buchanan's patent-office commissioner (1857-59), postmaster general (1859-60), and secretary of war (December 31, 1860–March 4, 1861), Holt became the first judge advocate general under the July 1862 act. Virtually from the moment he took office, he was inundated with the work of organizing, conducting, and reviewing the results of the seemingly endless stream of legal cases that came under his authority, many of which demanded careful analysis, thorough reconsideration and review, and the production of additional and often lengthy written reports. Holt's duties required him to consult directly and on a regular basis with President Abraham

---

[1] J. W. Clous, "Judge Advocate General's Department," http://www.history.army.mil/ books/R&H/R&H-JAG.htm. See also U.S. House of Representatives Report No. 74, Army Staff Reorganization, 42nd Cong., 3rd sess., February 2, 1873 (Washington, D.C., 1873), 204-7, in which Holt provides an excellent history of the post. See also Thomas Keys Bland, "Were the Lincoln Conspirators Dealt Justice?" *Lincoln Herald* 80 (1978): 38, and Mary Bernard Allen, "Joseph Holt: Judge Advocate General (1862-1865)" (PhD dissertation, University of Chicago, 1927), 86-87.

Lincoln, whose opinion and decision-making power were frequently essential components of the process, especially in cases where a defendant faced dismissal from the army or execution. Investigation into the court-martial files of the judge advocate general's office during this period indicates that Lincoln, Holt, and the president's secretary, John G. Nicolay, typically met in the morning, Holt making the half-block trip to the Executive Mansion from his War Department office on Seventeenth Street NW, near F Street. On some occasions, the trio considered more than seventy cases in a single sitting; at least once, they spent six straight hours in consultation.[2]

For each case that he brought to Lincoln's attention, Holt summarized the charges, the evidence, the sentence, the opinions presented by previous reviewers, and his own recommendations. When Holt and the president disagreed on how to handle a particular case, it was typically Holt who took the harder line, though his often extended written opinions also reveal him to be capable of demonstrating "compassionate good sense." Moreover, Holt was disinclined to try to impose his will on the president. "I certainly have no disposition to oppose the impulses of your kind heart in the matter," he wrote on one occasion, regarding a case where their opinions differed sharply. Holt himself admitted that Lincoln's overarching desire to save a life, if he could do so, tended to make him the more forgiving

---

[2] Thomas P. Lowry, *Don't Shoot That Boy!: Abraham Lincoln and Military Justice* (New York, 2002), 93; see also Lowry's The Index Project, Inc. (www.theindexproject.com). In Roy P. Basler, ed., *Collected Works of Abraham Lincoln*, 9 vols. (New Brunswick, N.J., 1953-55), 8:539, it is indicated that Lincoln and Holt reviewed seventy-one cases on April 21, 1864. There were many other days on which they viewed thirty or forty cases. There are also a number of notes in Holt's papers from John Nicolay, summoning him to meet with Lincoln. See, for example, John Nicolay to Joseph Holt, June 1, 1863, container 39; John Nicolay to Holt, February 13, 1864, container 42; John Nicolay to Holt, April 13, 1864, container 43, Joseph Holt Papers, Library of Congress, Washington, D.C. (hereafter Holt Papers, LC). See also Holt to Nicolay, February 13, 1864, Abraham Lincoln Papers, Library of Congress, Washington, D.C. (hereafter Lincoln Papers, LC). In addition to all of his regular responsibilities as judge advocate general, Holt received scores of letters from strangers as well as friends, relatives, and acquaintances, seeking his assistance with a host of different concerns. See, for example, John B. Bland to Holt, January 16, 1863, container 36; George P. Finlay to Holt, February 20, 1863, container 37; Jane P. Holt to Holt, August 24, 1863, container 39; Nannie W. Dorsey to Holt, October 3, 1864, container 45; S. E. Moseley to Holt, December 7, 1864, container 45; Washington Dorsey Gibbs to Holt, December 14, 1864, container 46, Holt Papers, LC.

of the two men. Holt, too, valued life. But he was also determined to punish rigorously those who strove to destroy the nation, as well as those who were derelict in their duty to save it. Nevertheless, if one detailed analysis of more than fifteen thousand cases that came under Lincoln and Holt's review during the war is in fact correct, the president and his judge advocate general agreed more than 90 percent of the time.[3]

When he appointed Holt judge advocate general, Lincoln was on the verge of issuing two major proclamations, both of which he fully expected Holt to endorse and implement. The first came just days after Federal forces drove Confederate general Robert E. Lee to abandon his invasion of Maryland following the battle of Antietam. On September 22, Lincoln issued his preliminary Emancipation Proclamation, which built upon the foundation of the Second Confiscation Act that Congress had passed two months earlier, providing that slaves of all those who supported or aided the rebellion would be free when they came within Union control. In addition, the act empowered the president to employ freed slaves for the purpose of suppressing the Confederate rebellion, even as soldiers. Lincoln's preliminary Emancipation Proclamation broadened the implications of the Second Confiscation Act by putting Americans on notice that as of January 1, 1863, "all persons held as slaves, within any state, or designated part of a state, the people whereof shall then be in rebellion against the United States shall be then, thenceforward, and forever free." Thanks to the action of Congress that summer, these former slaves could now be enlisted to serve the Federal cause, militarily and otherwise.[4]

Two days after he issued his preliminary Emancipation Proclamation, Lincoln also suspended the writ of habeas corpus, opening the door wide for the military trial not just of enlisted men and their

[3] Lowry, *Don't Shoot That Boy!*, ii, 13, 18, 21, 53; Holt to Abraham Lincoln, February 17, 1865, container 3, Lincoln Papers, LC.

[4] James M. McPherson, *Ordeal by Fire: The Civil War and Reconstruction* (New York, 2001), 316-17. On emancipation, see Allen C. Guelzo, *Lincoln's Emancipation Proclamation: The End of Slavery in America* (New York, 2006); Michael Vorenberg, *Final Freedom:, The Civil War, the Abolition of Slavery, and the Thirteenth Amendment* (New York, 2004).

officers but also, by means of military commissions, of "all Rebels and Insurgents, their aiders and abettors within the United States, and all persons discouraging volunteer enlistments, resisting militia drafts, or guilty of any disloyal practice," such as "affording comfort to Rebels against the authority of the United States." As a result, on top of all the strictly military cases for which they were responsible, it fell to Judge Advocate General Holt and his assistants to evaluate the evidence against civilians accused of disloyalty in any form and to determine whether or not those civilians should be subjected to trial in a military court. Clearly, both Holt's workload and his sheer power in connection with the interpretation, application, and enforcement of military law over soldiers as well as civilians were immense. So, too, was his sense of personal and professional accountability for ensuring the safety and survival of the nation by maintaining order in the army, keeping Federal soldiers focused on and committed to their goal of destroying the Confederacy, and disarming civilian enemies of the state and its military arm wherever they appeared.[5]

Although each of Lincoln's September 1862 proclamations was distinct in terms of its specific content, the consequences of the two were tightly intertwined. Among other things, both proclamations indicated that eighteen months into the war, Lincoln was prepared to renounce his earlier "soft war" tactics by which he had originally sought to train the sights of the Federal army as completely as possible on the enemies in Confederate uniform rather than on the civilian supporters of the rebellion and their human and other property. Lincoln's revised "hard war" approach identified Confederate civilians and any of their allies located in the border states and across the North as just as responsible for the war as the army and the political leadership of the Confederacy. The suppression of the support of

---

[5] McPherson, *Ordeal by Fire*, 317. Lincoln originally suspended the writ of habeas corpus on April 27, 1861; in May, the Supreme Court ruled this suspension unconstitutional, but Lincoln did not bend to the ruling. The September 24, 1862, proclamation was a restatement and expansion of his previous position, grounded on the notion that "the Constitution provided for suspension [of the writ] in cases of rebellion or invasion where public safety required it." See E. B. Long, *The Civil War Day by Day: An Almanac, 1861-1865* (New York, 1971), 79. President Andrew Johnson restored habeas corpus on April 2, 1866.

civilians for the Confederate war effort—even, if necessary, their demoralization by means of the loss of their property—had become as much a Federal war aim as victory on the battlefield. Henceforth, civilians on either side of the border between slavery and freedom could much more easily be held legally liable for endangering the welfare of the nation and the Federal soldiers.[6]

Slaveholders, moreover, faced not just the possible loss of their human property but also the specter of men whom they had held in bondage being handed weapons and ammunition to fight them. As such, it is hardly an exaggeration to say that Lincoln's September 1862 proclamations, and his appointment of the famously stern and resolute Holt to help enforce and implement them, raised the emotional stakes in the war to an unprecedented level. For unwavering Unionists willing to sacrifice some measure of civil liberty in order to win the war, save the nation, and free the slaves, Holt's appointment along with Lincoln's proclamations offered cause for celebration. For those who aimed to preserve slavery by destroying the Union, however, they offered reasons to fight even harder. And for many in the North and on the border who had supported what they understood to be a war for the reestablishment of the Union *as it was*, the combination of the preliminary Emancipation Proclamation, the suspension of the writ of habeas corpus, and the appointment of Holt served as an incitement to consider joining the opposition.[7]

Holt fully recognized the many implications for public sentiment, soldiers' morale, and even the abolitionists' optimism of Lincoln's September 1862 proclamations, and not long after he accepted his new job, he took the opportunity to make his own position clear. In an open letter to Hiram Barney, the staunchly pro-Lincoln, antislavery Republican collector of customs for the port of New York,

[6] For a thorough discussion of the difference between the "soft war" and "hard war" approaches, see Mark Grimsley, *The Hard Hand of War: Union Military Policy toward Southern Civilians, 1861-1865* (New York, 1995).

[7] "The Speech of Hon. C. A. Wickliffe, of Kentucky, on the Bills to Confiscate the Property and Free from Servitude the slaves of Rebels, and other Matters," May 26, 1862, Washington, D.C., 7, 15, Kentucky Historical Society Collections, Kentucky Historical Society, Frankfort, Kentucky.

Holt wrote vigorously in favor of the president's recent course of action and the preservation of the Union at all costs. The suspension of habeas corpus, Holt argued, was a necessary act in order to suppress debilitating opposition to the heroic efforts of the Federal army. And then, although he had been raised in a slaveholding family and had owned slaves himself, Holt openly and unequivocally acknowledged that slavery and the Union could no longer both be saved, and that in his mind there was no question of sacrificing the latter for the former. Slavery, Holt insisted, was not only a great pillar of Confederate strength but also a ghastly offense against human rights. "No human institution," he declared, "no earthly interest shall ever by me be weighed in the scales against the life of my country," especially "an institution, the fountain of whose being—the African slave-trade—the laws of my country have for more than forty years denounced as a crime worthy of death." Here Holt came down firmly on the side of the opponents of slavery. For the rest of his life, it was a stance he neither changed nor regretted.[8]

In his letter to Hiram Barney, which Barney subsequently had published in the *New York Times*, Holt also made it clear that he saw no other option for defeating the Confederacy than the hard-war approach. At the same time, however, he knew better than to believe that all Unionists in the North and along the border believed the same way. Indeed, he expressed considerable concern about the emergence of what he called a "conspiracy" of troublemakers within the Democratic Party in the North who sought to end the war as quickly as possible and restore the Union with slavery intact. For Holt, these so-called Peace Democrats, or Copperheads, constituted an exceedingly dangerous source of aid and comfort to the rebellion. In his mind, Copperheads were hardly different from the fire-eating southern nationalists who had started the war in the first place. Both groups, though few in number, were nevertheless mighty in spirit and corrupting influence. Significantly, both had demonstrated their ability

[8] T. S. Bell to Holt, March 24, 1863, container 38, Holt Papers, LC; Jesse Kincheloe to Holt, January 18, 1863, container 36, ibid.; Holt to Hiram Barney, October 25, 1862, quoted in the *New York Times*, November 13, 1862.

to turn the heads of the otherwise typically moderate and law-abiding masses of their regions and across the nation, making it necessary for the government to fight a war on two fronts against the Confederate South and against the Copperheads. Still, Holt's primary focus was on the battlefield, where he hoped to hear soon that the Federals had made "an immediate, bold and aggressive movement upon the enemy." "If those who are in the front will not go forward," he wrote, "the public safety will demand that they be assigned to positions in the rear." Here there is no doubt that Holt was thinking specifically of Major General George B. McClellan, whose repeated failures to launch decisive attacks on the Confederate armies he confronted, especially in light of his stunning hubris, had stretched the patience of many in the administration, including Holt, Secretary of War Edwin M. Stanton, and Lincoln himself. As it turned out, just two weeks after Holt wrote to Barney, Lincoln fired "Little Mac" once and for all. "I congratulate you on having reach[ed] the goal, upon which your eyes have long been fixed," wrote his longtime Louisville friend, T. S. Bell, when he heard the news. "If it had been done 8 or 9 months ago, the land would now be rejoicing in the prospect of a thorough settlement of all its troubles."[9]

As his letter to Barney makes clear, from the moment he took office Holt's intention was to support the president and his policies unwaveringly, to put his muscle and that of his staff firmly behind emancipation, and to make use of all the legal means at his command to move immediately and boldly against the enemies of the nation, wherever he found them. O. M. Dorman of Baltimore wrote with enthusiasm, "when I [say] that there is no voice in the whole land which can touch the patriotic heart of Americans like yours, it is not flattery." Not all of Holt's correspondents were so supportive, however. Hugh Campbell was certain that Lincoln's proclamations would severely

[9] Hiram Barney to Holt, November 7 and 11, 1862, container 35, Holt Papers, LC; Holt to Hiram Barney, October 25, 1862, quoted in the *New York Times*, November 13, 1862. See also T. S. Bell to Holt, November 16, 1862, container 35, Holt Papers, LC. For a thorough study of the wartime history of the Copperheads, see Jennifer L. Weber, *Copperheads: The Rise and Fall of Lincoln's Opponents in the North* (New York, 2008). On McClellan, see Stephen W. Sears, *George B. McClellan: The Young Napoleon* (1988; repr., Cambridge, Mass., 1999).

damage the ship of state the president was attempting to pilot. In an earlier letter, Campbell had implored Holt to advise the president that a "dignified retreat" from his recent policies, particularly on the point of emancipation, offered the only hope for peace. "Can you not prevail on him," Campbell had groaned on that occasion, "to be entirely silent on 'negro-ology?'" Now, although he admitted that Holt's letter to Barney offered a good example of his felicity of language and his "unconditional patriotism," Campbell's feelings about the dangers of emancipation had only grown stronger.[10]

For his part, Holt was hardly blind to the potential impact of emancipation on the commitment of the border states to remaining loyal. "Is it not too much," inquired an old friend from Kentucky, "for the government to ask of its friends, who have put in peril all, even life for its defense, to submit to robbery & outrage from its representatives?" Indeed, one good reason for paying close attention to what his own (and Lincoln's) critics had to say was that those same critics offered information about how wartime public opinion was shaping up on the border. In the fall of 1862, the military situation in Kentucky had become perilous. The cause of trouble was an invasion by Confederate forces under the command of General Braxton Bragg, whose troops had recently occupied Bardstown; Federal forces under Major General Don Carlos Buell were stationed about twenty-five miles away at Elizabethtown. On September 23, John Speed informed Holt that many of the women and children of the region had been sent across the Ohio River to Indiana but that the men who remained were bravely steeling themselves for "a capital Kentucky fight," though Speed himself lacked confidence in Buell's abilities and those of the largely untested Federal soldiers he commanded.[11]

[10] O. M. Dorman to Holt, November 13, 1862, container 35, Holt Papers, LC; Hugh Campbell to Holt, September 26, 1862, container 34, ibid.; Hugh Campbell to Holt, November 15, 1862, container 35, ibid.

[11] Jesse W. Kincheloe to Holt, November 26, 1862, container 35, ibid.; Alice Key Pendleton to Holt, December 17, 1862, container 36, ibid. Earlier in 1862, John Hunt Morgan's Confederate cavalry had also invaded the state, and he raided Kentucky again later in the war. "Such raids," Lowell H. Harrison writes, "were annoying, sometimes even embarrassing, but

197

The battle Speed anticipated finally came at Perryville, about fifty miles east of Elizabethtown, on October 7 and 8. Some fifteen thousand Confederate and twenty-three thousand Federal soldiers were engaged, and in the end, as had been true at Antietam, the inability of the Confederates to claim the field after the shooting stopped, combined with their failure to find much active sympathy within the population of Kentucky, resulted in their retreat to more friendly terrain. But a good deal of damage had been done. T. S. Bell grumbled on October 12 that "the vile treason & piracy of Jeff. Davis's disunion are reveling in the devastation of Kentucky." Bell particularly bemoaned the fact that the Federals—and especially the Kentuckians among them—had not done more to demolish the enemy forces while they had the chance. Somewhat less discouraged than Bell, John Speed's son, James, reported late in October 1862 that the departure of the Rebel army had greatly disappointed the Confederate leadership in Richmond. Still, like Holt, he remained doubtful that General Buell was up to the task of protecting Kentucky in the future. As it turned out, Lincoln had the same concerns, and on October 24 he relieved Buell of command, replacing him with Major General William S. Rosecrans. And by early November, even James Speed had grown confident that the Confederate sympathizers of Kentucky were losing ground.[12]

they did not pose a serious threat to Union forces in the state." See Lowell H.Harrison, *The Civil War in Kentucky* (Lexington, Ky., 1975), 39, (quote, 57). See also John Speed to Holt, September 23, 1862, container 34, Holt Papers, LC.

[12] T. S. Bell to Holt, October 12 and 20, 1862, and November 1, 1862, container 35; James Speed to Holt, October 23, 1862, November 8, 1862, and November 25, 1862, container 35; James Speed to Holt, November 27, 1862, container 41; James Speed to Holt, December 12, 1861, container 31; Gordon Granger to James F. Robinson, November 22, 1862, container 35, all in Holt Papers, LC; Holt to Abraham Lincoln, October 8 and 28, 1862, Lincoln Papers, LC; Harrison, *Civil War in Kentucky*, 47. According to Harrison, "The 1862 invasion of Kentucky was the high-water mark of the Confederacy in the West. The state would be the scene of numerous minor actions during the rest of the war; but after Bragg and Kirby Smith led their weary troops into Tennessee, the Confederate threat to seize Kentucky was at an end" (ibid., 57). In a late November conversation with "unconditional Union Kentuckians," Lincoln announced that he "would rather die" than rescind his emancipation policy. At this meeting, Holt's name was lifted up as one who could be sent through the state at an appropriate time in order to build support for the idea of ending slavery. See *New York Tribune*, November 24, 1862, in Basler, ed., *Collected Works*, 5:503. See also Holt to Secretary of War, April 9, 1863,

Still, Speed worried about the overall effects of the militarization of Kentucky and the nation, which he believed produced a form of "military despotism" in which the people turned increasingly to representatives of the armed forces for solutions to their disputes. At the same time, Speed noted the disturbing lack of discipline he had seen among the Federal forces who had stood bravely against Bragg the previous month, but who had otherwise proved themselves, in many cases, little more than "mere marauders," and he regretted that ill-behaved soldiers and their equally ill-behaved officers could not just be shot without first obtaining the approval of the president. As the person most responsible, next to the president, for arbitrating cases involving soldiers' offenses against military law and discipline, as well as civilians' "disloyal practices" of all sorts, Holt shared Speed's concern. His own general inclination was to respond to breaches of law, discipline, and professional responsibility—not to mention, loyalty—with severity rather than leniency. Just weeks into his new job in what became one of the most famous and controversial cases of the war and of his entire career, Holt had a dramatic opportunity to demonstrate his firmness on these matters.[13]

The charges were against Major General Fitz John Porter of Portsmouth, New Hampshire, a West Point graduate (class of 1845), a veteran of the Mexican War, and a dedicated and outspoken supporter of the recently deposed General McClellan. Porter had served with the Army of the Potomac courageously for over a year. However, he was accused of having violated the ninth and the fifty-second Articles of War by disobeying the orders of his commanding officer in the newly created Federal Army of Virginia, General John Pope, during the August 1862 second battle of Bull Run, where the Federals had once again suffered a humiliating defeat. Prior to the battle, Porter

---

The War of the Rebellion: A Compilation of the Official Records of the Union and Confederate Armies, 128 vols. (Washington, D.C., 1880-1901), series 2, vol. 5:456-57 (hereafter *OR*). Kentucky did not ratify the Thirteenth Amendment until 1976.

[13] James Speed to Holt, November 8, 1862, container 35, Holt Papers, LC. Eighteen months later, General William T. Sherman also complained to Holt about this "problem"; see William T. Sherman to Holt, April 6, 1864, *OR*, series 2, 7:18-19. See also Joseph Holt to William T. Sherman, April 7, 1864, ibid., 7:20.

had openly criticized Pope for his hard-war, antislavery views and his staunch opposition to McClellan. To disagree with or even to despise one's commander privately was not a crime, of course, but to speak out against him publicly was a serious problem and to disobey him in battle was a violation of military discipline punishable by death. For his part, Pope blamed the embarrassing failure of the army at second Bull Run on Porter's "shameful" refusal to follow his orders on several occasions, which he in turn traced back to Porter's blind allegiance to McClellan.[14]

In early November 1862, having already been relieved of command by Lincoln, Porter appeared before a court-martial organized by the new judge advocate general and presided over by Major General David Hunter to face the charges against him. Over the course of the next several weeks, witnesses—many of whom were striving to preserve or restore their own reputations in connection with the unsavory outcome of the battle—alternately praised Pope for his heroism and condemned Porter for his betrayal or commended Porter's faithfulness and damned Pope for his incompetence. In the end, although Porter had pleaded not guilty to all of the charges and specifications against him, the court—for which Holt served as both lead prosecutor and recorder—found him guilty and sentenced him to be cashiered from the army and "forever disqualified from holding any office of trust or profit under the Government of the United States." When the documents Holt subsequently prepared in connection with the case reached the president's desk for review in early 1863, Lincoln approved the proceedings, findings, and sentence, and the former rising star of the Federal army was discharged.[15]

---

[14] The Articles of War under which the U.S. army operated during the Civil War were approved in 1806 and not revised again for a century.

[15] Special Order, No. 350, November 17, 1862, *OR*, series 1, 12;, part 2, 506. On November 25, Special Order No. 362 dissolved the commission and organized a court-martial in its place. The court-martial was to begin meeting in Washington on November 27 or as soon after that as possible. Special Order, No. 362, November 25, 1862, ibid., 507. Documents pertaining to the case begin on 505. See also ibid., 821-1134 (supplement), and Holt's report to Lincoln on the case: Holt to Lincoln, January 19, 1863, Joseph Holt Papers, Huntington Library, San Marino, California (hereafter Holt Papers, Huntington).

Even while it was still underway, the Fitz John Porter case, widely covered in the national press, proved bitterly controversial, taking place as it did in the public arena where opinions about the war and its progress were diverse and against the backdrop of sharply conflicting estimates of McClellan's competence and his responsibility for the failure to make much headway against the Rebels in the eastern theater. "My first emotion when I heard of Fitz-John Porter's condemnation," wrote New Yorker George Templeton Strong in his diary, "was sorrow for the downfall of an old friend, and regret that he should have put himself in a technically false position." "But as I look further into the matter," he continued, "it assumes another aspect, and [his] name now seems to me likely to hold the lowest place in our national gallery but one—that of Benedict Arnold." "Holt's review of the evidence for and against him," Strong concluded, "is crushing."[16]

In contrast, McClellan's supporters were convinced that Porter was the victim of a vicious plot led by Pope, Stanton, and Holt to use the defendant to further discredit "Little Mac" even after he had been removed from duty and to advance Lincoln's hard-war policies—including emancipation—against the sadly misguided South. Porter himself was sure that he had been railroaded, and he and many of his influential allies (his cousins included admirals David G. Farragut and David D. Porter) strove to set the record straight. Several months after the trial was completed, Pope informed Holt that some of the New York newspapers had been publishing intimations that Reverdy Johnson—a prominent Maryland attorney and Democrat, who had served as attorney general of the United States from March 1849 to July 1850, had defended John F. A. Sanford in the landmark Dred Scott case in 1857, and had been Porter's attorney at the trial—was

---

In addition to General Hunter, the members of the court were Major General E. A. Hitchcock and brigadier generals Rufus King, Benjamin Prentiss, James Rickets, Silas Casey, James Garfield, Napoleon Bonaparte Buford, and John P. Slough.

[16] See Lincoln to Holt, January 12, 1863, in Basler, ed., *Collected Works*, 6:54; Allan Nevins and Milton Halsey Thomas, eds., *The Diary of George Templeton Strong*, 4 vols. (New York, 1974), 3:291.

preparing a pamphlet designed to vindicate his client's reputation.

The rumors were true; in the spring of 1863, Johnson published an attack on the Porter trial whose fundamental premise was that "never in the history of jurisprudence, civil, criminal or military" had a judgment been handed down that "so shocked and startled the sense of public justice." Although he had made no such claims either during or immediately after the trial itself, Johnson charged that Lincoln had stacked the court against the defendant from the start, had rewarded the members of the court for their guilty verdict with promotions and more favorable assignments, and had wrongly deferred the examination of the evidence in the case to Holt, who, Johnson was certain, had eschewed objectivity in order to do Lincoln's bidding. He further charged that Holt had manipulated, distorted, and concealed portions of the evidence in order to reach the harsh verdict that Lincoln had predetermined. When he finally had the opportunity to read Johnson's pamphlet that summer, John Pope declared it to be "so grossly unfair" and so full of "deliberate misrepresentations" that "it would be idle to answer it in detail."[17]

Still, answer it he did, in the form of an eloquent rebuttal penned by his ally and friend, Andrew Dickson White. In a series of articles in the *Washington Chronicle* that were later compiled as a pamphlet, White vigorously disputed Reverdy Johnson's claims and accused him of trying to embarrass the Lincoln administration and of wrongly striving to protect Porter "from the merited scorn of our people by unblushing falsehood, distortion of evidence, and an appeal to prejudice." Johnson, White declared, seemed content to "trample upon the many distinguished men connected with this trial"—including Holt—"as heedlessly as a maddened bull paws the sands beneath his feet." White defended the court and Holt's performance throughout the proceedings, reminding readers that the charges against Porter could well have yielded a death sentence. "The wonder of military men, who understand the atrocity of Porter's offence in all its bear-

[17] Reverdy Johnson, *Reply to the Review of Judge Advocate General Holt* (Baltimore, 1863), 6; John Pope to Holt, August 25, 1863, container 40, Holt Papers, LC.

ings," White concluded, "is, not that he was condemned, but that his life was spared."[18]

Rufus King, who had served as a judge in the case, agreed. "*You know how utterly false & unjust this charge is*," King wrote bracingly to Holt, whose sensitivity to criticism and attacks on his integrity was no secret. After the Porter trial concluded, King recalled that Reverdy Johnson himself had commented on Holt's wise and evenhanded supervision throughout, which had made the trial "the fairest and most impartial he ever saw." T. S. Bell also sent words of support to his beleaguered friend. "With what kind of a face Reverdy Johnson can lend himself to bolstering up such a man as Fitz John Porter," he wrote, "I cannot imagine. He must have cheeks of something harder than brass." Bell summed up his perspective by noting that "the man who can suppose that any power could seduce you into an act inconsistent with professional honor and integrity . . . does not know the first element of your character." In the end, Bell assured Holt, such "surges of personal wrath" were sure to "fall harmlessly at [Holt's] feet."[19]

Holt rose to the position of Lincoln's judge advocate general not because he lacked a temper or was impervious to criticism but because of his widespread reputation for being a brilliant, rational, stunningly articulate, painstakingly careful attorney and because he was a fearlessly determined supporter of the Union and the Lincoln administration, including Lincoln's policies on civil liberties, slave emancipation, and the need for a hard-war approach to crush the

---

[18] Andrew Dickson White, *Reply to the Hon. Reverdy Johnson's Attack* (Baltimore, 1863), 3, (quotes, 6, 8-9, and 19). White later became the first president of Cornell University.

[19] Rufus King to Holt, September 5, 1863, container 40, Holt Papers, LC; T. S. Bell to Holt, October 16, 1863, ibid. For a negative view of how the Porter case was handled, see Donald R. Jermann, *Fitz-John Porter: Scapegoat of Second Manassas* (Jefferson, N.C., 2008).

The reverberations from the Porter trial went on for many years as his defenders sought to have the results of the case overturned and have him restored to the army. President Chester Arthur finally reversed Porter's sentence in May 1882, although his critics remained vocal. Subsequently, he was restored to the army and retired as a colonel. President Grover Cleveland pardoned him completely in 1886. See also John Y. Simon, *The Papers of Ulysses S. Grant*, 32 vols. (Carbondale, Ill., 1967-2012), vol. 17, *January 1–September 30, 1867* (Carbondale, Ill., 1991), 327-40

Confederate rebellion. "I believe there is no power on earth [that] could induce you to stop working for Old Abe," wrote one friend in the fall of 1863. For his part, Lincoln was deeply grateful for Holt's fidelity, talents, apparent tirelessness, firm hand, and adherence above all to the principle that the Union *must* be preserved. Indeed, the nation was immensely fortunate to have Holt on its side.[20]

But it must also be acknowledged that precisely those characteristics that made Holt such a faithful servant of the Federal cause, combined with the more prickly and sensitive features of his basic temperament, made him supremely vulnerable as a lightning rod for the antipathies of those who were either outright enemies of the government or whose views about how to preserve it differed from those that Lincoln's policies reflected. As Lincoln's judge advocate general, other people's responses to Joseph Holt personally could no longer be separated from the fortunes of the army as well as its internal conflicts. As such, from September 1862 forward, Holt's actions as the lead arbiter of military law were interpreted largely according to whatever stance a particular observer took with regard to the rebellion, Lincoln, the progress the Federal government and the army were making, and the observer's own views on how the government and the army should proceed against its enemies.

Predictably, then, the bitterly contentious Fitz John Porter case, taking place virtually at the start of Holt's tenure as judge advocate general, contributed powerfully to the emergence of sharply divergent images of Holt, how he operated in his professional capacity, what he accomplished, and how, ultimately, he should be remembered. To uncompromising, pro-Lincoln Unionists wherever they lived, Holt continued to be seen as a stern but wise, careful, talented, courageous, and evenhanded jurist who sacrificed his time, energy, health, wealth, privacy, and personal and family relationships for the national cause. To ardent Confederates and their sympathizers North and South, however, Holt assumed the character of a corrupt, self-interested, shamelessly vindictive autocrat who was determined to suppress the

[20] Mary W. Cash to Holt, October 14, 1863, container 40, Holt Papers, LC.

slaveholders' legitimate revolution and crush as brutally as possible anyone he suspected of providing the revolution with either overt or covert support. No doubt, Holt's nature—austere and reserved, on the one hand, gracious, charming, and refined, on the other—lent itself readily to such caricatures, as did his passion and his intense commitment both to the Union and to his privacy. Moreover, over time the public promulgation of sharply delineated caricatures of Holt unavoidably *shaped* his behavior and his perspective. In particular, attempts to challenge his integrity and undermine his reputation for upstanding professionalism by suggesting that his labor on behalf of the national welfare was anything but righteous, just, and honorable drove Holt to defend himself, his efforts, and his cause ever more fiercely, not always in ways that were to his best advantage.

Fortunately, most of the cases Holt handled during his years as Lincoln's judge advocate general were both less high-profile and less controversial than the Fitz John Porter case, even when they shared, on a much smaller scale, some of the same features. For one thing, the majority of purely military cases he dealt with resulted in sentences of neither summary execution nor dismissal from the army but instead a period of imprisonment (often at hard labor), or the loss of some pay, or a demotion in rank, or some combination of the three. Upon review, many cases elicited Holt's forbearance in a way that Porter must have envied, and more than once Holt demonstrated that he could be flexible when it came to analyzing the circumstances that lay behind a charge of disobedience of orders or even desertion. Holt typically took a range of different circumstances into account when shaping his recommendations for a given case, but he demonstrated little tolerance for blatant displays of disloyalty to the nation, outright cruelty towards subordinates, or cold-blooded murder. Generally speaking, as judge advocate general Holt proved himself a stickler for legal detail, and when he believed that a defendant's legal rights had been violated in any significant way, he was inclined to overturn the sentence.[21]

---

[21] Abraham Lincoln to Holt, January 3, 1863, *OR*, series 1, 14:979; Basler, ed., *Collected*

It is simply impossible within the scope of this article to examine in detail the tens of thousands of cases that Holt dealt with during his tenure as Lincoln's judge advocate general. But it would be wrong not to point out that some of the most interesting and important cases he handled, particularly after Lincoln issued his final Emancipation Proclamation on January 1, 1863, involved slaves and former slaves whose legal, civil, and human rights had been violated. In these cases, Holt—the former slaveholder—repeatedly and energetically rose to the defense of blacks, even when they initially appeared in the case records as perpetrators of crimes against whites. Such was true for West Bogan of Arkansas, convicted of murdering his former owner with an axe. When he reviewed Bogan's case, Holt agreed that the defendant should be treated "as a whole man" in terms of his responsibility for having killed another human being. At the same time, however, Holt made clear that he considered Bogan to have been acting in self-defense. Bogan's former owner, Holt explained, was known for being "cruel and exacting," for having forced his slaves, under threat of punishment, to work extraordinarily long hours with few if any breaks, and for whipping at least one slave every day. Following the Emancipation Proclamation, Bogan had briefly remained on his former owner's farm, but then he had begun to move about more freely, laying claim to the promises of the proclamation. One day, his former owner threatened to beat or even kill Bogan if he did not stop "running about and going away from home" without permission, and this time the normally quiet and cooperative Bogan lost his temper. The two men fell to fighting, in the midst of which Bogan grabbed an axe and hit the white man twice in the neck, nearly

Works, 6:35; Holt to Abraham Lincoln, January 26, 1863, *OR*, series 1, 14:979-83; H. W. Benham to Holt, February 27, 1863, container 37, Holt Papers, LC; Special Order, No. 256, "Proceedings of a Military Commission," September 23, 1862, *OR*, series 1, 12, part 2, 766-805; Lowry, *Don't Shoot That Boy!*, 33-34, 70, 127, 134-35, 172-76, 190-91, 194-95, 202, 210-11, 221; Holt to Edwin M. Stanton, May 16, 1863, *OR*, series 2, 5:528-29; Holt to Henry Halleck, April 29, 1863, ibid., 5:536-37; Holt to Abraham Lincoln, March 11, 1864, ibid., 6:1029-33; Thomas P. Lowry, *Confederate Heroines: 120 Southern Women Convicted by Union Military Justice* (Baton Rouge, 2006), 53-55; Joseph Holt, "On the application of Capt. Benjamin P. Walker," December 1, 1862, *OR*, series 2, 5:3-5.

severing his head. In his review of the case, Holt disagreed with the murder conviction, declaring Bogan a free man who had killed only after he had "doubtless borne the oppressions of his taskmaster till endurance seemed to him no longer possible." In Holt's mind, the white man deserved what he got for behaving in a manner that "under the changed relations of the white and black population of the Southern States, he had no right to do." Bogan, Holt insisted, had acted out of passion in response to a great and inexcusable provocation.[22]

Similarly, in the case of John Glover of Tennessee, a freedman convicted by a military commission of murdering a white man, Holt stepped in to save the black man from hanging. "There can be no doubt," he wrote in his review of the case, "that the prisoner discharged a pistol at [George] Redman, the result of which was his [Redman's] death." From Holt's perspective, however, Glover's violence—like West Bogan's—was justified by the circumstances. Glover and another black man, identified only as "Dave," had crossed the Mississippi River into Arkansas solely in order to rescue Dave's daughters, whom the elderly Redman had been holding in slavery "against their father's will and in violation of the President's emancipation proclamation," promising to kill anyone who tried to free them. Dave and Glover had decided to go and get the girls anyway, and they had just managed to slip away with one and were going back for the other when Redman came after them with a gun. Initially, the black men tried to run back to where their boat was waiting, but Redman kept up the pursuit and at last, Glover, who was also carrying a gun, turned and fired. Redman died a few days later from his wounds.[23]

In reviewing the case, Holt admitted that some might question why, in the first place, Glover had participated in the mission that

[22] For the archival records of the tens of thousands of cases Holt considered during the war, see the vast files of Record Group 153, Records of the Office of the Judge Advocate General, National Archives and Records Administration, Washington, D.C. (hereafter NARA). For Bogan's case, see Joseph Holt, "Opinion in the Case of West Bogan," May 30, 1864, container 38, Holt Papers, LC.

[23] Joseph Holt, "Opinion in the Case of John J. Glover," June 6, 1864, container 43, Holt Papers, LC.

led to Redman's death. "It is true," Holt wrote, that Glover "had no personal interest in the rescue of the two girls," who were, after all, not his children but Dave's. Still, in light of the Emancipation Proclamation, Holt considered the rescue effort in and of itself "a lawful and justifiable act," making Glover's participation in it "no less justifiable and lawful." Moreover, Glover had not meant to murder Redman but only to help a friend "in the delivery of his children from bondage." But when Redman came after him with a gun, Glover had feared for his own life and had acted in self-defense. That Glover had armed himself before setting out on the rescue mission should not be a cause for criticism either, Holt argued, given "the extreme severity with which offenders of his race are treated by their white masters." For Holt, the case was one in which a white man had "rashly thrown away his [own] life in an endeavor to enslave a feeble young woman in defiance of the proclamation of the President which had declared her free."[24]

Holt wrote his opinion in the Glover case in June 1864, seventeen months after Lincoln issued his final Emancipation Proclamation and almost two years after black men had begun enlisting in the Federal army. Indeed, just a month after the Second Confiscation Act passed in July 1862, Secretary of War Stanton had quietly begun to authorize the recruitment of freedmen as Federal soldiers; their numbers would reach almost two hundred thousand by the time the war was over. From the start, Holt was as supportive of the idea of arming black men in the national service as he was of the Emancipation Proclamation itself, which he made clear when he responded that fall to Stanton's request for his opinion. Holt's immediate response

---

[24] Ibid. See also Joseph Holt, "Opinion in the Case of Fountain Brown," May 24, 1864, container 43, Holt Papers, LC; *OR*, series 2, 7:159-62; Holt to Edwin M. Stanton, November 22, 1864, ibid., 7:1151; Basler, ed., *Collected Works*, 7:357. And see Lowry, *Don't Shoot That Boy!*, 247, where he discusses the case of Private William Elliott of the Eighth U.S. Infantry, who, while his regiment was stationed at Rectortown, Virginia, attempted to rape a black woman, Kate Brooks. Commenting on the case, Holt described Elliott's act as "a brutal attempt at rape on a gray-haired Negro woman between 60 and 70 years of age" and declared him unequivocally guilty. With Lincoln's approval, Elliott was sentenced to spend the rest of his life in prison.

was an emphatic endorsement.[25]

A year later, in August 1863, he penned a more extended and thorough statement on the question, in which he reiterated the right of the government "to employ for the suppression of the rebellion persons of African descent held to service or labor under the local laws." This right, Holt declared, had two distinct legal foundations. First, the U.S. Constitution recognized slaves as *property*, and the Federal government had the authority to seize enemy property and make use of it however the government saw fit, even putting uniforms on "it," giving "it" guns, and sending "it" into battle. Second, the Constitution recognized persons of African descent as *persons* for the purpose of representation in Congress. They were, therefore, constituents of the government, and since all male constituents were required to bear arms "in defense of the Government under which they live, and by which they are protected" (provided they were physically able to do so), and as it was the duty of the government to call upon its male constituents to bear arms against an enemy "whenever the public safety may demand it," black men could, and should, serve as Federal soldiers.[26]

Moreover, Holt pointed out, the "tenacious and brilliant valor" and the "obstinate courage" black soldiers had already displayed at battles like Port Hudson, Milliken's Bend, and Fort Wagner demonstrated their potential as effective soldiers, which the nation would be foolish to ignore. "A man precipitated into a struggle for his life on land or sea," Holt wrote, "instinctively and almost necessarily puts forth every energy with which he is endowed, and eagerly seizes upon every source of strength within his grasp." Likewise, "a nation battling for existence, that does not do the same, may well be regarded as neither wise nor obedient to that great law of self preservation, from which are derived our most urgent and solemn duties." On the

---

[25] McPherson, *Ordeal by Fire*, 379. See also Elizabeth D. Leonard, *Men of Color to Arms! Black Soldiers, Indian Wars, and the Quest for Equality* (New York, 2010); D. S. Curtiss to Holt, April 4, 1863, container 38, Holt Papers, LC; Benjamin P. Thomas and Harold M. Hyman, *Stanton: The Life and Times of Lincoln's Secretary of War* (Santa Barbara, Calif., 1980), 234.

[26] Holt to Edwin M. Stanton, August 20, 1863, container 39, Holt Papers, LC.

question of what black soldiers should be led to expect once the war was over, Holt responded that they should expect and be permitted to enjoy all of the rights that the Constitution they had so bravely defended grants to its citizens. Holt's opinion on the place of black men in the Federal armed services heartened the many supporters of the policy, not least those who were certain, as Lincoln was, that the war could not be won without their help. At the same time, however, Holt's support for black male enlistment only further hardened the sentiments of his opponents, who believed that he, like Lincoln, had once again gone much too far and that his primary reason for saving the Union was to transform it into a racially egalitarian state.[27]

Holt's official opinion on the legitimacy of black men's military service offers a good reminder that as judge advocate general, he did more than serve as the supreme adjudicator of military law of the War Department; he also profoundly influenced its formulation and development. Among other things, he contributed materially to the production of probably the most famous set of instructions relating to the behavior of armies in the field during this period: the Lieber Code, which was promulgated in April 1863 as General Order No. 100 and which remains a keystone in the international rules of war today. Indeed, from the time Holt became judge advocate general, Francis Lieber—a German legal scholar who had immigrated to the United States in the late 1820s and, at the time of the war, was a professor of history and political economics at Columbia University—was one of his regular correspondents. During the period when he was crafting the code, Lieber consulted with Holt several times, including in February 1863, when he asked Holt to have a look at a draft of what he had written and to return it with his suggestions and revisions.[28]

---

[27] Ibid.; Holt to Edwin M. Stanton, August 17, 1863, *OR*, series 2, 6:209-11; Holt to Abraham Lincoln, August 19, 1863, ibid., 6:216-18; Holt, "The writer of this letter," December 4, 1863, ibid., 6:604. For a thorough discussion of black men's service in the Federal army during the Civil War, see Joseph T. Glatthaar, *Forged in Battle: The Civil War Alliance of Black Soldiers and White Officers* (Baton Rouge, 2000).

[28] William E. Boulger to Holt, November 18, 1862, container 35, and Francis Lieber to Holt, February 22, 1863, container 37, Holt Papers, LC. For an overview of legal changes during the Civil War, in many of which Holt's hand can be seen, see Christian G. Samito,

In addition to assisting Lieber in the development of the Lieber Code, Holt later published an extensive, alphabetically organized compilation of his own opinions on a wide range of military legal matters—from his interpretations of the Articles of War to his view on what sorts of remuneration a witness in a military trial could properly expect—which appeared in 1865 as the *Digest of Opinions of the Judge Advocate General of the Army* and later in a number of revised editions. Meanwhile, of course, Holt also continued to manage with energy, focus, and dedication the massive responsibilities of his office, to which were soon added the protracted and politically thorny mess brought on by the activities of a particularly ardent "Peace Democrat," U.S. congressman Clement L. Vallandigham of Ohio. On May 1, 1863, Vallandigham had defied Major General Ambrose E. Burnside's General Order No. 38, published on April 13, warning that public expressions of support for the Confederacy would no longer be tolerated in the Department of the Ohio, where Burnside was in command, and that offenders would be arrested immediately and brought before a military commission for trial. Ignoring Burnside's warning, Vallandigham made a speech at Mount Vernon, Ohio, in which he declared the war a failure, attacked the principle of emancipation, and criticized the suspension of habeas corpus. Four days later, he was arrested, and on May 6, a military commission authorized by Holt convened in Cincinnati to try him for "expressing public sympathy for those in arms against the Government, and declaring disloyal sentiments and opinions, with the object and purpose of weakening the power of the Government in its efforts to suppress an unlawful rebellion." Ten days later, the commission—whose jurisdiction Vallandigham had unsuccessfully challenged—reached the unanimous conclusion that he was guilty

ed., *Changes in Law and Society during the Civil War and Reconstruction: A Legal History Documentary Reader* (Carbondale, Ill., 2009) and Stephen C. Neff, *Justice in Blue and Gray: A Legal History of the Civil War* (Cambridge, Mass., 2010). In April 1863, Holt called for a stern policy against both men and women who demonstrated themselves to be "incorrigible rebels." Holt to Edwin M. Stanton, April 24, 1863, *OR*, series 2, 5:515. Lieber built this policy into his code. See Francis Lieber to Holt, June 11, 1863, and July 17, 1863, container 39, Holt Papers, LC.

as charged. The court sentenced Vallandigham to imprisonment at Fort Warren in Massachusetts for the duration of the war.[29]

This was the first major case for Holt and the Lincoln administration involving a civilian dissident against the civil-liberties policies of the administration and, like the Fitz John Porter case, it vehemently polarized public opinion. Those who believed that Copperheads like Vallandigham must be silenced in order for the Union war effort to succeed were pleased with Holt's management of the trial and its outcome. Those who sympathized with either the Confederacy or the principle of a citizen's freedom to speak freely regardless of the setting and the consequences—or both—were outraged and condemned Holt in particular for what they considered his collusion in Lincoln's repressive, unconstitutional measures. In the end, in any case, Vallandigham did not go to jail. Instead, on May 19 Lincoln commuted his sentence to banishment into the Confederacy, at least in part because the president realized that Vallandigham's antiadministration, antiwar, antiemancipation allies threatened to transform the convicted man into a First Amendment martyr. Subsequently, Vallandigham slipped away to Canada, and from there appealed his conviction (and also ran for governor of Ohio). Holt, in turn, wrote at length to the members of the U.S. Supreme Court providing extensive detail about the case and asking that Vallandigham's appeal be denied. "The Supreme Court," Holt argued boldly, "might with as much propriety be called upon to restrain by injunction the proceedings of Congress" as to "reverse the proceedings of the military authorities in time of war." Handing down its decision in *Ex parte Vallandigham* in February 1864, the Supreme Court ruled against the defendant. Sometime later, Vallandigham brazenly returned to the

---

[29] *Digest of the Opinions of the Judge Advocate General of the Army* (Washington, D.C., 1865); McPherson, *Ordeal by Fire*, 374; Holt to the U.S. Supreme Court, December 1863, *OR*, series 2, 6:620-24. For a critical look at the government handling of the Vallandigham case, see Frank L. Klement, *The Limits of Dissent: Clement L. Vallandigham and the Civil War* (New York, 1998). See also Mark Neely Jr., *The Fate of Liberty: Abraham Lincoln and Civil Liberties* (New York, 1992) and see Lincoln's reply to a series of critical resolutions regarding the case from a group of citizens in Albany, New York, in Abraham Lincoln, *The Truth from an Honest Man: The Letter of the President* (Philadelphia, 1863).

United States, where he gave a number of powerful speeches and helped write the Democratic platform for the fall 1864 elections, in which George McClellan appeared as the presidential candidate of the Democratic Party. Vallandigham was not arrested again, however, and his power and influence ultimately collapsed.[30]

Even without Vallandigham at full throttle, the Copperheads were managing to stir up a good deal of trouble as the war ground through its third brutal year, particularly in the Old Northwest—Ohio, Indiana, Illinois—and along the border between slavery and freedom. So much trouble did they generate, in fact, that on July 12, 1864, Secretary of War Stanton ordered Holt to proceed personally and immediately to Kentucky. Traveling back to his home state for the first time since the summer of 1861, and now as chief of the newly created Bureau of Military Justice of the War Department, Holt arranged to meet with Governor Thomas E. Bramlette and Major General Stephen G. Burbridge to discuss military and political affairs in Kentucky and across the region. In addition, he prepared to investigate the operations of any secret organizations that were suspected of giving aid and comfort to the enemy and undermining the Federal cause.[31]

Not long after his arrival in the west, Holt reported to Stanton that the situation in Kentucky was grave. Secret organizations of Confederate sympathizers were only a part of the problem. In addition, he explained, guerrilla warfare was tearing the state apart. No one seemed to be able to stand up to the "thieves and murderers" who, moving in parties of between four and twenty, rode the "fleetest

---

[30] Holt to the U.S. Supreme Court, December 1863, OR, series 2, 6:620-24; John W. Forney to Holt, February 16, 1864, container 42, Holt Papers, LC. Holt took a similarly hard line against other political prisoners accused of trying to undermine the Federal government and the army. See Holt to J. H. Martindale, June 24, 1863, OR, series 2, 6:38-39.

[31] Harrison, *Civil War in Kentucky*, 83-85; Holt to Stephen G. Burbridge, May 14, 1864, OR, series 2, 7:144-45; Stephen G. Burbridge to Holt, May 20, 1864, ibid., 7:155; E. D. Townsend to Holt, July 12, 1864, ibid., series 1, 52, part 1, 567-68; Clous, "Judge Advocate General's Department," ibid., series 3, 4:774; Holt to Edwin M. Stanton, June 29, 1864, and Joseph Holt, Oath of Office, June 29, 1864, in H834 CB 1864, Record Group 94, Records of the Adjutant General's Office, 1780s-1917, Letters Received by the Commission Branch of the Adjutant General's Office, 1863-1870, Roll 96, 1864, H579-H835, NARA.

and best horses of the country" and were "thoroughly armed with weapons, which they conceal in their boots and under their clothes." To a great extent, Holt attributed the increase in guerrilla activity across the region to Lincoln's initial Proclamation of Amnesty and Reconstruction, issued in December 1863, in which the president had proposed a reasonably mild process for returning states to the Union once they came under the control of the Federal army. Although he recognized the proclamation as a reflection of Lincoln's generosity, forgiveness, and forbearance, Holt was convinced that many Rebels saw it simply as an opportunity to be exploited. "So far as Kentucky is concerned," Holt wrote, "the rebels have used this proclamation . . . only as a means for returning to the State, visiting their friends, making observations upon our military affairs, and then arming, mounting, and equipping themselves either for the Confederate service or for the career of robbers and cut-throats." In addition, Holt reported that although the recruitment of regional blacks into the Union army was proceeding at a reasonably good pace, many of the runaway slaves who were trying to enlist or simply seeking safety within the Federal lines were instead being "waylaid, beaten, maimed, and often murdered." Holt urged Lincoln to suspend wartime reconstruction, at least in Kentucky.[32]

In a subsequent report, Holt focused on the secret, antigovernment organizations he had gone west to investigate. That fall, Brigadier General Henry B. Carrington reported from Indianapolis that he had captured confidential materials—including information about "rituals, signs, passwords, and plans"—from a number of organizations whose purpose was to stir up trouble across the North should Lincoln be reelected in November. More generally, Holt's contacts

---

[32] T. S. Bell to Holt, June 28, 1864, and Mary Ann Stephens to Holt, July 4, 1864, container 44, Holt Papers, LC. Lincoln's so-called 10-percent plan offered full pardons and the restoration of property (except human property) to most Rebels who took the oath of allegiance to the United States. It also authorized Rebel states to reenter the Union whenever 10 percent of those who had voted in the 1860 election had taken the oath and had adopted a new republican state government that recognized emancipation. See McPherson, *Ordeal by Fire*, 425; Holt to Edwin M. Stanton, July 22, 1864, *OR*, series 1, 39, part 2, 198; Holt to Edwin M. Stanton, July 31, 1864, ibid., 212-15.

convinced him that antigovernment organizations such as the Order of the American Knights were more than just a rumor. They were real and extremely effective, and their members were armed, drilling for revolution, and dedicated to the preservation of slavery and the overthrow of the Federal government. To Holt, such organizations represented a radical and influential fraternity and, like the fire-eating southern nationalists who had started the war in the first place or the Know-Nothings even earlier, a manifestation of the power of a few "conspirators" to corrupt the minds of otherwise mild-mannered people, arousing in them a fiercely "parricidal spirit" and driving them into violent action against the benevolent institutions and leadership of the Republic and its loyal citizens. Collectively, and more than ever before, they represented a raging fire at the rear of the army.[33]

Upon reading Holt's lengthy report about the "hellish conspiracy" of virulent Copperheads that he had uncovered in the West, Francis Lieber expressed his dismay. "I can hardly command sufficient calmness to write to you," he confessed. The Columbia professor's horror "at the loathsomeness of this huge mass of crime" was mixed with grief regarding the state of affairs Holt had described, and he urged Holt to disseminate his informative report quickly and widely. As it turns out, the report only served to sharpen the antigovernment animus that was directed against Holt in particular, as at least one anonymous but shrill correspondent from Oswego, New York, made clear. Enclosing a newspaper article about the recent investigation, this writer made light of Holt's Democratic credentials and called him a traitor to his party and his birthplace whose name, henceforth, would evoke only scorn and contempt among those who had witnessed his betrayal. Back in Washington in the fall, Holt dismissed as best he could such hostile reactions to his ongoing attempt to save the Union. Instead, he focused on continuing to identify and crush the fomenters of the madness he had witnessed on the border and

---

[33] T. S. Bell to Holt, August 8, 1864, container 44, Holt Papers, LC; Henry B. Carrington to Holt, November 4, 1864, *OR*, series 2, 7:1089 and ibid., 7:930-53. On antigovernment organizations during the war, see Weber, *Copperheads*; Frank L. Klement, *Dark Lanterns: Secret Political Societies, Conspiracies, and Treason Trials in the Civil War* (Baton Rouge, 1984).

in the West. In his view, the very life of the Union—not to mention Lincoln's reelection in November—depended just as much on suppressing the internal enemies of the nation as it did on battlefield victories against the Confederate army. In essence, this is what he had meant to do when he urged the Supreme Court to sustain Clement Vallandigham's conviction in December 1863. In October 1864, he sought to do it again when he oversaw the trial of Lambdin P. Milligan, arrested in Indiana and charged with treason.[34]

By the time he was taken into Federal custody, Milligan, an ardent Democrat, lawyer, and politician, had long been recognized as a purveyor of antigovernment, antiwar sentiment in the Old Northwest. As early as July 1862, Milligan had publicly declared the war a lost cause. In August 1863, despite the encouraging Federal victories at Gettysburg and Vicksburg, Milligan had expressed his conviction that the North could not possibly win the war in the end and that the western states would do well to tie their fortunes to an independent South instead. That same year, he successfully argued the case of an Indiana legislator who, like Vallandigham, had violated Burnside's General Order No. 38. Subsequently, Milligan became widely known as a leader in the Indiana branch of the Order of the American Knights, whose stated goal was to instigate an antiwar rebellion across the North by raiding government arsenals, attacking Federal prisoner-of-war camps and liberating incarcerated Confederate soldiers, and then massing those released soldiers (and their liberators) in Louisville to create a serious distraction for the Federal forces. This, the members of the organization believed, would destroy confidence in the Lincoln administration and ensure its demise.[35]

[34] Francis Lieber to Holt, October 16, 1864, and Mary Ann Stephens to Holt, October 31, 1864, container 45, Holt Papers, LC; Anonymous to Holt, October 15, 1864, ibid.; Joshua F. Speed to Holt, September 8, 1864, container 44, ibid.; Joshua F. Speed to Holt, September 30, 1864, container 45, ibid.; Roger J. Bartman, "The Contribution of Joseph Holt to the Political Life of the United States" (PhD dissertation, Fordham University, 1958), 253-54.

[35] See Kenneth M. Stampp, "The Milligan Case and the Election of 1864 in Indiana," *Mississippi Valley Historical Review* 31 (1944): 41-48; Stephen E. Towne, "Dissent and Treason: Lambdin P. Milligan, Indiana, and the Civil War," (unpublished conference paper, September 20, 2007; see www.in.gov/judiciary/citc/files/towne-milligan-remarks.pdf); Benn Pitman, ed.,

In the end, of course, the plot failed when Federal informants infiltrated the Order and revealed its plans to the authorities. By early October, Milligan and others were in jail in Indianapolis. Their trial before a military commission on charges of conspiring against the government, giving aid and comfort to the rebels, inciting insurrection, engaging in disloyal practices, and violating the laws of war began on October 21. Prosecuted for the government by Colonel Henry L. Burnett, Holt's trusted judge advocate for the Department of the Ohio, Milligan's case was as public and dramatic as those of Porter and Vallandigham had been, and key to the effort of the government to convict him and the others was that a number of their fellow conspirators had turned state's evidence. The trial lasted about six weeks, during which—thanks in large part to General William T. Sherman's stunning occupation of Atlanta—Lincoln was resoundingly reelected. In early December, Milligan and his codefendants were found guilty and sentenced to death by hanging.[36]

As the Vallandigham case had done the previous year, Milligan's case generated a great deal of controversy around the question of what sorts of offenses committed by civilians could be considered sufficiently disloyal and detrimental to the Federal war effort to justify imprisonment or execution. The Milligan case also added considerable fuel to the fire being stoked by those who questioned the scope and reach of the military-justice system of the War Department and Holt himself, including its—*his*—seemingly boundless jurisdiction over civilian behavior in the form of military commissions. Like Lincoln's suspension of the writ of habeas corpus—which Congress had legitimized with its Habeas Corpus Act (March 1863)—and the restrictions of the Federal government on civil liberties generally, the question of the right of the military to try cases involving civilians

---

The Trials for Treason at Indianapolis, 1864 (Cincinnati, 1865) and Klement, *Dark Lanterns*. It was, writes Stephen E. Towne simply, "an ambitious plot."

[36] The members of the court were Brevet Brigadier General Silas Colgrove, and colonels William E. McLean, John T. Wilder, Thomas I. Lucas, Charles D. Murray, Benjamin Spooner, Richard P. DeHart, Ambrose A. Stephens, Ansel D. Wass, Thomas W. Bennett, Reuben Williams, and Albert Heash. See Pitman, ed., *Trials for Treason*, 44.

had already become a thorny topic; it generated even more vexed debate in the wake of the Milligan trial. For his part, it is clear that Holt remained unequivocally committed to limiting civil liberties and extending the legal powers of the military-justice system in order to win the war and save the Union. As was true of Lincoln, Holt's understanding of the concept of "constitutionality" was inseparable from his understanding of what it would take to save the Constitution in the first place, which included protecting and defending the president, his administration, and his policies; suppressing the rebellion and its allies with force; delivering the Union from the diabolical enemies who were arrayed against it; and restoring the public peace. Tolerance and magnanimity would simply have to wait until the war was over, the South was punished, treason was crushed, and the future of the freedpeople was secure.[37]

In late November 1864, in the wake of the resignation of Attorney General Edward Bates, a newly reelected Lincoln demonstrated his appreciation for Holt's ongoing and dedicated service to the Union, his administration, and his war policies by offering the judge advocate general Bates's post in the cabinet. Deeply honored, Holt nevertheless turned the president down. Holt, recalled Nicolay and Hay, "with that modesty and conscientiousness which formed the most striking trait of his character, believed that the length of time which had elapsed since he had retired from active service at the bar had rendered him unfit for the preparation of cases in an adequate manner before the Supreme Court, and therefore he declined the appointment." Indeed, this was precisely the reason Holt gave for saying no. "After the most careful reflection," he explained to the president, "I am satisfied that I can serve you better in the position which I now hold, at your hands, than in the more elevated one to which I have been invited." Holt insisted that his decision had not

---

[37] See *OR*, series 2, 6:620-24, for Holt's justification of the use of military commission generally, and in the Vallandigham case specifically, and for his explanation of the jurisdiction of the military commission. On Lincoln, habeas corpus, and civil liberties, see Daniel Farber, *Lincoln's Constitution* (Chicago, 2004) and Brian McGinty, *Lincoln and the Court* (Cambridge, Mass., 2009).

been an easy one to make and that he had "reached this conclusion with extreme reluctance & regret." At the same time, he assured Lincoln of his gratitude for the offer, which reflected the president's confidence and also provided him with new energy to pursue the work he had already taken on. In his place, Holt recommended that Lincoln appoint their mutual friend, James Speed.[38]

By the time James Speed took his cabinet seat in early December 1864, the war was almost over. Soon, congressional passage of the Thirteenth Amendment to the Constitution, in February 1865, would virtually guarantee the permanent end of slavery in the United States. For these things, Holt was wonderfully thankful. But as the war wound down, he was also exhausted. In a March 1865 report to Stanton, he indicated that just since November 1863, the Office of the Judge Advocate General had reviewed almost thirty-four thousand records of general courts-martial and military commissions and had made about nine thousand reports "as to the regularity of proceedings on applications for restoration to the service, the pardon of offenders, the remission or commutation of sentences," and other miscellaneous questions.[39]

Moreover, as winter gave way to spring, Holt could not escape the deep sadness that his own wartime losses had evoked, including the death of his only sister, Elizabeth Holt Sterett, in early 1863, and the apparently permanent rupturing of his relationships with almost every other member of his family and many of his friends back in Kentucky and across the South, most of whom were, from start to finish, enthusiastic supporters of the rebellion. During the war,

---

[38] In his journal, Secretary of the Navy Gideon Welles speculated that Lincoln also offered the post to Holt because he deemed it politically wise at this stage in the war to appoint someone from one of the border states. Gideon Welles, *Diary of Gideon Welles*, 3 vols. (New York, 1911), 2:183. Welles thought Holt erred in turning the attorney generalship down. "No man," Welles wrote, "should decline a place of such responsibility in times like these, when the country is unanimous in his favor" (ibid., 187). See also John G. Nicolay and John Hay, *Abraham Lincoln: A History*, 10 vols. (New York, 1904), 9:346-47; Holt to Abraham Lincoln, November 1864 (precise date unclear), container 45, Holt Papers, LC; Holt to Abraham Lincoln, December 1, 1864, ibid.

[39] Holt to Edwin M. Stanton, March 2, 1865, *OR*, series 3, 4:1216.

Holt found it simply impossible to sustain many of his once richly affectionate bonds with those persons—even those to whom he was linked by blood—who seemed committed to undermining everything he himself was struggling to protect. At the same time, he could not help worrying about the future. In January, an old friend had written describing the grim state of affairs in Breckinridge County, where Holt was born almost sixty years earlier. "We are having a hard time in this part of the state," this friend explained. "The country is at the mercy of the guerrillas, or Southern soldiers as they term themselves. They hesitate at nothing, take homes, kill & steal, and whatever they choose to do. The country is ruined, every man is in fear of his life, & if he saves it he will indeed be lucky. We have no way to defend ourselves & have to submit to every & any thing they choose to inflict without a murmur." Holt's friend reported that his own slaves were now all gone, but that he was content to have been able to get his children to adulthood and to come through the conflict "in a better condition that many others."[40]

On April 2, the Federal army captured the Confederate capital of Richmond, putting President Jefferson Davis and the remaining members of his collapsing administration to flight and signaling the imminent end of the war. Two days later, W. G. Snethen described "the enthusiasm that glowed on all sides in the faces" of Baltimore's "Union-loving friends" now that Federal victory was at hand. "Baltimore street was red with the Stars and Stripes," Snethen wrote, and "soldiers were marching under arms from point to point to prevent

[40] Mary Ann Stephens to Holt, January 13, 1863; C. C. Green to Holt, January 19, 1863; Thomas Holt to Holt, February 3, 1863, container 36; Mary Ann Stephens to Holt, June 3, 1863, container 39; Margaret Sterett to Holt, May 7, 1863, container 38; Mary Ann Stephens to Holt, March 10, 1863, container 37; Mary Ann Stephens to Holt, August 7, 1863, container 39; William Sterett to Holt, September 15, 1863, container 40; William Sterett to Holt, July 2, 1864, container 44; C. C. Green to Holt, January 30, 1864, container 42; Mary Ann Stephens to Holt, February 10, 1864, container 42; John R. Holt to Holt, October 15, 1864, container 45; F. K. Hunt to Holt, December 22, 1862, container 36; C. W. Wooley to Holt, February 23, 1863, container 37; Nathaniel P. Banks to Holt, May 5, 1863, container 38; James O. Harrison to Holt, May 14, 1863, container 38; James O. Harrison to Holt, December 26, 1864, container 46, all in Holt Papers, LC. For conditions in Breckinridge County, see William Sterett to Holt, January 13, 1865, container 46, ibid.

the pent-up anger of loyal men from bursting forth in deeds of violence against the wretched minions of Jeff Davis and slavery." A week later, on April 11, Holt's passionately secessionist brother, Robert, sadly confirmed the demise of the Confederacy. "It is now manifest," wrote Robert, "that the cause of the south has failed and is rapidly approaching the most disastrous end." Although he had anticipated this conclusion for almost a year, Robert still felt stunned. It was almost impossible, he admitted, to grasp the damages that the South had sustained over the course of four years of bloody conflict. "Fully seven tenths of our able bodied males between the ages of 17 and 50 years have perished," he wrote. "Our fields every where lie untilled, naked chimnies [*sic*] and charred ruins all over the land mark the spots where happy homes, the seats of refinement and elegance, once stood. Their former inhabitants wander in poverty and exile wherever chance or charity affords them shelter or food. Childless old age, widows, and helpless orphans, beggared and hopeless, are every where." Surely, Robert surmised, "our offence must have been great, that God has thus scourged us by the hands of our Demoniac enemies."[41]

Just a few days before Robert wrote, Mary Goldsborough of Frederick, Maryland, tucked "some dear little violets" into a letter in which she invited Holt to come and spend the Easter holiday at her home. Holt, however, had other obligations. Indeed, Good Friday, April 14, 1865, found him in Charleston, South Carolina, participating in the ceremonies surrounding the raising of the U.S. flag over Fort Sumter in the wake of Lee's surrender on April 9 to General Grant at Appomattox. There, Holt attended a dinner at the Charleston House, where he also gave a speech entitled "Treason and its Treatment" to a rapt audience. "From the first moment" the Rebel conspiracy "disclosed its cloven feet in the Capital until now," Holt thundered,

---

[41] W. G. Snethen to Holt, April 4, 1865, container 47; Robert Holt to Thomas Holt, April 11, 1865, container 47; Robert Holt to Holt, April 12, 1865, container 47, Holt Papers, LC. On the condition of the South and the attitudes of Confederates after the war, see Mark Grimsley and Brooks D. Simpson, eds., *The Collapse of the Confederacy* (Lincoln, Neb., 2001) and Jason Phillips, *Diehard Rebels: The Confederate Culture of Invincibility* (Athens, Ga., 2010).

"I never doubted of my own duty, and had the entire race of man confronted me on the question, my convictions in regard to that duty would not have been the less complete." As Holt understood it, his duty had been, simply, to do whatever he could to ensure a Federal victory. And in that victory, which Americans across the North, and even some in the South, were celebrating, lay the proof "that the republic which was born on the 4th day of July 1776, was born not for death, but for immortality, and that though its bosom may be scarred by the poignards of conspirators, and though its blood may be required to flow on many fields," still "neither the swords nor the bayonets of traitors can ever reach the seat of its great and exhaustless life."[42]

But what next? Victory itself brought new dangers, Holt pointed out, dangers that were "quite as great as those that marked the battle, though of a totally different character." Above all, Holt hoped and prayed that in the weeks and months ahead, "the fruits of this prolonged and sanguinary conflict," especially universal liberty, might endure. This, however, meant that the remnants of treason, in all of its forms, must be obliterated and that every single "root of that cancer of slavery which has been eating into the national vitals" must be destroyed. Otherwise, the "thousands of millions of treasure" the nation had expended, and the sacrifice of the bravest of its sons "on the red altars of war," would have been in vain. "Let it then be our fond and solemn trust," Holt implored his audience, "that the Government will maintain to the end the position which it has occupied from the beginning—that this is, in very deed, a war upon crime and criminals—criminals with whom we cannot fraternize, with whom we can make no compromises, without, in the judgment of mankind, and at the bar of history, becoming criminals ourselves." As Stanton had also done in a cabinet meeting on April 11, Holt recommended that the states of the former Confederacy be placed under military rule, at least for a time, until they completely and irrevocably renounced

---

[42] Mary Goldsborough to Holt, April 5, 1865, container 47, Holt Papers, LC; Joseph Holt, "Treason and its Treatment," April 14, 1865, Holt Papers, Huntington.

their wicked ways and accepted emancipation and Federal supremacy. "While the ballot box is the rightful source of authority over loyal men," Holt explained as forcefully as he could, "the legitimate and reliable foundation for the authority of the Government over traitors is the sword."[43]

Even as Holt spoke these stern words, back in Washington his beloved and deeply respected commander in chief, Abraham Lincoln, lay mortally wounded on the floor of the presidential box at Ford's Theater.

[43] Joseph Holt, "Treason and its Treatment," April 14, 1865, Holt Papers, Huntington.

BLUEGRASS AND VOLUNTEER—SISTER STATES OR ENEMY STATES?

By Benjamin Franklin Cooling

Were Kentucky and Tennessee sister yet also enemy states during the Civil War and Reconstruction? One recent book uses that theme. *Sister States, Enemy States* is an anthology edited by Kent T. Dollar, Larry H. Whiteaker, and W. Calvin Dickinson. It is catchy in title and assuredly rich in content. It provides a convenient springboard for revisiting the subject matter of Bluegrass and Volunteer States in the throes of rebellion, conflict, stabilization, and reconstitution. From 1860 to 1877, regional, state, and local (even personal) history played out in ways defying simplification. Kentucky and Tennessee illustrated the point. Suggestions of similarities and differences raise the questions of where to begin, where to end, how deep to posthole the subject, and what to conclude from it all. These issues have been written and discussed over the years; however, the sesquicentennial generation should be excited about revisiting old themes, topics, personalities, and judgments. The proverbial old wine in new bottles can be found, for instance, in recent works by Lincoln scholar William C. Harris and Kentucky reconstruction historian Anne Marshall as

BENJAMIN FRANKLIN COOLING retired from the National Defense University in Washington, D.C. He received his PhD from the University of Pennsylvania and is the author of numerous books and articles, including *Forts Henry and Donelson: The Key to the Confederate Heartland* (1987), *Fort Donelson's Legacy: War and Society in Kentucky and Tennessee, 1862-63* (1997), *To the Battles of Franklin and Nashville and Beyond: Stabilization and Reconstruction in Tennessee and Kentucky, 1864-1866* (2011), and *Arming America through the Centuries* (2022).

well as Elizabeth Leonard and Aaron Astor.[1]

The realities of the era were laid down long ago in official documents, diaries, letters, and reminiscences. Many have found publication; others await discovery. Decades of interpretive layering by scholars, the public, and descendants still have not exhausted questions seeking answers. Archives and attics across the two states and beyond continue to hold keys to the past. So, too, do the physical landscapes of battlefields and other cultural resources. Thanks to the National Park Service and state and local equivalents or the Civil War Trust (formerly the Civil War Preservation Trust), and even here and there a sensitive private landowner, the sesquicentennial generation may gain a sense of places like the Water Battery at Fort Donelson, Peach Orchard at Shiloh, the H. P. Bottom farm at Perryville, and the Carter House at Franklin. It is to be hoped that this array of "tools" will evoke more curiosity and respect than mere armchair entertainment or historical tourism. With such recognition will always come more questions than answers and more thrill and frustration than satisfaction to excite the future as they inform the present.

Moreover, evidence combines with generational interests. Civil War interpretation for Kentucky and Tennessee long ago affected historical waves of Union triumphalism and Lost Cause exceptionalism. Then the twentieth-century penchant of "using" history for domestic and international purposes conveniently advanced liberal democracy and nation-building by our forefathers for shaping continued American acceptance of a political and economic system in the face of totalitarianism. Our contemporary predilection for nation-building and humanitarian interventionism offers fresh opportunities for exploring past events and people in the dark and bloody ground of rebellious and destabilized states such as Kentucky and Tennes-

---

[1] William C. Harris, *Lincoln and the Border States: Preserving the Union* (Lawrence, Kans., 2011); Anne E. Marshall, *Creating A Confederate Kentucky: The Lost Cause and Civil War Memory in a Border State* (Chapel Hill, 2010); Kent T. Dollar, Larry H. Whiteaker, and W. Calvin Dickinson, eds., *Sister States, Enemy States: The Civil War in Kentucky and Tennessee* (Lexington, Ky., 2009); Elizabeth D. Leonard, *Lincoln's Forgotten Ally: Judge Advocate General Joseph Holt of Kentucky* (Chapel Hill, 2011); and Aaron Astor, *Rebels on the Border: Civil War, Emancipation, and the Reconstruction of Kentucky and Missouri* (Baton Rouge, 2012).

see. Thus, we may use our recent experiences in the Middle East and southwest Asia to explore Civil War–era Bluegrass and Volunteer States. This approach suggests various areas of interest: (1) failing and failed states; (2) paroxysms of violence; (3) social dislocation and revolution; (4) privation and destruction; and (5) reconstitution and readjustment. My approach is suggestive, not definitive.

The Anatomy of Success Turned Failure

The United States of America by the close of 1860 was a "failing" state. Within the year, it passed to the category of "failed state." In a recent study, David Goldfield posits a very traditional yet reawakened realization. The Civil War, he observes, was both the completion of the American Revolution and the beginning of a modern nation. It was "also America's greatest failure." Tennessee and Kentucky were microcosms of such success and failure. Although they had contributed to a rising nation before the 1850s, failure set in by 1861 for a Tennessee that continued under brief Confederate suzerainty and Federal occupation from 1862 to 1865 and for a Kentucky that disintegrated in similar if not precise comparison, while remaining part of the Union. The two helped populate a failed-state chapter of our national story. But what exactly is meant by these terms—"failing" and "failed state"? How might they be instructive for dissecting an epoch one hundred fifty years ago?

Common characteristics of a "failing" state relate to a weak, even ineffective, central government that has little practical control over much of its territory. Perceived wisdom today also suggests breakdown of public services, widespread corruption even criminality, displaced populations or refugees, and sharp economic decline. The term "failed state" connotes: (1) loss of control of its territory or state monopoly on legitimate force; (2) erosion of legitimate authority for collective decision-making; (3) inability to provide public services; and (4) inability to interact with other states as a full member of a national and international community. Just how many of these criteria fit the United States after the election of 1860 depends upon how narrowly or strictly they are applied. One can certainly see a more mixed application of the term "failing" to Kentucky and Tennessee when the new Confederacy "failed" and the rump United States reversed its own 1860 trajectory.[2]

Just as American uniqueness and search for empire is hardly new, Kentucky and Tennessee were part of that "manifest destiny" emerging with the early republic. The two states contributed to and at some point were actually on the edge of the psychological and physical frontier of America. They identified with the expansive spirit of enterprise, the art of the possible, and individualism expressed in commonality of mission, goal, and achievement. They also reflected a strong Anglo-Saxon mistrust of power, especially government (but also special-interest) as reflected by intrusion into the affairs of the Common Man. They offer an antebellum window for better appreciating cause and effect, trends, and directions as well as the impact of the human landscape.

The Age of Jackson and Clay with Tennessee and Kentucky in tandem—obviously along with Calhoun and Webster from elsewhere—featured exemplary, nationally focused statesmen. Yet they were politicians attached to locale and special interests in focus and bias. The antebellum period provides opportunities to study the great issues of constitutionalism, federalism, nullification (if not secession) and, above all, compromise and communalism as they played out on state and local stages. Moreover, these issues conditioned how the greatest attribute of the nineteenth century—nationalism—performed in North America. Curiously, too, the Bluegrass and Volunteer States were not only part of that general phenomenon. By 1860, both (or elements within both) were ready to become pawns of another nationalist movement, the Southern Confederacy. Thus, one might posit that Kentucky and Tennessee as states in the American federal system were quite prepared to exchange one identity for yet another new destiny. This is to say, as shown in the quandaries of Upper South Unionists in the secession crisis of 1860-61 or even

---

[2] Stewart Patrick, "'Failed' States and Global Security: Empirical Questions and Policy Dilemmas," *International Studies Review* 9 (2007): 644-62; David Goldfield, *America Aflame: How the Civil War Created a Nation* (New York, 2011), i.

thereafter, that divisiveness provided a mystery when applied to Kentucky and Tennessee in particular.[3]

Of course, geostrategically, this appeared as part of an ongoing, renewable cycle of sovereignty assertion (popular, state, and national). Is it not always a matter of progress versus status quo, the unknown versus the known, with the forces of history ever moving men in strange and mysterious ways? Add in that other great phenomenon of the nineteenth century—industrialism—in parallel with nationalism. Perhaps Tocquevillian America was only beginning to appreciate how the technologies of steam power, canals, railroads, and telegraph shrank time and distance to promote political and social unity as well as supplying mechanization to civilization in a New America. Eventually, the nationalism and industrialism knocked down limits of provincialism, localism, and parochialism. That, however, would happen long after "the late unpleasantness" was overtaken by modernism and world events.

Meanwhile, this trio stood erect and defiant in affairs of the 1860s. Kentucky and Tennessee provided models of such behavior. The United States itself remained unformed, "invertebrate" as suggested by Allan Nevins. Questions of governance (national versus state and local government focus and power) vied with the role of the regime in stimulating and forming the economy through internal-improvement projects and creation of opportunities (or simply deferring) to market-driven development. So, too, did the impact of social movements (gender and ethnic rights, and religious fervor in what Carroll Van West styles "the land, the people, and the culture") for creating identities. What made a distinctive Tennessean or Kentuckian, for instance, or even "the American"? And were they models of

---

[3] Daniel W. Crofts, *Reluctant Confederates: Upper South Unionists in the Secession Crisis* (Chapel Hill, 1989) as well as William W. Freehling, *The South vs. The South: How Anti-Confederate Southerners Shaped the Course of the Civil War* (New York, 2001); Robert Tracy McKenzie, "Prudent Silence and Strict Neutrality: The Parameter of Unionism in Parson Brownlow's Knoxville, 1860-1863," in *Enemies of the Country: New Perspectives on Unionists in the Civil War South*, ed. John C. Inscoe and Robert C. Kenzer (Athens, Ga., 2001), 73-96; McKenzie, *One South or Many? Plantation Belt and Upcountry in Civil War–Era Tennessee* (Cambridge, Eng., 1994).

the Jacksonian Common Man or the Whiggish elite?[4]

Underappreciated then and now, however, were linkages, matrices, patterns even more than conflict spawned by one or two issues taken by some as irrepressible. As a people, we were just as unformed as the state and far less congealed as to direction. Or at least, true to American form, the definition of that direction was as distinct as individuality amidst commonality in an era before socially wired media communication. Kentuckians and Tennesseans may have thought themselves distinct or different from each other or the rest of the country. But separation merely by state boundaries did not preclude sisterhood. True, a quintuple physiographic region Bluegrass and a tripartite grand divisional Volunteer identification suggest internal differences that cut across politics, economics, and sociocultural divides. Still, such east-west definition within these states defies an alternative, and impressive north-south orientation as antebellum affairs came to a crossroads over (we are told) the singularly most divisive issue of the time. The forming economic ties between Upper Midwest, Upper Heartland, and Deep South by inland or "interstate" connectors, soon enhanced by rail service, and sociocultural ties went unheeded because of the incendiary issue of human bondage as part of labor and capital.

Inevitably, slavery as the blot on the American escutcheon—whether part of a labor-capital system or a human-rights issue—gridlocked the nation. States like Kentucky and Tennessee were swept into this witches' brew by the middle of nineteenth century. That issue, set in the context of economic and political, even sociocultural growing pains, the unending search for self-governance, the brittle glue of political parties, and nativist racial attitudes, yielded the storyline for history books. Slavery and abolition resonate in the sesquicentennial climate. They wrap themselves into the historical question of inevitability versus avoidance—the great secession–Civil War quandary. When did one transpose to the other? How did Tennessee

---

[4] See Allan Nevins, *The War for the Union: The Improvised War, 1861-1862* (New York, 1959), "Giant in Swaddling Clothes," chap. 13; also Carroll Van West, ed., *Tennessee History: The Land, the People, and the Culture* (Knoxville, 1998), esp., title, subtitle, and preface.

and Kentucky stand at the center of the storm? What happened to the generation of Jackson and Clay and its talent for ameliorating confrontation? Were Kentuckians and Tennesseans every bit as guilty of the impasse as South Carolina and New England zealots? Was the nonperpetuation of ideas and blood (the curse of political dynasties and parties) predictable? Was something predestined in supplanting Clay, Jackson, Webster, and even Calhoun with the likes of Isham G. Harris, Andrew Johnson, Beriah Magoffin, and Thomas E. Bramlette?

For that matter, were those four politicians necessarily so inadequate to the challenge that fate dealt them? Was it not more the death of the second political party system (Democrat–Whig) or rise of a radicalized "tea party" destabilizer called Free-Soil Republicans, which conclusively answered the inevitability question? At some point, was it simply human fatigue—fatigue with media blasts, constant politicking, repeated compromising, and the transition of that "distant black cloud on the horizon" to some raven-like (perhaps buzzard-like might be more apt) shadow over everything men talked, wrote, or thought about which altered forever America's virginal landscape? That cursed institution, sanctioned if not ingrained in founding documents and antebellum American economics, power, and political control, coupled with the manifest destiny of westward expansion, had the power to simply render all else moot—even in the sister states.

From Failing to Failed

Surely, there was more to it as we look back one hundred fifty years. Our great American catastrophe—symbol and fact of a failed state—depended upon men's attitudes, actions, and events at all levels—national, regional, state, and local. Disunion, destabilization, reunification, and nationalization (nation-building) as human activities provided tests for both states. Separate segments of the period from 1860 to 1877 reflected levels of political, economic, and sociocultural issues and quandaries. They also suggest different moments when the die might have been cast otherwise but was not.

Kentucky might be said to have experienced four phases of trauma: (1) antebellum compromise and neutrality; (2) Confederate presence, even occupation; (3) Federal-state cohabitation (occupation and destabilization); and (4) postwar quasi-separation. Tennessee similarly passed through: (1) antebellum compromise followed ultimately by secession; (2) Confederate-state cohabitation and disaster; (3) Union instability, occupation, and reconstruction; and (4) postwar readjustment. Certainly, affairs often played out on different timelines within the grand divisions of Tennessee and the five regions of Kentucky.

Opportunities opened and closed politically for external as well as internal reasons in the two states. Combat and insurgency, political oppression, and socioeconomic revolution resulted from the frictional, systemic, transformative interaction of national, state, and local people and events. Passage through that most traumatic moment warrants appreciation of horizontal and vertical complexities, as illustrated in the Bluegrass and Volunteer States.

The great antebellum national issues of internal improvements, economic development, demographic and sociocultural changes, and the politics of party system and governance had unique grassroots expression in the upper heartland. Andrew Johnson, like Andrew Jackson, was a disciple of something called "laissez-faire constitutionalism" or opposition to overweening federal-government promotion of special interests rather than the general welfare. But were not special interests simply conglomerate manifestations derived from the general populace? In the end, by 1860 the throw of the dice involved a battle between special interests—ironically with common cause (single-crop agriculture and cloth manufacturing) fighting over one pivotal issue—labor. The interlocked economic matrix of Upper and Lower South suppliers and consumers with Eastern and Midwestern suppliers and consumers failed to hold. At issue basically was slavery—involving property, investment, and human capital. A presidential year pitted three of four candidates as sons of the upper heartland locked on this issue, and it culminated in disaster—the failed American State.

Neither Kentucky sons Lincoln and Breckinridge nor John Bell of Tennessee as candidates could hold the Sacred Union together.

Regular Democratic candidate Stephen Douglas, too, was a man be-yond which the affairs of men had passed. In fact, each candidate contributed to the demise through a political system that polarized the electorate and fractured the last political pillar of the old na-tion—Douglas's Democratic Party. In sum, the election put into the White House the spokesman of the radical, revolutionary party of that time. Lincoln came as a distrusted minority president and one who was such a cipher that only South Carolina thought it perceived his real meaning and dared test his determination. Other Lower-South states soon followed the Gamecock lead to try to forge a new nation. Interestingly, early secession did not include either Upper South Tennessee or border-state Kentucky.

Most Volunteer and Bluegrass voters passed over Lincoln. Their Unionist backing of Bell suggested avoidance of polarizing rhetoric and precipitous action concerning slavery or other reasons to break up the Union. Tennessee and Kentucky during what became styled "the Secession Winter" were among those political entities holding together a cascading house of cards. Perhaps less glamorous than Deep South demagoguery or zealot advocacy of northern aboli-tionists, the pro-Union, procompromise threads that lingered with sister-state politicians mitigated the impact of governors Harris and Magoffin. Wiser heads counseled patience concerning Lincoln and maybe even his native Kentucky counterpart, the president of the Confederacy, Jefferson Davis. To a point, neither of these men was quite positioned yet as chief executive to act other than through agents to resolve the grand dilemma. Indeed, a secession winter which dragged into spring reflected inertia born of uncertainty, misdirection spawned from irresolution.[5]

Response to a second incendiary event changed everything.

[5] Crofts, *Reluctant Confederates*, esp. epilogue as well as Freehling, *The South vs. The South*, 40-41, 52-54; *Sister States Enemy States*, ed. Dollar, Whiteaker, and Dickinson, part 1; William E. Hardy, "Reconstructing Andrew Johnson: The Influence of Laissez-Faire Constitutionalism on President Johnson's Restoration Policy," *Tennessee Historical Quarterly* 65 (2006): 71-92, and the visualization map of political sentiment in the 1860 presidential election in Kenneth C. Martis, *The Historical Atlas of the Congresses of the Confederate States of America: 1861-1865* (New York, 1994), map 2 on 14.

Conventional wisdom has the Volunteer State of Tennessee seceding from the Union after Fort Sumter. That same wisdom holds that Bluegrass Kentucky remained part of the United States. Unconventional wisdom might suggest that the Volunteer State returned to the Union before Appomattox with the Bluegrass State, according to E. Merton Coulter's famous quip (echoed recently by Gary W. Gallagher), joining the Confederacy *after* that culminating event. Thus, two peas in the pod of the Upper South heartland slave states followed different courses for the era of the Civil War and Reconstruction. Or did they? Both sister states were reluctant debutantes when it came to disunion—at least at first. Neither Harris of Tennessee nor Kentuckian Magoffin gained an immediate popular mandate for "going south." The time was simply not ripe in the hearts and minds of rank-and-file citizenry. Two fractionalized states in a dividing Union, this was a period for watchful waiting and searching yet for some sign. Their representatives in Washington like Andrew Johnson, Horace Maynard, and John J. Crittenden remained steadfast to the Union. There might still be time. The fact is that the sacred ties of Union were still a binding theme throughout much of America—Kentucky and Tennessee included.[6]

Of course, in retrospect, it was not, and time for compromise evaporated. The political issues were clear. Still, the true test became one of the fascinating ironies—escalation by secession to open conflict. Kentuckians would be front and center in that test also. The "Secession Winter" reflected the spirit of Clay when one of his successors, John J. Crittenden, sought desperately to counter Montgomery, Alabama, hotheads. Nothing came of compromise, and overheated rhetoric hardly betokened an atmosphere for negotiation. Electoral ballot counting and then presidential inauguration preceded Lincoln's moving into the White House. The political leaders of Tennessee called for a new "Union Party" in defense of what remained of the old nation. It was a season long on talk, short on patience. Yet nobody was quite ready for precipitous hostile action. If slavery

---

[6] Gary W. Gallagher, *The Union War* (Cambridge, Mass., 2011), 6.

stood at the root of the failed nation, secession and disunion would not transition to war over that issue as such. Slavery inflamed men's senses. Those senses found a new cause célèbre in April.[7]

Lincoln and Davis would be joined by another son of the Bluegrass at the storm's center as two (not one) American republics tested first and enduring principles, rule of law, and just who Americans thought they were after six or seven decades of independence. The presidential pair from the upper heartland seemed to have the key as to whether or not 1861 and succeeding years would be ones of peace and union or disunion and conflict. Remarkably, Lincoln, who thought losing Kentucky meant losing everything, adroitly maneuvered fellow Kentuckian Davis into the crucial first move that meant war. Determined to defend United States property under the Constitution, Lincoln went toe-to-toe with Davis over an indefensible fort in the Charleston, South Carolina, harbor. Quietly manipulative, Lincoln maneuvered hot-headed South Carolinians with Davis's sanction into firing the first shot.

But a third Kentuckian, U.S. Army Major Robert Anderson, actually occasioned the two nations' Rubicon by moving to defend Fort Sumter in the first place. Even then a war of rebellion (as the United States termed the Civil War for decades thereafter) or a war for independence (one of the titles bestowed by generations of Southerners) resulted more from Lincoln's next step than Davis's initial move. The day after Anderson's surrender at Fort Sumter, the sixteenth president of the United States used constitutional war powers to call upon state governors to supply militia to suppress domestic insurrection.

Herein lay the moment when Tennessee chose "enemy state" status by secession and admission to the Confederacy. Governor Harris announced that Tennessee would not furnish a single man "for the purposes of coercion." Kentuckian Magoffin was just as adamant, declaring famously, "Kentucky will furnish no troops for

---

[7] "Historians' Forum: The American Civil War's Centennial vs. the Sesquicentennial," *Civil War History* 57 (2011): 380-402.

the wicked purpose of subduing her sister Southern states." But he got no further in officially following Harris into Confederate ranks. Kentucky wobbled into remaining loyal (neutrality was but a shibboleth holding no viability), thus creating the stereotypical image of sister states now enemy states. Both sides spent the rest of 1861 reacting to Bluegrass neutrality, yet recruiting actively from her native white sons as well as her material resources. A "phony war" resulted. Both Union and Confederacy prepared for active military activities and tiptoed around Bluegrass "neutrality."[8]

Sisters as Enemies?

Were Kentucky and Tennessee necessarily at a tipping point in 1861? Were containment and deterrence still possible involving Kentucky and Tennessee? Or was simple geography prohibitive, given the fact that two rivers bounded the neutrality of the Commonwealth? Two more rivers bisected both Kentucky and Tennessee, obviating any necessity for an invader to even set foot on Bluegrass soil. Most of the secessionist Volunteer State could be controlled from waterways. Nashville, its capital, could be captured by means of the Cumberland. The Tennessee River could carry Union forces all the way to north Alabama. Steamboats on the western rivers were mostly northern-owned and northern-based; a Union river battle fleet was soon under construction.

Moreover, Kentucky neutrality upset the Confederate forward land defense and preemptively scuttled establishing a geographically northern frontier on the Ohio and Mississippi Rivers. So Kentucky pursued Magoffin's fragile neutrality yet concentrated its military power for deterrence of both sides. Tennessee mustered military strength in self-defense as the real western frontier of the Confederacy and hoped to push that line to the Ohio with the Bluegrass

[8] Useful points of departure include Lowell H. Harrison, *The Civil War in Kentucky* (Lexington, Ky., 1975); Lowell H. Harrison and James C. Klotter, *A New History of Kentucky* (Lexington, Ky., 1997), chaps. 13 and 14; and James L. McDonough, "Tennessee in the Civil War," *Tennessee History,* ed. Van West, 155-79; Magoffin quoted in Lewis and Richard H. Collins, *History of Kentucky*, 2 vols. (Covington, Ky., 1874), 1:87.

as a buffer to Yankee invasion. Under two state regimes, as well as two national governments, men and materiel increasingly merged uncertainty with certainty. Managing neutrality, containment, deterrence, and mobilization are delicate procedures even today. Both sides discovered that truth in the 1860s.[9]

Sam Summer, a detached Yankee observer, wrote home in late April 1861 to his father in Troy, Vermont, from a teaching post in Bourbon County, Kentucky. He nonetheless reported that he was still "going on with my school the same as ever but war has commenced and great excitement prevails here." Military companies were forming everywhere, although most "are what they call home guards." Some places saw the Secession flag hoisted, while the "Stars and Stripes" were flown elsewhere with money being raised to send to France for arms. Sumner had "no notion of becoming a Southern Mercenary," he assured his father, but had Northerners only accepted the Crittenden amendments "this scheme of secession would have proven abortive." Advocates of disunion would have been "robbed of their thunder" in his opinion, and he did "not believe that a single State with the exception of South Carolina would have left the Union." But now, Sumner thought that, "The 15 Slave states will go together." "When an old Patriot like J C Crittenden offered measures of reconciliation, the North should have offered to the South guarantees that they did not intend to interfere with the institution of Slavery either directly or indirectly" was his Green Mountain assessment.[10]

Neither state wanted to be a battleground, but each became just that by their actions during the first year of the war. Tennessee and Confederate impetuosity finally punctured the bubble of the delusional neutrality of Kentucky. Generals Leonidas Polk and Gideon Pillow (neither a professional soldier) set up shop on the Columbus

---

[9] See Earl J. Hess, *The Civil War in the West: Victory and Defeat from the Appalachians to the Mississippi* (Chapel Hill, 2012), chaps. 1 and 2; Benjamin Franklin Cooling, *Forts Henry and Donelson: The Key to the Confederate Heartland* (Knoxville, 1987), chaps. 1-4.

[10] Samuel Sumner to "Dear Father," April 27, 1861, *A War of the People: Vermont Civil War Letters*, ed. Jeffrey D. Marshall (Hanover, N.H., 1999), 22-23; Damon R. Eubank, *In The Shadow of the Patriarch: The John J. Crittenden Family in War and Peace* (Macon, Ga., 2009), chaps. 1 and 2; Albert D. Kirwan, *John J. Crittenden: The Struggle for the Union* (Lexington, Ky., 1962).

Bluffs in the Jackson Purchase section of Kentucky by early September. Federal moves from north of the Ohio soon followed in what was the greater coup. By taking Paducah and Smithland, the Federal, not the Confederate, government would control access to the inland waterways and might simply outflank the Columbus fortress that Polk and Pillow established to interdict the Mississippi trade route to the outside world. By October, Confederate theater commander Albert Sidney Johnston stretched his western departmental defense line longitudinally across the Bluegrass. He would spend six months marching and countermarching his understrength legions to create yet another illusion—numerical sufficiency. An equally chimerical Confederate state government, first under George W. Johnson, then Richard Hawes, vied for power with the regular, loyal Frankfort regime under both Magoffin and his successor James F. Robinson. Washington remained wary of Kentucky loyalty, and this affected state-national wartime relations accordingly. But Kentucky Confederate politicians chose exile south as did Tennessean Harris who managed to remain only a limited time at Nashville (before the defeats at Forts Henry and Donelson sent him packing), yet long enough, with national Confederate help, to stifle loyalist opposition in East Tennessee; his trampling on civil liberties eventually became the wartime norm in both Volunteer and Bluegrass States.[11]

The muster of the pro-southern State Guard versus the loyalist Union Home Guard in Kentucky reflected Bluegrass political disarray. "There is encamped here [Camp Boone near Clarksville, Tennessee] three regiments of Kentuckys, and a finer set of men I never saw," wrote William M. Matthews of the Second Kentucky,

---

[11] On the somewhat detached situation in East Tennessee, see Noel C. Fisher, *War at Every Door: Partisan Politics & Guerrilla Violence in East Tennessee, 1860-1869* (Chapel Hill, 1997); W. Todd Groce, *Mountain Rebels: East Tennessee Confederates and the Civil War, 1860-1870* (Knoxville, 1999); Robert Tracy McKenzie, *Lincolnites and Rebels: A Divided Town in the American Civil War* (New York, 2006); Brian D. McKnight, *Contested Borderland: The Civil War in Appalachian Kentucky and Virginia* (Lexington, Ky., 2006); and Kenneth W. Noe and Shannon H. Wilson, eds., *The Civil War in Appalachia: Collected Essays* (Knoxville, 1997); Richard N. Current, *Lincoln's Loyalists: Union Soldiers from the Confederacy* (Boston, 1992), chaps. 2 and 6; and the reprint of Oliver P. Temple's classic, *East Tennessee and the Civil War* (1899; repr., Johnson City, Tenn., 1995).

C.S.A. (which became part of the so-called "Orphan Brigade" of Bluegrass Rebels) to his aunt on September 5, "They are all healthy and true Kentuckians." In Tennessee, impressionable young men like Thomas B. Wilson of Davidson County anxiously searched around, often without finding a unit with space available. Wilson canvassed his neighbors and together they pooled the meager number willing to sign up. "The officers were all elected by ballot, Wilson remembered after the war, "and as I knew only a small part of the crowd my chances for an office were slim. But, I was patriotic enough just then not to care about that or whether I went as cavalry or infantry, but I learned better afterwards." There was not a counterpart Unionist military organization in sight, although pockets of closet loyalists existed throughout Tennessee. Summer, fall, and early winter provided a false security in the sister states. The recruits laughed and drilled and dropped like flies from camp diseases that claimed their young lives far from the glory for which they enlisted.[12]

Paroxysms of Violence

A second paradigm for examining the upper-heartland states

[12] Representative pieces for this critical and fascinating political period include J. Milton Henry, "The Revolution in Tennessee, February, 1861, to June, 1861," *Tennessee Historical Quarterly* 18 (1959): 99-119; Charles M. Cummings, "Robert Hopkins Hatton: Reluctant Rebel," *Tennessee Historical Quarterly* 23 (1964): 169-81; S. Kittrell Rushing, "Agenda-Setting in Antebellum East Tennessee," in *The Civil War and the Press*, ed. David B. Sachsman et al. (New Brunswick, N.J., 2000), 147-59; Charles Lufkin, "The Northern Exodus from Memphis during the Secession Crisis," *The West Tennessee Historical Society Papers* 42 (1988): 6-29; Benjamin F. Stevenson, "Kentucky Neutrality in 1861," in Loyal Legion of the United States, Ohio Commandery, *Sketches of War History: Papers Read before the Commandary*, ed. R. M. Kelly, 6 vols. (Cincinnati, 1888-1908), 2:44-45, and Kelly, "The Secret Union Organization in Kentucky in 1861," ibid., 3:278-91. For military matters, see Peter Franklin Walker, "Building a Tennessee Army: Autumn, 1861," *Tennessee Historical Quarterly* 16 (1957): 99-116; Harris D. Riley Jr. and Amos Christie, "Deaths and Disabilities in the Provisional Army of Tennessee," *Tennessee Historical Quarterly* 43 (1984): 132-54; Dillard Jacobs, "Outfitting the Provisional Army of Tennessee: A Report on New Source Materials," *Tennessee Historical Quarterly* 40 (1981): 3, 257-71; Ben L. Bassham, *Conrad Wise Chapman: Artist and Soldier of the Confederacy* (Kent, Ohio, 1998), 58-70; Bassham, ed., *Ten Months in the "Orphan Brigade": Conrad Wise Chapman's Civil War Memoir* (Kent, Ohio, 1999); George W. Johnson letters, fall 1861, Filson Historical Society, Louisville, Kentucky, and Thomas B. Wilson Reminiscences, 17-21, Southern Historical Collection, University of North Carolina, Chapel Hill, North Carolina; John K. Ross Jr., "Civil War Letters: Update," *Journal of the Jackson Purchase Historical Society* 29 (1991): 31-32.

and two nations sprang from the first. The die may have been cast with fanatic Edmund Ruffin's first cannon shot fired from the Charleston Water Battery. Still, the old order in Kentucky and Tennessee changed more because of singular events the next winter. Mill Springs in southern Kentucky and Forts Henry and Donelson just across the line in upper-middle Tennessee (January and February 1862, respectively) provided catalysts that altered the direction for the two states in virtually every unpredictable way. The three contests demolished the Confederate defense of the upper heartland (if not the desire to place their national frontier on the Ohio River and control Bluegrass soil). The three swept Federal arms up the inland rivers to the eventual occupation of most of Middle and West Tennessee (although postponing Lincoln's cherished wish to succor East Tennessee loyalists). Isolated behind the invaders lay the ardently secessionist Jackson Purchase section of western Kentucky.

The three battles shattered illusions of using both states' resources for the Confederacy; the battles cost invaluable if not irreplaceable stockpiles of clothing, foodstuffs, and munitions, and they sacrificed the first Confederate state capital, Nashville, to Federal control. A Rebel army corps equivalent (including prominent Confederate Kentuckians like Roger Hanson with Simon Bolivar Buckner and thousands of their men) departed for Yankee prison pens and set in motion a reputedly alcoholic, Union brigadier's road to the White House. Dreams of quick and managed violence evaporated and started the train of civil-military, sociocultural, and economic difficulties that rendered the two enemy states far more like sister states under national occupation, management, and supervision. Both states became the test bed for partisan or guerrilla warfare. Cavalry raids and savage intertribal conflict as well as civil disobedience upset commerce and communication, governance, and sociocultural comity far more than Confederate counterthrusts.[13]

[13] The war involving Kentucky and Tennessee can be studied in Hess, *Civil War in the West*, chaps. 3, 6, 10-11, 13-14, as well as Cooling, *Forts Henry and Donelson: Fort Donelson's Legacy: War and Society in Kentucky and Tennessee, 1862-1863* (Knoxville, 1997); and *To the Battles of Franklin and Nashville and Beyond: Stabilization and Reconstruction in Tennessee and Kentucky,*

Works studying the combat side of war in the western theater are legion. The war years themselves, a period of unprecedented, unbridled violence that has so fascinated generations of Americans, suggest a pyramid. The top layering focuses on great leaders, heroic soldierly deeds, traditional combat, and "what ifs" of strategy, operational art and tactics, and mighty armies (and fleets) traversing the landscape. Make no mistake; this tip of organized violence has unarguable importance. The centrality of battles and leaders always remains the focal point of wartime. Nonetheless, a second layer suggests auxiliary military operations known as raiding—by organized units or cavalry or infantry or what today is called "combined arms" of infantry, cavalry, and artillery or even "joint" army-navy expeditions. Even a third, much-broader layering concerns the unbridled, destabilizing violence of counterinsurgency and partisans or guerrillas, plus in the dying stages of organized war—plain banditry. Victims in each layer are always civilians regardless of gender, race, or economic, social, and political considerations. All three layers engulfed the sister–enemy states from 1861 to 1877.[14]

The fact that war includes more than battles and leaders is nowhere more apparent than in Kentucky and Tennessee. In the first place, the Confederacy failed three times (at least) to secure Kentucky and two of those occasions failed also to redeem Tennessee. In between, Mill Springs, Forts Henry and Donelson, Shiloh, Richmond, and Perryville, Stones River, Tullahoma, Chattanooga, Franklin, and Nashville peppered the landscape with cemeteries, broken hearts and bodies, and localized destruction. Today, those events populate books and i-pods. These Tennessee and Kentucky battles (seemingly only three of real note for the Bluegrass) helped determine the fate of mid-America and the United States as a whole. No doubt they shall continue to enrapture military professionals, battle "buffs," the curious public, tourists, and genealogists. Devotion of so much of the September 2007 issue of the scholarly journal *Civil War History*

1864-1866 (Knoxville, 2011).

[14] Thomas Hardy, *The Dynasts* (1904-1908), part II, section 5, famously observed that "war makes rattling good history; but Peace is poor reading."

to the "battle question" attests to the popularity of this sector.[15]

One can even make a case for the military side of battles and generals truly beginning and ending on Kentucky and Tennessee soil. Something as simple as one Southerner's Union victories at Mill Springs, Kentucky, in January 1862 and Nashville, Tennessee, in December 1864 provides this ironic twist—bookends to the war in the American heartland. That Southerner was a confirmed loyal Virginian, George H. Thomas, an outsider from start to finish in the pantheon of Ulysses S. Grant's Midwestern officers, who themselves cut their martial teeth in the Bluegrass and Volunteer States. By the same token, it could be argued that the war was essentially set in course, if not indeed settled by the Union capture of Forts Henry and Donelson on the Tennessee–Kentucky borderland of the inland rivers. It was only a matter of time whereby those highways reduced duration and distance for Union reduction of Confederate resistance and redemption of "wayward sisters" all the way to the Gulf of Mexico. Moreover, Mill Springs lay on the route for liberating the loyal people of East Tennessee to complete one of Lincoln's favorite war aims. Battles like Mill Springs and Forts Henry and Donelson doomed the Confederacy. Of course, it may not have seemed so in the winter of 1862.[16]

Counterfactual history also proves attractive at this point. What if some Kentucky equivalent of Richmond and Perryville had been fought at Bowling Green that first war winter or even spring? What if such decisive battles for the upper heartland like Forts Henry and Donelson or even Shiloh had occurred six months earlier in February 1862—on Kentucky soil? Or what if Albert Sidney Johnston had ridden out on the February battlefield at Fort Donelson to lead the Rebel breakout—and caught that Yankee (or maybe it was a Rebel) bullet then and there? The question has always been—should he

---

[15] See Frank Joseph Wetta, "Battle Histories: Reflections on Civil War Military Studies": Introduction, 229-35; Kenneth W. Noe, "Jigsaw Puzzles, Mosaics, and Civil War Battle Narratives," 236-43; George C. Rable, "The Battlefield and Beyond," 244-51; and Carol Reardon, "Writing Battle History: The Challenge of Memory," 252-63, all in *Civil War History* 63 (2007).

[16] Benson Bobrick, *Master of War: The Life of General George H. Thomas* (New York, 2009).

have gone in person to conduct a decisive winter battle rather than ignominiously retiring with William J. Hardee's Army of Central Kentucky, thus sacrificing all of the Bluegrass and virtually all of Middle and West Tennessee to the advancing northern host? Such are the provocative possibilities of armchair reinterpretation and re-directional thinking about what we know of battles, leaders, or what one author terms "a new geostrategic paradigm." Thus, speculative details of men and battles will always fill bookshelves for any Kentucky–Tennessee library of the war years.[17]

There is more to the "legacies" that stretch from Mill Springs and Forts Henry and Donelson in the layers of our paradigm. The "real war" that poet Walt Whitman alluded to grows closer when we dig through successive substrata of conflict. A second stratum emerges, rich with importance for the sister–enemy states in the war and thereafter. Here lay the authorized and organized military raids (mounted or otherwise) against logistical infrastructure of the armies as well as political stability and public will. Conducted by officially sanctioned instruments of state, such operations yielded the familiar names and glories of John Hunt Morgan, Nathan Bedford Forrest, or Joseph Wheeler (state icons even today for Kentucky, Tennessee, and Alabama) and their followers (commands). Less-well-known, generals Alvin Gillem, Lovell H. Rousseau, Samuel Carter, or Benjamin Grierson, even naval commander Samuel L. Phelps provided Union counterparts.

All traversed sections of Volunteer and Bluegrass terrain spreading hope, mayhem, transitory presence, and elusive success as well as varying degrees of destruction and violence sufficient also to fill the record. Today, they remain heroes or villains. Confederate demigods (underscoring a certain eternity to Lost Cause persuasion) contested invading predators from north of the Ohio. Still, heroic Union volunteers in uniform also came from divided Kentucky and Tennessee. They were dedicated to chasing rabble-rousing Rebels, a threat to the

---

[17] Spurgeon King, "Confederate Leadership in the West: Towards a New Geostrategic Paradigm," *Tennessee Historical Quarterly* 70 (2011): 142-49. See also James C. Bresnahan, ed., *Revisioning the Civil War: Historians on the Counterfactual Scenarios* (Jefferson, N.C., 2006), chap. 4.

Union but mostly to their own homes and families.[18]

In a sense, the raiders while detached from, yet part of, the armies did bridge the demarcation between organized violence and home fronts. Mobile raiders, like continuing battles, reflected the immediate inconclusiveness of conflict after Forts Henry and Donelson. The war would continue and whereby main-force military operations transcended time and place, an increased breakdown between clearly defined combat and noncombat zones (war zones and home front) emerged. Perhaps now we will take more comprehensive note of the colorful West Kentucky brigadier, Hylan B. Lyon, whose late-war rampage in the Bluegrass contributed virtually nothing to his main mission of supporting Confederate general John Bell Hood's "besieging" Nashville in December 1864—en route to a possible winter in the Bluegrass. Lyons burned Kentucky courthouses that served as administrative centers for oppressive Yankee occupation. This only further inflamed upper west Tennessee and western Kentucky, which were already on the brink of pure brigandage, murder, and breakdown of rule of law. Lyon earned the dubious sobriquet of the "courthouse burningest general." In any event, Lyon (or for that matter Morgan in a similar late-war foray to redeem his Commonwealth home) blurred this second-tier strata of legal, organized military operations with a third, involving a breakdown of law and order in the upper heartland.[19]

It was truly at the cusp of war and home front where a more holistic integration begins for understanding the Civil War and Reconstruction in Kentucky and Tennessee. Here ghosts of Vietnam, Bosnia, Iraq, Afghanistan, and Libya converge with our own epic struggle. True, Indian wars, the Philippine Insurrection, banana wars,

---

[18] For these colorful characters wending their way through Kentucky–Tennessee wartime history, see Cooling, *Fort Donelson's Legacy* and *To the Battles of Franklin and Nashville*; James D. Brewer, *The Raiders of 1862* (Westport, Conn., 1997); and James Alex Baggett, *Homegrown Yankees: Tennessee's Union Cavalry in the Civil War* (Baton Rouge, 2009). See also the essays in *Sister States, Enemy States*, ed. Dollar, Whiteaker, and Dickinson, part 2.

[19] Edward M. Coffman, ed., "The Memoirs of Hylan B. Lyon Brigadier General, C.S.A.," *Tennessee Historical Quarterly* 18 (1959): 35-53, and B. L. Roberson, "The Courthouse Burn'est General," ibid., 23 (1964): 372-78.

chasing Pancho Villa in Mexico, and other escapades lie in between (world wars and Korea notwithstanding). But, then and now, blurring lines between combatants and noncombatants in a tremulous mix of political, military, economic, and sociocultural affairs replicated occupied Volunteer and Bluegrass States. Such violence shaped hearts and minds of civilians and partisans, regular warriors, and just plain bandits and felons wrapped in the mantle of "irregulars." Hunter B. Whitesell declared fifty years ago of the Jackson Purchase during the Civil War, "notwithstanding the fact that the [region] was a portion of a loyal state, to Federal occupation authorities it represented hostile territory" with its citizenry "predominantly southern in their way of life, sympathy, and support [of the irregulars' war]."[20]

In fact, Kentucky and Tennessee linked the long continuum from prewar "Bloody Kansas" to the degradations of the Ku Klux Klan, corruption, and vendetta after the war. Tennessee and Kentucky were closer to the civil war practiced in Missouri and Kansas than the gentrified carnage in Virginia. Kentucky and Tennessee provided a middle ground that climaxed west of the Mississippi. Blue and gray, uniformed and civilian, soldiery and veterans, law-abiding and lawless alike—they could be found not only in the likes of Kentucky Confederate partisan rangers Tom Woodward (a West Pointer) and Adam Rankin Johnson but also in brutal loyalist, West Tennessee colonel Fielding Hurst; Stewart County, Tennessee, vigilante Old Jack Hinson; and Appalachian avenger Champ Ferguson. Significantly, William Clarke Quantrill, that arch-perpetrator of trans-Mississippi atrocities ended his days seeking refuge in Kentucky. He was mortally wounded and captured by local, dubiously reputed Bluegrass Union home guards near Taylorsville in Spencer County, south of Louisville. He died in a Louisville military prison. Ferguson went to the gallows from an appropriate trial after Appomattox.[21]

[20] Hunter B. Whitesell, "Military Operations in the Jackson Purchase Area of Kentucky, 1862-1865," *Register of Kentucky Historical Society* 63 (1965), part 1,141-67; part 2, 240-67, and part 3, 323-48.

[21] The growing body of literature of this genre of Civil War history includes William J. Davis, ed., *The Partisan Rangers of the Confederate States Army: Memoirs of General Adam R.*

A favorite piece in my personal Civil War memorabilia collection is an envelope containing the property of John H. Hart of Hardin County, Kentucky. At the time of the Civil War, he owned a farm on Youngers Creek about twenty miles from Elizabethtown, the county seat of Hardin County. Kentucky being a border state, stated Hart's great-grandson in a signed and notarized affidavit, "there were numerous partisans of both sides operating in this area and the settlers in Youngers Creek received frequent visits." Hart collected and retained four pieces of paper money that would pass down through the family—a U.S. ten-cent note; a State of Georgia Merchants Planters Bank, Savannah, two-dollar note; a Bank of Allegan, State of Michigan five-dollar note; and a Confederate ten-dollar note. As the great-grandson declared, "These bills were kept by my great-grandfather as souvenirs of the 'payments' he received for feed and livestock taken by the partisans of both sides." All that leads to yet another sister–enemy state paradigm.[22]

Social Dislocation and Revolution

A third paradigm for Kentucky and Tennessee did not automatically begin where battles left off. The Union military presence (Kentucky) or occupation (Tennessee) sparked fertile dimensions of "dark and bloody ground" for both states. Visualization of Federal control comes through the shrinking physical dimensions of the Confederacy as shown in Kenneth C. Marti's groundbreaking his-

Johnson (1904; repr., Austin, Texas, 1995); James Louis Head, *The Atonement of John Brooks: The Story of the True Johnny "Reb" Who Did Not Come Marching Home* (Geneva, Fla., 2001); Robert R. Mackey, *The Uncivil War: Irregular Warfare in the Upper South, 1861-1865* (Norman, Okla., 2004); Thomas D. Mays, *Cumberland Blood: Champ Ferguson's Civil* War (Carbondale, Ill., 2008); Tom C. McKenney, *Jack Hinson's One-Man War: A Civil War Sniper* (Gretna, La., 2009); Clay Mountcastle, *Punitive War: Confederate Guerrillas and Union Reprisals* (Lawrence, Kans., 2009); Sean Michael O'Brien, *Mountain Partisans: Guerrilla Warfare in the Southern Appalachians, 1861-1865* (Westport, Conn., 1999); John Sickles, *The Legends of Sue Mundy and One Armed Berry: Confederate Guerrillas* (Merrillville, Ind., 1999); Thurman Sensing, *Champ Ferguson: Confederate Guerrilla* (Nashville, 1942); Daniel E. Sutherland, *A Savage Conflict: The Decisive Role of Guerrillas in the American Civil War* (Chapel Hill, 2009) and Sutherland, ed., *Guerrillas, Unionists, and Violence on the Confederate Home Front* (Fayetteville, Ark., 1999).
[22] John Glenn Hart III, paper money and affidavit, author's collection.

torical atlas of Confederate congresses. Forts Henry and Donelson produced military occupation, wartime reconstruction, and home-front oppression and resistance only randomly brushed by promise of Confederate redemption. Social revolution and demographic dislocation followed. Understanding the permeability of violence and normality, and stability and resurrection from 1862 on in Kentucky and Tennessee is a prerequisite for exploring gender and ethnic studies. Linked inextricably to the third tier of violence through military and civil administration, logistical and strategic infrastructure, guerrillaism, and plain banditry, the civilian sector produced particular political, ideological, and survival issues.[23]

Women beyond the battlefield, hospital, and service sector, as well as children and elderly noncombatants found themselves vulnerable. They encountered ill-disciplined rabble and flotsam passing as uniformed representatives of both national armies as well as the irregular jetsam of those militaries. One recent book, *Occupied Women*, suggests how this experience shaped southern women of all classes. Their focus and their memories, reflected in surviving letters, diaries, and family folklore, shaped their subsequent attitudes, as well as our own understanding of that age-old problem of noncombatants in a combat zone. Civilians of all political stripes, class, or economic status—and most certainly race—faced the shadowy uncertainty of informants and spies, felons of dubious affiliation, and the so-called partisans. As the war progressed, almost separate groupings emerged—mostly bandits and criminals as well as a vagabond, displaced refugee population of blacks and whites. Broken families and shattered hopes symbolized splintered communal trust and weakened underpinnings of society all across Kentucky and Tennessee.[24]

---

[23] Martis, *Historical Atlas*, maps 2-5, on 14-17, and maps 13, 15, 17, 19, 21, 23, on 42, 44, 46, 48, 50, 52; also Stephen V. Ash, *When the Yankees Came: Conflict and Chaos in the Occupied South, 1861-1865* (Chapel Hill, 1995) and *Middle Tennessee Society Transformed, 1860-1870: War and Peace in the Upper South* (Baton Rouge, 1988); Freehling, *The South vs. The South* as well as Cooling, *Fort Donelson's Legacy* and *To the Battles of Franklin and Nashville*.

[24] LeeAnn Whites and Alecia P. Long, eds., *Occupied Woman: Gender, Military Occupation, and the American Civil War* (Baton Rouge, 2009); Bradley Clampitt, "'Not Intended to Dispossess Females': Southern Women and Civil War Amnesty," *Civil War History* 56 (2010): 324-49.

247

To be sure, the firestorm of slavery that produced one failed nation and undergirded the spawning of another, translated from liberation to emancipation. What resulted amounted to a freedpeople's revolution. Bluegrass and Volunteer African Americans as well as whites helped accomplish that revolution. Neither group necessarily accepted the result with equitable felicity. Just as events and men had prompted the political revolution of secession turned war, events and men of wartime itself transposed social and economic revolution. In turn, they produced a clangor of well-intended postwar legalization through national constitutional amendments and rewritten state constitutions that in many ways only further exacerbated a cesspool of racial enmity, violence, and disquietude. Wartime experiences and attitudes continued to offer a red flag to returning veterans in Kentucky and Tennessee, as well as home-front victims for an unrepentant generation of Southerners and an emasculated body of loyalists in the sister states. Furthermore, a detached, almost disinterested body of victorious Northerners as well as defeated Southerners (Kentuckians and Tennesseans among them) moved west after Appomattox. Freedpeople as well as most whites who were unable to relocate were left to fend for themselves in an inhospitable postwar South.[25]

This intricate sociocultural picture of war years in Kentucky and Tennessee brushes squarely against politics and the military story. A new Civil War history based on ethnic and gender demographics offers enough horror tales, heroic acts of resistance, patriotism (of both blue and gray), and impact upon hearts and minds to resurrect *Gone with the Wind, Horse Soldiers, Cold Mountain,* and *Outlaw Josey Wales,* countering a more antiseptic Ken Burns trudge through the war years. Again, Forts Henry and Donelson, Shiloh, and subsequent encounters of summer and fall 1862 chronologically broke apart a structured war. They opened the veins of venomous occupation, phony emancipation and nonenforcement of fugitive-slave law,

---

[25] Follow this theme in Heather Cox Richardson, *West from Appomattox: The Reconstruction of America after the Civil War* (New Haven, Conn., 2007); Marshall, *Creating a Confederate Kentucky;* and Andrew L. Slap and Gordon McKinney, eds., *Reconstructing Appalachia: The Civil War's Aftermath* (Lexington, Ky., 2010).

social revolution, and destruction of accustomed social-stratification patterns. Affected was the comity of home and hearth, family and surroundings, and neighborhood and region.

As soon as any Union soldiers or sailors came to conquer, the world changed. Nannie Haskins in Clarksville, Eleanora Williams at Cumberland Furnace, Dickson County, or Maury County farmer Nimrod Porter—all Tennesseans—captured that life-shattering recognition in the accounts they left us. So, too, did Kentucky diarists George Richard Browder and Thomas W. Parsons and Unionist Lexingtonian Frances Peter as well as Rebel Amelia Bourne of Somerset. Investigative work by National Park Service historian Susan Hawkins at Fort Donelson illustrates the synthesis of the black and white experience in that very crucial community that witnessed four years of main-force operations, strategic-hamlet occupation, and counterguerrilla operations on the site of both Confederate and Union river guard posts.[26]

Confiscation acts, conscription laws, partisan-ranger laws and rules, violations of civil liberties, declarations of martial law, and suspension of habeas corpus numbered among Union and Confederate government war measures affecting the populations of Kentucky and Tennessee. Occupation of churches, schools, and private structures along with suppression of press freedom and a passport system for passage behind, much less passage through, combatant lines—all spoke to a similar pattern in the Upper Heartland. In both Kentucky and Tennessee, a true civil war between brothers and sisters became part of suppressed corporate memory for the next

---

[26] Susan Hawkins, "Forts Henry, Heiman, and Donelson: The African-American Experience" (MA thesis, Murray State University, 2004), available from NPS main site: http://www.nps.gov/history/history/park histories/index.htm reference Fort Donelson; John David Smith and William Cooper Jr., eds., *A Union Woman in Civil War Kentucky: The Diary of Frances Peter* (Lexington, Ky., 2000); Richard Troutman, ed., *The Heavens are Weeping: The Diaries of George R. Browder, 1851-1886* (Grand Rapids, Mich., 1987); Frank F. Mathias, ed., *Incidents and Experiences in the Life of Thomas W. Parsons from 1826 to 1900* (Lexington, Ky., 1975); Eleanora Williams diary, Special Collections, University of Tennessee Library, Knoxville, Tennessee; Nannie Haskins Diary, Special Collections, University of North Carolina Library, Chapel Hill, North Carolina; and Nimrod Porter Journals, 1861-1871, 1880-1898, 5 vols., UNC microfilm, Tennessee State Library and Archives, Nashville, Tennessee.

one hundred fifty years. It was even stoked by legitimate logistics gone awry. Kentuckians in 1864 suffered through "the Great Hog Swindle" whereby Union quartermasters short-changed Bluegrass pork suppliers until exposed and corrected. Political ramifications for the actions of military supply agents searching for "best value" and bottom-line efficiency in procurement activities parallels present-day operations of the military-industrial complex. It was alive and well in Civil War sister–enemy states. One might cite similar plausible but controversial actions of military governor and Brigadier General Andrew Johnson of Tennessee for having unintended consequences amongst the populace.[27]

Assuredly, the straw that broke the proverbial camel's back was the social revolution attending the evolution of the conflict itself. Passage from a war for the Union or the Confederacy into a war of liberation and emancipation unnerved both loyal and dissident whites in Kentucky and Tennessee. African Americans stood at the apex of how the civilian population as well as the fighting forces changed in composition and attitude over the course of the war. That saga flowed from a question of liberation of human beings to the pure labor issue of lost property and productive enterprise. That progression reached a culmination in the determination of the Federal government that black males might become not merely drovers and haulers (free rather than enslaved) but also fighting men, recruited, even conscripted, to effect their own liberation (and, incidentally, offset white-male shortages for the combat slaughter pens). Where did preservation of the Union, the constitution "as it is," and property protection migrate to some other war aim?[28]

Loyal slaveholding Kentucky and Tennessee citizens scratched their heads and bitterly resented heavy-handed recruitment and

---

[27] On political reverberations of a purely military logistical issue, see E. Merton Coulter, *Civil War and Readjustment in Kentucky* (1926; repr., Gloucester, Mass., 1966), 222-24; Harrison, *Civil War in Kentucky*, 100-101; and Marshall, *Creating a Confederate Kentucky*, 23.

[28] See Victor B. Howard, *Black Liberation in Kentucky: Emancipation and Freedom, 1862-1884* (Lexington, Ky., 1983); Darrel E. Bigham, *On Jordan's Banks: Emancipation and Its Aftermath in the Ohio River Valley* (Lexington, Ky., 2006); and John Cimprich, *Slavery's End in Tennessee, 1861-1865* (University, Ala., 1985).

impressments of black labor. Their Rebel kinfolk reacted just as negatively to the government resource extraction of goods and services through conscription and impressments by the Confederate government at Richmond. Still, that intractable prewar issue of slavery remained the burr under Kentucky and Tennessee saddles during the wrenching wartime experience. Society had to adjust to a revolution imposed from above and individually inspired acts of dissidence from below. This displacement of labor from a closed to an open system in the end concluded at the very apex of the greatest fears of southern whites—placing firearms and legitimacy in the hands of their former slave "mudsills," thus nailing the coffin shut on an institution, a system, a way of life. As one former slave apocryphally declared, "the bottom rail is now on the top." When the process from enslavement to freedom passed so harshly through refugee facilities like Camp Nelson, Kentucky, can we really wonder that white and black attitudes remained so sour when the organized fighting eventually stopped?[29]

Slaveholding politician and closet-racist Andrew Johnson (who really presided only over those portions of Tennessee where he and Union arms actually exerted control) stands out in the internal struggle in the Volunteer State. So, too, the whirlwind passage across Kentucky by dedicated but oppressive soldier-bureaucrats like Jeremiah Boyle, Stephen Burbridge, or E. A. Payne (who terrorized Middle Tennessee before shifting to Paducah, Kentucky) clarifies the Bluegrass story. That story included military and civilian Union officials mixing counterguerrilla suppression, punishment of treason, and African American recruitment to the discomfort of loyal and disloyal citizens alike. Contemporary comments confided to personal diaries proclaimed the feelings of Rebel sympathizer Eleanora Williams who wrote of "melancholy days" from Cumberland Furnace, Tennessee, on October 1, 1862. "Cousin Robert has just returned from Nashville," she penned in her diary. "Every thing there looks

[29] Mary Clay Berry, *Voices from the Century Before: The Odyssey of a Nineteenth-Century Kentucky Family* (New York, 1997); Richard D. Sears, *Camp Nelson, Kentucky: A Civil War History* (Lexington, Ky., 2002).

very gloomy and the Northern invaders are exercising their ill gotten power to the fullest extent to which tyrant spirits prompt them. May our God soon free our Country from the pollution of their foul spirits!" No less impassioned, Lexington schoolgirl Frances Peter noted in her diary in mid-March 1864 that the threat of Confederate invasion might prompt even a counterrevolution against the Lincoln government "which will greatly aid the rebel army in taking the state out of the Union." Times appeared "stormy," she suggested, "but the old ship of state weathered the first storm in 1861 and I expect she will weather this one also."[30]

Colonel Nathaniel Collins McLean (an Ohio veteran of the war in the East, but by April 1864 relegated to headquarters duty under Burbridge), wrote his wife on April 12 how he had gone to a public meeting and heard ardent Unionists Dr. Robert Breckinridge and Charley Anderson speak. "They both made stirring and effective appeals but their very speeches brought out in the audience, or a portion of them, the evidence of a dangerous feeling which must be carefully watched and rigidly put down as Kentucky will blase [sic] up the rebellion, under a false name." The Rebel-sympathizing locals near Lexington, he suggested, "are evidently expecting a raid and many of them are preparing their affairs so that they can meet with no loss." "A feeling of excitement is constantly kept up by the disloyal which prevents the growth of a healthy Union sentiment and I am sorry to say that this feeling is largely aided by many officers here in our army who are of the [Frank] Woolford [sic] school." Wolford and other Unionist Kentuckians were unhappy about emancipation, black military recruitment, and heavy-handed treatment of Kentucky by Washington. Thus, McLean had his hands full, although forced to admit that in their remarks and actions, he found "nothing strong enough for me to take hold of." Still, like Burbridge, McLean's intimidating presence guaranteed ill feelings for the duration of the Union military presence in the Bluegrass. Authoritarian military ac-

---

[30] Eleanora Williams diary, October 1, 1862, Special Collections, University of Tennessee; Smith and Cooper, eds., *A Union Woman*, 197; Bryan S. Bush, *Butcher Burbridge: Union General Stephen Burbridge and His Reign of Terror over Kentucky* (Morley, Mo., 2008).

tions prejudiced "hearts and minds" of the time and help us better understand the raw edges of civil war in the region.[31]

Destruction and Privation

Conventional wisdom also portrays the next paradigm as two states "burned out and "eatin' out" by the close of the war. Lee Anderson of Company B, 153rd Illinois, wrote his cousin Nelson from Tullahoma, Tennessee, on March 22, 1865:

> Most of the people in this part of the world have fled, either North or South, and if they ever return they will find a sorry looking place, fields gone, plantations destroyed, buildings burned, and their *niggers free* & in short everything is entirely "gone up" & what "always white trash" is left, are as igno- rant as the heathen theirselves in walking the streets 1/2 the persons you meet are Soldiers 2/5 negroes & the rest are mostly "American citizens of African descent."

Four days earlier, William H. Green of Company F, Forty-fifth New York Veteran Volunteers, had walked out on the Nashville battle-field to be greeted with a gruesome sight: "the field is covered with dead horses and bones of all kinds," but he "did not see any Skulls there, I suppose they were all buried." He was more enamored with a private cemetery caught up in the fighting, the marble headstones mixing with those of humble wood, the gender segregation, and flowers he "picked from the Battle field." He wished his sister "to press them and lay them away for me." Memories and impressions were indelibly etched on the witnesses as well as participants as the war ended in Kentucky and Tennessee.[32]

As intriguing, if somewhat opaque, for both Kentucky and Ten-nessee is the economic facet of sister states–enemy states. Perhaps here is the phoenix-like story that links the darkness of failed state and a rejuvenated "reconciled" Kentucky of Coulter and Marshall with a "restored" Tennessee beyond Andrew Johnson. In a sense,

---

[31] N. C. McLean to his wife, April 12, 1864, author's collection.

[32] William H. Green to his sister, March 18, 1865, and Lee Anderson to his cousin Nelson, March 22, 1865, both in ibid.

that story in itself is a waystation en route to a New South in a new reunified America. But how may we judge the economic impact of various military incarnations rolling across the two states? How do we measure the economies of human conflict—their logistical umbilical cords strung out behind armies and fleets feeding local economies as much as sucking them dry? These cords caused destructive disruption resulting from pilfering and creation of displaced vagabondage, conscription, home-guard persecution, black liberation, breakdown of law and order, and prohibition of peacetime commercial intercourse.

War interrupted customary trading patterns, even local sustainment. Kenneth Martis's mapping, which combined data, text, and illustrations, might be profitably supplemented by a wider analysis from John Solomon Otto's *Southern Agriculture during the Civil War Era* (1994). Harrison and Klotter's *New History* (1997) has a useful subsection on economic aspects of the war for Kentucky, supplemented by the "destructiveness in the Confederacy" thesis of Paul F. Paskoff. As Bluegrass historian Lowell Harrison so eloquently put it, although "Kentucky did not experience as much physical damage as some of the other states in which the war was fought," there were few of her citizens whose lives were not in some manner affected "by the demands of the great conflict." Echo the same, and more, for sister state Tennessee.[33]

Harrison gave a balanced appraisal when he observed that a number of towns suffered considerable damage: "Economic losses were certain when troops passed through a region, and the color of their uniforms made little difference." Fences for camp firewood and vanished orchards, corncribs, and chicken coops attested to capital losses for providers, and consumable gains for the acquirer. Fodder, grain, and livestock (hogs and cattle especially) supplemented army-

[33] Harrison, *Civil War in Kentucky*, 80, 94; Harrison and Klotter, *New History*, 207-9; Martis, *Historical Atlas*, maps 9-11, on 38-40; John Solomon Otto, *Southern Agriculture during the Civil War Era, 1860-1880* (Westport, Conn., 1994), 2, 6-7, 9-10, 12, 15, 21, 23, 26, 32, 40, 43-44, 50, 59, 63, 65-66, 71, 74, 85-87, 98, 100-101, 107, 110, 115-16, and Paul F. Paskoff, "Measures of War: A Quantitative Examination of the Civil War's Destructiveness in the Confederacy," *Civil War History* 54 (2008): 35-62.

supplied provender. Horses and mules were worth their price in gold as precursors to horseless carriages. Regardless of requisitioning cavalrymen, procurement officials, and itinerant robbers, the four-footed contributors to the war effort were, as Harrison picturesquely put it, "volunteered for military service." Human capital was similarly procured. The white volunteers and conscripts for both sides and the liberated and enslaved blacks similarly were impressed for hard labor and service in the ranks. Moreover, while Harrison did not focus on it, the Kentucky hemp industry (already in possible decline anyway) never recovered the loss of its Deep South cotton markets. As James F. Hopkins stated in his classic study of that industry, the United States prohibited shipment of rope and bagging into the South, "thereby outlawing the trade from which a part of Kentucky had derived its livelihood."[34]

Statistics plus human recall translate to understanding how a society so economically rent one hundred fifty years ago might continue to react attitudinally for years thereafter. Had econometrics reached sophisticated analysis in either Washington or Montgomery and Richmond at the time, there might not have been secession and war in the first place. Perhaps the same could be said for Frankfort or Nashville, or even Louisville, Paducah, Memphis, Knoxville, or Chattanooga. One doubts it, for inflamed passions and politics meant that war came anyway. With it came the inherently governmental responsibility of mobilizing resources by modern planning and analysis to tap the emotions in 1860-61. Institutional responses from the national and state governments by the spring and summer of 1861, mostly cobbled together by both sides, served as an economic stimulus as state and national officials saw mobilization for deterrence, containment, or, at most, a short war. That changed when the destructiveness of protracted struggle drained breadbaskets and stock pens of the sinews of war. The destructiveness of war conditioned the economies of the sister states in ways still requiring

[34] James F. Hopkins, *A History of the Hemp Industry in Kentucky* (1951; repr., Lexington, Ky., 1998), chap. 6, esp. 193; see also the classic Byrd Douglas, *Steamboatin' on the Cumberland* (Nashville, 1961), chap. 5.

more reexploration.

In a section on the "Kentucky World of 1865," Harrison and Klotter noted that of the approximately one hundred forty thousand Bluegrass sons who went off to fight, thirty thousand or 21 percent never returned. "Their graves were scattered across a large, war-ravaged area," with thousands more wounded, maimed physically or mentally. "An entire era had been blighted" with all to show for it—empty sleeves, legless bodies, permanent damage to the mind, the very things the second decade of the twenty-first century confronts from its particular forays. The authors continued about the loss of leaders—"what art, literature, or statecraft would have resulted from those lives?" A generation would grow to maturity without those lost talents. Even more so for the Volunteer State, as James L. McDonough declared regarding the arrival of peace in the spring of 1865, "The conflict had been a tragedy without parallel for the state of Tennessee," as "the loss of life and the destruction of property had been appalling." He added that the stigma of rebellion would endure for decades with "part of that cost [being] the loss of power in national politics," a thought that echoed for loyal Kentucky.[35]

Paskoff's discussion hints at the reality but only for Tennessee. In one table, he suggests that of eighty-four Volunteer counties, 58 percent could be labeled "war counties." With 63 percent of 42,150 total square miles, holding a black and white population of 109,801, 70 percent of the land fit the "war category," affecting 69 percent of whites and 76 percent of blacks. Of a total of 36,844 slaveholders, 74 percent resided in "war counties." Notwithstanding his determination that neither side intended nor authorized wholesale "total war" like that of the Thirty Years' War or the Hundred Years' War, his additional charts and statistics suggest that events overtook intent. Of nineteen Tennessee towns and cities, eleven (58 percent) fit "war zone" criteria. Yet none were destroyed, however much demographic changes or privation affected them. Of local seats of government—county courthouses—while many counties conducted

[35] McDonough, "Tennessee in the Civil War," 176; Harrison and Klotter, *New History*, 215.

business in something other than a dedicated building, only five distinct structures or 10 percent of the "war county" courthouses were destroyed. The fact that these courthouses and their towns became Federal military enclaves for controlling the region and its inhabitants meant that Kentucky suffered far more proportionally, because of Hylan Lyon, than because of any Yankee invader. Official business, faced with loss of court and other official records, suffered accordingly after the war.[36]

Still, Paskoff's impersonal computations of percentage decreases in the value of farm implements and machinery between the 1860 and 1870 censuses prove frankly astonishing. Of Tennessee's supposed "nonwar counties," a decline of 8 percent was the lowest in the defeated Confederacy, as was the 2 percent values for "war counties." Obviously, this anomaly between conflict, destruction, and statistics points to the huge change in human, not physical, capital. Moreover, fecundity of agriculture over a decade hardly reflected the immediate postwar privation when absence of working animals and other livestock should be factored in. Nor, perhaps, did passage from slave to free (even if indentured) labor. As Harrison and Klotter more picturesquely suggest, "the conflict left behind its toll of physical destruction," because "crops had been lost, livestock taken, and property destroyed." Then the agricultural sector that had seemed so promising from 1850 to 1860 (according to census counts) had been drastically altered. "There were 89,000 fewer horses, 37,000 fewer mules, and 172,000 fewer cattle in Kentucky in 1865 than at the start of the war," they note. The amount of land under cultivation plummeted, as did land values.

One might question similar effects in cities like Louisville in Kentucky or Memphis, Nashville, Chattanooga, and Knoxville in Tennessee. Nevertheless, "neglected farms . . . roads and paths overgrown with weeds, and almost no business of any kind being carried on"

[36] Paskoff, "Measures of War," tables 1 and 2 on 42, 47; compare Coffman, "Lyon Memoirs" and Roberson, "Courthouse Burn'est General" with Dan Lee, "'Success Beyond My Most Sanguine Expectations': General Hylan B. Lyon's Kentucky Raid, 1864," *North & South* 14 (2012): 54-61, which completely omits the broader impact.

greeted one returning Bluegrass veteran at war's end. Kentucky had been "hobbled" write Harrison and Klotter, and that phrase fit Tennessee as well. But postwar physical recovery for agriculture would occur in direct proportion to the need for subsistence and market. As echoes of armies, pilferage of brigands, and privations of civilians (white and black) faded, new challenges awaited survivors.[37]

Paskoff's third sector of physical capital destructiveness included the railroads. Despite a state like Tennessee or Kentucky sustaining memorable hits (according to historical accounts or, say, the Louisville & Nashville Railroad annual reports), Paskoff concluded that "at most" 47 percent of the Confederacy's total 9,415 miles of railroad track could have been destroyed. This assumed that Union troops tore up every mile of track in the "war states." His calculations for Tennessee's eighty-four counties with 231 stations and 1,341 miles of trackage record 38 stations (16 percent) and 298 miles (22 percent) in "nonwar counties," 193 stations (84 percent) and 1,043 rail miles (78 percent) in "war counties." Paskoff does not provide the same statistics on actual damage to such capital. Moreover, his conclusion that Volunteer State railroad damage (to rails, rights-of-way, locomotives and rolling stock, infrastructure of bridges, water towers, roundhouses, and depots) may have been negligible seems questionable, especially since military and railroad records (not to say personal accounts) suggest otherwise.

Railroads that had been seized and managed by the military or handled roughly, like James Guthrie's privately operated Louisville & Nashville line, experienced rehabilitation and rebuilding by the end of the war. This war-induced upgrading laid the groundwork for a rapid return to normal or even improvement for upper-heartland postwar railroading. Overlooked also is the experiential factor seemingly captured, once again, by Allan Nevins when he spoke in 1960 to a later war-trained managerial and administrative generation that emerged from the butchery better for the experience of handling modern business operations and logistics of bigger enterprises like

---

[37] Paskoff, "Measures of War," table 3 on 51; Harrison and Klotter, *New History*, 216.

railroads (or steamboat lines for that matter).[38]

Forrest, Morgan, Wheeler, and the partisans may have conducted their destructive "railroad war" to warm Rebel hearts, but at the same time Union minions developed skillful innovations to keep supply lines operable from Cincinnati and Louisville to Chattanooga and beyond. These same innovators improved the uncompleted Nashville and Northwestern Railroad as a military line servicing a Johnsonville supply base on the Tennessee River. Several rail lines in Kentucky experienced similar military-induced improvements to support localized operations. Today, one can see a legacy of working freight rail on rights-of-way that the Civil War ripped up and put back together again in Kentucky and Tennessee. Ironically, other significant transportation elements central to war and peace—steamboats or the telegraph—seemingly escape Paskoff's cliometrical findings. Yet they were indispensable to judging the impact of the war on the economic infrastructure and commerce of the two states.[39]

The fascinating story of seized or confiscated property (human and material) has yet to be adequately told. Certainly, there was redress after the war—if you could prove your wartime loyalty to the United States! The exchange of Stanton McGuire's seized steamboat *Baldwin* was such a case in point. Here was an instance of an innocent Tennessee boat owner caught up in secession, the Confederate blockade of river trade in 1861-62, and the fall of Fort Donelson. He lost his means of earning a living, first to Rebel authorities who confiscated and used the steamboat and then to United States authority and use after the fall of that fort and the city of Nashville. The *Baldwin* then passed to Federal quartermaster usage before, unbeknownst to McGuire, being sold in court for half its value. In February 1865, he petitioned for thirty thousand dollars in damages. This business of wartime loss and postwar recovery (or permanent loss of real and personal property) fairly begs for research, study, and analysis before we can properly pronounce upon the economic

[38] Allan Nevins, *The War For The Union: The Organized War, 1863-1864* (1960; repr., New York, 1971), chaps. 7 and 8.
[39] Paskoff, "Measures of War," table 4 on 53 as well as 52-54.

impact of the war on Kentucky and Tennessee.[40]

"Lost Cause" and "Great Alibi" rationales of postwar Southerners about depredations and privations do not obviate Paskoff's
striking conclusion—"that the extent and intensity of that physical
destruction were considerably less than has been thought does not
mean that the war was not deadly, destructive and traumatizing." War
created many widows and half-orphans, he asserts, and "impoverished
even non-slaveholding families by the loss of the labor of men to
battle and family heirlooms and silver to looters," many in Union
blue. Such losses and accompanying emotions "were tragedies for
the families and individuals who experienced them," notes Paskoff,
echoing Harrison and Klotter. But to Paskoff, the individual traumas,
numerous as they appear from historical accounts "did not amount
to devastation or explain the demonstrable lag in the performance
of the southern economy in the decades following the war." He, like
others, suggests that "the war killed slavery, and, with it, an entire
system of valuating capital, labor, and wealth." That would have been
true not merely for those rebellious states that left the Union, such
as Tennessee. Four loyal slave states, with Kentucky as an example,
reflected that same truth. As such, then, if "the war did not, however,
destroy the South's capacity to generate wealth," it certainly crippled
it for a time in the Bluegrass and Volunteer States.[41]

Reconstitution and Readjustment

Reconstruction of the Union began when the first Federal troops
crossed the Ohio and Potomac Rivers. We have been loath to embrace
so-called "Reconstruction" since the years 1865-77 hardly reflect well
on American democracy. Tennessee and Kentucky in many ways
mirror the national picture. When reconstruction (always identified in Kentucky as "readjustment" and "restoration" in Tennessee
by one scholar, perhaps to differentiate them from the other more
onerous "R" word) actually ended remains unclear in comparison

[40] Stanton P. McGuire petition, February 15, 1865, McGuire Papers, Filson Historical
Society; see also Douglas, *Steamboatin' on the Cumberland*, 174-80.
[41] Paskoff, "Measures of War," 55-57.

with the national version. Coming to terms with this final paradigm should be a priority for the sesquicentennial. In some ways, it can even better illumine the permeability question of conflict generally as well as sociocultural, political, and especially economic dimensions of destruction and recovery. Unfortunately, the focus of current Civil War studies seems to preclude a more holistic or rationalized examination. The field suggests that slavery was merely replaced by race as the lodestone of both wartime and postwar reconstruction in the sister states. Yet, even here, there remains an economic as well as sociocultural and political prism worth considering.[42]

A disruption of economics and trade, the politics of occupation and the sociocultural revolution all depended upon this single, defining lightning rod—slavery followed by emancipation. Yet, in both states exploring the restoration of civil government and constitutional reform in Tennessee (thanks to Johnson, "Parson" Brownlow, and the radicals); the agonizing readjustment battles of Bramlette and Burbridge (later Major General John M. Palmer) as well as several successor civilian governors; the return of conservative veterans from both sides in Kentucky all suggest structural as well as attitudinal factors at work. The military dimension, whether through wartime presence of Federal and state troops in the Upper South hinterland or resurrection of some form of normal state militia (the Tennessee State Guard, the Kentucky National Legion) for law and order enforcement, stability, or population control after the war, remains an important theme. Recent works underscore this assertion.[43]

[42] Start with the classic Coulter, *Civil War and Readjustment in Kentucky*, chaps. 13–19 before moving to Marshall, *Creating a Confederate Kentucky*; Slap and McKinney, *Reconstructing Appalachia*, as well as Benjamin Franklin Cooling, "After the Horror: Reconstruction in Kentucky," in *Sister States, Enemy States*, ed. Dollar, Whiteaker, and Dickinson, 320-62. Likewise, for Tennessee, start with James Welch Patton, *Unionism and Reconstruction in Tennessee, 1860-1869* (1934; repr., Gloucester, Mass., 1966) and Thomas B. Alexander, *Political Reconstruction in Tennessee* (1950; repr., New York, 1968); thence to Jonathan M. Atkins, "The Failure of Restoration: Wartime Reconstruction in Tennessee, 1862-1865," in *Sister States, Enemy States*, ed. Dollar, Whiteaker, and Dickinson, 299-319, as well as Robert Tracy McKenzie, "Civil War and Socioeconomic Change in the Upper South: The Survival of Local Agricultural Elites in Tennessee, 1850-1870," in *Tennessee History*, ed. Van West, 201-33.

[43] Ben H. Severance, *Tennessee's Radical Army: The State Guard and its Role in Reconstruction,*

Perhaps Reconstruction came to an end when sizeable Federal contingents finally departed both states. A single regular army post with forty-seven personnel remained on Tennessee soil well past 1876. Admittedly, this was a far cry from the state roster of 16,065 African American and white garrison numbers in September of 1865. Or perhaps it can be said to end when Tennessee rejoined the Union (1866) or finally ratified a new state constitution in 1870 reflecting the existence of the Thirteenth Amendment. Perhaps Kentucky finally made peace with a restored nation, although official approval of Amendments Thirteen, Fourteen, and Fifteen came only in 1976! And, if we are to believe cliometricians, some accommodation of free but indentured labor or peonage of sharecropping or other un-equal provision of labor and wages for ex-slaves denoted recovered upper-heartland economies during the decade after Appomattox.

Patrick A. Lewis and others have suggested that the bitter Recon-struction years of racial violence, resistance to the national consti-tutional amendments, and a continuing "war against federal policy" generally carried Kentucky "into communion with the South"— a "new community" that castigated African Americans and many whites in the Republican eastern counties and fought racial equality (like former Confederate state Tennessee) for the next century.[44]

Conclusion

So, were Kentucky and Tennessee "enemy" states or "sister" states in the Civil War years? Yes, on both counts. Kentucky and Tennessee were antebellum "sister states" that passed briefly to official "enemy-state" status during the early war years, even as they mutually suffered like "sister states" from Federal governmental supervision for the

1867-1869 (Knoxville, 2005) and Patrick A. Lewis, "The Democratic Partisan Militia and the Black Peril: The Kentucky Militia, Racial Violence, and the Fifteenth Amendment, 1870-1873," *Civil War History* 56 (2010): 145-74.

[44] In addition to Severance and Lewis, see Hambleton Tapp and James C. Klotter, *Kentucky: Decades of Discord, 1865-1900* (Frankfort, Ky., 1977), chaps. 1-3; Alan W. Trelease, *White Terror: The Ku Klux Klan Conspiracy and Southern Reconstruction* (New York, 1971); and E. Merton Coulter, *William E. Brownlow: Fighting Parson of the Southern Highlands* (1937; repr., Knoxville, 1999).

duration. Ironically, they may have actually reverted to "enemy state" status—but in reverse—for a generation after the conflict. The war certainly did not end with Forts Henry and Donelson. Yet, the war thenceforward defined Kentucky and Tennessee. "Actions-other-than-war" provided one legacy, more battles still another. The military presence affected the civil sector, destabilizing before restructuring both Kentucky and Tennessee.

Ultimately, one is left not by "what-ifs" but "what was." Kentucky was saved for the Union—a fragile prospect before and after the twin-rivers Yankee victory. Perhaps Kentucky departed for the Confederacy after Appomattox, at least in attitude. Tennessee meanwhile was reconstructed early—an agonizingly complex ordeal that resembles Afghanistan and Iraq more than we care to admit or recognize. Military governor Johnson in Tennessee and elected civilian governors Bramlette in Kentucky, later William Brownlow and John Stevenson in the respective states, set a tone. Their administrations saw a swirl of violence, human degradation and prejudice, and disruption of governance, economics, and institutions that demand better accounting of cost and result.

Wartime Kentucky and Tennessee endured military liberation and emancipation through property confiscation and later military enlistment and conscription. They suffered government-enforced loyalty oaths and incarceration, persecution of disobedience, and possibly unjustified executions that remain a dark spot on the escutcheon of this country and the sister states. Brigandage, felonies, murder, rape, and human-rights violations by both sides followed in the years after Forts Henry and Donelson. This side of the story demands retrieval from the mists of the past to stand side by side with the mute glories of battlegrounds and cemeteries. This war, like any war, projected a Janus-like image. Yet new perspectives will emerge with new generational focus.

A different semantic even now appears as one historian suggests rethinking revolution, using a paradigm of reconstruction as an insurgency. Mark Grimsley, who studied the Civil War as "hard"

263

or unremitting conflict, offers a contemporary link between the Civil War and Reconstruction, and the mid-twentieth-century civil rights movement and the southern conservative white resistance. By so doing, he extends our outlook to more recent times, much as this essay has suggested integrating the continuum of wartime and postwar reconstruction for comprehending a failed but resurrected nation. Nation-building is a never-ending process. The United States began its modern era with attempts to help liberate and then democratize peoples during the Civil War. Somehow incorporated in the national DNA, the crusade continues today. We might think of that perspective at the grass-roots as well as the country levels. The sister states–enemy states of Kentucky and Tennessee provide a point to begin our quest for understanding.[45]

Test the hypotheses in this essay. A continuous flow of new materials—presentations, articles, and books based on new hypotheses, analyses, and syntheses will enable the effort. Move beyond the previously cited Harris and Marshall volumes. James A. Ramage and Andrea S. Watkins provide a panoramic *Kentucky Rising* that treats democracy, slavery, and culture in the antebellum Bluegrass. Aaron Astor's study of civil war, emancipation, and reconstruction in Kentucky and Missouri offers the same type of comparative approach used by Brian D. McKnight for the contested Appalachian borderland of Kentucky and Virginia. Rich detail of a Kentuckian in Lincoln's cabinet comes from Elizabeth D. Leonard's study of judge advocate general Joseph Holt. Lindsey Apple dissects Henry Clay's family legacy. Broader investigations include Bradley Clampitt's portrait of civilian morale in the Confederate heartland, while Yael A. Sternhell serves up an innovative study of "the world of movement" in the Confederate South. Kristen Streater's exploration of

---

[45] Mark Grimsley, "Wars for the American South: The First and Second Reconstructions Considered as Insurgencies," *Civil War History* 57 (2012): 6-36; Mike Few and Mark Grimsley, "Rethinking Revolution: Reconstruction as an Insurgency: An Interview with Mark Grimsley," *Small Wars Journal* at http://smallwarsjournal.com/jrnl/art/rethinking-revolution-reconstruction-as-an-insurgency.

"'She-Rebels' on the Supply Line" illumines gender conventions in Civil War Kentucky, although fairly begging for equal insights for the Unionist side. William A. Dobak's integrating treatment of the United States Colored Troops, recruited heavily from both Kentucky and Tennessee, adds an ethnic dimension. Essays in Andrew L. Slap's complementary work to that of McKnight suggests the return of scholarly focus to regional and local dimensions of what Michael Fitzgerald terms our "splendid failure" or postwar Reconstruction of the American South.[46]

Indeed, fresh scholarship will always produce new revelations. Witness veteran historian Gary Gallagher's rediscovery that the North truly went to war not to free slaves but to preserve the Union or Mark Grimsley's postulate about wars for the American South embracing two reconstructions (traditional, 1865-77) and (civil rights era) but "considered as insurgencies." Here are our contemporary paradigms—nation-building and insurgency—applied to the past. And they definitely relate to Kentucky and Tennessee. Sister states and enemy states were part of both an old nationalism and then a brief (if disastrous) flirtation with a new nationalism, represented by the southern Confederacy. Andre M. Fleche correctly places our Civil War in just such a context—in the international Age of Nationalist Conflict. For us, that experience produced insurgency and counterinsurgency wrapped in a civil war. The result was a churning, expansive, modernizing nation-state that vaulted onto the world stage at century's end. Bluegrass and Volunteer sister states helped pave

[46] See, for example, McKnight, *Contested Borderland;* James A. Ramage and Andrea S. Watkins, *Kentucky Rising: Democracy, Slavery, and Culture from the Early Republic to the Civil War* (Lexington, Ky., 2012); Lindsey Apple, *The Family Legacy of Henry Clay: In the Shadow of a Kentucky Patriarch* (Lexington, Ky., 2012); Aaron Astor, *Rebels on the Border: Civil War, Emancipation, and the Reconstruction of Kentucky and Missouri* (Baton Rouge, 2012); Bradley T. Clampitt, *The Confederate Heartland: Military and Civilian Morale in the Western Confederacy* (Baton Rouge, 2011); Leonard, *Lincoln's Forgotten Ally;* William A. Dobak, *Freedom By The Sword: The U.S. Colored Troops, 1862-1867* (Washington, D.C., 2011); Andrew L. Slap, ed., *Reconstructing Appalachia: The Civil War's Aftermath* (Lexington, Ky., 2010); Kristen L. Streater, "'She-Rebels' on the Supply Line, Gender Conventions in Civil War Kentucky," *Occupied Women*, ed. Whites and Long, 88-102; and *Sister States, Enemy States*, ed. Dollar, Whiteaker, and Dickinson, part 3.

the way for Henry Luce's "American Century" and today, however blemished the recent past may seem for civil rights travesties, imperial pretensions, and maldistribution of great wealth.[47]

[47] Gallagher, *The Union War;* Grimsley, "Wars for the American South," *Civil War History* 57 (2012): 6–36; Andre M. Fleche, *The Revolution of 1861: The American Civil War in the Age of Nationalist Conflict* (Chapel Hill, 2012).

A "SISTERS' WAR": KENTUCKY WOMEN AND THEIR CIVIL WAR DIARIES

By Anne E. Marshall

On February 18, 1862, Woodford County resident and Confederate sympathizer Martha Buford Jones penned a brief entry in her diary: "We had news of the fall of Fort Donelson—feel badly enough about it." Just twenty miles away, on the same date, Frances Dallam Peter reported in her journal that a salute of forty guns was fired in Lexington that evening to commemorate the victory of Federal forces in Tennessee. An ardent Unionist, Peter was in full sympathy with the celebration.[1]

The fall of Fort Donelson had a much more personal impact on another Kentuckian, Unionist Josie Underwood. Her family home, a sizeable farm just outside Bowling Green, had been occupied since the previous September by Confederate brigadier general Simon Bolivar Buckner and his bivouacking forces. Upon their arrival, Josie had written in her diary: "The Philistines are upon us!" Josie's father, Warner Underwood, was committed to the Union cause, and the family endured continuous harassment and anxiety during the Confederate occupation of their property. In early January 1862, the Rebels forced the family to leave their home and settle temporarily

ANNE E. MARSHALL is the director of the Ulysses S. Grant Presidential Library at Mississippi State University. She is the author of *Creating a Confederate Kentucky: The Lost Cause and Civil War Memory in a Border State* (2010).

[1] Martha McDowell Buford Jones, *Peach Leather and Rebel Gray: Bluegrass Life and the War, 1860-1865: Farm and Social Life, Famous Horses, Tragedies of War: Diary and Letters of a Confederate Wife*, ed. Mary E. Wharton and Ellen F. Williams (Lexington, Ky., 1986), 81; Frances Peter, *A Union Woman in Civil War Kentucky: The Diary of Frances Peter*, ed. John David Smith and William Cooper Jr. (Lexington, Ky., 2000), 8.

behind Union lines. It was only with the fall of Forts Henry and Donelson that the Confederates retreated from Bowling Green, freeing the Underwoods to return to their home. Josie's joy was short-lived, however, as the family arrived to find their house still smoldering from Confederate arson. Josie declared in a March 1, 1862, entry: "Ruin devastation, desolation everywhere!"[2]

Harrodsburg native Lizzie Hardin, too, found herself in the midst of chaos in the wake of the fall of Fort Donelson. At the time, Lizzie, her mother, and her siblings were visiting Nashville. A zealous Confederate, she later wrote in her diary: "I beheld a city upon which the foe was advancing. Those who have once witnessed such a scene need no description . . . the streets were filled with carriages, horses and human beings from the doomed city. Men, women, children, the rich, the poor, white and black mingled in one struggling mass which gave way for nothing but the [retreating Confederate] soldiers marching through the city." Shortly after the Confederate defeat, the Hardins returned to Kentucky.[3]

These Kentucky diarists had several common characteristics. They were female, relatively young (Peter, Underwood, and Hardin were in their late teenage years and early twenties during the war—only Martha Jones was over the age of thirty); they were white and relatively affluent. And as residents of Kentucky, they felt the impact of the nation's most catastrophic war in a border state torn by divided political and national loyalties and splintered personal and familial relations. Whether they were Confederate or Union, issues of community and family division pervade their description of wartime life.[4]

Writing on the occasion of the Civil War centennial in his short

---

[2] Josie Underwood, *Josie Underwood's Civil War Diary*, ed. Nancy D. Baird (Lexington, Ky., 2009), 99, 103, 156.

[3] Elizabeth Pendleton Hardin, *The Private War of Lizzie Hardin: A Kentucky Confederate Girl's Diary of the Civil War in Kentucky, Virginia, Tennessee, Alabama, and Georgia*, ed. G. Glen Clift (Frankfort, Ky., 1963), 33.

[4] For general and concise treatments of the Kentucky Civil War experience, see Lowell H. Harrison, *The Civil War in Kentucky* (1975; repr., Lexington, Ky., 2009); Harrison and James C. Klotter, *A New History of Kentucky* (Lexington, Ky., 1997), 181-212. For an excellent treatment of the divided families of Kentucky, see Amy Murrell Taylor, *The Divided Family in Civil War America* (Chapel Hill, 2005).

volume, *The Legacy of the Civil War: Meditations on the Centennial,* Kentucky native Robert Penn Warren claimed that the Civil War was for Americans "our only 'felt' history—history lived in the national imagination. . . . It is an overwhelming and vital image of human, national, experience." Today, fifty years later, and one hundred and fifty years after the Civil War raged, Warren's statement rings no less true. Of all the ways of connecting to and "feeling" the war, reading diaries of people who lived through it is one of the most compelling. In Kentucky, as elsewhere, female diarists wrote some of the most revealing and candid commentaries on the war. While the Civil War in the Bluegrass State is so often referred to as a "brothers' war," they prove that the war belonged no less to Kentucky sisters. This essay will focus on some of common themes and revelations present in the published wartime diaries of Kentucky women and also will address how their experiences both reflect and complement recent shifts in historiography on women's Civil War home-front experience.[5]

The two best-known published diaries penned by Kentucky women are those of Frances Dallam Peter and Elizabeth Pendleton ("Lizzie") Hardin, two women who endured very different wartime experiences. Frances was the daughter of prominent Lexington physician and Union supporter Dr. Robert Peter. The Peters resided in a house located on what was then known as "Little College Lot" (present-day Gratz Park) near Transylvania University in downtown Lexington. This prime geographical location put Frances at the center of military events as Union troops bivouacked on the Little College Lot and officials converted parts of Transylvania University into a military hospital. That same ground filled with Confederate troops during Kirby Smith's occupation in the fall of 1862. One of the truly fascinating aspects of her diary is just how extensive her

[5] Robert Penn Warren, *The Legacy of the Civil War: Meditations on the Centennial* (New York, 1961), 4. For further reading on the significance of women's diaries, see Jane F. Schultz, "Civil War Diaries," *Companion to Southern Literature: Themes, Genres, Places, People, Movements, and Motifs,* ed. Joseph M. Flora, Lucinda Hardwick MacKethan, and Todd W. Taylor (Baton Rouge, 2002), 207-11, and Margo Culley, "Introduction to A Day at a Time: Diary Literature of American Women from 1764 to 1985," *Women, Autobiography, Theory: A Reader,* ed. Sidonie Smith and Julia Watson (Madison, Wis., 1998).

knowledge of happenings and events was, given that as a sufferer of epilepsy she was rarely able to leave her home. With her avid newspaper reading, her family members serving as her eyes and ears, and her neighborhood teeming with action, Peter was, as the editors of her diary note, part of a "female network" in the city that "sustained friendships, provided support in times of anxiety, offered humor to release tension, and monitored the activities of enemies." Sadly, Frances Peter, who kept her diary between January 1862 and April 1864, died from epilepsy in August 1864 at the tender age of twenty-one.[6]

One of the most interesting aspects of the wartime experience of Kentucky women is that, whether Unionist or secessionist in sentiment, many engaged with community members and even family members of the opposite persuasion on an almost daily basis. The Peter residence stood across the Little College Lot from the home of Rebel cavalry raider John Hunt Morgan's mother, Henrietta, giving Frances a perfect vantage point from which to observe the considerable goings-on at what became a hub of Confederate activity. Peter delighted when Mrs. Morgan endured Federal officials searching her houses for Confederates or regularly complained to Union army officials about one thing or another. She reported contemptuously when any of Morgan's Confederate friends or family members paid a visit. When John Hunt Morgan's famed regiment rode through the streets during the Confederate occupation in September 1862, Peter wrote, "A nasty, dirty looking set they were . . . They looked like the tag, rag & bobtail of the earth & as if they hadn't been near water since Fort Sumter fell."[7]

Lizzie Hardin, perhaps the most oft-quoted Kentucky Civil War diarist, held John Hunt Morgan in much higher regard than Peter. She was kin to several prominent Kentuckians, including her cousin, Confederate brigadier general (and Lincoln in-law) Benjamin Hardin Helm. The Harrodsburg native, who was twenty-two at the outbreak of the war, was a die-hard Rebel and stated so again and again in her

[6] Peter, *A Union Woman in Civil War Kentucky*, 31, xxi, xxvii.
[7] Ibid. 3-4, 79-80, 30-31 (quote, 30).

diary. In fact, it was Hardin's support of John Hunt Morgan on his July 1862 raid through Harrodsburg that eventually sent her along with her sister and her mother into exile for most of the war. "At last I saw John Morgan!" she remembered of the notorious raider's entrance "and was not disappointed! He was exactly my ideal cavalryman. Tall and well formed with a very handsome face, shaded by light hair and adorned by mustache and beard of the same color . . . his whole dress was scrupulously clean and neat." According to Hardin, Morgan greatly appreciated his female loyalists and told her mother: "Madam, when I entered Harrodsburg and found that here in the very center of Kentucky the ladies had assembled to welcome me, it was the proudest and happiest moment of my life. Oh! If the men of Kentucky had but the spirit of the women she would have long since been free."[8]

Soon, however, Hardin's very public Confederate sympathies attracted the attention of Union authorities, who arrested and tried her, her mother, and sister for waving their handkerchiefs and cheering Morgan's men as they rode through town. Officials offered to release them only if they signed the oath of allegiance to the United States, and when they refused, local Provost Marshal William Riley sent them to the headquarters of Brigadier General Jeremiah T. Boyle in Louisville. Boyle then sentenced them to leave the state and to relocate behind Confederate lines. The Hardins fled to Tennessee and Alabama before settling in Eatonton, Georgia, until the end of the war. Since its publication in 1963, Hardin's candid commentary on wartime life in a range of locales has made her diary a favorite source for Civil War historians like George Rable, Drew Gilpin Faust, and Anya Jabour. For those interested in the Kentucky Civil War experience in particular, Hardin's diary is valuable for its description of civilian discord and her secessionist vantage point, as well as her portrayal of postwar Kentucky.[9]

---

[8] Hardin, *Private War of Lizzie Hardin*, 86-87.

[9] Ibid., 122-23. For examples of works which cite Hardin's diary, see George Rable, *God's Almost Chosen People: A Religious History of the Civil War* (Chapel Hill, 2010); Anya Jabour, *Scarlett's Sisters: Young Women in the Old South* (Chapel Hill, 2007); Drew Gilpin Faust, *Mothers*

The diary of Martha Buford Jones, published along with a number of her letters as *Peach Leather and Rebel Gray: Bluegrass Life and the War, 1860-1865,* also sheds light on the struggles of Kentuckians of Confederate sympathy. Martha and her husband Willis lived outside Versailles on a verdant and productive estate, Edgewood Farm. Willis was a successful horse-breeder, and Jones's diary offers insight into the lives of the most prominent human and equine citizens of Kentucky during the Civil War era. The Joneses were the parents of five children, including an infant who died during the war, and Martha's journal offers a fascinating account of her efforts to maintain the farm and support her children after Willis joined the Confederate army in September 1862. Her husband's devotion to the Confederate cause—one which she apparently shared—put Martha at odds with the views of her own father, who was a committed Unionist at the outset of the war. As she explained in a letter to her father, who had urged Willis to return home after the death of their infant daughter in the fall of 1862,

> I feel sure no other than the best of motives can prompt you—but at the same time I deem it my duty to place before you as briefly as possible my reasons for not concurring with you. . . . He has linked his fortunes with the southern people, from an unalterable conviction of the justice of the cause and believing that the principle for which they are fighting must ultimately triumph, and bring the blessing of civil liberty once more to our country.[10]

Like Frances Peter, Martha Jones was part of a network of women (albeit a Confederate one) who shared information and offered one another support and camaraderie. She reported making numerous visits to Henrietta Hunt Morgan's home, and one wonders if Frances Peter might have spied her on some of her calls. One of Jones's closest friends was Issa Desha Breckinridge, wife of W. C. P. Breckinridge, a colonel in John Hunt Morgan's cavalry. The two kept each

---

of Invention: Women of the Slaveholding South in the American Civil War (Chapel Hill, 1997).

[10] Jones, *Peach Leather and Rebel Gray,* 88-89.

other company while their husbands were gone to war, and in 1864, they fled to Toronto, Canada, together to avoid being apprehended by Federal officials under a military order which called for the arrest of all wives of Confederate officers in Kentucky. While she was gone, she left her children in the care of her mother-in-law. She was able to return to Kentucky in September 1864.[11]

The entry in which Martha describes her return to the United States was the final one of her diary, but the editors of *Peach Leather and Rebel Gray* have done an able job of filling in the details of the short and tragic remainder of her life. Sadly, only a month after Martha's return to Kentucky, Willis Buford died in battle near Richmond, Virginia. In early 1865, Martha applied directly to President Lincoln for a pass to go to Richmond and see her husband's grave and retrieve his personal effects, including his servant Ben, whom she promised to manumit on return to Kentucky. Lincoln acceded and wrote her a pass in his own hand. The text of both of these documents is included in the edited volume. Martha herself became ill soon after her husband's death and died at the age of thirty-seven in February 1866.[12]

The most recent Kentucky Civil War diary to appear in published form is that of Josie Underwood, the typed copy of which ended up in the archives of the Kentucky Library at Western Kentucky University under very interesting circumstances in 1976. Josie was the daughter of Warner Underwood, a former Whig who was elected to the U.S. House of Representatives as a member of the American Party in 1855 and 1857. The 1860 census showed him owning twenty-eight slaves, putting him among the wealthiest residents of Bowling Green. Josie inherited from her father a keen interest in the politics of disunion, and while speaking publicly about such matters was considered unladylike during the time in which she lived, she reveals in her diary, which she began keeping in December 1860, that she was not afraid to enter the heated political fray.[13]

[11] Ibid., 160-68.
[12] Ibid., 175-78.
[13] Underwood, *Josie Underwood's Civil War Diary*, xiii-xv, 4.

As a resident of Bowling Green, Underwood had a bird's-eye view of the Confederate occupation of that city in 1862. The family's fortunes declined after bivouacking Rebels destroyed their home in March 1862, but improved when Abraham Lincoln offered Warner Underwood a position as a U.S. consul in Glasgow, Scotland, as a reward for his efforts to keep Kentucky in the Union. Josie accompanied her father on a visit to Washington, D.C., in the summer of 1862, during which she met the president and Mary Todd Lincoln, and several other political and military luminaries. Josie's diary comes to an abrupt end as she prepares to set sail for Scotland in September 1862.[14]

While the situations and wartime loyalties of these Kentucky women diarists varied, they each speak to experiences and anxieties that are in some ways universal to civilians during war but also particular to the status of Kentucky as a border state. Strained personal and family relationships are a common refrain in their writings. In February 1861, Josie Underwood observed: "There begins to be unpleasant feelings between old friends who take different sides. When Lizzie Wright [a good friend] and I met today we both got too excited—just what we said I won't try to recall—but when we parted I had a hot feeling through me and Lizzie's face was flushed and though we were both polite—we did not kiss each other as usual on parting." As the secession crisis wore on, Josie reported that young people in particular had trouble containing their heated opinions and that "the school boys all 'carry chips on their shoulders'—ready to fight at the slightest provocation." Josie, who like many young unmarried women of her age, was quite occupied with romantic and marital prospects, found herself turning down would-be suitors because of their secessionist views. Of one, a handsome Mississippi planter and attorney named Tom Grafton, she remarked: "he seems to me everything a girl might love, except, alas! his desire to break up our country, which is a broad gulf in our sympathies." Underwood

---

[14] Ibid., 182-88, 201. A "second" Underwood diary was found in Louisville, Ky. It has been edited and is forthcoming as a special issue of the *Register*.

later grieved when he died in battle in September 1862.[15]

Throughout her journal, Josie continually described the difficulties of maintaining friendships amid a divided populace. In October 1861, she wrote: "I started to make some calls today, but didn't get very far in the list. There is no use trying to keep up visiting with the 'secesh' girls—and we are too intensely interested, too wrought, too suspicious, too distrustful of each other to make any intercourse pleasant." Lizzie Hardin echoed these sentiments; when she returned to Harrodsburg in 1862, she reported, "I have never seen such bitter feeling as there was between the two parties. Social intercourse had almost ceased." By 1863, Frances Peter remarked that Rebel sympathizers took "very little notice of Union people, or even show them the cold shoulder" in public. Yet, through the terrible discord, ties of friendship and family endured. Martha Jones continued to communicate warmly with her father despite his Union proclivities, and Josie Underwood remained very close with her sister Juliette, whose husband fought for the Confederacy. Josie also took pains to reconcile with her estranged friend Lizzie before leaving for Scotland.[16]

Another common theme among all the diarists is their support for slavery. Perhaps this is not surprising, given that most white Kentuckians of their socioeconomic level owned slaves and depended upon them for labor. Though their slaveholdings tended to be small, five or six bondspeople on average, by 1850, 28 percent of Kentucky families owned slaves. This is a higher percentage than in any other southern state except Missouri. Many of these slaveholders were Unionists who believed that their best chance of preserving slavery lay within the Union. Many apparently asked, as Josie Underwood did in January 1861, "But why not fight for southern rights *in* the Union—why wish to divide this great country that your forefathers and mine sacrificed so much to establish." Several times in her diary,

---

[15] Ibid., 62, 85, 46.

[16] Ibid., 112; Hardin, *Private War of Lizzie Hardin*, 59; Peter, *A Union Woman in Civil War Kentucky*, 171; Jones, *Peach Leather and Rebel Gray*, 88-89; Underwood, *Josie Underwood's Civil War Diary*, 165, 199.

she echoes the sentiments of her father, Warner Underwood, who from his position of infl uence worked mightily in 1860 and 1861 to keep Kentuckians from seceding. Though he was no supporter of Lincoln and had served as an elector for John Bell of the Constitutional Union Party, as Josie wrote:

> He opposes secession *most*—out of his love for the South, for disunion will be her ruin—for if there is war—it will surely be in the South and the whole land desolated and laid in waste and slavery will certainly go if the Union is dissolved. The only way, he thinks, is for the South to remain in the Union if she would maintain *any* of the "Southern rights" she is clamoring for.[17]

Underwood was particularly clear about her own identity and that of her family as "southern people loving the south—yet opposing the breaking up of the Union." Josie's mother, Lucy Underwood, also shared these views. "Ma has always been the most intense Southerner I ever know," wrote Josie in 1861,

> and hated Abolitionists as envious meddlers and had little use for anything above 'Mason and Dixies [*sic*] Line' and she says now to think that the South will be so foolish as to break up the country for which their fathers fought, bled, and died and give up the old fl ag, to the Yankees—instead of staying in the Union and fi ghting for their rights under the Constitution of our fathers—is more than she can bear.

Lizzie Hardin, whose family also owned slaves, professed much less trust in the Federal government to preserve the peculiar institution. "My love for the Union," she wrote, "arose only from an idea that it was beneficial to the South. I never doubted the will but the power of the North to injure us."[18]

Even as the war started, many Union families like the Underwoods had a hard time staking out their position. Josie reported in

[17] Underwood, *Josie Underwood's Civil War Diary*, 34, 39; Harrison and Klotter, *New History of Kentucky*, 168.

[18] Underwood, *Josie Underwood's Civil War Diary*, 112, 59; Hardin, *Private War of Lizzie Hardin*, 3.

June 1861, that her brother Henry engaged in a "'fast and furious' fight with some secessionist boys of his age after they called him an 'Ab'"—or abolitionist, a term that "no southern boy will stand being called." She noted that secessionists also benefitted from having a sympathetic figure, Jefferson Davis, representing their cause, "whilst the Kentucky Unionists despise Lincoln and fear his policy and it is doubly hard to stand firm for a principle and true to the Union under these circumstances and requires a high order of patriotism to be a Kentucky Union man."[19]

As the war continued and emancipation emerged more clearly as one of Lincoln's war aims, support for the Union cause began to dissipate among many white Kentuckians. The unpublished diary of one woman, Ellen McGaughey Wallace, which resides at the Kentucky Historical Society, offers unambiguous insight into this phenomenon. At the time of the war, Wallace lived in western Christian County outside of Hopkinsville. Her husband Albert owned a considerable amount of land and, according to the 1860 census, thirty slaves. Wallace's diary provides a fascinating and, at times, disturbing proof of just how closely Unionist disaffection with the Federal cause was tied to the increasing commitment of the Union to emancipation throughout the war. In April 1861, Wallace had hoped, in terms much like those of Josie Underwood, that Kentucky would not secede, stating that the state "had nothing to gain by such a course but ruin." But she also wrote frequently about her opposition to the Lincoln administration, the Republican Party, and what she perceived as his abolitionist intent.[20]

Though Lincoln strategically excepted the loyal border slave states

---

[19] Underwood, *Josie Underwood's Civil War Diary*, 85, 61.

[20] Diary of Ellen Kenton McGaughey Wallace, April 19, 1861, Ellen Wallace and Annie Starling Diaries, 1849-1932, folder 2, box 2, mss. 52, Kentucky Historical Society Collections, Kentucky Historical Society, Frankfort, Ky. (hereafter Wallace and Starling Diaries, KHS Collections); for Wallace's views on Abraham Lincoln, see entries for May 11, August 14, and October 16, 1862. Census information regarding the slaves owned by Albert Wallace is located in the text of the finding aid for these papers. See also Amber C. Nicholson, "Border State, Divided Loyalties: The Politics of Ellen Wallace, Kentucky Slave Owner, during the Civil War" (MA thesis, University of New Orleans, 2011).

from his emancipation proclamations in 1862 and 1863, most Kentucky whites realized that they portended the death of the peculiar institution everywhere. When Lincoln announced his preliminary emancipation in September 1862, Ellen Wallace predicted nothing less than racial insurrection:

> Lincoln's proclamation emancipating all the slaves is justly creating great indignation. The consequences of it are too awful to contemplate. The blood of women, children, and helpless aged will flowintorrentsifits[*sic*] carried into ef-fect. The vile wretch ought to suffer all the torments that could be inflicted on him, body and soul. Then to place innocent women and helpless infants at the mercy of black monsters who would walk in human shape.

"Servile insurrection will be the consequence [of emancipation] unless the strong arm of the nation prevents it," she wrote in December 1862, "and the blood of helpless women and children will flow in torrents if [Lincoln's] wicked and fanatical policy is not over ruled." She predicted that it might end up "St. Domingo all over again."[21]

Reflecting the anger of many of her fellow Kentucky whites, Ellen Wallace was even more outraged by Lincoln's policy of arming and enlisting African Americans in the Union army. More than anything, this move caused many Unionists to distance themselves from their former cause. Ellen Wallace's entries describe candidly the social and racial turmoil this represented to whites:

> [Lincoln] has made the negro the master of the white man as far as his power goes putting arms in their hands. Stationing negro pickets at the toll gates and bridges where they defy their former masters to pass on peril of their lives. The white man has to turn his horse's head and obey Lincoln's negro troops with clenched teeth. . . . The hot blood of our best Union men is up. They feel keenly the insults heaped upon them by the negro administration.

[21] Diary of Ellen Wallace, September 29, December 13, and December 23, 1862, Wallace and Starling Diaries, KHS Collections.

A year later, Wallace's sentiments toward the Union cause had shifted completely. As several thousand Confederate troops marched into Hopkinsville and took possession of the town, she wrote, "Oh how our hearts leaped for joy at the sight, after being subjected to Negro bayonets and black republican outrages. I could not refrain from weeping as I saw the brave heroes, half clad and half frozen pass, with a song of defiance on their lips, to their northern foes, who well fed and well clad had fled on their approach with their black hords [sic]."[22]

Some Kentucky Unionists were more measured in their feelings regarding emancipation and black enlistment in the Union army. While she shared some of Wallace's racial prejudices, Frances Peter was rather dismissive of the threat of both. On the subject of emancipation, she remarked, "For my part I say whip the rebels first and let the ballot box decided the slavery question if there are any slaves left." Likewise, though she did not approve of the idea, she did not seem to fear the prospect of black troops. "From all I observed of the negro," she wrote in February 1863, "he is much to [sic] averse to work, too timid to make a good soldier, and has got it into his head that liberty means doing nothing. I think it is acting against the Constitution to make soldiers of the blacks, and however much the abolitionists may say to the contrary, they will find in the end that this arming & equipping of negro regiments is a mere waste of time and money." She did, however, recognize the consequences of black enlistment on the racial status quo, and a few months later in June 1863 stated, "I am afraid now that the negros have got arms in their hands, and so many notions of freedom in their heads that before the war is over it is not improbable that we may have to fight them as well as the secesh."[23]

While Kentucky white women left no doubt about their thoughts and feelings on these issues, we are left wondering what their African American counterparts might have said of wartime challenges and possibilities in their state. Unfortunately, no black Kentucky women,

[22] Ibid., December 25, 1863; December 12, 1864.
[23] Peter, *A Union Woman in Civil War Kentucky*, 170, 96, 136

slave or free, left the kinds of extensive accounts that white diarists did. We can, however, catch glimpses of their reactions to the opportunities that war presented them within the writing of white diarists. In January 1864, for example, Frances Peter reported that the local Methodist minister "lost" two of his slaves, "two whom he thought a great deal of and to whom he had been very kind and indulgent," and one of whom, Peter noted, had nursed his children. Rather than believe that the slave woman's life within the clergyman's household could have been so bad, she conjectured: "it was thought beyond the possibility of a doubt that it was a prearranged scheme and that very likely they had help from some of the Abolitionists scattered through every northern regiment." In July 1864, a family member informed Martha Buford Jones that her escaped slave Charlotte was in a jail in Nicholasville. Charlotte may have been on her way to nearby Camp Nelson, a Union recruiting center that became a refugee camp for many Kentucky slaves. Unfortunately for Charlotte, however, Martha Jones regained custody and sold her less than a month later, intending to use the proceeds to pay off some household debts. A full year and a half after the Emancipation Proclamation had freed slaves in Confederate states, Kentucky was one of only four states in which such a sale would have been allowed. Ellen Wallace complained in her diary of the challenge of dealing with her increasingly challenging slave, Jinny, and placed the blame with the Union army: "Yankey [*sic*] interference with our Negroes would ruin the best servant in the world." She remarked on the increased frequency with which slaves were leaving their masters, "The Negroes have become so unmanageable that it will be a relief to their masters for them to go." In March, she reported that some slaves belonging to her household were also planning to leave, likely heading to Union encampments in Tennessee.[24]

In July 1865, Lizzie Hardin, who had by then returned to Kentucky, was very concerned about the "liberty fever" that had broken out among her family's slaves. The Hardins' two female slaves, Debby

[24] Ibid., 187-88; Jones, *Peach Leather and Rebel Gray*, 115-17; Diary of Ellen Wallace, February 14, 20, and March 22, 24, 1864, Wallace and Starling Diaries, folder 3, box 2, KHS Collections.

and Ellen, entreated Lizzie's grandfather for permission to obtain a pass that would allow them to travel freely throughout and outside of the state. "I thought, notwithstanding some anticipations of the glory of freedom, they desire to attain it in a manner that will not displease us." Hardin, however, did not think the family slaves had the capacity to appreciate the meaning of freedom: "Martha is not much troubled, not having risen to the intellectual standard where ideas of any kind obtrude themselves upon the brain, and having a day or two ago attended a circus, she finds all her longing for a higher sphere of being satisfied." Though she lamented the prospect, she clearly anticipated the complete demise of slavery, expecting any day that "our negroes" will "blossom into freedom." While we cannot know exactly what these African American women were thinking, we can see them, through the words of white writers, straining and grabbing for freedom that must have seemed just outside of their grasp. We can understand, too, how wartime confusion, dislocation, and stress meant for them something entirely different from what it did for the white women who wrote of their experiences.[25]

In their edited forms, the diaries of Frances Peter, Lizzie Hardin, Martha Buford Jones, and Josie Underwood make for absorbing reading, and each of their accounts offers unique insight into life in Civil War–era Kentucky. Their experiences also underscore an interpretational shift that is taking place in scholarship on women and the southern home front. During the past twenty years, historians writing about southern women in the Civil War have concentrated on both the challenges and the opportunities the war posed for white women, as well as the ways it did and did not permanently alter social gender structure in the South. They have primarily focused their arguments on whether or not women desired their changing wartime roles and responsibilities, and on how and for how long the wartime experiences of these women affected their social and legal standing in society.[26]

[25] Hardin, *Private War of Lizzie Hardin*, 285, 284.
[26] Examples of this scholarship include: Catherine Clinton and Nina Silber, eds. *Divided Houses: Gender and the Civil War* (New York, 1992); Faust, *Mothers of Invention*; George Rable.

Recently, however, a number of Civil War scholars have shifted their focus. Instead of looking at the impact of the war on women, they have concentrated on the effect women had on the war, particularly in occupied areas of the South. In the process, they have begun to redefine the relationship between the home front and battle front. As historian LeeAnn Whites has written, "In the war of occupation, the home front and the battlefield merged, creating a new kind of battlefield and an unanticipated second front, where some civilians, many of whom were women—continued resisting what they perceived as illegitimate domination." In her recent volume, *Confederate Reckoning*, Stephanie McCurry has argued along the same lines, asserting: "As war exacted its toll and old assumptions crumbled, politicians and military men in the Civil War South ended up contending with the women—even, some charged, making war on women. In the occupied South, Union forces struggled to limit the damage done by Confederate women and were eventually forced to recognize them as enemies of war. Women would be forced to take oaths of allegiance, subjected to Union court-martial, and clapped in prison."[27]

While McCurry is focused on the states that made up the Confederacy proper, the experiences of our Kentucky diarists emphasize the high stakes of women's disloyalty in the war and the readiness of Union army officials to quell it. The Kentucky diarists also underscore the many ways in which women, whose sex supposedly deemed them apolitical and above and outside of war, actually became embattled participants in the eyes of both military officials and their fellow citizens. Their experiences embody McCurry's contention that the Civil War disabused both Confederate and Union authorities of the conviction "that women were outside war, that they were innocent parties, entitled to protection, even perhaps from enemy men."

Civil Wars: Women and the Crisis of Southern Nationalism (Urbana, Ill., 1989); and LeeAnn Whites, *The Civil War as a Crisis in Gender: Augusta, Georgia, 1860-1890* (Athens, Ga., 1995).

[27] LeeAnn Whites and Alecia B. Long, eds., *Occupied Women: Gender, Military Occupation, and the American Civil War* (Baton Rouge, 2009), 3; Stephanie McCurry, *Confederate Reckoning: Power and Politics in the Civil War South* (Boston, 2010), 3-4.

As the war evolved, and as our Kentucky writers reveal, southern women, whatever their sectional sympathies, became very politically and militarily engaged. Josie Underwood, for example, read every speech her father gave as he traveled the state preaching the cause of Unionism before the war. Though Warner Underwood repeatedly begged her "not to get excited in arguments" with other people on the subject, she confessed, "I can't help it." The views he espoused became weapons in Josie's own arsenal as she entered the fray of heated political talk that inevitably came up even during personal visits and balls in late 1860. Lizzie Hardin was, like the Underwoods, a John Bell supporter in 1860, and was perfectly able to articulate her political convictions but was restrained from doing so by the prevailing gender conventions and, of course, a woman's inability to vote. As she stated: "Having only the boy's privilege of 'hollering for my candidate,' and being denied even that, except in very secluded situations, I determined to leave the country in the hands of the men."[28]

In the framework of recent scholarship, the experiences of our Kentucky diarists not only underscore the notion of women as battlefront participants, they put a fine point on it. Perhaps nowhere did Federal troops have to work so hard and for so long to control enemy women as in Kentucky and other border states. When the Civil War began, Union officials believed that they needed to treat Kentucky citizens of all sympathies gingerly so as not to push them towards the Confederacy. Quickly however, they realized that, as Major General George B. McClellan directed Brigadier General Don Carlos Buell in 1861, that "where there is good reason to believe that persons are actually giving aid, comfort, or information to the enemy it is of course necessary to arrest them." Buell, who commanded the Department of the Ohio in which Kentucky lay, and other Union officials and civilians alike, recognized quickly enough that secessionist women were primary among people providing aid to the enemy. Frances Peter's diary provides a list of female pro-

---

[28] McCurry, *Confederate Reckoning*, 96; Underwood, *Josie Underwood's Civil War Diary*, 48, 30-31; Hardin, *Private War of Lizzie Hardin*, 1.

Confederate offenses. Henrietta Hunt Morgan was her favorite target, and she recounted an incident in 1862 in which Mrs. Morgan and her daughter, under questioning from a Federal official, denied sheltering a Confederate officer. As the Federals searched the house, the fugitive attempted to escape and was arrested. Morgan offered as her excuse that "the man had come there for protection and she did not think it would be kind to betray him."[29]

Along with her routine complaints regarding the activities of Mrs. Morgan, Frances Peter recorded myriad other abuses by Confederate women. During a funeral procession for a dead Confederate, Mrs. Morgan's daughter, Henrietta Morgan Duke, hissed at Union officials "all the way to the cemetery." She also reported occasions of Rebel sympathizers spitting on and verbally abusing Union soldiers. In 1863, she wrote of the particularly audacious behavior of two of Lexington's most prominent and, under other circumstances, genteel Confederate women, Mrs. Hart Gibson and Mrs. Ella Duncan. When Major General Ambrose Burnside, the commander of the Department of the Ohio, visited town, the sisters entered a home at which he was calling, and "continually hissed" at him as he addressed a crowd there. "When the band played national airs these women sung 'Bonny Blue Flag' 'Dixie' and other secesh songs." Later, Peter wrote bitterly, these "same creatures had the impudence to come down and send for Gen Burnside to come out into the hall and meet with them."[30]

Perhaps Mrs. Gibson and Mrs. Duncan gave the general extra incentive to crack down on secessionist women, for less than a week after Peter reported this incident, Burnside issued his General Order

[29] For excellent studies of women's Civil War experience in the border South, see LeeAnn Whites, "'Corresponding With the Enemy': Mobilizing the Relational Field of Battle in St. Louis" and Kristen L. Streater, "'She-Rebels on the Supply Line:' Gender Conventions in Civil War Kentucky," both in Whites and Long, eds., *Occupied Women*, and Streater, "'Not much a friend to traiters no matter how beautiful': The Union Military and Confederate Women in Civil War Kentucky," *Sister States, Enemy States: The Civil War in Kentucky and Tennessee*, ed. Kent T. Dollar, Larry H. Whiteaker, and W. Calvin Dickinson (Lexington, Ky., 2008), 245-66. McClellan quoted in Streater, "Not much a friend," 246; Peter, *A Union Woman in Civil War Kentucky*, 3-4.

[30] Peter, *A Union Woman in Civil War Kentucky*, 11, 125, 136, 121-22.

No. 38, which made it illegal to criticize the Union war effort or its soldiers. The order stated: "hereafter all persons found within our lines who commit acts for the benefit of the enemies of our country, will be tried as spies or traitors, and, if convicted, will suffer death." The order applied to a number of offences, including "all persons within our lines who harbor, protect, conceal, feed, clothe, or in anyway aid the enemies of our country." These were all acts that fell primarily on women of secessionist sentiment. The order continued: "The habit of declaring sympathies for the enemy will no longer be tolerated in the department. Persons committing such offences will be at once arrested, with a view to being tried as above stated, or sent beyond our lines into the lines of their friends." This order very clearly reflected the fact that Union officials had come to recognize secessionist women as agents of war, and wrote them into military policy as such.[31]

In the days after Burnside issued Order No. 38, Peter reported several arrests of secessionist women. Union officials offered them a choice of exile in the South or taking the oath of allegiance. She recounted an incident in Louisville where several secessionist women left a theatre dramatically as a band played patriotic music. The following evening, according to Peter, "the manager came on the stage and announced that the band was about to play some national airs and all those who were too much opposed to the government had now an opportunity to leave. As on the previous night a number of ladies got up and flirted [sic] out of the room but at the door they were met by the Provost guard who marched them off to jail."[32]

While General Order No. 38 was the policy applied most widely to crack down on female insubordination, neither of the Confederate diarists profiled in this article left the state under this order. Lizzie Hardin's forced exile from the state came prior to the issuance of the order. The harsh reaction of Union officials to what in some ways seems like trivial actions—voicing support and waving hand-

---

[31] Streater, "Not much a friend," 248-49.
[32] Peter, *A Union Woman in Civil War Kentucky*, 124-25, 129-31.

kerchiefs—that Lizzie Hardin and her family gave to Morgan and his men seems largely symbolic and unworthy of imprisonment. Their arrests came, however, as part of a larger effort to clamp down on secessionist civilians who supported guerrilla warfare. As Kristen Streater has noted, however, in Kentucky, "The nature of guerrilla warfare increased the reliance on civilian support by the Confederacy; thus the need of the Federals to suppress Confederate home-front support also increased." Meanwhile, it was General Order No. 66, which mandated that wives of Confederate soldiers swear an oath of loyalty to the Union or be exiled, which compelled Martha Jones to leave Kentucky for Canada. For all the unsparing assessments of secessionists of her own sex, Frances Peter also recognized their efficacy as combatants on the home front. She noted, "Secesh ladies can do a great deal in the way of giving information. It is known pretty certainly by the officers here that a southern mail leaves nearly of every night . . . It is thought that it is not carried by men but by boys or ladies." Thus she was convinced that, "If we fight them on the field we should keep them down at home too."[33]

Confederate women were not the only combatants in Civil War Kentucky, however. Union women certainly did their part to resist and antagonize Confederate partisans and military forces during times when they invaded their locales. Frances Peter reported the story of Lexington woman Mrs. J. Wilgus who fended off three guerrillas who came looking for her husband. When one tried to enter her home, she wrested his gun away from him and declared that "if only she knew how to use it she would blow his brains out." Peter also recounted the tale of a Miss Mary Williams, who, upon receiving a letter meant for his fiancé, another Miss Mary Williams, from Charlton Morgan, younger brother of John Hunt Morgan, promptly turned it in to Union authorities who used the information in it to

---

[33] Streater, "Not much a friend," 252; Jones, *Peach Leather and Rebel Gray*, 112; Lewis Collins and Richard H. Collins, *Historical Sketches of Kentucky*, rev. ed., 2 vols. (Covington, Ky., 1882), 1:123; Peter, *A Union Woman in Civil War Kentucky*, 82.

apprehend him.[34]

The Civil War diaries of Kentucky women demonstrate that the "women-as-war-combatant" phenomenon was heightened in Kentucky because of the divided nature of the population. Unlike many southern women in Confederate states, Hardin, Jones, and other secessionist women in Kentucky did not have to wait for invading Union armies to "occupy" their fields and streets. All of our diarists had neighbors of opposite sympathies that at times took on the function of enemy troops. Furthermore, both the pervasiveness of guerrilla warfare and the myriad military campaigns that rolled through the Bluegrass State meant that, whether they were Unionist or Secessionist, nearly every Kentucky woman had the opportunity to engage very personally with the enemy.

Whether in their capacity as civilian combatants or simply as young women writing about the chaos around them, these young diarists demonstrate that there are few better ways to remember and connect with the most disharmonious chapter in the history of Kentucky than by reading the words of those who lived through it. In the closing of *The Legacy of the Civil War*, Robert Penn Warren elucidated why the story of the Civil War mattered still to Americans. "Looking back on the years 1861-65," he wrote, "we see how the individual men, despite failings, blindness, and vice, may affirm for us the possibility of the dignity of life. It is a tragic dignity that their story affirms, but it may evoke strength. And in the contemplation of the story, some of that grandeur, even in the midst of the confused issues, shadowy chances, and brutal ambivalences of our life and historical moment, may rub off on us." When Warren penned these words fifty years ago, the Civil War was, for many, largely a story of "individual men," with only a few published female accounts of the war accessible to an American public ready to ponder the meaning of the bloody struggle one hundred years before. Fortunately for us today, the published diaries of at least four Kentucky women can

---

[34] Peter, *A Union Woman in Civil War Kentucky*, 68, 102.

be found in bookstores and public libraries across the state, ready to offer readers insight into the great struggle that belonged no less to them than it did the men on battlefields and in public office. With their very real tales of fear, struggle, dislocation, loss, and death, Kentucky women certainly embodied the "tragic dignity" about which Warren wrote. "And that," as he concluded, "may be what we yearn for after all."[35]

---

[35] Warren, *Legacy of the Civil War*, 108-9

THE FREEDMEN'S BUREAU IN THE JACKSON PURCHASE REGION OF KENTUCKY, 1866-1868

By Patricia A. Hoskins

On July 25, 1866, a member of the Fourth United States Colored Heavy Artillery (USCHA) boarded a train on the Mobile & Ohio Railroad in Columbus, Kentucky, a small town on the Mississippi River in the Jackson Purchase region of the Bluegrass State. The soldier caught the eye of two white employees of the railroad as he entered the railcar. Union soldiers were nothing new in the area. The Jackson Purchase, often referred to simply as "the Purchase," had been under Union control since February 1862 when Confederate major general Leonidas Polk abandoned the region to Union troops following the battles of Forts Henry and Donelson. As it had done during the war, the sight of an African American in Federal uniform provoked extreme ire among the white men that hot July day. Columbus almost erupted in riot when the two railway employees attacked the African American soldier. The men ordered the "colored boy" to remove the buttons from his coat. When the soldier refused, they "came to blows and from blows the white men used knives rather freely and cut and bruised the colored boy considerably." Other freedmen who witnessed the attack followed the white men off the train, where they drew the attention of "authorities." In the ensuing melee, two freedmen were severely wounded.[1]

PATRICIA HOSKINS is a native of Hyden, Kentucky. She received her BA and MA in history from Eastern Kentucky University in Richmond, Kentucky, and her PhD in history from Auburn University in Auburn, Alabama. She is professor of history and college historian at Limestone University in Gaffney, South Carolina.

[1] Lewis Collins and Richard H. Collins, *History of Kentucky*, 2 vols. (Covington, Ky., 1874),

The thwarted riot in Columbus that summer was nothing new to various areas of the South following the Civil War. Though a border state, Kentucky would experience continued racial unrest during the late 1860s, leading the Bureau of Refugees, Freedmen, and Abandoned Lands or, as it was more popularly known, the Freedmen's Bureau, to locate in the state. From 1866 to 1868, the Purchase was designated one of three branches of the bureau in Kentucky.[2]

The road that led the bureau to the Purchase was a long and bloody one. In 1865, the region, located in the far western corner of Kentucky and separated from the rest of the state by the Tennessee River, comprised seven counties—Ballard, Calloway, Fulton, Graves, Hickman, Marshall, and McCracken.[3] Bounded to the north by the Ohio River and to the west by the Mississippi River, the area was a virtual peninsula. Added to Kentucky in 1819, the region developed a separate identity because of immigration patterns, agriculture, and politics. Primarily agricultural, the largest town in the area was Paducah, which served as the commercial hub for western Kentucky, western Tennessee, and southern Illinois. In stark contrast to Whig-leaning Kentucky, the voters of the Purchase were staunch Democrats in the decades leading up to war. Despite its late formation, Purchase farmers relied on slavery and became its staunch defenders. By 1840, dark-fired tobacco had become the staple crop in the area, and though the Purchase could never compete with the Bluegrass and Pennyroyal regions of the state in terms of slavery, by 1860 20 percent of the population was enslaved. With the exception of a few people in Paducah, the vast majority of Purchase citizens supported the South during the secession crisis and called for Kentucky to

---

1:173; *Louisville Daily Journal*, July 25, 1866; *New York Times*, July 25, 1866. The South was plagued by a series of race riots in the summer of 1866. The largest occurred in Memphis in early May and in New Orleans in late July.

    [2] Lowell H. Harrison and James C. Klotter, *A New History of Kentucky* (Lexington, Ky., 1997), 235-38; "Freedmen's Bureau," *The Kentucky Encyclopedia*, ed. John E. Kleber (Lexington, Ky., 1992), 356-57; Marion B. Lucas, *From Slavery to Segregation, 1760-1891*, vol. 1 of *A History of Blacks in Kentucky*, 2 vols. (Frankfort, 1992), 186-88.

    [3] An eighth county, Carlisle, was carved out of Ballard County and added to the Purchase in 1886. See "Carlisle County," *Kentucky Encyclopedia*, 163.

withdraw from the Union and join the fledgling Confederacy. When the state declared neutrality, several vociferous secession supporters called for the Purchase to secede from Kentucky and join Tennessee. In the ensuing call to arms, the Purchase would contribute more soldiers to the Confederacy than any other area of Kentucky.[4]

The war came to the Purchase in September 1861 when Confederate major general Leonidas Polk occupied Columbus. Three days after Polk's invasion, Union brigadier general Ulysses S. Grant occupied Paducah. After the battles of Forts Henry and Donelson in February 1862, the Confederates withdrew from Columbus, leaving the Purchase in the grip of Federal troops for the remainder of the war. From 1862 until the end of the war, the Purchase was overrun with guerrillas, bushwhackers, and home guards, both Union and Confederate. The violence was caused when the guerrillas and bushwhackers attacked loyal families. The Union army, in turn, reacted violently when guerrillas or anyone accused of aiding them were caught. Exacerbating the violent climate was the fact that Union trade boards, charged with issuing trade permits, turned a blind eye to illegal commerce which operated freely up and down the Tennessee and Mississippi Rivers. During the last three years of the war, the area was stuck in a violent cycle whereby illegal trade led to raids by irregulars upon towns and communities, which then attracted the attention of Union soldiers who often held the local population in contempt and doubted professed Union support from loyal citizens.[5]

---

[4] For more on the history of the Jackson Purchase, see Patricia Hoskins, "'The Old First Is With the South': The Civil War, Reconstruction, and Memory in the Jackson Purchase Region of Kentucky" (PhD dissertation, Auburn University, 2009). See also John E. L. Robertson, "Paducah," *Kentucky Encyclopedia*, 705-6; Jasper B. Shannon and Ruth McQuown, *Presidential Politics in Kentucky, 1824-1948: A Compilation of Election Statistics and an Analysis of Political Behavior* (Lexington, Ky., 1950), 1-3, 14-18, 24-36; 1860 U.S. census, Slave Schedules, for Ballard, Calloway, Fulton, Graves, Hickman, McCracken, and Marshall Counties, Kentucky, http://www.ancestry.com. For more on the secession crisis in the Jackson Purchase, see Berry F. Craig, "The Jackson Purchase Considers Secession: The 1861 Mayfield Convention," *Register of the Kentucky Historical Society* 99 (2001): 339-61 (hereafter *Register*).

[5] Hoskins, "Old First is with the South," 62-220. For more on the Civil War in western Kentucky, see Benjamin Franklin Cooling, *Fort Donelson's Legacy: War and Society in Kentucky and Tennessee, 1862-63* (Knoxville, 1997) and *To the Battles of Franklin and Nashville and Beyond: Stabilization and Reconstruction in Tennessee, 1864-1866* (Knoxville, 2011). "Irregulars" is an elastic

Adding to the chaos brought about by divided loyalties and Union occupation was the presence of African American refugees and soldiers in the Purchase. After Lincoln's issuance of the Emancipation Proclamation, slaves from the Purchase and western Tennessee flocked to the Union fortifications at Columbus and Paducah. In January 1864, acting upon the request of powerful Unionist congressional leader Lucian Anderson of Graves County, Lincoln designated Paducah the first area in Kentucky where the Union army could recruit black soldiers. Consequently, the black population of the city soared when the soldiers' families followed them to camp.[6]

The presence of black soldiers in the Purchase enraged Confederate major general Nathan Bedford Forrest, who led the largest raid on the area in late March 1864. Forrest led approximately two thousand men, a vast majority of whom were natives of the Purchase, on an audacious attack on Paducah. For hours they fired on Fort Anderson, the Union stronghold in the town. The Purchase soldiers in Forrest's ranks were overheard swearing "to kill every damned nigger" inside the fort.[7]

Forrest's raid led Lucian Anderson and members of the local Union League to write Lincoln and beg for a new Union commander to quell the activity of irregulars that plagued the area. In July 1864,

term which covers guerrillas, bushwhackers, or common brigands who took advantage of the tumult of war.

[6] *The War of the Rebellion: A Compilation of the Official Records of the Union and Confederate Armies*, 128 vols. (Washington, D.C., 1880-1901), series 3, 4:178-79, 436-38 (hereafter OR). For more concerning the recruitment of African American soldiers in the Purchase, see James E. L. Robertson, *Paducah: Frontier to Atomic Age* (Charleston, S.C., 2002), 40-53; "Paducah Letter," *Louisville Journal*, January 26, 1864; John David Smith, "The Recruitment of Negro Soldiers in Kentucky, 1863-1865," *Register* 72 (1974): 364-90; Michael T. Meier, "Lorenzo Thomas and the Recruitment of Blacks in the Mississippi Valley, 1863-65," in *Black Soldiers in Blue: African American Troops in the Civil War*, ed. John David Smith (Chapel Hill, 2002), 249-76; Lucas, *From Slavery to Segregation*, 160. See also Victor B. Howard, *Black Liberation in Kentucky: Emancipation and Freedom, 1862-1884* (Lexington, Ky., 1983).

Lucian Anderson, a prominent Mayfield lawyer, was the most powerful and vocal Union leader in the Jackson Purchase. For more on Anderson, see James Larry Hood, "For the Union: Kentucky's Unconditional Unionist Congressmen and the Development of the Republican Party in Kentucky, 1863-1865," *Register* 76 (1978): 197-215.

[7] OR, series 1, part 1, 32:540-49; Frank Moore, ed., *The Rebellion Record: A Diary of American Events*, 11 vols. (New York, 1865), 1: 499-510.

Union brigadier general Eleazer A. Paine took command of the Purchase. He was, however, removed in November 1864 after Paducah townspeople accused him of extortion, bribery, banishing southern sympathizers to Canada, and executing over forty people. Paine's so-called "reign of terror," combined with what many saw as crushing Federal authority, a strained atmosphere rife with both Confederate and Union irregulars, and the dissolution of slavery, had a profound impact on the Purchase. Thus, when the war finally ended, the majority of people undoubtedly hoped to resume the normal rhythms of life. Like many former slave states, however, Kentucky's journey back to "normal" was only just beginning.[8]

Two issues plagued most of the whites in the Purchase in the first few weeks after the end of the war: the removal of the Union army and the status of former slaves. They particularly worried over the thousands of black soldiers stationed at Paducah and Columbus. In just over a month after Lee's surrender, Purchase residents complained to the Federal government about black soldiers. In May, it was reported that they had committed "unparalleled depredations" during a recruiting mission in the Purchase and northwest Tennessee. Several citizens complained that the soldiers performed "shameful outrages on persons and property," broke "into the courthouse and public offices," and utterly destroyed "all State and county records, court papers . . . dockets, judgments, and title papers." The inflicted damages, they insisted, were more than "the losses of the war combined." Citizens begged for "immediate relief."[9]

Indeed, reports of supposed outrages committed by freed blacks dominated the summer of 1865. One of the more unusual cases to come before the provost marshal was the case of Louis Knox, Arthur

---

[8] Information on General Eleazer A. Paine and his command, removal, and court-martial can be found in "Explanations of Brigadier General E. A. Paine, recently in command of the Western District of Kentucky required by the report of Brigadier General Joseph Holt, MM1609, folders 3 and 4, RG 153, Judge Advocate General of the United States, Washington, D.C." in Records of the Field Office of Judge Advocate General (Army) Court-martial Case Files, 1809-1894, National Archives and Records Administration, Washington, D.C. (hereafter NARA).

[9] OR, series 1, 49, part 2, 905-6.

Hinton, and John Ayers. The three African American men were accused of taking up arms and joining with disgruntled Confederate guerrillas in Hickman County. The court charged two additional men, George Nivin and Dan Nailin, with rape. The men supposedly "forcibly and feloniously and against her consent, carnally knew one Mrs. Susan Carroll, white woman of Hickman." Knox, Hinton, and Ayers were sentenced to thirty days in jail, while Nivin and Nailin were "sentenced to hang by the neck." George Hardesbrook of the Twelfth USCHA faced similar charges; he was accused of inducing "fifteen year old Emma Rust into his headquarters without knowledge of her lawful protectors" where he had "carnal knowledge of her." He received a "severe reprimand in front of his regiment." Another incident occurred when John Thomas of the Fourth USCHA entered the home of Mrs. Alice Young of Columbus and "feloniously assaulted her daughter Miss Maggie Young with a bayonet and forced her to sit beside him and intended to rape her."[10]

According to Union army major N. H. Foster, however, it was the soldiers and freedmen who received constant contemptuous treatment. From his command at Paducah, he reported, "From all information I am able to obtain from this section of the state, it appears that the people are in an open revolt—discharged colored soldiers are beaten, driven from their homes, in some instances all blue clothing and U.S. uniforms found in their possession taken from them and burned; and they are otherwise persecuted by the returned rebel soldiers."[11]

The primary reasons for the chaotic situation concerning black soldiers and freedmen in the Purchase were the intense racist attitude of the majority of whites in the area and the overall uncertainty about the status of African Americans in Kentucky in the immedi-

---

[10] Records of the Provost Marshal, General Court-Martial Orders, entry 2182, 1865, nos. 62, 65, 1866, nos. 62, 65, 1866, nos. 1, 7, RG393, Records of the U.S. Army Continental Commands, NARA. There are no records to determine whether Niven and Nailen were actually executed for their alleged crime.

[11] Major N. H. Foster to Colonel Grier, January 10, 1866, Records of the Provost Marshal, miscellaneous records, E964, RG393, ibid.

ate postwar era. As Frank Cooling notes, the prewar investment of Kentuckians in slaves, accompanied by a lack of strong abolitionist sentiment and weak Unionism, made acceptance of the Thirteenth Amendment unpalatable for most Kentuckians. Moreover, the wartime experiences of Kentuckians with Federal occupation and the suspension of habeas corpus created an obsessive desire among Kentucky politicians to resist what they perceived as further encroachment. Federal authorities in the state, however, considered African Americans free with the proposal by Congress of the Thirteenth Amendment in January 1865. The Kentucky legislature, however, had in February and after the summer elections rejected the amendment, which had bolstered slaveholders who refused to free their former chattel. Indeed, until December 1865, when two-thirds of the states had finally ratified the amendment, over sixty-five thousand slaves remained in bondage in Kentucky. Making the situation even murkier was the fact that the Kentucky General Assembly repealed its Wartime Act of Expatriation which allowed former Confederates the right to regain political offices and positions of power.[12]

Moreover, there was the desperate situation facing African American refugees within the state. As they did throughout the war, thousands of former slaves flocked to Kentucky cities following Lee's surrender, increasing the already large refugee population in places such as Louisville, Columbus, Paducah, and Camp Nelson south of Lexington. To remedy the situation, the Federal commander of Kentucky, Major General John M. Palmer issued Order No. 32 in May and Order No. 49 in June. Both allowed refugees and ex-soldiers to leave camps to seek employment. Thousands of African Americans accordingly crossed the Ohio River to seek jobs, while hundreds

---

[12] Lucas, *From Slavery to Segregation*, 178-79; James F. Bolton to John Donovan, August 18, 1866, Letters Sent, Columbus, Records of the Bureau of Refugees, Freedman, and Abandoned Lands, RG105, M1904, NARA, Southeast Region, Atlanta, Georgia (hereafter BRFAL records). For more on Kentucky and the Thirteenth Amendment, see B. Franklin Cooling, "After the Horror: Kentucky in Reconstruction" in *Sister States, Enemy States: The Civil War in Kentucky and Tennessee*, ed. Kent T. Dollar, Larry H. Whiteaker, and W. Calvin Dickinson (Lexington, Ky., 2009), 343-47; Harrison and Klotter, *New History*, 240-41; amendments to the constitution, 5, United States House of Representatives, http://house.gov/house/constitution/amend.html.

more sought employment with the Federal army in the quartermaster stores, as laborers, cooks, and laundresses. Many others sought out and reunited with long-lost loved ones.[13]

The freedom to move about, however, had the effect of bringing even more freed blacks to the refugee camps. In the months after the end of the war, African American families in the Purchase flocked to Paducah and Columbus for employment and the protection of the Federal army. Housing and food were in short supply, and disease ran rampant in the unsanitary camps. In Paducah, destitute, old, and sick freedmen and women died in the streets, prompting blacks in the town to organize a Freedmen's Aid Society and the Freedmen's Sanitary Commission. Lack of funds, however, prevented any significant change. When the city council attempted to appropriate funds to house and feed the destitute freedmen, they were met with protests of "I am not going to pay out any money to assist the 'damned niggers.'"[14]

In December, acting on demands from those concerned about the status of freed blacks, Major General Oliver O. Howard, head of the Freedmen's Bureau, finally recommended that a branch of the bureau be organized in the Bluegrass State. Howard believed that the bureau was desperately needed to combat "the rascally rebellious revolutionists in Kentucky." Because the state lay beyond the arm of the bureau, Howard chose the director of the agency in Tennessee, Major General Clinton B. Fisk, to organize offices in Kentucky. In late December, Fisk announced the plans to establish branches of the bureau in Kentucky. In February 1866, the Kentucky senate passed resolutions condemning the bureau, but by March Fisk had

---

[13] Lucas, *From Slavery to Segregation*, 178-79; John M. Palmer, *Personal Recollections of John M. Palmer: The Story of an Earnest Life* (Cincinnati, 1901), 242-45.

[14] Superintendent John H. Donovan to Major General John Ely, May 4, 1866, Letters Sent, Paducah, BRFAL records (quote); John Smith to Donovan, June 16, 1867; Letters Sent, Columbus, ibid.; James F. Bolton to John Donovan, August 18, 1868, Letters Sent, Columbus, ibid. See also Lucas, *From Slavery to Segregation*, 198. John H. Donovan was appointed chief superintendent of the Freedmen's Bureau in Kentucky and served from April to December 1866. The letters of Donovan, John Bolton, and John Smith document the reluctance of local whites to help the former slaves.

organized three subdistricts within the state with headquarters at Lexington, Louisville, and Paducah.[15]

The Freedmen's Bureau at Paducah and its subdistrict at Columbus would operate from April 1866 until July 1868. At Paducah, the first chief superintendent in charge of the bureau office was John H. Donovan. He was followed by W. James Kay, P. T. Swaine, and A. Benson Brown, who would oversee the closure of the branch. Lieutenant James F. Bolton became supervisor of the office at Columbus. Donovan and Bolton's goals for the bureau were to provide assistance to destitute freedmen, secure their rights by establishing courts, instituting schools, facilitating labor contracts between farmers and freedmen, and reuniting families. To the majority of whites in the Purchase, the bureau seemed to be nothing more than a new phase of Federal occupation. In his first letter to his superior, General John Ely, Donovan noted that "great prejudice and hostility" existed against the bureau. Indeed, the outlook for organization was less than promising:

> the presence as well as the assistance of troops will be absolutely necessary in order to carry out the business of the bureau . . . so much hostility appears to exist to the prejudice of Freedmen's Rights . . . The more respectable and intelligent portion of the Farmers, Manufacturers, and Mechanics—The class who represent the solid interest of the county are all disposed towards the Bureau. They believe its existence important to the best interests of both the whites

[15] Lucas, *From Slavery to Segregation*, 182-87; *New York Times*, February 15, 1866; Victor B. Howard, "The Black Testimony Controversy in Kentucky, 1866-1872," *Journal of Negro History* 58 (1973): (quote, 144); Ross Webb, "'The Past is Never Dead, Its Not Even the Past': Benjamin Runkle and the Freedmen's Bureau in Kentucky, 1866-1870," *Register* 84 (1986): 343-60. See also Victor B. Howard, *Black Liberation in Kentucky: Emancipation and Freedom, 1862-1884* (Lexington, Ky., 1983). Fisk served as director of the Kentucky branch of the bureau from December 1865 to June 1866. He appointed Brevet Brigadier General John Ely chief superintendent for the bureau in Kentucky. Ely was replaced by Major General Jefferson C. Davis who headed the bureau until January 1867. He was succeeded by Brigadier General Sidney Burbank who oversaw the agency until June 1868. Major General Benjamin P. Runkle presided over the closure of the agency in 1869. See Pamphlet Describing Microfilm Collection M1904, NARA, Records for the Field Office of Kentucky, Bureau of Refugees, Freedmen, and Abandoned Lands (Washington, D.C., 2003), 2-5.

and blacks . . . they treat the Freedmen humanely . . .the majority of the people comprising lawyers, doctors, bankers, later speculators in slaves retired gentlemen . . . merchants, Hotel Keepers, newspapers editors, rum sellers, Bar Room loafers, gamblers, politicians, and the low breed and disaffected rabble—are with exceptions pregnant with hostility.[16]

By April 30, three of his county superintendents had resigned because of "hostility" and three families of freedpeople in Ballard and Hickman Counties had been assaulted by white men who "blackened themselves up." Soon enough, Donovan himself reported an attempt on his life. In late fall, while sitting at his desk in Paducah, someone fired a shot at him. The ball went through his hat and lodged in the wall behind him.[17]

As in the formerly Confederate states, the bureau in Kentucky worked diligently to establish schools for freedmen and their families. Between 1866 and 1870, the educational division of the agency, under the leadership of army chaplain Thomas K. Noble, organized 219 schools in Kentucky. The building of schools became one of the first ventures of the agency in the Purchase. James Bolton reported to Donovan that several loyal Union men in Hickman and Ballard Counties pledged support of a school serving both counties, exclaiming that "with the right kind of teacher I know that the colored children will learn as fast as the white children." In 1866 and 1867, centers of learning were erected at Paducah, Columbus, and Hickman. Initial attempts to build a school in Paducah met with white disdain. John C. Noble of the *Paducah Herald* no doubt spoke for the majority of Purchase citizens when he scoffed at the idea of educating blacks, noting "to talk about educating the drudge is to talk without thinking." That resentment was manifested in violence in April 1866 when

[16] John Donovan to General Ely, June 30, 1866, monthly reports, no. 101, BRFAL records. James F. Bolton was superintendent at Columbus during the entire duration of the bureau. In April 1868, Captain Emerson H. Liscum oversaw the closure of the office. See Pamphlet Describing Microfilm Collection M1904, 8.

[17] John Donovan to General John Ely, April 7, 18, 30, and November 13, 1866, Letters Sent, Paducah, BRFAL records.

white students attacked the first freedmen's school at the instigation of "the community at large." Superintendent John Donovan reported that the "scholars were assaulted . . . the windows broken in and the teachers compelled to flee." He added that "women were seen to encourage the attack." Donovan complained of the incident in a letter to Paducah mayor John Fisher who "paid not the slightest [attention] to my communication and nothing has been done by the civil authorities." Donovan placed guards outside the school to protect it from further harassment and later answered the request of the teacher of the white school to "erect a fence separating the colored playground from theirs."[18]

Attempts to build a school at Mayfield in 1867 also met with extreme violence. In Graves County, Lucian Anderson gathered the local freedmen together where they were treated to a "sumptuous dinner" and speeches that helped raise two hundred dollars for the erection of a brick school building. Anderson's efforts once again went for naught. Not long after the dinner, fifty Klansman appeared in Mayfield and ordered the teacher to leave town. They likewise entered the houses of several freedmen and robbed and whipped them. In Hickman, the white teacher, Ohio native Jenny Mead, was "insulted many times in the streets" and "threatened with death." Mead also reported the murder of one of her pupils in late 1868.[19]

There were, however, stories of success. Jennie Fyfe, a native of

[18] *Paducah Herald*, June 28, 1866; "Freedmen's Schools," *Kentucky Encyclopedia*, 357; Harrison and Klotter, *New History of Kentucky*, 237; James Bolton to John Donovan, October 6, 1866, Complaints, Affidavits, and Evidence Relating to Court Cases, BRFAL records; John Donovan to Levi Burnett, April 17, 1866, Letters Sent, ibid. John Fisher, a German immigrant and local brewer, served as mayor of Paducah from 1863 to 1868. See John E. L. Robertson, *Paducah* (Charleston, S.C., 2004), 32, and "Paducah," *Kentucky Encyclopedia*, 705-6.

[19] C. D. Smith to John Ely, June 31, 1867, Letters Received, Paducah, BRFAL records. Smith served as subassistant and chief agent at Paducah from February to November 1867; Noble to Alvord, M803, Records of the Education Division of the Bureau of Refugees, Freedmen, and Abandoned Lands, 1865-1871, Kentucky School Reports, January 12, 1869, NARA. The name of Mead's student who was murdered has not been located. It is not known if the Klansmen who appeared in Mayfield were from the Purchase. Several groups of Klansmen operated across the Tennessee line in Paris, Jackson, and Dresden. Several references to "masked" groups of men are scattered in the Freedmen's Bureau papers and in some newspapers, but it is not indicated if they were actual members of the Klan.

Michigan who first came to Paducah during the war as a nurse, taught in Paducah in 1865 and 1866. In July 1865, she described her school to her sister back in Michigan as "a very singular one . . . unlike any you ever visited, with about forty pupils in number from the age of six . . . to forty years. My pupils are all shades of complexion from nearly white to coal black." By February 1866, the school had 160 pupils and had held its first "colored school exhibition." Fyfe faced heavy persecution during her first year of teaching and "was unable to find a boarding place" in Paducah. Donovan, who described her as "a most energetic and highly accomplished lady," noted that "the prejudice against her is so great." Fyfe reported that the "the scholars certainly did splendidly . . . far exceeded our expectations and made us very proud of them." She was particularly pleased with a sixteen-year-old pupil, a girl who was "sold from her mother" and claimed that her former master was her father. Fyfe also commented on the achievements of the girl's brother, who came to school unable to read or write but by February had advanced to "Intellectual Arithmetic and Geography." By July 1866, the school had formed a band and performed a concert in which the pupils "sang so pretty." Between 1866 and 1868, three more schools were built in Paducah, two headed by black teachers. At Columbus a school of 115 students operated in 1865 and one year later the bureau opened a brick schoolhouse built by freedmen. In Hickman, a local black carpenter, Warren Thomas, donated fifty dollars to build a school; with additional funding from the bureau the school opened in 1866.[20]

In addition to establishing schools, the Freedmen's Bureau attempted to address the grievances of former slaves by establishing "freedmen's courts" within the districts of the bureau. Like most southern states, the Kentucky prewar black codes prohibited African

---

[20] Jenny Fyfe to Nell Fyfe, June 15, 1865, and June 19, 1866, Fyfe Family Papers, Special Collections, Bentley Historical Library, University of Michigan, Ann Arbor, Michigan; John Donovan to Levi Burnett, June 21, 1866, Monthly Reports, No. 72, BRFAL records; W. James Kay to Thomas Noble, April 4, 1867, Letters Sent, Paducah, ibid.; James F. Bolton to W. James Kay, December 12, 1867, Letters sent, Columbus, ibid.; Kay to Runkle, February 5, 1868, Letters Sent, Paducah, ibid.

Americans from testifying against whites. In January 1866, General Fisk announced that bureau-designated courts would handle cases involving freedmen until Kentucky passed laws accepting black testimony. In 1872, five years after the dissolution of the bureau, the state legislature finally allowed African American testimony.[21]

In the Purchase, the bureau found trying cases involving freedmen almost impossible because of the apathy or outright hostility of the county courts. In June 1866, Chief Superintendent Donovan tried a case involving a former slave, a youth named George Morton, in one of the courts. Morton accused his former owners and current employers, William R. Brame and his sixteen-year-old son John of "assault and battery and inhumane treatment." Morton was unable to try his case in civil court because "no white witnesses" would "testify in his favor to the unjust and inhumane treatment inflicted" upon him. The case was tried before the freedmen's court which found Brame and his son guilty and imposed a fine upon them. Donovan disgustedly reported that "rebel lawyers" in Paducah advised Brame not to pay the fine but to "enter a protest in the Circuit Court." The state circuit court of appeals issued an injunction in the case and forbade Donovan or any other Bureau official from collecting the fine.[22]

County courts in the Jackson Purchase constantly thwarted Dono-

---

[21] Howard, "Black Testimony Controversy in Kentucky," 140-45.

[22] Ibid. For details of the case, see John Donovan to Major General John Ely, Reports, June 30, 1866, No. 100, BRFAL. In 1860, William R. Brame was listed as a forty-year-old farmer with seven slaves and an estate valued at fourteen thousand dollars. His son J. M. Brame was ten years old in 1860. See 1860 U.S. census for McCracken County, Kentucky, http://www.ancestry.com. In 1867, as a result of several court rulings, freedmen's courts ceased to operate. Because the state denied black testimony, the bureau used the Civil Rights Act of 1866 to have cases involving freedmen tried in the U.S. District Court. In 1867, the U.S. Court of Appeals ruled that the denial of black testimony in Kentucky was in conflict with the Civil Rights Act of 1866. Only through the intervention of the Federal government and the threat of indictment did state judges begin allowing testimony. By 1871, most judges were complying with the law. See Howard, "Black Testimony Controversy in Kentucky," 140-45, and Lucas, *From Slavery to Segregation*, 311-13. Judge Bland Ballard, a strong Unionist, Republican, and supporter of black rights, presided over the cases. Ballard County, ironically, was named for Ballard's father, a Kentucky pioneer also named Bland Ballard. See Mary Lou Madigan, "Bland Ballard," *Kentucky Encyclopedia*, 44, and H. Levin, ed., *Lawyers and Lawmakers of Kentucky* (1897; repr., Easley, S.C., 1982), 145-46.

van and the efforts of his agency and even threatened their lives on occasion. In August 1866, J. Bond Thompson sent an urgent letter to Donovan, signed "in haste," begging the superintendent to send troops to Smithland, a small town east of Paducah. Thompson was charged on three different indictments for trying to uphold the authority of the bureau. One of the charges was for extorting money from a citizen upon whom he had imposed a fine. In the courtroom, he was charged as a "traitor" working for the "Nigger Bureau" and was found guilty by Judge Wiley Fowler, a vocal Confederate sympathizer who was arrested by Federal troops during the war. He was ordered to pay a fine or go straight to jail. Surrounded in the courtroom by a group of "rebels" who assaulted him like a "lawless mob," he escaped only through the kindness of the town sheriff. Donovan confronted Judge Fowler who claimed the bureau was a "usurpation" by the Federal government placed on the people of Kentucky and that every agent and supporter of the bureau should be "thrown in the state penitentiary."[23]

Donovan himself faced a similar situation in November 1866 after he arrested Mayfield resident Samuel Orr for imprisoning former slave Amanda Anderson in his home and beating her in an "outrageous" and "unmerciful" manner. Donovan sent a detachment of ten soldiers to Mayfield to arrest Orr. Orr was tried before the magistrate and court in Paducah and released because of laws preventing Anderson from testifying against a white man. Indignant at the ruling, Donovan demanded that Orr appear before a Freedmen's court. Instructed by his lawyers to ignore the summons of the bureau, Orr failed to show up for his trial. Donovan had him rearrested and held as a military prisoner. Orr's lawyers demanded that a "posse" be organized to arrest Donovan for defying the state courts. Donovan asked in a letter to his superiors, "how is the negro to obtain justice" against those that "groan and sweat over their lost property in slaves?"[24]

[23] J. Bond Thompson to John Donovan, August 15, 17, 23, 1866, Complaints, Affidavits, and Evidence Relating to Court Cases, BFRAL records.

[24] Donovan to John Ely, November 1, 1866, Complaints, Affidavits, and Evidence

Superintendent Donovan soon discovered that the foremost desire among the freedmen was the reunion of their families. Only a handful of former slaves had been able to locate long-lost family members. At Paducah, Louise Lauderdale was reunited with her two sons who served in the Union army, while Andrew Webb went to live with a long-lost son in Iowa. Most were not so lucky, especially those attempting to remove their children from former masters who claimed them as "apprentices." Kentucky state law allowed county courts to apprentice African American orphaned and delinquent minors, giving white farmers a welcome supply of free labor. From his office in Columbus, Bolton, whose district comprised Hickman, Fulton, and Ballard Counties, reported that "the county courts of each of the counties over which my jurisdiction extends have apprenticed orphans and Abandoned minors of the Freedmen." Bolton investigated several cases of apprenticed children in Ballard County and concluded that the court "appears to be determined to grind under foot or disregard all orders and instructions of the Bureau." Bolton and local Unionists claimed recently pardoned former Confederate colonel Edward Crossland canvassed the county persuading others to "reenslave the niggers" by apprenticing former slave children.[25]

James Tisdale of Ballard County threatened his former slave Mary Reynolds when she tried to reclaim her children. Reynolds had fled Ballard County in July 1865 to find work across the river in Illinois, leaving her children at Tisdale's farm. In July 1866, she and her new husband attempted to reunite with her children and move them to their new home in Metropolis, Illinois. Tisdale responded by refusing to return her children and threatening to "blow her brains out" should she come back. Austin Tyler of Fulton County also refused to give up a young slave girl to her family, claiming that state laws allowed him to maintain custody of her.[26] In Graves County, Malinda Neel

Relating to Court Cases, ibid.

[25] Bolton to Donovan, November 9, 1866, Letters Sent, Columbus, ibid.

[26] James F. Bolton to John Donovan, August 24, 1866, Letters Sent, Columbus, ibid. In 1860, James Tisdale was forty-eight-years old and owned an estate worth nine thousand dollars. See 1860 U.S. census, Ballard County, Kentucky. In 1860, Austin Tyler was a fifty-

refused to return Sarah Ann, Dana, and Jerry Hobbs, the children of Emiline Hobbs. James L. Dunbar of Mayfield claimed that seven children between the ages of two and sixteen legally belonged to him since the county courts authorized former owners to apprentice minor orphans.[27]

Ann Ezell of Calloway County likewise appealed to the Freedmen's Bureau that her employer, A. G. Ezell of Calloway County, held her child. She complained that Ezell beat her over the head with a stick when she asked him to return the child to her. Compounding Ann Ezell's problem was that "returned rebels and guerrillas" treated "the negroes with great cruelty and oppressiveness." In addition, the county judge, "a violent rebel," was accused of "binding children, men, and women." In Paducah, Belcher Baker sought the assistance of the bureau in regaining his wife, Lucy Martin Baker, from their employer P. C. Martin. Baker accused him of abusing and beating his wife. He claimed that Martin slapped his wife "several times in the face and refuses to pay her for her labor."[28]

One of the more alarming cases involved Sylvia Leach Johnson, former slave of a man named Joe Leach of Paducah. When she went to retrieve her child from her former owner, Leach beat her with a broom handle. After the broom handle broke, he used an ax to

nine-year-old farmer with eight slaves and an estate valued over twenty-eight thousand dollars. In 1870, his income increased to over thirty thousand dollars. See 1860 U.S. census, Fulton County, Kentucky and Slave Schedules for Fulton County, Kentucky; 1870 U.S. census, Fulton County, Kentucky, http://ancestry.com.

[27] Complaint of Emiline Hobbs to Superintendent John Donovan, September 23, 1866, Complaints, Affidavits, and Evidence Relating to Court Cases, BRFAL records; James Dunbar to Superintendent John Donovan, April 13, 1866, ibid. In 1860, James L. Dunbar was listed as a wealthy farmer worth $23,270 and the owner of fifteen slaves. By 1870, his fortunes had declined considerably to $7,200. In 1870, the home next to his was occupied by the family of Frank Dunbar, an African American farmhand with five children. The children match the ages of five of the seven children James Dunbar claimed as apprentices in 1866. See 1860 U.S. census, Graves County, Kentucky and Slave Schedules, Graves County, Kentucky; 1870 U.S. census, Graves County, Kentucky, http://ancestry.com.

[28] Sworn Testimony of Belcher Baker, April 20, 1866, Complaints, Affidavits, and Evidence Relating to Court Cases, Paducah, BRFAL records; J. T. Bollinger to Superintendent W. James Kay, Chief Superintendent North West Sub District, January 28, 1866, Letters Received, Paducah, ibid.

continue his assault. More disturbing, Leach beat Sylvia's eighteen-month-old child in front of her, picked the youngster up by hair, and attempted to throw him into the fireplace. He narrowly missed, but the child's hair was burnt.[29]

Complaints of violence against freedmen whose former owners had a difficult time accepting their newly freed status swamped the Purchase bureau offices. Oscar Turner, one of the wealthiest and largest slaveholders in Ballard County, became enraged after one of his former slaves, Ann Turner, spilled some cider. He subsequently "whipped her with switches" and cut "her right hand until the blood came." The young woman left Turner's employ to work for a Mr. Scott. Several weeks after the incident, Oscar Turner located Ann at her new employer's home and removed her "by force with a stick" and returned home. He "took her into the field and tied her to a fence rail, stripped her clothes off, and whipped her with switches in the body," and "put her in the hay press . . . all night." The next morning, Oscar Turner called Maria, Ann's mother, whom he blamed for her daughter's earlier escape, to the house where he cursed her saying "god damn your soul you god damned bitch . . . I will learn you to run my negroes off." He tied her to a peach tree, stripped off all her clothes, "except an undergarment which he made a little girl pull above my waist" and whipped her. Maria Turner's cries brought the intervention of Oscar Turner's wife who untied her. Maria subsequently fled to the Freedmen's Bureau Office at Paducah, where she pleaded to officials to punish Oscar Turner and rescue her remaining five children from Turner's farm.[30]

[29] Testimony of witnesses in the case of Joe Leach v. Sylvia Leach Johnson, Complaints, Affidavits, and Evidence Relating to Court Cases, ibid.

[30] Complaint of Maria Turner to John Donovan, n.d., 1866, Letters Received, Paducah, ibid. Oscar Turner was one the earliest settlers in the Jackson Purchase after it opened for settlement in 1819. A staunch Democrat and supporter of secession before the war, he became a state legislator and member of Congress after the war. His treatment of his slaves is not surprising. Turner's mother, who was notorious for her cruel treatment of her slaves, was murdered in Lexington by her carriage driver Richard in 1844. Oscar Turner put out a five-hundred-dollar reward for the man's arrest. By all accounts, the man was never captured. The event was so notable that Robert Penn Warren referenced the murder in his novel *All the King's Men* (1946). For Turner's mother, see *Lexington Observer and Reporter*, August 24, 1844, and

A similar complaint was made by freedman Alexander Flint, who complained to Chief Superintendent Donovan that his employer "collared" and hit him "across the head with a stick of strong wood" and tore his shirt from his body. He ordered Flint to work or "he would get his pistol and blow my *god Damned* heart out."[31] Robert Robertson of McCracken County fared worse. Robertson caught his employer, a Mr. Titsworth, whipping his children and ordered him to stop. After threatening Robertson with the same punishment, Titsworth mounted his horse and started for Paducah. Robertson, too, headed to Paducah to lodge a complaint with the Freedmen's Bureau. There he encountered Titsworth, who told him "by God be off and don't you come back no more." After ignoring the order, Robertson turned away and Titsworth shot him in the back. As he turned to face his assailant, Titsworth fired again, hitting the freedman in the thigh. Titsworth rode home and attempted to kill Robertson's wife, but failed after his own wife shielded her.[32]

A particularly gruesome case involved Mary Dillworth, who testified that her former owner W. H. Dillworth imprisoned her and abused her repeatedly. At Dillworth's trial, his own family testified that he assaulted Mary in ways "no man has ever treated a slave." Several witnesses gave evidence of Dillworth's sadomasochistic treatment of Mary. Dillworth's daughter claimed that her father tied Mary down "with four stakes driven in the ground stretching out her feet and hands as far as he could" and whipped her "naked body with a paddle made rough by nails in it—until the blood would form in puddle on the floor." His son corroborated his sister's accusations,

---

for Oscar Turner, see J. H Battle, W. H. Perrin, and C. G. Kniffen, *Histories and Biographies of Ballard, Calloway, Fulton, Graves, Hickman, McCracken, and Marshall Counties* (Louisville, 1885), 34.

[31] Complaint of Alexander Flint to John Donovan, n.d., 1866, Letters Sent, Padcuah, BRFAL records.

[32] Complaint of Robert Robertson to Superintendent John Donovan, August 7, 1866, Letters Received, Paducah, ibid. Mr. Titsworth could be Joseph Titsworth who would have been approximately twenty years old in 1866. In 1860, there were ten people with the last name Titsworth living in McCracken County. In 1870, there were twenty-one people with the last name, only three of whom were white. 1860 and 1870 U.S. censuses, McCracken County, Kentucky, http://www.ancestry.com.

adding that after the beating his father would leave Mary tied for hours and "rub salt" in her wounds.[33]

Accusations of abuse also were made against a Dr. Mileum of Graves County. A neighbor of the doctor's wrote the bureau to complain that Mileum "takened up a fence rail and beat and bruised" a "honest and industrious colored lady" named Caroline Burnett in his employ. The neighbor accused Milieum of "being one of Col. Faulkner's vilians of 'the' so called Confederacy" and pleaded that the freedwoman "should have rights." Similar reports of violence were also made. In Paducah, three black children were wounded by "squirrel shot" when someone shot at them while they bathed in the Ohio River. Charles Slaughter, a young invalid whom bureau agents had moved to a Freedmen's Bureau hospital in Louisville, was thrown overboard by the captain of the *Silver Springs* after refusing to take the "damned nigger anywhere." In addition, three accusations of rape of black women by white men were reported in Paducah in August 1867.[34]

Murders also plagued the Purchase during the tenure of the bureau. In August 1865, Jenny Fyfe noted that two black men were lynched in the streets of Paducah. She was horrified when her pupils asked her "to turn out school" to watch the spectacle. In October 1866, Superintendent James F. Bolton reported the murder of John H. Elliot, who was shot by Benel Howell and his brother in Fulton County after accusing the freedman of "a number of depredations in some three or four houses in the neighborhood." Despite the ef-

---

[33] Testimony of Witnesses in Case of W. H. Dillworth, June 25, 1866, Complaints, Affidavits, and Evidence Relating to Court Cases, BRFAL records. W. W. Faulkner had been the colonel of the Twelfth Kentucky Calvary Regiment, CSA. His "villains" harassed Union outposts in the Purchase during the war, and some of the men also operated as irregulars while on leave in the area. Faulkner himself was killed by his own men shortly before the end of the war. See Henry George, *History of the 3rd, 7th, 8th, and 12th Kentucky CSA* (Louisville, 1911), 139-40.

[34] Complaint of W. H. Ham to Superintendent John Donovan, July 24, 1866, Letters Received, Paducah, BRFAL records. Dr. Thomas Mileum of Feliciana was listed on the 1870 census as worth $2,300 in property; John Donovan to John Ely, August 4, 1866, Monthly Reports, no. 138, ibid; October 29, 1866, No. 140, ibid.; W. James Kay to Sidney Burbank, August 30 1867, Monthly Reports, no. 143, ibid.

forts of Bolton, local magistrates and the county judge of Fulton claimed they were unable to find the Howell brothers, who were "secreted back in the country" and had "friends on the lookout." In January 1867, Jesse Meshew, an ex-Confederate soldier known to hold a grudge against freedmen, shot and killed Washington Gardner "without provocation" in Columbus. Though authorities promised to "spare no pains in making an arrest," Meshew evaded capture. Five months later, Bolton reported that the ex-Confederate was roaming about the country amongst "a gang of outlaws, burglars, thieves, and robbers" and intended to "make a descent on" the office of the bureau in Columbus.[35]

In December 1867, a local white man named John Whitsell murdered a Marshall County freedman on the Kentucky-Tennessee line. Whitsell had overheard the freedman bragging that he had "plenty of money in his possession." Whitsell lured the man into the woods and shot him in the head. With the help of friends, Whitsell "threw the corpse into a well." To Whitsell's indignation, the "plenty of money" the freedman bragged about turned out to be eight dollars. In Paducah in April 1868, Cleary Hardy and R. Thomas shot Richard Williams in the head. The next month, a group of masked white men, "representing themselves to be dead rebels," shot and killed a freedman named Cato in Hickman, Fulton County. The men also pulled Jacob Kyle from his home and shot him in the stomach. The white men traveled across the county threatening freedmen and robbing them of their firearms and ammunition. Several African American witnesses recognized the voices of the "young villains" as "sons of the wealthiest people" in Fulton County. The fathers of the young white men warned the freedmen that if "they talked of the affair they would be murdered by the Ku Klux Klan." The superintendent at Columbus doubted that justice could be done as the "people who

---

[35] Jenny Fyfe to Nell Fyfe, June 18, 1865, Fyfe Family Papers; James F. Bolton to Donovan, October 27, November 6, 1866, Letters Sent, Columbus BRFAL records; Bolton to W. James Kay, June 6, 1867, Letters Sent, Columbus, ibid. Jesse Meshew was a corporal in the Seventh Kentucky Mounted Infantry; see National Park Service, Civil War Soldiers and Sailors System, Jesse Meshew, http://www.itd.nps.gov/cwss/soldiers.cfm.

own all the property about this section . . . wink at this thing and take no measures against it."[36]

Another issue that thwarted the success of the bureau was the preoccupation with local and state elections in 1867. Democrats in the area hoped to sweep the election and in the process remove the hated bureau and all Federal presence from their midst. In May, Purchase whites participated in the first postwar balloting that allowed former Confederate soldiers to vote. Challenging the incumbent Democrat, U.S. congressman Lawrence S. Trimble, an ardent supporter of the former Confederacy, was "Carpetbagger" George G. Symes, who had established a law practice in Paducah after his tenure as commander of Federal forces in the Purchase. Trimble won, receiving over nine thousand votes to Symes's paltry 1,780. Symes, backed by Lucian Anderson and his fellow Republicans, promptly challenged the election results, claiming that Trimble had won through the assistance of sheriffs, magistrates, clerks, and former Confederate soldiers who "intimidated and overawed" local Union men. T. A. Duke, another local Republican, confirmed the accusations, stating that "three fourths" of the election officers "were men who have, during the late rebellion, aided, counseled, or advised the separation of Kentucky from the federal union by force of arms . . . or engaged in said rebellion." In a last bid to regain some semblance of their former power, Anderson and his cohorts waved the "bloody shirt" in an effort to remind voters that Democrats had started the war and dredged up old accusations that Trimble was pro-Confederate and involved in illegal smuggling activities during the war. They also reminded the congressional committee that Trimble was arrested during the election of 1863 for making "anti-administration" speeches in several Purchase counties. In a hearing before the Committee

---

[36] Captain Emerson H. Liscum to Brigadier General Sidney Burbank, June 26, 1868, Letters Sent, Columbus, BRFAL records; Kay to Benjamin Runkle, April 1868, Letters Sent, Paducah, ibid.. The freedmen who testified in the murder of Cato accused Jeffery Alexander, sixteen; Samuel McConnell, seventeen; and Robert McConnell, twenty-one, of Fulton County of being among the masked men. They likewise accused Marsh Glenn, twenty, of Obion County, Tennessee. Two other men, Charlie Mills and David DeBeaugh, were also involved. Unknown author to Benjamin Rankle, December 2, 1867, Letters Sent, Columbus, ibid.

on Elections in Washington, D.C., in June and July 1867, Trimble denied the charges, stating that "democrats and conservatives were threatened with Reconstruction, confiscation, and military rule, if they did not vote" for Symes. He further accused Symes of "publicly denouncing Congress as a set of Jacobins and revolutionists" during several political meetings over the past year. After considering the evidence, the committee upheld Trimble's victory.[37]

The majority of whites in the Purchase also closely watched the national congressional elections of 1867. Northern Democrats in states such as Ohio and Pennsylvania made great gains in the October contests, which highlighted the weakening of Republican strength and which bolstered many in the South. Across the South, many celebrated Democratic Party victories and the repeal of black suffrage and the Reconstruction acts. In Paducah, Bureau Superintendent Smith reported:

> The bitter feelings existing toward the republicans of the north, and the white unionists and freedmen of the south, to all appearances remains unchanged, there was great rejoicing here over the Democratic gains and victories of some of the northern states and especially over the defeat of negro suffrage, and saying many bitter things against the north for trying to force negro suffrage on the south when they will never accept it at home, calling it the consistency of the north radicals. At times it seems as though it was almost impossible for any of the citizens here to express themselves bitter enough against some of the leading men of the north.

[37] Zachariah Smith, *The History of Kentucky* (Louisville, 1885), 782-83; *United States House of Representatives Committee on Elections, Digest of Election Cases: Cases of Contested Elections in the House of Representatives from 1865 to 1871* (Washington, D.C., 1870), 329-40. Lawrence S. Trimble left Paducah in 1879 and moved to Albuquerque, New Mexico. He was the only Democrat representative to the New Mexico Constitutional Convention in 1889. He died in 1904. See Levin, *Lawyers and Lawmakers of Kentucky*, 413. George G. Symes also left Paducah in the 1870s, moving to Montana where he served as an associate supreme court judge. In 1874, he moved to Denver, Colorado, where he worked as an attorney for the Citizens Water Company and the Western Beef Association. In November 1893, Symes committed suicide by poison. See *New York Times*, November 4, 1893.

With most here the feeling is anything but friendly toward any person entertaining northern or union principles.[38]

At Columbus, bureau superintendent Bolton reported similar reactions to the elections, noting "when we received news of the result of the elections in Pennsylvania & Ohio they had a great illumination here and openly boasted that they should have their slaves back again . . . the great object of the whites here is to keep the freedmen down and reduce them to slavery or something worse."[39]

Democrats in the Purchase eagerly anticipated the 1868 presidential election between one of their old occupiers, General Ulysses S. Grant, who was running on the Republican ticket, and former governor of New York, Democrat Horatio Seymour. Though Grant went on to win the election, the Democratic Party in Kentucky registered its largest victory in the history of the two-party system. Approximately three out of four voters cast their lot with Seymour, who received 75 percent of the vote in Kentucky. Indeed, the Bluegrass State recorded the largest percentage of Democratic voters in the nation. In the Purchase, the Democratic victory was astounding, with four of the counties giving more than 90 percent of votes to Seymour. The remaining three counties polled between 80 and 89 percent of their vote to Democrats. The overwhelming support for Democrats in local and national elections was, in essence, a repudiation of the efforts of the bureau and, indeed, a threat to its very existence.[40]

In 1868, despite protestations from the superintendents in the Purchase, the bureau announced that it would cease operations in western Kentucky. In March 1868, W. James Kay made one of his last reports to the chief superintendent of Kentucky, Benjamin Runkle. The bureau had been in operation in the Jackson Purchase for over

[38] Smith to W. James Kay, November 27, 1867, Letters Sent, Paducah, BRFAL records.

[39] James F. Bolton to Kay, October 26, 1867, Letters Received, Columbus, ibid.

[40] Shannon and McQuown, *Presidential Politics in Kentucky, 1824-1948,* 41-44. For more on the complicated postwar party system in Kentucky, see Harrison and Klotter, *New History of Kentucky,* 240-43; Hambleton Tapp and James C. Klotter, *Kentucky: Decades of Discord, 1865-1900* (Frankfort, Ky., 1977); and Thomas L. Connelly, "Neo-Confederatism or Power Vacuum: Postwar Kentucky Politics Reappraised," *Register* 64 (1966): 257-69.

two years, but Kay had little to report in the way of changing attitudes towards freedmen:

> The condition of the freedmen in this Sub-District is generally as good as could be expected when the fact is considered that under the laws of Kentucky they have no rights in the courts . . . and that they are surrounded by those who because they are not permitted to hold them as slaves are the enemies of the African race, who leave nothing undone that would in itself have the slightest tendency to degrade and injure them. A large number of Freedmen are awaiting the pay due them. It is almost impossible to persuade the freedmen to leave towns for homes in the country. When contracts are made . . . a quarrel is made by the employer and the freedmen are compelled to leave their homes. The majority prefer to stay about the towns and pick up a precarious living by doing small jobs of work to the risk of being abused and cheated by the planters. Captain Bolton reports the case of a shooting that occurred in Ballard County . . . and he complains there is no U.S. Commission in his subdistrict before whom complaints can be brought.[41]

In the Purchase and elsewhere in Kentucky, the agency ultimately failed to achieve its intended reforms. It faced constant financial problems, partly because Congress failed to provide funds to Kentucky offices until June 1866, leaving it to officials to feed, clothe, shelter, and protect sick and homeless freedmen and women during the first six months. Another problem was lack of agents. Between 1866 and 1868, the seven counties of the Purchase were never staffed by more than a total of eight superintendents, subassistants, and clerks. Graves, Marshall, and Calloway Counties never did have any agents of the bureau.[42]

The lack of Federal troops within the state compounded the problem. At the close of the war, close to ten thousand black troops

---

[41] W. James Kay to Benjamin Runkle, March 27, 1868, Monthly Reports, BRFAL records.
[42] Lucas, *From Slavery to Segregation*, 186–87.

were stationed in Kentucky, but by October 1865 the number had been reduced to six thousand. As the need for troops in the Deep South grew, the number of troops in Kentucky was constantly reduced until almost all had been discharged by mid-1866. In Paducah, the last African American Federal troops withdrew in April 1866, prompting Q. Q. Quigley, a local lawyer, to write, "The last troop of Negroes left here, leaving us for the first time in over four years to revel in visions of peace. The town begins to assume somewhat of its old looks and habits." Though a small number of troops were sent in August 1866, they were unable to quell the violence and hatred directed toward the bureau. And unfortunately, the troops that were sent often displayed violent, racist attitudes towards the freedmen and their families. Agent Charles Smith informed superiors that he received almost daily complaints by local citizens and police of Paducah of attacks by soldiers on freedmen. In July 1867, a soldier shot an African American man named John Martin and wounded a white man who attempted to intervene. Another complaint was made by freedman Bob Murray who accused a private of knocking down his door and "chasing and frightening" his children. When the Paducah constable tried to intervene, the soldier "outrageously cursed and abused" him with "opprobrious language."[43]

Yet another factor that played into the failure of the agency was the racist attitudes of bureau officials themselves. In several reports, agents complained of the allegedly lazy, mischievous, mendacious, and childlike nature of the freedmen. In late April, John Donovan noted that "dances and shindigs are frequented amongst the negroes

---

[43] Lucas, *From Slavery to Segregation*, 186-87; George Langstaff Jr., ed., *The Life and Times of Quintus Quincy Quigley, 1828-1910: His Personal Journal, 1859-1908* (Brentwood, Tenn., 1999), 81; Charles Smith to James Kay, July 17, 1867, Letters Sent, Paducah, BFRAL records. Smith noted that the troops were made up largely of men from southern Illinois and southern Indiana counties just across the Ohio River who held racist views. Large numbers of Kentuckians settled in these counties before the war. See Thomas Mackey, "'Not a Pariah, but a Keystone': Kentucky and Secession," *Sister States, Enemy States*, ed. Dollar, Whiteaker, and Dickinson, 27, and Chandra Manning, *What This Cruel War Was Over: Soldiers, Slavery and the Civil War* (New York, 2007).

of this city and vicinity. These places . . . give occasion for a variety of mischiefs and have the demoralizing affect upon the Freedmen and especially upon the females whose habits are of such an evil character as will bring on in the course of time a species of moral and physical degeneracy that will compromise the existence of the race." Donovan made similar disparaging remarks concerning the work ethic of local freedmen, stating that "many of their difficulties grow out of their stubborn indolence and lack of respect to their employers and superiors." He added that, "They think that because they are *'free'* they have perfect license to do about as they please . . . they have yet to learn the difference between natural and civil liberty and to comprehend the relation that properly exists between the different classes and orders of society." When V. A. Brown, a local freedwoman complained that her employer "knocked her senseless" for refusing "to get on her knees and scrub the kitchen floors," Donovan said Brown "brought it on herself." Other agents expressed similar opinions. An agent investigating the beating of a man by a "gang of horsemen" believed whites who insisted that the incident never happened. Calling the man a "liar," the agent dismissed the man's claims because he recanted to authorities after being arrested and "examined" under mysterious circumstances.[44]

Most important, the agency could not survive the intense hatred of the freedmen and the mistrust of it that existed among whites in the Purchase. The few who attempted to help the freedmen often displayed an intense racism that left no room for equality. The case of Mary Ann Gerald highlights that dichotomy. In May 1866, Gerald, a former slave, walked into the newly established Freedmen's Bureau office in Paducah. In her hand, Gerald held a written complaint against her former owner, R. Y. Gerald of Ballard County, who refused to release one of her children. The letter detailed her attempts to regain her child, noting that Gerald "beat her numer-

---

[44] John Donovan to Ely, April 30, 1866, Letters Sent, No. 4, BRFAL records; John Donovan to Ely, August 4, 1866, Letters Sent, No. 134, ibid.; John F. Smith to John Donovan, August 13, 1866, Letters Sent, ibid.

ous times and threatened to kill her if she came back again." The author of the letter was Gerald's current employer, a young farmer from Woodville, McCracken County, named Edward S. Thornton. Thornton informed Superintendent Donovan that he believed Mary Ann Gerald's accusations of cruelty against the former slaveholder, noting that she arrived at his farm "almost naked and destitute." He further believed that the former slave should be "treated humanely." Thornton, however, stopped short of promoting equal rights for freedmen, stating, "Sir, I am not the advocate of the Negro against the white-man, nor the advocate of Negro equality, or any thing of that sort. I did all in my power to keep them in bondage . . . I would further state that I am not interested at all so far as the child is concerned—if she gets it, it will be an expense and no profit to me."[45]

Similar attitudes were expressed by local whites during the trial of W. H. Dillworth. Of the eight witnesses called to testify, all agreed that he had been an unusually cruel master to his former slave, Mary. Yet, six of the witnesses excused Dillworth's behavior. One believed Mary deserved the treatment because she was "a bad sort," while another witness called her an "idiotic girl" and "one of the worst Negroes the county affords." Indeed, one witness testified to actually observing the horrid beatings of Mary but stated that she did "not think it unusual to tie down negroes when they are whipped."[46]

As 1868 came to a close, whites in the Purchase found much to celebrate. The despised Freedmen's Bureau was gone, its last agents having left in June. For the first time in seven years, the area was free

[45] Edward S. Thornton to Superintendent John Donovan, May 16, 1866, Letters Sent, Paducah, BRFAL records. R. Y. Gerald went so far as to obtain an order to keep Mary Ann Gerald's children in his employ after he convinced bureau officials that the children's supposed father signed them over to his custody. Mary Ann Gerald denied the claim, stating that "the man who claims to be the father of her children never was her husband, that she is the only legal parent." Three months after her complaint, the freedwoman's children remained in Gerald's hands. Edward S. Thornton was a native of Johnson County, Missouri, who fought under General Sterling Price in the Second Missouri Confederate Infantry. He moved to McCracken County ca. 1865-66. See National Park Service, Civil War Soldiers and Sailors System, Edward S. Thornton, http://www.itd.nps.gov/cwss/soldiers.cfm.

[46] Testimony of Witnesses in Case of W. H. Dillworth, June 25, 1866, Complaints, Affidavits, and Evidence Relating to Court Cases, BRFAL records.

of what most viewed as Federal occupation. Democrats like Lawrence S. Trimble packed local and state offices in the area, while Unionists like Lucian Anderson left politics entirely. And while the Democrats had lost the 1868 election nationally, the steady transformation of Kentucky into a Democratic stronghold bolstered the Purchase. A political anomaly during the antebellum era, the Purchase ironically could boast that Kentucky followed *her* lead. Indeed, the next few decades would see the Purchase and the Bluegrass State grow even closer culturally, as they both grasped on to the Lost Cause ideology that enveloped the South.[47]

Yet for African Americans in the Purchase, equality remained a distant dream, as across the countryside former slaves toiled in the same fields they worked prior to the war. In the last three decades of the nineteenth century, cotton and tobacco production as well as railroad construction brought a steady influx of African American laborers to the Purchase. The increase in the black population led in turn to an exponential growth in violence against blacks. Between 1869 and 1873, eleven black men were lynched in the Purchase. By 1916, over forty blacks had lost their lives to white lynch mobs in the area. The Purchase, like the rest of the state, would struggle throughout the twentieth century to come to terms with the legacy of slavery, war, and reconstruction.[48]

Back in June 1865, Freedmen's Bureau teacher Jenny Fyfe addressed a prophetic letter to her sister in Michigan. Looking out her window one morning, Fyfe was startled at the number of returned Rebel soldiers in the streets still in uniform. Christening them "greybacks," she noted that many walked with an air of defiance: "Many alas! are as rebel at heart as ever they were—'Conquered but not defeated' they say 'and we will see that our children are reared to

---

[47] See Anne Marshall, *Creating a Confederate Kentucky: The Lost Cause and Civil War Memory in a Border State* (Chapel Hill, 2010) and Michael Flannery, "Kentucky History Revisited: The Role of the Civil War in Shaping Kentucky's Consciousness," *Filson History Quarterly* 71 (1997): 27-51.

[48] George C. Wright, *Racial Violence in Kentucky, 1865-1940* (Baton Rouge, 1990), 1, 72-73; *New York Times*, August 18, 1871.

think as we think, to feel as we feel."' The young Yankee nurse and Freedmen's Bureau teacher from Michigan had no way of knowing how true her words would ring.[49]

---

[49] Jenny Fyfe to Nell Fyfe, June 16, 1865, Fyfe Family Papers.

PIONEER BLACK LEGISLATORS FROM KENTUCKY, 1860s–1960s

By Peter Wallenstein

The 1860s created, or at least made possible, a whole new political world in Kentucky—and in all the South, indeed across America. Universal emancipation came late to Kentucky with the Thirteenth Amendment. The Civil Rights Act of 1866, followed by the Fourteenth Amendment, declared African Americans to be citizens. And the Fifteenth Amendment conferred voting rights on all black men. Only one American of known African ancestry gained election to any state legislature before 1865, but even before 1870 any number of others did.

A survey of pioneer black members of American state legislatures offers an illuminating approach to calibrating the historical contours of African American political power. The ability to run as a black candidate and win—in a race not just for a minor local office but for a seat in the state legislature—is a key historical marker of black political power, as well as a means for attaining a diminished regime of white supremacy and black exclusion. And Kentucky is a representative state for the 1860s and after—a slave state during the Civil War but not a member of the Confederacy; a state subject to the three post–Civil War constitutional amendments but not subject to the Congressional Reconstruction legislation of 1867; a state with proportionately far fewer African Americans than in most states of

PETER WALLENSTEIN is a professor of history at Virginia Tech in Blacksburg, Virginia. His books include *Cradle of America: A History of Virginia* (2014), *Race, Sex, and the Freedom to Marry: Loving v. Virginia* (2014), and *Virginia Tech, Land-Grant University: History of a School, a State, a Nation* (2021).

the South but far more than in the states outside the South during the Civil War era.[1]

Alexander Lucius Twilight, the only legislator with African ancestry elected before the Civil War, served in Vermont in 1836–37. Even before the Fifteenth Amendment took away from states the authority to deny voting rights on the basis of racial identity, other black legislators gained election in some states—Edward G. Walker (son of David Walker, author of *Walker's Appeal*) and Charles L. Mitchell in Massachusetts in 1866, soon followed by black candidates in ten states of the former Confederacy.[2]

Black men from Kentucky gained election to state legislatures in three categories. Some promptly won seats in other southern states, including Arkansas and South Carolina. Some became legislators outside the South, including the adjacent states of Illinois and Ohio. And—finally—native black Kentuckians found themselves winning an occasional election to the Kentucky state legislature, though never

---

[1] This exploration of pioneer black legislators from Kentucky rests in part on two compilations: Notable Kentucky African Americans Database: Legislators, Kentucky, http://www.uky.edu/Libraries/nkaa/subject.php?sub_id=116; and Notable Kentucky African Americans Database: Legislators, Outside Kentucky, http://www.uky.edu/Libraries/nkaa/subject.php?sub_id=117. A significant resource for the wider subject, though not for officeholders in Kentucky, is Eric Foner, *Freedom's Lawmakers: A Directory of Black Officeholders during Reconstruction* (1993; rev. ed., Baton Rouge, 1996). Leading studies of pioneer black legislators in other southern states are Luther Porter Jackson, *Negro Office-Holders in Virginia, 1865-1895* (Norfolk, Va., 1945); Charles Vincent, *Black Legislators in Louisiana during Reconstruction* (Baton Rouge, 1977); Thomas Holt, *Black over White: Negro Political Leadership in South Carolina during Reconstruction* (Urbana, Ill., 1977); Merline Pitre, *Through Many Dangers, Toils, and Snares: The Black Leadership of Texas, 1868-1900* (Austin, Texas 1985); Canter Brown Jr., *Florida's Black Public Officials, 1867-1924* (Tuscaloosa, Ala., 1998); Blake J. Wintory, "African-American Legislators in the Arkansas General Assembly, 1868-1893," *Arkansas Historical Quarterly* 64 (2006): 385-434; and Richard Bailey, *Neither Carpetbaggers nor Scalawags: Black Officeholders during the Reconstruction of Alabama, 1867-1878* (1991; rev. 5th ed.; Montgomery, Ala., 2010).

[2] Michael T. Hahn, *Alexander Twilight: Vermont's African-American Pioneer* (Shelburne, Vt., 1988); http://www.blackpast.org/?q=aah/walker-edward-garrison-1831-1901. Vermont voters did not make a habit of electing black officials. The next black legislator in that overwhelmingly white state was William J. Anderson (1876-1959), elected more than a century later by overwhelming majorities, though his was the only black family in his hometown of Shoreham. He served two terms, from 1945 to 1949. See Elsie B. Smith, "William J. Anderson: Shoreham's Negro Legislator in the Vermont House of Representatives," *Vermont History* 44 (1976): 203-13.

more than one at a time until a century after the Civil War. Each of these three clusters supplies a window on the new political possibilities in post–Civil War America. Each relates as well to other dimensions of black citizenship and equality in the long aftermath of the 1860s.

Migration patterns, as reflected in the movement of pioneer black legislators who had been born in Kentucky, reveal that the borders of the Bluegrass State were easily passed through. Before the Civil War, slaves from Kentucky were sold farther south, and free blacks left for free states. During and immediately after the war, black Kentuckians left for greener pastures, where freedom came sooner or was more full-bodied. At first, that might be the Cotton South of the former Confederacy. For far longer—for generations after the war—they left for states outside the South, especially the states of the Northwest Ordinance or the Louisiana Purchase.

Black Kentucky Natives Elected in Other Southern States

Benjamin Franklin Randolph (?–1868) was born free in Kentucky. When he was still young, his family moved to Warren County, Ohio, and there he attended elementary school. He enrolled at Oberlin College in Oberlin, Ohio, in 1854, first in the preparatory department to complete high school, then in the college. After graduation in 1862, he was ordained a minister in the Methodist Episcopal Church (North) and subsequently served as a chaplain with U.S. Colored Troops in South Carolina. After the war, Randolph worked with the American Missionary Association and the Freedmen's Bureau in South Carolina, and he edited two newspapers in Charleston. Both a minister and a politician, he worked with the Union League to organize the Republican Party, and he was elected to the 1868 South Carolina Constitutional Convention and then later that year to the state senate. Randolph did not hold back in his advocacy of a radically new racial order. He called for integrated public schools, arguing that "we must decide whether the two races shall live together or not," and he supported legislation to ban racial discrimination in public accommodations. In October 1868, still in his first year as an elected official, he was assassinated, one of many black politicians in

South Carolina to meet that fate.[3]

By one recent count, seven of the eighty-four African Americans who served in the Arkansas legislature between 1868 and 1892 had been born in Kentucky. Among them, William H. Furbush (1839–1902) was a Carroll County native, probably born a slave, but he was free by 1860 and operating a photography studio in Ohio. Then he worked for a time in Phillips County, in a Union-occupied part of Arkansas, but late in the war he joined the Union army. In 1866, he moved to Liberia, but after eighteen months he returned to Ohio. By then, black men had gained the right to vote in the former Confederacy, and by 1870 he had moved back to Phillips County. In 1872, he won election as a Republican to the Arkansas House of Representatives. The next year, when he and three other black men were refused service at an establishment in Little Rock, they sued the barkeeper under the new Arkansas civil rights act of 1873, and, represented by two black lawyers, they won—a victory said to be the only one ever obtained under that law. Between 1873 and 1879, Furbush served as sheriff of Lee County, a new county (carved out of Phillips and adjacent counties) that he had successfully promoted in the legislature, named after Robert E. Lee to help attract support from his fellow legislators. But then, given the tangled history of partisan and fusion politics in Arkansas in the 1870s, he ran in 1878 as a Democrat in a campaign to return to the legislature, and he won, likely the first black Democrat in any state legislature. The next year, Furbush moved on again, this time to Colorado, where he worked in mining and gambling, and then to Ohio again, where he taught music, before returning to Arkansas, this time as a lawyer. Still a Democrat, he tried to attract black voters to the ranks as an alternative to the "lily-white" Republicans. But he grew increasingly disenchanted at the narrowing options in the Arkansas political universe, as his fellow Democrats passed new laws in the 1890s that disenfranchised many black men and segregated railway passenger cars. He moved to South Carolina, and then to Georgia, and finally to Indiana, where

[3] Daniel W. Hamilton, "Randolph, Benjamin Franklin," in *American National Biography*, ed. John A. Garraty and Mark C. Carnes, 24 vols. (New York, 1999), 18:120-21.

he died while living in the National Home for Disabled Veterans.[4]

Any number of other southern black legislators from the 1870s and 1880s may have been born in Kentucky, including several in Reconstruction Texas. Thomas Beck (1819?–?), for one, having arrived in Texas in his twenties, around 1842, gained election to the Texas House of Representatives in 1874 and again in 1878 and 1880. His legislative triumphs included obtaining passage of a law to bar people from putting children to work without their parents' consent and funding for a black land-grant college, Prairie View A&M. Charles Caldwell (1832?–75), another possible Kentucky native, was elected to the Mississippi constitutional convention of 1868 and then in December 1869 to the state senate, where he served with distinction and courage from 1870 until his assassination in 1875.[5]

Outside the South

William Jefferson Hardin (1830?–89) was born free in Kentucky but left for California in the 1850s and never again lived in his native state. Rather, after serving briefly in the U.S. Army during the Civil War, he made his way all around the West. In Colorado, he spoke out against a restrictive voting measure passed by the territorial legisla-

[4] Identified as Kentucky natives in addition to Furbush are Edward A. Fulton (born a slave in 1833), Lewis W. Daniel (1851?-1932), Howard McKay (1858-?), William Murphy (1810?-?), Granville Ryles (1831-1909), and John W. Webb (1824-?). See Wintory, "African-American Legislators in the Arkansas General Assembly, 1868-1893," 385-434, and "William Hines Furbush: An African American, Carpetbagger, Republican, Fusionist, and Democrat," *Arkansas Historical Quarterly* 63 (2004): 107-65; see also Christopher Warren Branam, "'The Africans Have Taken Arkansas': Political Activities of African-Americans of the Arkansas Legislature, 1868-1873" (MA thesis, University of Arkansas, 2011).

[5] Herbert Aptheker, "Mississippi Reconstruction and the Negro Leader Charles Caldwell," *Science and Society* 11 (1947): 340-71; the Notable Kentucky African Americans Database identifies Caldwell as a Kentucky native, and perhaps he was, although Foner (*Freedom's Lawmakers*, 36) follows the 1870 U.S. census in identifying him as born in Mississippi. As for Texas, one source identifies legislator Richard Allen as having been born a slave in "Virginia or Kentucky" and Silas Cotton as a slave born in "South Carolina or Kentucky." It also says of Thomas Beck that he was born in "Mississippi or Kentucky" (the 1880 U.S. census, Grimes County, Texas, which identifies Beck's occupation as "legislator," reports Kentucky). See http://genealogytrails.com/tex/state/aapolitics.html. For more on pioneer black legislators in Texas, see Pitre, *Through Many Dangers, Toils, and Snares*, and J. Mason Brewer, *Negro Legislators of Texas* (Dallas, 1935).

ture, and he lobbied Congress, which passed the Territorial Suffrage Act, enfranchising African Americans in all the territories in January 1867. An effective public speaker, he engaged civic issues everywhere he went. In Wyoming, he gained election in 1879 and 1881 to two successive terms in the territorial legislature. In 1882, following his impassioned speech in support of repealing a law that banned interracial marriage, the legislature did so. Given his appearance—his father was white, his mother biracial—it is not clear that his African ancestry was always recognized, so it is hard to know the degree to which his accomplishments came in the face of racial prejudice and helped to dispel it. But the issues he took on had mostly to do with African Americans' rights as citizens, such as voting and education.[6]

The first victories by black candidates in legislative elections in the states of the Midwest, just across the Ohio River from Kentucky, also came in the late 1870s and early 1880s. Illinois was first in 1876, soon followed by Ohio in 1879, and Indiana in 1880. The first African American in the Illinois House of Representatives, John W. E. Thomas (1847–99), voiced his identification with the Republican Party when he wrote in 1875: "What we are, the Republican Party made us. And the success of the Republican Party is our success and the downfall of it will be our downfall." A teacher and then a grocer, he was elected to a two-year term in 1876 and then twice more in the 1880s. Born a slave in Alabama, Thomas had moved north soon after the Civil War, and in the national centennial year he celebrated an electoral victory from a district with far more white voters than black. His party failed to nominate him, or indeed any African American, for the next two elections, but he triumphed again in 1882 and 1884. In 1885, in what proved to be his final term in

[6] Eugene H. Berwanger, "Hardin and Langston: Western Black Spokesmen of the Reconstruction Era," *Journal of Negro History* 64 (1979): 101-15; Roger D. Hardaway, "William Jefferson Hardin: Wyoming's Nineteenth Century Black Legislator," *Annals of Wyoming* 63 (1991): 2-13; Gary Kimball, "William Jefferson Hardin: A Grand but Forgotten Park City African American," *Utah Historical Quarterly* 78 (2010): 23-38; Berwanger, "Reconstruction on the Frontier: The Equal Rights Struggle in Colorado, 1865-1867," *Pacific Historical Review* 44 (1975): 313-29.

the legislature, Illinois enacted a state civil rights act after the U.S. Supreme Court overturned the 1875 federal civil rights act. Thomas continued to seek election through 1890 when he ran for a seat in the state senate.[7]

Taking the seat previously held by Representative Thomas was George French Ecton (1846–?), who had been born a slave in Clark County, Kentucky. Ecton moved across the Ohio River into Cincinnati in 1865—after the end of the Civil War but before the Thirteenth Amendment, so he and a friend traveled with freedom papers forged by an abolitionist. He found a wide variety of employment as well as some schooling and in 1873 moved on to Chicago, Illinois, where he was dining-room headwaiter at the Hotel Woodruff when he was elected to the Illinois House of Representatives in 1886. He won reelection in 1888 but had left the district before he could run again in 1890.[8]

In Ohio, like Illinois, black citizens active in the Republican Party wanted to do more than vote for white Republicans. Among those men was a newcomer, George Washington Williams (1849–91), a native of Pennsylvania who attended school there and in Massachusetts but then, in 1863, when black men could enlist, lied about his age so he could do so. Over the next four years, he fought in Virginia and South Carolina, suffered a serious wound, spent time as a soldier in postwar Texas, joined the Mexican army, and fought in the U.S. cavalry against the Comanche in 1867. A civilian again by 1868, he returned to New England and in 1874 became the first

[7] David A. Joens, "John W. E. Thomas and the Election of the First African American to the Illinois General Assembly," *Journal of the Illinois State Historical Society* 94 (2001): 200-16; Joens, *From Slave to State Legislator: John W. E. Thomas, Illinois's First African American Lawmaker* (Carbondale, Ill., 2012), (quote, 11), 109-16. In Indiana, the first black legislator was James Sidney Hinton (1834-92); born free in North Carolina, he migrated with his family to Indiana in 1848; he later joined the Union army and gained election in 1880 to a two-year term representing Indianapolis. See Etta Russell, "Hinton, James Sidney," in *The Encyclopedia of Indianapolis*, ed. David J. Bodenhamer and Robert G. Barrows (Bloomington, Ind., 1994), 683; Ronald D. Snell, "Black Spokesman or Republican Pawn," *Negro History Bulletin* 32 (1969): 6-10.

[8] William J. Simmons, *Men of Mark: Eminent, Progressive, and Rising* (Cleveland, 1887), 358-60; Joens, *From Slave to State Legislator*, 133-35, 158, 163; *Blue Book of the State of Illinois, 1921-22* (Springfield, Ill., 1921), 648-51.

black graduate of Newton Theological Seminary. As a preacher, he had a church in Boston, then in Washington, D.C., and, beginning in 1876, in Cincinnati, where he was a blur of activity. In 1877, Republicans found, in a competitive political environment, that they had to offer black constituents the opportunity to vote for a black Republican, and they nominated two black candidates for the Ohio House of Representatives. Williams ran for a seat from Cincinnati but lost, as did the other black candidate for the house, John P. Green in Cleveland. Williams redirected his energies, resigning his church post, starting a newspaper, and studying law. In 1879, he ran again, and this time, with sufficient white Republican support for a black candidate, he won and became, at age thirty, the first black state legislator in Ohio. One of the measures he pressed for in the house of representatives—though without success, in the first session or the second—would have repealed the Ohio law against interracial marriage. In addition, his exclusion from an eating establishment near the statehouse at which Ohio legislators routinely ate—during his very first week as a representative, with the Civil Rights Act of 1875 still in effect—led him to elicit from his colleagues a resolution against such racial discrimination. He proved to be an active member of the legislature in committee and on the floor. He also began his major life work, writing a pioneering history of African Americans. After one term as a lawmaker, having proved that a black candidate could win a legislative race in Ohio, he stayed in Columbus but moved on to other activities, especially his work as an historian. As for John P. Green, he won election in 1881, the second black legislator in Ohio, and pushed, though without success, for school integration.[9]

Later in the 1880s, Kentucky native Robert J. Harlan (1816–97) gained election as a Republican candidate with African ancestry to the Ohio House of Representatives. Harlan's mother was a fair-skinned slave; his father was quite likely Judge James Harlan—the father of

[9] John Hope Franklin, "George Washington Williams, Historian," *Journal of Negro History* 31 (1946): 60-90, and *George Washington Williams: A Biography* (1985; repr., Durham, 1998), xvii-100; David Gerber, *Black Ohio and the Color Line, 1860-1915* (Urbana, Ill., 1976), 223-30, 236-37.

John Marshall Harlan, the Supreme Court justice who famously dissented in *Plessy v. Ferguson* (1896). In the 1840s, Robert J. Harlan lived more or less as a free man in Kentucky, and in 1848 James Harlan officially manumitted him. Formally free at last, the fair-featured thirty-something followed the lure of the California Gold Rush, which made him a wealthy man in the 1850s. He lived most of the rest of his life across the Ohio River in Cincinnati, though from the late 1850s to the late 1860s he lived in England. The Thirteenth Amendment ended slavery for all his nonwhite kin back in Kentucky, and it ended slaveholding for his white family. Moreover, an 1869 Ohio law brought political rights to black men in Ohio, just as the Fifteenth Amendment did for black men in Kentucky. In 1877, Harlan lost the Republican nomination for the Ohio legislature that went to George Washington Williams. In 1885, however, he was nominated, in Cincinnati, as were two other African American candidates—Jere A. Brown (c. 1842–?) in Cleveland and Benjamin W. Arnett (1838–1906) from Greene County—and all three won. Working in a much more favorable political environment than had Williams or Green, Representative Harlan and his colleagues obtained passage in 1886 of a bill to repeal both the Ohio antimiscegenation law and the separate-school law. After the Ohio Senate passed the measure in early 1887, the state had reached a new level of racial nondiscrimination.[10]

Matthew Oliver Ricketts (1858–1917), born near New Castle, Kentucky, to slave parents late in the era of slavery, moved as a child with his newly freed family to Boonville, Missouri (near Columbia), where he attended school and his father became a minister. He graduated in the 1870s from the Lincoln Institute (later Lincoln University) and became a teacher. Then he went to Nebraska, where he became

[10] James W. Gordon, "Did the First Justice Harlan Have a Black Brother?" *Western New England Law Review* 15 (1993): 159-238; Franklin, *George Washington Williams*, 62-64; Gerber, *Black Ohio and the Color Line*, 230-44. See also Davison M. Douglas, *Jim Crow Moves North: The Battle over Northern School Segregation, 1865-1954* (New York, 2005), 88-94; David H. Fowler, *Northern Attitudes towards Interracial Marriage: Legislation and Public Opinion in the Middle Atlantic and the States of the Old Northwest, 1780-1930* (New York, 1987), 255-65.

the first black graduate of Omaha Medical College. Still in his thirties, a physician and political leader among African Americans in Omaha, Dr. Ricketts was elected to the Nebraska House of Representatives in 1892, the first black legislator in that state, and he was reelected in 1894. In addition to getting other black Nebraskans jobs in state or local government, a notable accomplishment during his time in the legislature was the strengthening of the state civil rights law (first passed in 1885) regarding discrimination in public facilities—at about the same time that southern states were moving in the opposite direction. But in the Republican primary in 1896, he lost to a white candidate in a bid for a seat in the state senate.[11]

During the long interlude between black electoral success in the post–Civil War, post–Confederate South and the resumption of black representation in state legislatures there in the 1960s, black Kentuckians continued to gain election in states outside the South—states where black voters were too few to be greatly feared but sufficient in number to be effective and even courted. This phenomenon reflected both the continuing possibility of black victories in the North during those years and the continuing black migration out of the South. Thus the rising black population in the North could translate into an increase in black electoral success there—in turn increasing the relative attractiveness of areas outside the South. Black natives of Kentucky who gained election to public office, wherever they did so, cumulatively helped to alter the world of the era of Civil War and Reconstruction and bring on the world of the 1960s.

These men included Kentucky native Henry T. Eubanks (1853–1913), who was elected in 1903 and again in 1908 in Cleveland, Ohio. In the next generation, Harris B. Gaines Sr. (1888–1964) served in the Illinois legislature in the 1930s, and Dr. Richard Pollard Mc-

---

[11] www.blackpast.org/?q=aaw/ricketts-matthew-oliver; Quintard Taylor, *In Search of the Racial Frontier: African Americans in the American West, 1528-1990* (New York, 1998), 205; "Lively Time at Primaries," *Omaha Daily Bee*, September 19, 1896; my thanks to Corinne Jacox at the Creighton University Law Library in Omaha, Nebraska. Ever since the 1930s, Nebraska has had a unicameral legislature, but such was not the case in the 1890s; Ricketts is sometimes said to have been elected to the Nebraska Senate, but in fact it was to the lower house.

Clain (1890–1965) served in the Ohio legislature. Subsequent black legislators born in Kentucky but elected elsewhere before the 1960s include James S. Hunter (1900–65), who served in the Indiana House of Representatives from 1941 until his death, and David S. Holmes Jr. (1914–94), who served in Michigan, also for a quarter-century, first in the house and then in the senate, from 1959 until his death.[12]

Kentucky at Last

Already by the early 1870s, black Kentuckians had occasion to show their impatience at white Republicans telling them that the time had not yet come for black candidates to run for legislative office.[13] Yet so much terror was visited upon advocates in Kentucky, white or black, of black political rights that the running of black candidates for office there and getting elected hardly seemed possible. In early November 1872, just before the elections, members of the Ku Klux Klan went to the house of Samuel Hawkins, a black farmer who had been registering black voters. Having already warned him to stop, they took not only Hawkins himself but also his wife, Mahala, and his oldest daughter, Francie, and hanged them all from a tree. The atrocity served as a stark warning to anyone else who might act as he had.[14]

[12] Notable Kentucky African Americans Database: Legislators, Outside Kentucky; Alan F. January and Justin E. Walsh, *A Century of Achievement: Black Hoosiers in the Indiana General Assembly, 1881-1986* (Indianapolis, 1986), 29. Also listed in the database are the fathers of Georgia legislator Julian Bond and Illinois legislator (and Chicago mayor) Harold Washington. The database reports that Opal L. Tandy (1917-83) was elected to the Indiana legislature in 1956, but the biographical sketch in the Opal L. Tandy Collection at the Indiana Historical Society in Indianapolis, Indiana, indicates he lost that election.

[13] Victor B. Howard, *Black Liberation in Kentucky: Emancipation and Freedom, 1862-1884* (Lexington, Ky., 1983), 146-59.

[14] The story broke in the *New York Times* on November 5, 1872, election day. George C. Wright, *Racial Violence in Kentucky, 1865-1940: Lynchings, Mob Rule, and "Legal Lynchings"* (Baton Rouge, 1990), 48-52; names are from the 1870 U.S. census of Jessamine County, Kentucky; see also Anne E. Marshall, *Creating a Confederate Kentucky: The Lost Cause and Civil War Memory in a Border State* (Chapel Hill, 2010), 58-68. News stories, one of which used the name Samuel Hawkins, the other George Hawkins, placed the event in neighboring Fayette County (in the Hickman precinct), and the 1870 census listed a Samuel Hawkins there as well, but he was far too young—and he and his growing family appear there again in the 1880 census. Jessamine County had a Little Hickman precinct.

The time for a black legislator in Kentucky had not yet come—white Republicans maintained that claim into the 1910s and beyond. In the 1890s, for the first time, Republicans won key offices in Kentucky, including William O. Bradley as the first Republican Kentucky governor (1895–99). Nor was that the only instance of statewide victories by Republican candidates, as they continued thereafter to win the governorship every third or fourth term. Black Republicans in Louisville had in mind running as candidates themselves. A group of them wanted to see attorney Nathaniel R. Harper as a candidate for the legislature in 1895, but white Republicans engineered a change in the rules for nominations so as to block such a development. William H. Wright, a black lawyer and businessman, sought a nomination in 1909. Public schoolteacher Lee Brown did the same in 1913. Whites told them all that the time had not come—and then ensured that this was the case. A half-century after the election of native black Kentuckians to state legislatures farther south as well as to the north, none had yet cracked the Kentucky General Assembly.[15]

William Warley, a newspaper editor and civil rights activist who had won a case, *Buchanan v. Warley* (1917), in the U.S. Supreme Court attacking a residential-segregation ordinance in Louisville, sought a legislative seat in 1919. Again, he received no significant white or Republican Party support. Nothing had yet worked, and in 1921 some black insurgents formed the Lincoln Independent Party, on whose ticket bank president Wilson Lovett ran for the lower house and newspaper editor I. Willis Cole ran for the state senate. According to the official vote count, the independent effort was squashed. But the victorious Republicans made significant concessions to the black independents. The city administration began hiring black policemen and black firemen—and establishing a new fire station staffed by black firemen—and it also hired black workers for white-collar jobs in city government.[16]

[15] George C. Wright, *Life behind a Veil: Blacks in Louisville, Kentucky, 1865-1930* (Baton Rouge, 1985), 176-93; 1910 U.S. census, Jefferson County, Kentucky; J. Blaine Hudson, "Harper, Nathaniel R.," in *The Encyclopedia of Louisville*, ed. John E. Kleber (Lexington, Ky., 2001), 369.

[16] *Buchanan v. Warley*, 245 U.S. 60 (1917); Wright, *Life behind a Veil*, 204, 246-53; Russell

Black Kentuckians had been running for legislative office, and winning, in a variety of states, in the South and outside the South, as far back as 1868. In the 1930s, the time for black representation in the Kentucky state legislature at last arrived, as black voters in Louisville demonstrated by electing a black legislator. Unable to secure Republican backing, a young lawyer and African Methodist Episcopal Zion (AMEZ) minister, Charles Ewbank Tucker (1896–1975), ran in 1933 for a seat from Louisville and lost—to the white Republican candidate. But the Democratic Party had backed him, happy to divide the black and Republican vote. The move worked for the Democrats, who regained the mayoralty in Louisville after a number of years out of office. And it worked for black residents, in that the new Democrats in office appointed various black men as deputy officials and to other posts, and they established a second black fire station. Those immediate benefits did not, however, put an African American in the legislature. In 1935, the Democrats backed Tucker again. This time, the Republicans finally moved to nominate a black candidate, so, for one seat in the Kentucky House of Representatives that year, black Democratic candidate Tucker faced off against black Republican candidate Charles W. Anderson Jr.[17]

Sixty-five years after the Fifteenth Amendment, Charles W. Anderson Jr. (1907–60) became the first black candidate to be elected to the Kentucky state legislature, and beginning in 1936 in fact he gained election to six consecutive two-year terms. A native of Louisville, his father a doctor, he had graduated from Kentucky State College in Frankfort, the black land-grant school in Kentucky, and had then left the state to earn a law degree. Shortly after finishing law school at Howard University in 1931, he returned to his hometown. Immediately plunging into local politics and civil rights endeavors, he became a force at a time when a real prospect of securing the Re-

Wigginton, "'But He Did What He Could': William Warley Leads Louisville's Fight for Justice, 1902-1946," *Filson History Quarterly* 76 (2002): 427-58.

[17] Wright, *Life behind a Veil*, 259-60; "Tucker, Charles Ewbank," *Encyclopedia of Louisville*, 893-94.

publican nomination to a seat representing black voters in Louisville had finally materialized.[18]

Even before his campaign for the legislature, Anderson had in effect called for an end to the black exclusion from higher education in the state that had forced him to go out of state to attend law school. As a rookie legislator, Representative Anderson continued his push for the desegregation of white institutions of higher education, in particular the University of Kentucky or, as an alternative, state funds to assist black Kentuckians to obtain advanced degrees out of state. The legislature passed the measure as the Anderson–Mayer State Aid Act of 1936. In the context of the time, this was a substantial advance over the current situation black Kentuckians faced, although already in 1935–36 Maryland state courts were ruling, as in 1938 the U.S. Supreme Court did in a case from Missouri, that such an approach was a constitutionally inadequate means of addressing black educational rights or needs.[19]

Anderson resigned his office in 1946 to accept appointment as assistant commonwealth's attorney in Louisville. Soon, however, an African American presence returned to the Kentucky House of Representatives. Dennis Henderson (1901–79), elected in 1947, served one term, and then taking his place and serving two terms was the third black Kentuckian to be elected to the Kentucky legislature, Jesse H. Lawrence (1900–66). Holding degrees from Howard University and Indiana University, Lawrence owned a funeral home, and he picked up the cause of black access to higher education where Charles W. Anderson Jr. had left off. Elected in 1949, later in the same

[18] George C. Wright, *In Pursuit of Equality, 1890-1980*, vol. 2 of *A History of Blacks in Kentucky*, 2 vols. (Frankfort, 1992), 156-60; John Benjamin Horton, *Not Without Struggle* (New York, 1979), 76-80; Karen C. McDaniel, "Anderson, Charles Jr.," *Encyclopedia of Louisville*, 34-35.

[19] Wright, *In Pursuit of Equality*, 158, 160-61; Horton, *Not Without Struggle*, 77-79; Mark V. Tushnet, *The NAACP's Legal Strategy against Segregated Education, 1925-1950* (Chapel Hill, 1987), 70-77; Vernell Denae Larkin, "Dreams Fulfilled and Dreams Denied: The Ironies and Paradoxes of Being a Student under the Anderson-Mayer State Aid Act 1935-1936" (EdD dissertation, University of Kentucky, 2001). See also Michael J. Klarman, *From Jim Crow to Civil Rights: The Supreme Court and the Struggle for Racial Equality* (New York, 2004), 148-52, 160-62.

year that black Louisville teacher Lyman T. Johnson won a federal court order to be admitted to the University of Kentucky graduate program in history, Representative Lawrence successfully proposed a bill to amend—in effect it largely undid, at the college level—the Day Law of 1904, the measure that had absolutely forbidden integrated schools in Kentucky. Berea College was thus permitted once again to enroll both black and white students, and historically white public institutions of higher education also moved to change their undergraduate admissions policies to permit desegregation.[20]

The first candidate to win a seat in the Kentucky legislature as a Democrat was the Reverend Felix S. Anderson (1891–1983), an African Methodist Episcopal clergyman in Louisville elected to the house of representatives for three terms beginning in 1954. A migrant himself from North Carolina, he reflected the continuing shift by black voters, in Kentucky and nationwide, away from the party of Lincoln and into the party of the New Deal. Early in his first term, a legislative colleague introduced a bill to repeal the Day Law. Where the issue in the past had been segregated or nonsegregated higher education, by this time it had become one of segregation in elementary and secondary schooling. Anderson, convinced that such a bill could not pass, proposed instead an amendment to the Day Law that would simply permit local school districts to make their own policies. In the end, legislators showed that they were happy to wait and let the U.S. Supreme Court decide for them as it did in *Brown v. Board of Education*, a ruling that came down in May.[21]

Four years later, Felix Anderson was still at his post, and civil rights issues remained high on just about everyone's agenda, whatever

---

[20] John A. Hardin, *Fifty Years of Segregation: Black Higher Education in Kentucky, 1904-1954* (Lexington, Ky., 1997), 100; Elizabeth S. Peck, *Berea's First 125 Years, 1855-1980* (Lexington, Ky., 1982) with a final chapter by Emily Ann Smith, 39-62, 194-95. To put a finer point on the law as it passed, black and white students could both attend a school, public or private, in Kentucky provided that the all-black Kentucky State University did not offer a comparable course of study.

[21] Tracy E. K'Meyer, *Civil Rights in the Gateway to the South: Louisville, Kentucky, 1945-1980* (Lexington, Ky., 2009), 46-48, 308nn2, 4; 1930 U.S. census, Jefferson County, Kentucky.

their position. In late 1957, Louisville city fathers began considering a public-accommodations bill, but then the city law director advised them that they could act only if they first obtained state authority. Whereupon the sole black member of the legislature proposed a bill that would permit municipalities to pass civil rights ordinances. Anderson was an important voice, but he had only one vote, and the legislation failed that year. African Americans in Louisville soon adopted direct action to press for change in the laws and change in the behavior of restaurants and other such "private" businesses. And in the following session, black Democratic representative William H. Childress Jr. (1911–93), elected in 1959, introduced and championed the 1960 bill that created the Kentucky Commission on Human Rights, which, in the years to come, monitored and tried to promote progress in such areas as employment, education, and housing.[22]

The 1960s brought countless newly enfranchised black voters to the polls in the former Confederate states in an environment that featured the Voting Rights Act of 1965 as well as legislative reapportionment mandated by the Supreme Court in 1964 in *Reynolds v. Sims* and other cases.[23] Again and again across the South, black candidates gained election as state legislators, often touted as "the first" in their state "since Reconstruction."

In Kentucky, the 1960s began before those twin revolutions in black electoral politics and built upon what had been developing since the 1930s. There was, though, a twist as to gender. Winning candidates included the first black women to hold seats in the Kentucky legislature. Amelia Moore Tucker (1902–87), a native of Alabama, moved with her husband to Louisville in the 1920s. The Reverend Amelia Tucker had served as minister at Brown Temple AMEZ

---

[22] K'Meyer, *Civil Rights in the Gateway to the South,* 80, 141-42, 230, 252-54, 273; Horton, *Not Without Struggle,* 69-70. Felix Anderson received notice in the *New York Times* when he became the first African American to chair a standing legislative committee in Kentucky: "Negro Heads Kentucky Panel," *New York Times,* January 18, 1958. He did not make it into the *Encyclopedia of Louisville,* however, nor did Childress.

[23] *Reynolds v. Sims,* 377 U.S. 533 (1964); Richard C. Cortner, *The Apportionment Cases* (Knoxville, 1970).

Church, and her husband was Bishop Charles Ewbank Tucker—who had run twice with Democratic backing for the house of representatives in the 1930s. Elected in 1961 as a Republican, she served one term as the first black woman in the Kentucky legislature. Amelia Moore Tucker pressed in 1962, as Felix Anderson had in 1958, for a public-accommodations act. Like him, she failed. But unlike him, she saw passage of an enabling act authorizing Kentucky cities to pass their own civil rights measures.[24]

The first black Kentuckian elected to the state senate, a Democrat, was Georgia Davis Powers (b. 1923), also the first woman, black or white, to sit in that chamber. A native of Springfield, Kentucky, she first gained election from Louisville in 1967 and served five four-year terms (1968–88). Senator Powers explained in an interview some years later how she had come to run for the legislature, after spending time there lobbying for a public-accommodations bill in 1966:

And those legislators were just so snobbish when I asked them to vote for the bill, and they just really looked down their nose at me and I didn't like it. And I thought, "well, okay, so what I need to do is get my own seat here." Never thought about sex, race, nothing. I just needed a seat up here because if I get a seat up here, I'm gonna know how to vote and I'm gonna vote right. That's what I thought in '66. So I didn't think much about it until '67 when I was sitting in the kitchen there reading the paper and I saw where the senator from this district was moving in the East End. Well, I knew if he moved out of the district, he'd have to give up the seat. And the thought just came to me [snaps finger], you know, to run for that seat. So, I'd worked on those campaigns five years, and I'd watched other candidates, how they organized the precincts, how they got endorsements, and how they raised money. And I thought, well I'm ready. The very next day I went down to the courthouse and filed

---

[24] "Tucker, Amelia Moore," *Encyclopedia of Louisville*, 893.

for the state senate. And nobody thought I could win, but I thought I could. I've always thought I could do anything I set my mind to do.[25]

Powers had gained considerable political experience as logistical leader of a march on Frankfort in March 1964—some months before Congress passed the Civil Rights Act of 1964—in support of a state-level civil rights bill that would ban racial discrimination in both jobs and such public accommodations as restaurants and theaters. Immediately upon taking her legislative seat, she pressed successfully for passage of a fair-housing bill.[26] During her time in the Kentucky Senate, she embodied a century's worth of black Kentuckians' aspirations to be recognized not only as voters but also as people for whom voters could cast their votes—not only as parties interested in the outcome of legislative tussles but as people who could act directly in the legislative process by casting their votes themselves on the house or senate floor in Frankfort. As Senator Powers said in her interview, "I just needed a seat up here because if I get a seat up here, I'm gonna know how to vote and I'm gonna vote right."[27]

Historical and Historiographical Significance

Offering additional context for the Kentucky trajectory to the election of African American legislators are two overlapping surveys—of the former slave states contiguous to Kentucky and of other Border South states. Virginia, for example, one of the ten former Confederate states to undergo Congressional Reconstruction, began to see black legislators in both houses as early as the first post–Restoration session in 1869, and many more gained election to

[25] Georgia M. Powers, interview, October 19, 1990, Kentucky Legislature Oral History Project, Louie B. Nunn Center for Oral History, University of Kentucky Libraries, University of Kentucky, Lexington, Kentucky, accessed at http://kdl.kyvl.org/cgi/b/bib/oh2.php?cachefile=1990OH285_LEG019_Powers.xml&kw=1990-10-19. Georgia Davis Powers, *I Shared the Dream: The Pride, Passion and Politics of the First Black Woman Senator from Kentucky* (Far Hills, N.J., 1995), dwells fairly little on her life after 1968—her first year in the legislature as well as the last year in the life of her close friend Martin Luther King Jr.

[26] K'Meyer, *Civil Rights in the Gateway to the South*, 101-8, 141-42.

[27] Powers interview, October 19, 1990.

both houses throughout the 1870s and 1880s. None, however, was elected after 1889, with the seating of a final cluster just before the curtain fell on black power there, until 1967 in the Virginia House of Delegates and 1969 in the Virginia Senate.[28]

Tennessee, the sole former state of the Confederacy not to go through a period of military rule beginning in 1867, nonetheless saw its first black legislator, Sampson W. Keeble, elected in 1872. Among the fourteen black legislators elected in Tennessee in the nineteenth century—or before 1964—all but he and one other gained election in the 1880s—an even more pronounced pattern along those lines than in Virginia. The sole other exception, Jesse M. H. Graham, though elected in 1896, was refused his seat by the men who would have been his fellow legislators. That is, he was seated only provisionally and then had his seat declared vacant, on the reported grounds that he had spent insufficient time in his home district.[29]

The first black legislator of West Virginia, Charles Payne, was elected in 1896, and others soon followed. The second, James M. Ellis, gained election in 1902, like Payne from Fayette County, a center of black political and labor activity in West Virginia. In the late 1910s, three black men served in the West Virginia House of Representatives: Harry J. Capehart, an attorney in Keystone; John V.

[28] Jackson, *Negro Office-Holders in Virginia*; Peter Wallenstein, *Cradle of America: Four Centuries of Virginia History* (Lawrence, Kans., 2007), 372.

[29] Joseph H. Cartwright, "Black Legislators in Tennessee in the 1800s: A Case Study in Black Political Leadership," *Tennessee Historical Quarterly* 32 (1973): 265-84; "19th Century African American Legislators of Tennessee," http://www.tn.gov/tsla/exhibits/blackhistory/bios/graham.htm. None of the Tennessee black legislators appear in Eric Foner, *Reconstruction: America's Unfinished Revolution, 1863-1877* (New York, 1988), 356-59; some black officeholders in the early post-Civil War years are referenced there, though few are named. Foner names twenty such officeholders in his encyclopedic *Freedom's Lawmakers*, 257, but, as he explains in the introduction to that work (xiii, note to Table 1), he did not include men who held office after the "end of Reconstruction," which he defines for each state as "the election that produced simultaneous Democratic control of the governorship and both houses of the state legislature." This occurred in 1870 in Tennessee. All but one black Tennessee legislator, however, had been elected after 1877, so even the conventional later date would have left out all but Keeble. Foner's focus, moreover, remains fixed on the "South," as is the case with most scholars of the Civil War era, so developments of that sort in states outside the region do not appear in his compilation.

Coleman, a coalminer in Fayette County; and T. G. Nutter, a lawyer in Charleston. Together, they successfully promoted legislation to establish a number of new institutions: the West Virginia Colored Deaf and Blind School at Institute; the West Virginia Home for Colored Girls in Huntington; the West Virginia Industrial Home for Colored Boys in Lakin; and the West Virginia Hospital for Colored Insane, also at Lakin. In 1928, Minnie Buckingham Harper became the first African American woman to serve in the West Virginia legislature when Governor Howard Gore appointed her to the seat representing McDowell County that her husband, E. Howard Harper, had held at the time of his death. She did not run to succeed herself in the elections later that year.[30]

Charlton H. Tandy (1836–1919) was born in Kentucky into a free-black family in the Lexington area but moved to St. Louis, Missouri, in 1857, where he joined the Missouri state militia during the Civil War. An all-purpose activist against racial discrimination in schools, on streetcars, and in politics, he helped establish Lincoln Institute in the 1870s. Although elected in 1894 to the Missouri legislature, he was not permitted to take his seat. A quarter-century passed before the first black legislator of Missouri, Walthall M. Moore (1878–1928?)—an Alabama-born waiter from St. Louis (by way of Indiana)—was elected in 1920 and again in 1926. His first election resulted from the organization in 1919 of the Citizens Liberty League which sought the election of black candidates to political office. In 1921, he successfully proposed that what had become the state black land-grant school, Lincoln Institute, be named Lincoln University, and the legislature also began supporting the establishment of black high schools in urban areas.[31]

[30] John R. Sheeler, "The Negro in West Virginia before 1900" (PhD dissertation, West Virginia University, 1954), 211; Thomas E. Posey, *The Negro Citizen of West Virginia* (Institute, W.Va., 1934), 58-62; Joe William Trotter Jr., "African-American Heritage," http://www. wvencyclopedia.org/print/Article/27; I. D. "Duke" Talbott and Charles M. Murphy, "Minnie Buckingham Harper," http://www.wvencyclopedia.org/articles/259.

[31] Notable Kentucky African Americans Database: Legislators, Outside Kentucky; http://www.umsl.edu/~whmc/guides/whm0135.htm; http://www.stlmedia.net/sonderman/january/01-05hist.pdf; http://shs.umsystem.edu/outreach/mohist/april6.html; J. Clay Smith

In Delaware, the first African American was elected to the general assembly even later than in Kentucky, but as with Kentucky, black representation proved nearly continuous after that. The first black legislator of Delaware was William J. Winchester, elected to the house of representatives in 1948. The next, Paul F. Livingston, gained election to the house in 1952 and served until his death in 1963. Herman M. Holloway Sr. won a special election in 1963 to take Livingston's place, but he subsequently served in the Delaware Senate until his death in 1994.[32]

David Robinson ran as a Republican for the Maryland House of Delegates in 1921 but was defeated. Harry A. Cole (1921–99) finally won a seat in the Maryland Senate in 1954, though Dr. Furman Templeton lost his bid that year for a seat in the lower house just as Coleman had four years earlier. In 1958, when Cole ran for reelection, he was defeated by a black Democrat, J. Alvin Jones. That year, two black female Democrats, Verda Welcome and Irma Dixon, gained election to the Maryland House of Delegates.[33]

In Oklahoma, Albert Comstock (A.C.) Hamlin (1881–1912) was elected in 1908 to the first state legislature. During his only term, he sponsored laws that appropriated state funds for a black school for deaf, blind, or orphaned children, and he also sponsored a law that called for genuinely equal, though segregated, railroad-passenger facilities. Defeated in a bid for reelection, he fell victim to a state constitutional amendment introducing the Oklahoma "grandfather

Jr., *Emancipation: The Making of the Black Lawyer, 1844-1944* (Philadelphia, 1993), 360n122.

[32] Carol E. Hoffecker, *Democracy in Delaware: The Story of the First State's General Assembly* (Wilmington, Del., 2004), 190, 212, 245, 252-53; "William J. Winchester," *New York Times*, January 4, 1952; for Livingston, Senate Bill 386 (1984), http://delcode.delaware.gov/sessionlaws/ga132/chp385.shtml; "Hon. Herman M. Holloway Sr.," *Congressional Record* 140, No. 28, March 15, 1994, http://www.gpo.gov/fdsys/pkg/CREC-1994-03-15/html/CREC-1994-03-15-pt1-PgS22.htm.

[33] Hayward Farrar, *The Baltimore Afro-American, 1892-1950* (Westport, Conn., 1998), 57-85, tracks black Marylanders' long years of relative futility in electoral politics but then points toward the 1950s—after the years of his study—when black residents of Baltimore made their way back into political office and, for the first time, into the state legislature. See *Baltimore Afro-American*, August 26, 1921; November 13, 1954; November 8, 1958; Simeon Booker, "Baltimore: New Negro Vote Capital," *Ebony*, December 1959, 129-36; "Harry Cole, First Black on Maryland High Court," *Baltimore Sun*, February 16, 1999.

clause." President Theodore Roosevelt had made it known that he would reject statehood for Oklahoma if its constitution restricted black voting, so Democrats waited until after statehood to press for the change. Then they pounced on the sole black Republican. By the time the U.S. Supreme Court ruled against the measure, Hamlin had died.

No additional black candidates gained election to the Oklahoma legislature before 1964, when reapportionment made it far more likely that black candidates would be elected from Tulsa and Oklahoma City. That year, Edward Melvin Porter (b. 1930), who had lost an earlier bid for the Oklahoma House of Representatives as a Republican, ran as a Democrat and won a seat from Oklahoma City in the state senate.[34]

In every state in the South, black candidates were soon running for seats in their legislatures—and winning. The developments of the 1960s reflected a transformation in national politics, itself a result of black migration out of the South. Kentucky had been late to get started, but in the 1960s the rest of the South was catching up to what black Kentuckians had been accomplishing with some regularity ever since 1935—and the number of black legislators in Kentucky at any one time finally rose above the previous maximum of one.

The native black legislators from Kentucky who gained election in such states as Illinois and Ohio in the late nineteenth century prefigured the role of the later and much larger black migration that transformed the political landscape in the urban North and West. In California, for example, the first black legislator was Frederick M. Roberts (1879–1952), a Republican elected in 1918 from Los Angeles to the first of many terms whose four grandparents had all been

[34] Patrick G. Williams, "Hamlin, Albert Comstock," in Garraty and Carnes, eds., *American National Biography*, 9:933-34. Larry O'Dell, "Porter, Edward Melvin," http://digital.library.okstate.edu/encyclopedia/entries/P/PO017.html. Years before Oklahoma statehood, a black Exoduster from Tennessee named Green I. Currin (1842?-1918) was elected in 1890 to the territory's first house of representatives, and another Exoduster (from South Carolina by way of Texas), David J. Wallace (1850?-1928), won election two years later. "Exodusters," as they were called, were the thousands of black Southerners who fled the region for Kansas or neighboring areas, especially in 1879. Helen M. Stiefmiller, "Wallace, David J.," http://digital.library.okstate.edu/encyclopedia/entries/W/WA010.html; Bruce T. Fisher, "Curran, Green I.," http://digital.library.okstate.edu/encyclopedia/entries/C/CU005.html.

born in Virginia. In the Northeast, the first black legislator of New Jersey, Virginia native Dr. Walter Gilbert Alexander (1880–1953), the son of two former Virginia slaves, gained election from Orange as a Republican in 1920 to the first of two terms in the assembly. Both men proved to be successful proponents of significant civil rights legislation. And what historians term the "Great Migration" and generally date to a period beginning with World War I was barely underway, although substantial migration north from both Kentucky and Virginia began in the 1880s.[35]

Among the black legislators to gain election in the Deep South in the 1960s and 1970s—a second pioneer group, a century after the first—one who had Kentucky connections was Horace E. Tate (1922–2002), who in 1960 became the first African American to earn a doctorate (in educational administration) from the University of Kentucky. The University of Georgia did not begin admitting black students at any level until after Tate finished his degree at Kentucky—many years after the efforts of pioneer black Kentucky legislators Charles W. Anderson Jr. and Jesse H. Lawrence to open the state's institutions of higher education to African Americans. Dr. Tate had returned to his native Georgia, where he continued his career in education. He ran unsuccessfully for mayor of Atlanta in 1969 and then, in 1974, was elected to the Georgia Senate, where he served for the next eighteen years.[36]

The First . . . Since Reconstruction

The "first" since "Reconstruction"—the term appears repeatedly in reports, whether in newspapers or historical accounts, of elec-

---

[35] 1900 U.S. census, Los Angeles, California; 1920 U.S. census, Essex County, New Jersey; Peter Wallenstein, "Cartograms and the Mapping of Virginia History, 1790-1990," *Virginia Social Science Journal* 28 (1993): 90-110, at 100-103; http://www.blackpast.org/?q=aaw/roberts-frederick-m-1879-1952; http://blackcaucus.legislature.ca.gov/about; http://www.njsendems.com/release.asp?rid=1081; http://www.newjerseynewsroom.com/state/new-jerseys-first-two-african-american-legislators-remembered-at-statehouse.

[36] http://www.uky.edu/Education/hofamers/Tate.html; http://www.uky.edu/Education/news/Tate.html.

tions—often in the second half of the 1960s—of a black legislator or other officeholder. Yet historians conventionally date the end of Reconstruction as occurring in 1877, even if popular understanding simply points toward the last third of the nineteenth century. Clearly, when Charles W. Anderson Jr. gained election to the Kentucky legislature in the 1930s, no such statement could be made, since he was the first black candidate ever so elected in that state. In contrast to the states of the former Confederacy, no cohort of black predecessors had served in Kentucky back during the post–Civil War years.

The term scarcely applies, either, to northern electoral victories by black Kentucky natives, because in those states, Illinois in particular, a black legislative presence remained very much in evidence pretty much from the first black legislator on down to the present. Nor does the term necessarily seem well suited even for the former Confederate states, given such patterns as those for Kentucky's neighbors Tennessee and Virginia.[37] Patterns of change and continuity varied among the states or clusters of states but not in ways that the conventional periodization of "Reconstruction" helps us understand.

The pioneer black legislators of Kentucky remind us that the long electoral drought in so many southern states between the late nineteenth century and the 1960s did not apply everywhere. Kentucky came late to the party among the slave states of 1860 in electing a black candidate as a state legislator; it took seven decades after the Civil War for a black Kentuckian to be elected to such a post in his native state. Yet black Kentuckians, unlike their counterparts in any state of the former Confederacy, had black representation during most legislative sessions from the 1930s on. Even before the breakthrough election of Charles W. Anderson Jr. in 1935, by the 1920s their efforts to elect a black legislator sometimes brought real gains even in losing causes, at least in Louisville.

Patterns elsewhere varied. West Virginia had its first black leg-

---

[37] For a survey of the former Confederate South in the late-nineteenth century, see Peter Wallenstein, "Reconstruction Reconfigured: The Persistence of Southern Black Legislators Well Beyond 1877," Society of Civil War Historians conference, Lexington, Kentucky, June 2012.

islator in the 1890s, at just about the time disfranchisement—black exclusion from electoral politics—was closing its fist throughout the former Confederacy, nor did black success in legislative races there come to an end then. Oklahoma displayed black electoral success in the territorial era in the 1890s, and again at the beginning of statehood in the next decade—but not after that until the mid-1960s, as the Sooner State signed on with the broader southern pattern.

Reconstruction, when black men could no longer be barred by law from voting or running for legislative office on the basis of their race, created conditions in which biracial democracy might emerge. The Union victory in the Civil War, together with the postwar constitutional amendments, had opened new possibilities in American racial politics. How soon, how often, and how effectively it did so remained to be seen, in Kentucky and everywhere else.

Black citizens—men and, by the 1920s, women too—had the vote in Kentucky, and the two political parties soon thereafter found they had to contest for black votes. The first successful black candidates were Republicans, but by the 1950s Felix Anderson was running and winning as a black Democrat. The election in the 1960s of black candidates Amelia Moore Tucker and Georgia Davis Powers reflected the empowerment of women in American political life, first through the Nineteenth Amendment in 1920 and then through changing attitudes regarding gender. By the 1960s, race and gender both operated in Kentucky—and across the South, across America—in very different ways than at any time in the era of Civil War and Reconstruction. The triple changes of the 1860s, the 1920s, and the 1960s—combined—made it possible for the Kentucky legislature of the past half-century to take on its modern make-up. But it took Kentuckians, as voters and candidates alike, to make those changes in voting behavior and election results happen, and then it took the legislators to help make policy changes happen and give those political changes their greater significance.

AFTERWORD

By Benjamin Lewis Fitzpatrick

Historians of the Civil War have long acknowledged Kentucky's strategic import to both the Union and the Confederate war efforts. Bordered on the north by the Ohio River, to the west by the Mississippi River, and containing the Tennessee and Cumberland rivers, Kentucky was a bulwark between the Union and the Confederacy. As President Lincoln apprehensively stated in a letter to Senator O. H. Browning in 1861, "I think to lose Kentucky is nearly the same as to lose the whole game. Kentucky gone, we can not hold Missouri, nor, as I think, Maryland. These all against us, and the job on our hands is too large for us."[1] Throughout the conflict, the state experienced Union occupation, Confederate invasions, and bloody guerrilla warfare. However, going beyond the state's strategic significance and well-known battles, *New Perspectives on Civil War-Era Kentucky* provides insightful interpretations on a range of topics—from the nature of Unionism to the experiences of women on the home front to African American struggles for social and political equality during Reconstruction. The writers' essays teem with exemplary scholarship that charts an exciting course of future research for scholars of Civil War-era Kentucky.

From the essays of James C. Klotter, Elizabeth D. Leonard, Christopher Waldrep, Luke Harlow, and Aaron Astor, the reader gains a better understanding of how the profuse viewpoints on race and slavery informed Unionism in the borderland of Kentucky. Klotter's tracing of the origins of Kentucky's Unionism back to its great

BENJAMIN LEWIS FITZPATRICK is an assistant professor of history at Morehead State University. His research interests include the Civil War and Reconstruction, slavery, and Kentucky history.

[1] Abraham Lincoln to Orville H. Browning, September 22, 1861, in *The Collected Works of Abraham Lincoln*, 8 vols., ed. Roy P. Basler (New Brunswick, N.J., 1953), 4:532.

statesman, Henry Clay, elucidates why the spirit of secessionism did not dominate in Kentucky (except in the Jackson Purchase) even though the state contained the third highest number of slaveholders in the South. Clay's political "spirit" of moderation and compromise over slavery informed Kentucky's neutrality and, later, its Unionism, both of which helped to anchor the other border states, just as Lincoln had hoped, securing a northern victory. Native Kentuckian and President Lincoln's judge advocate general Joseph Holt, as described by Leonard, was an unconditional Unionist, an unwavering supporter of Lincoln's policies, from suspending habeas corpus to emancipating the slaves, even as he became a persona non grata among many pro-Confederate Kentuckians, some of whom were his relatives. Waldrep, Harlow, and Astor adroitly demonstrate how different viewpoints on race and slavery interacted with constitutional perspectives and evangelical Christianity to inform proslavery Unionism. Using different analytical approaches, the writers arrive at a similar conclusion: for many white Kentuckians, support for the Union primarily hinged upon the protection of slavery. Prior to the spring of 1862, Senator Garrett Davis had been a strong supporter of President Lincoln's efforts to defend the Union. However, as Waldrep recounts, when Lincoln unveiled his plans to emancipate the slaves, Davis began to view the president's policies as threats to Kentuckians' constitutional liberties. Conservative Unionists, as Astor describes, espoused Clay's spirit of political compromise as the best way to protect slavery from the radical forces of both secessionism and abolitionism, as did conservative white Christians, who, according to Harlow, advocated for political neutrality in order to maintain the Union and slavery.

Klotter's thesis implores historians to further examine the long-term influence of prominent antebellum Bluegrass politicians to better comprehend how and why the diverse political mindsets that divided Kentuckians on slavery, secession, and Unionism developed in the decades leading up to the Civil War.[2] However, as Waldrep, Harlow,

[2] For additional biographies of Henry Clay, see David S. Reynolds, *Waking Giant: America in the Age of Jackson* (New York, 2008); Robert V. Remini, *Henry Clay: Statesman for the Union* (New York, 1991), and David S. Heidler and Jeanne T. Heidler, *Henry Clay: The Essential American*

and Astor aptly demonstrate, in a state fraught with such political divisions, the threat of slave resistance and Federal policies meant to maintain control shattered Clay's legacy of nationalism, collapsed proslavery Unionism, and left staunch Unionists like Joseph Holt in a precarious minority. Hopefully, future scholarship will explore the roles that other demographics played in the construction of Unionism, particularly among eastern Kentuckians and African Americans. After neutrality failed in the fall of 1861, many mountaineers remained loyal, enlisting in the Union over the Confederacy by a ratio of four to one.[3] During Reconstruction, eastern Kentucky became an enclave of support for the Republican Party in the state.[4] Meanwhile, a large proportion of Kentucky's African Americans joined the Union army after the Federal government lifted restrictions on black enlistment in the spring of 1864.[5] Historians have dedicated substantial inquiries

(New York, 2010). Also see "Henry Clay," in Daniel Walker Howe, *The Political Culture of the American Whigs* (Chicago, 1979), and Merrill D. Peterson, *The Great Triumvirate: Webster, Clay, and Calhoun* (New York, 1987). Historians still need to mine the lives of prominent politicians Richard Mentor Johnson and John C. Breckinridge. For an important study of Breckinridge, see William C. Davis, *John C. Breckinridge: Statesman, Soldier, Symbol* (Baton Rouge, 1974). Other studies include Frank Heck, *Proud Kentuckian: John C. Breckinridge, 1821–1875* (Lexington, Ky., 1976), and James C. Klotter, *The Breckinridges of Kentucky* (Lexington, Ky., 1986). Despite his rise to the vice presidency in 1836, historians have largely ignored Johnson. Two dissertations tackle his political career: Jonathan Milnor Jones, "The Making of a Vice President: The National Political Career of Richard M. Johnson of Kentucky" (Ph.D. diss., University of Memphis, 1998), and Miles James Smith, "The Kentucky Colonel: Richard M. Johnson and the Rise of Western Democracy, 1780–1850" (Ph.D. diss., Texas Christian University, 2013). Most scholars have been interested in Johnson's relationship with Julia Chinn and the analysis on race relations that relationship provides. See Christina Snyder, *Great Crossings: Indians, Settlers, and Slaves in the Age of Jackson* (New York, 2017), and Thomas Brown, "The Miscegenation of Richard Mentor Johnson as an Issue in the National Election Campaign of 1836–1836," *Civil War History* 39 (1993): 5–30.

[3] Anne E. Marshall, "Civil War Memory in Eastern Kentucky Is 'Predominantly White': The Confederate Flag in Unionist Appalachia," in *Reconstructing Appalachia: The Civil War's Aftermath,* ed. Andrew Slap (Lexington, Ky., 2010), 355. In *Creating a Confederate Kentucky,* Marshall explains how even though African Americans and white Unionists in Kentucky did not shape public memory of the Civil War, they nevertheless were active participants in the public debates. The same approach needs to be taken concerning antebellum public discourse on Unionism. Anne E. Marshall, *Creating a Confederate Kentucky: The Lost Cause and Civil War Memory in a Border State* (Chapel Hill, 2010).

[4] Ibid.

[5] Historians have produced little work on the political activity of free blacks in antebellum Kentucky. Bridget Ford examines the strong presence of black evangelical antislavery activism

into why proslavery Unionism faltered and why white Kentuckians came to embrace the Confederacy after the war, but writers should pay more attention to Kentuckians who remained loyal to the Union during the era.

Although the states' rights argument had long been a part of Kentucky politics, it was not inevitable that white Kentuckians would come to embrace the Lost Cause. The Federal government's attempts to squelch Confederate guerrillas and sympathizers often led to resentment among whites, dissolving the state's fragile conditional Unionism. The essays of Christopher Phillips and Benjamin Franklin Cooling provide further penetrating analyses on this topic. The desire of the Federal government to maintain order in Kentucky during the war led it to enact the dominion system, as discussed by Phillips, with Federal and state officials declaring martial law, suppressing Confederate supporting newspapers, and requiring citizens to take oaths of allegiance. After the war, memories of the hated dominion system drove many white Kentuckians to resent the Union's harsh measures as a betrayal of their loyalty. Cooling's broad analytical framework of comparative inquiry within a context of U.S. foreign policy between Kentucky and Tennessee demonstrates that throughout most of the Civil War era the two were both "enemy" and "sister" states. They were sisters prior to the war but became enemies during the conflict even though they both suffered under Union policies. Future comparative studies between Kentucky and other border states can help position Kentucky within the larger context of southern and national politics during the era.[6] Furthermore, Cooling's and Phillips's works should coax scholars to conduct more investigations into the nature

in the face of resistance from proslavery Christians in Louisville during the mid-1840s. Bridget Ford, "Black Spiritual Defiance and the Politics of Slavery in Antebellum Louisville," *Journal of Southern History* 78 (2012): 69–106.

[6] For more on the border states, see William C. Harris, *Lincoln and the Border States: Preserving the Union* (Lawrence, Kans., 2011). For comparisons of Kentucky and other states during the Civil War era, see Aaron Astor, *Rebels on the Border: Civil War, Emancipation, and the Reconstruction of Kentucky and Missouri* (Baton Rouge, 2012), and Brian D. McKnight, *Contested Borderland: The Civil War in Appalachian Kentucky and Virginia* (Lexington, Ky., 2006).

of guerrilla warfare and the causes of postbellum violence that fostered Kentucky's national reputation for brutality.[7]

Anne E. Marshall's essay on women and the divisive nature of the war on the home front adds to the growing historiography on the experiences of women in the border states during the war.[8] The diaries of women, both Union and Confederate, illustrate that guerrilla warfare, Union army occupation, and social division increased the "women-as-war-combatant" experience for Kentucky women.[9] The diarists' comments also provide important perspectives on how the war strained personal and family relationships and in particular destroyed their social status bedrock, slavery, right before their eyes. Because Marshall uses diaries, her examination necessarily focuses on affluent white women since many African American and working-class white women were either illiterate or did not have the opportunity to create a written record. Because diarists did not always understand the behavior of black women and working-class white women that they encountered in their communities, scholars will need to use analytical frameworks that allow for the actions of these voiceless groups to be examined via the words of affluent whites.

Scholars have paid considerable attention to the war's effects on slavery in Kentucky, which contained the largest slave population of the border states. Initially, Federal officials assured slaveholders that their rights to human chattel were secure, but as the war progressed masters lost control of their slaves, many of whom fled to Camp Nelson to join the U.S. Colored Troops. Patricia Hoskins's and Peter

[7] For more on the nature of guerrilla warfare in Kentucky during the Civil War, see James B. Martin, "Black Flag Over the Bluegrass: Guerrilla Warfare in Kentucky, 1863–1865," *Register of the Kentucky Historical Society* 86 (1988) 352–75 (hereafter *Register*).

[8] For more on women's experience in the border states during the Civil War, see LeeAnn Whites, "'Corresponding with the Enemy': Mobilizing the Relational Field of Battle in St. Louis," in *Occupied Women: Gender, Military Occupation, and the American Civil War*, ed. LeeAnn Whites and Alecia P. Long (Baton Rouge, 2009); Kristen L. Streater; "'She-Rebels on the Supply Line': Gender Conventions in Civil War Kentucky," in ibid.; and Kristen L. Streater, "'Not much a friend to traiters no matter how beautiful': The Union Military and Confederate Women in Civil War Kentucky," in *Sister States, Enemy States: The Civil War in Kentucky and Tennessee*, ed. Kent T. Dollar, Larry H. Whiteaker, and W. Calvin Dickinson (Lexington, Ky., 2008).

[9] Anne E. Marshall, "A 'Sisters' War': Kentucky Women and Their Civil War Diaries," *Register* 110 (2012): 501.

Wallenstein's essays examine the bitter contest over black social and political equality that occurred after the fighting officially ended. Although the Freedmen's Bureau accomplished important work by establishing schools and courts for the freedpeople in the Jackson Purchase, according to Hoskins the Federal government sorely underestimated white resistance against the freedpeople and the Bureau. Simply put, the Freedmen's Bureau could not overcome the white supremacy of the region to fully achieve its mission. Hoskins's work adds to the scholarship of historians such as Berry Craig who have examined the career of secessionism and white supremacy in the Jackson Purchase during the era.[10] Furthermore, her essay adds to the work of scholars such as George Wright who have documented the racial violence that stifled black equality for generations after the war.[11] Yet, more work is needed on the role of the Freedmen's Bureau, one of the most "misrepresented" institutions of the postbellum period. Indeed, as Hoskins states, despite facing immense racism, the Freedmen's Bureau did have some accomplishments—for example, establishing 219 schools in the state.[12] Future local studies or even comparative analyses among the activities of the three branches of the Bureau would help to understand how Bureau agents in other subdistricts in the state dealt with strong white resistance.

Meantime, native black Kentuckians who left won legislative offices in other southern and midwestern states by 1868, while African

[10] Berry Craig, *Kentucky Confederates: Secession, Civil War, and the Jackson Purchase* (Lexington, Ky., 2014).

[11] For more on postbellum racial violence in Kentucky, see George C. Wright, *Racial Violence in Kentucky, 1865–1940: Lynchings, Mob Rule, and "Legal Lynchings"* (Baton Rouge, 1990); Patrick A. Lewis, "The Democratic Partisan Militia and the Black Peril: The Kentucky Militia, Racial Violence, and the Fifteenth Amendment, 1870–1873," *Civil War History* 56 (2010): 145–74; J. Michael Rhyne, "'We Are Mobbed & Beat': Regulator Violence Against Free Black Households in Kentucky's Bluegrass Region, 1865–1867," *Ohio Valley History* 2 (2002): 30–42; J. Michael Rhyne, "'Conduct . . . Inexcusable and Unjustifiable': Bound Children, Battered Freedwomen, and the Limits of Emancipation in Kentucky's Bluegrass Region," *Journal of Social History* 42 (2008): 319–40.

[12] Ross A. Webb, "'The Past Is Never Dead. It's Not Even Past': Benjamin P. Runkle and the Freedmen's Bureau in Kentucky, 1866–1870," *Register* 84 (1986): 345; Patricia Hoskins, "The Freedmen's Bureau in the Jackson Purchase Region of Kentucky, 1866–1868," included in this book (298).

Americans who remained in Kentucky only occasionally won a seat in the General Assembly in the century after the war. As Wallenstein illustrates, the careers of African American Kentucky politicians, from Reconstruction to the 1930s, laid the foundation for the civil rights movement of the 1950s and 1960s. Wallenstein's work poignantly reminds researchers that the efforts of African American leaders in the immediate postbellum period planted the seeds for the civil rights movement that bloomed decades later. Future scholarship should continue Wallenstein's lead by focusing on the prolonged influence of political and social activism of African Americans in the state. In 1935, the election of Louisville's Charles W. Anderson Jr. to the Kentucky House of Representatives paved the way for future black politicians, including groundbreaking black women, such as Senator Georgia Davis Powers and Representative Mae Street Kidd, Louisvillians who cosponsored and shepherded the state's Fair Housing Act through the General Assembly in 1968.[13]

There are still major tasks historians need to accomplish in the field. Namely, more work is needed on the three and a half decades of social and cultural transformations that occurred between 1865 and 1900. Additional institutional studies of the Freedmen's Bureau and the Republican Party would begin to address these historiographical omissions. The Freedmen's Bureau records are a rich source for studying African Americans. Over the past two decades, Reconstruction historians have written vibrant studies concerning the agency's efficacy vis-à-vis late nineteenth-century cultural assumptions about labor, gender, and dependency. Similar studies of the Bureau's complex relationship with black women in Kentucky are required

[13] For more on the careers of Georgia Davis Powers and Mae Street Kidd, see Georgia Davis Powers, *I Shared the Dream: The Pride, Passion and Politics of the First Black Woman Senator from Kentucky* (Far Hills, N.J., 1995); and Wade Hall, *Passing for Black: The Life and Careers of Mae Street Kidd* (Lexington, Ky., 1997). For additional information on African American political activity in Kentucky from the end of the Civil War into the early twentieth century, see George C. Wright, *Life Behind a Veil: Blacks in Louisville, Kentucky, 1865–1930* (Baton Rouge, 1985); George C. Wright, *History of Blacks in Kentucky*, vol. 2, *In Pursuit of Equality, 1890–1980* (Frankfort, Ky., 1992); and George C. Wright, "Black Political Insurgency in Louisville, Kentucky: The Lincoln Independent Party of 1921," *Journal of Negro History* 68 (1983): 8–23.

to understand the experiences of the black community's transition from slavery to freedom.[14] Also, a complete study of the Republican Party's evolving strategies and leadership from the nascent wartime Union Party to its maturity in 1895 with the election of William O. Bradley, the first Republican Kentucky governor, would shed light on the struggles between African Americans and white moderates over black representation in the party and provide crucial insights on how Republicans constructed a winning coalition in the face of riveting violence and competing factions that politically fractured the commonwealth.[15] Furthermore, full histories of the Civil War and Reconstruction and of slavery in Kentucky to update E. Merton Coulter's *The Civil War and Readjustment in Kentucky* (1926) and J. Winston Coleman's *Slavery Times in Kentucky* (1940), respectively, are necessities. Nevertheless, the essays in this book demonstrate that scholars of Civil War-era Kentucky continue to robustly investigate important questions about the religious, racial, political, and social issues that situate Kentucky within the larger historiography of the Civil War and Reconstruction.

[14] Mary Farmer-Kaiser examines how freedwomen who conformed to notions of northern gender roles and dependency in their appeals for assistance benefited from Bureau policy in Virginia, Texas, Louisiana, and Georgia. Mary Farmer Kaiser, *Freedwomen and the Freedmen's Bureau: Race, Gender, and Public Policy in the Age of Emancipation* (Bronx, N.Y., 2010). On gender and the Bureau, see Carol Faulkner, *Women's Radical Reconstruction: The Freedmen's Aid Movement* (Philadelphia, 2004); Sara Rapport, "The Freedmen's Bureau as a Legal Agent for Black Men and Women in Georgia, 1865–1868," *Georgia Historical Quarterly* 73 (1989): 26–53; and Paul A. Cimbala, *Under the Guardianship of the Nation: The Freedmen's Bureau and the Reconstruction of Georgia, 1865–1870* (Athens, Ga., 1997).

[15] A good overview of politics in the era can be found in Hambleton Tapp and James C. Klotter, *Kentucky: Decades of Discord, 1865–1900* (Frankfort, Ky., 1977). A solid analysis of Republican strategizing in postbellum Appalachia is Gordon B. McKinney's *Southern Mountain Republicans, 1865–1900: Politics and the Appalachian Community* (Chapel Hill, 1978). Thomas Louis Owen provides a useful assessment of the transition from the Union Party to the Republican Party in "The Formative Years of Kentucky's Republican Party, 1864–1871" (Ph.D. diss., University of Kentucky, 1981).